Viewpoints

Readings Worth Thinking
and Writing About

Viewpoints

FIFTH EDITION

Readings Worth Thinking and Writing About

W. Royce Adams

Santa Barbara City College, Emeritus

HOUGHTON MIFFLIN COMPANY
Boston   New York

Senior Sponsoring Editor: Mary Jo Southern
Development Editor: Kellie Cardone
Editorial Associate: Peter Mooney
Senior Project Editor: Nancy Blodget
Editorial Assistant: Celeste Ng
Senior Production/Design Coordinator: Jill Haber
Manufacturing Manager: Florence Cadran
Marketing Manager: Annamarie Rice

Cover image: The Image Bank © 2003 Ellen Schuster, "Three Open Windows to
Nature Over Desert"

Acknowledgments for reprinted materials appear on pages 445–449.

Printed in the U.S.A.

Library of Congress Catalog Card Number: 2002109346

ISBN: 0-618-26179-6

3 4 5 6 7 8 9—MP—08 07 06 05 04

Contents

v

PART 2
Readings Worth Thinking and Writing About

79

CHAPTER

4

CHAPTER

9

Rhetorical Table of Contents

Since few, if any, essays serve as exact models for one particular rhetorical mode, reading selections containing paragraph examples of several modes appear under more than one category.

Description

Narration

Analysis

Illustration and Example

Division and Classification

Comparison and Contrast

Definition

Cause and Effect

Argumentation

Preface

The fifth edition of *Viewpoints: Reading Worth Thinking and Writing About* is a thematic collection of readings intended for students who have difficulty writing compositions in English courses. The text is based on the premise that students who have difficulty writing essays usually have not or do not read much. To provide them with grammar drills is not enough. They need to know what to look for when they read; they need to understand what an essay is and how it is constructed; they need to be shown the relationship of reading and writing skills; they need to be exposed to various writing styles; they need to experience the range of emotions that good writing can convey; and they need to see how writers work and how that knowledge can work for them. But most importantly, students need to be introduced to and provoked by the world of ideas in readings that can stimulate their own thinking.

Overview of the Readings and Writing

The text is comprised of two parts. **Part I, Viewpoints on Reading and Writing Essays,** provides an overview of the required skills for thoughtful reading and writing. Chapter 1 covers the basic essay structure, its thesis, and the various rhetorical arrangements of support. To aid reading comprehension, the chapter shows how to separate main ideas from supporting details, how to distinguish fact from opinion, and how to draw inferences. It also provides suggestions for marking and note taking while reading, along with advice for writing summaries. Students are encouraged to keep a reading journal and to develop their vocabulary by learning unfamiliar words used in the essays they read. One goal of this text, then, is to show students how to approach and understand what may appear to be a difficult reading, rather than avoiding it. Inexperienced readers, if taught well, can respond positively to the challenge of material often considered "too difficult" for them.

To strengthen students' understanding of the ties between reading and writing, Chapter 2 draws upon the information provided in Chapter 1. It presents the three stages of writing: prewriting, drafting, and revising. This chapter teaches students that writing is not a linear procedure but a recursive one, with the three stages recurring throughout the writing process. Students are shown how to make a writing assignment their own; how to find and develop a working thesis; how to arrange supporting evidence; and how to revise, edit, and proofread their way to a final draft. Rhetorical patterns are explained as aids to both reading and comprehension. In this chapter and all the others, a section called "On the Net" provides students with useful Internet resources.

The Readings

Eight thematically organized reading chapters make up **Part II, Readings Worth Reading and Thinking About.** They offer collections of viewpoints on learning, human behavior, cultural heritage, social concerns, family and relationships, work, media, and capital punishment. Sixteen of the sixty-seven essays are new to this edition. Diverse viewpoints have been deliberately chosen to provoke student thinking on the issues presented. Exposing students to viewpoints worth thinking and writing about takes precedence over organizing essays by rhetorical modes, though a rhetorical table of contents is provided.

The Apparatus

Each chapter begins with photographs or cartoons and quotations that reflect the chapter's topic. Questions about the opening graphics and quotations help students focus on the topic of the chapter. Each essay in the chapter is preceded by questions that help prepare the student to read. A list of vocabulary words from the reading selection helps the student learn any words needed to better understand the essay.

Four sets of questions follow each reading selection: **Understanding the Content, Looking at Structure and Style, Evaluating the Author's Viewpoints,** and **Pursuing Possible Essay Topics.** The content of these four categories requires students to draw upon what they learned about reading and writing in **Part I.**

Most essays are short and accessible readings for students, but some are longer and more difficult. As with the readings, the questions and suggestions for essays reflect a graduated range of difficulty in order to provide for and challenge the diversity of ability usually found in developmental reading classes. If we are to help students become better readers and writers, we must provide challenging readings and assignments.

Each chapter ends with a student essay written in response to an assignment from that particular chapter's theme. In some cases, early drafts of student essays are used to illustrate specific writing problems and effective revision approaches. Seeing their peers' writing can benefit students by encouraging them to believe that they, too, can compose essays about what they read and think about.

While not meant to replace a handbook, **Appendix A, Essay Format and Proofreading Guide,** and **Appendix B, Quoting and Documenting Sources,** can be used to help the students understand what form the printed essay should take and how to document sources.

Suggestions for using the essays appear in the accompanying *Instructor's Manual.* It often calls attention to readings that work well when assigned in pairs.

Commentaries on each of the chapters and individual reading selections may help you decide which ones to assign during the course and in which order they might be assigned.

Acknowledgments

No text reaches its fifth edition without the help, aid, and suggestions of others. I would like to thank the many users and reviewers who helped with this edition: Helene J. M. Kozma of St. Vincent College; Tracey Smyser of the University of Baltimore; Dr. James Simon of Fairfield University; Dr. Lorna Anne Tran of Portland Community College; Lyn Buchheit of Community College of Philadelphia; and Yeonman Kim of Indiana University of Pennsylvania.

Thanks and appreciation also go to Maggie Barbieri and the staff at Houghton Mifflin, especially Mary Jo Southern, Nancy Blodget, Celeste Ng, and Peter Mooney.

W.R.A.

PART 1

Viewpoints on Reading and Writing Essays

1 Viewpoints on Reading Essays

TOPICS IN THIS CHAPTER

> *"Reading is to the mind what exercise is to the body."*
>
> —Joseph Addison

Take Time To Read... Together

American Library Association

R esearch shows that unless we keep notes and regularly review we will forget over 80 percent of what we learn within two weeks. Considering the time, energy, and money you put into learning, that's a big waste. For this class, a good way to make certain that you don't lose what you have read and studied is to keep some type of reading journal. To help you get into the "journal habit," periodically you are directed to stop reading in this book and to make various types of journal entries. Following are some suggestions for keeping a reading journal.

Keeping a Reading Journal

As a companion to your textbook, buy an 8 ½-by-11 spiral notebook for use only in this class. It should be used for three basic purposes: (1) keeping **notes** of the key points made in Part 1; (2) recording any **reactions, reflections,** or **questions** you may have regarding what you read; and (3) writing **summaries** of the essays you read in Part 2. You will be shown how to write summaries later in this chapter. Of course, anything else you want to keep in your journal, such as vocabulary words you want to learn or ideas for possible essays, is up to you. Keeping a journal for this class is not "busy work." It's a vital part of the learning process, and you'll find that you get much more from this class by keeping a journal than you might think.

Reading Essays

Take a minute to look at the table of contents in this book. Notice that the reading selections in Part 2 are grouped into chapters based on themes such as learning, human behavior, cultural heritage, family, and so on. Each chapter contains several readings expressing various viewpoints on that theme. The readings will provide you with (1) information on the theme, (2) ideas for possible essays of your own, (3) examples of ways to write essays, and (4) practice in developing your reading versatility.

In most chapters, you will find that authors' viewpoints on certain themes are different and frequently disagree. Some essays are longer than others, some better written than others, some more interesting to you than others. You will also discover as you read that there are many different styles of writing. But despite these differences, all essays share three particular features: a thesis or point the author wants to make about a subject, support for that thesis, and a logical arrangement of that support. This section shows you what to look for when you read essays; how to look more closely at the methods writers use to express their opinions, feelings, and experiences; and more detailed information on keeping a reading journal.

The Structure of an Essay

Not all essays are structured the same way. Some essays use what might be called the traditional form: the thesis or point the author wants to make appears in the first paragraph (the beginning), several paragraphs are used to develop or support that point (the middle), and the last paragraph draws a conclusion or summarizes the support used (the end). Many instructors use this basic form to teach beginning writers the essay structure.

In reality, essays don't always follow that form. Some writers may choose to withhold their main idea until the last paragraph, building up to the point they want to make. Some essays may begin with an anecdote or a story that consumes several paragraphs before the point is made. In some cases, the point is never stated directly in words, but instead is implied through what the writer says. As a reader, you will see the variety of forms used when you read the essays in Part 2. As a beginning writer, you may be asked to work on developing essays by the more traditional approach until you are able to break away from the mold.

Regardless of its form or style, an essay contains the three basic ingredients mentioned earlier: a thesis, either stated or implied; sufficient support of that thesis; and a logic behind the arrangement of that support. As a good reader, you need to identify these ingredients and understand how they function as a whole, no matter what the structure of the essay.

Thesis

Every good essay has a **thesis,** which is the main idea or point an author wants to make about his or her topic. The **topic** of an essay is a broad or general subject, such as teenage smoking. A thesis, on the other hand, is the point the author wants to make about the subject. On the subject of teenage smoking, a thesis might be "The increase of teenage smoking despite the evidence that smoking causes cancer is due to advertising directed at teenagers," or "The claim that teenage smoking is on the rise is exaggerated." In other words, a thesis is what the author thinks or feels about the subject of the essay. It's the purpose for writing, the main point around which everything else is written. If you fail to recognize an author's thesis, you may miss the whole point of the essay.

To help clarify the difference between a topic and a thesis, look at the examples below. Notice that topics are broad, general categories, whereas thesis statements are more specific.

Topic	*Possible Thesis Statements*
religion	The use of the Bible to swear in a witness at court trials actually establishes religion and is therefore unconstitutional.

	Recent biblical research, such as the translation of the Book of Q, suggests that Jesus was not the Messiah, but rather a roving sage who preached acceptance of one's fellow human beings.
marriage and family	Gay marriages should be legally recognized as long as the couple abides by the rules of love, to honor and cherish, through sickness and in health, for better or for worse.
	Evidence suggests that one of the important causes of social problems today is the absence of fathers from the lives of many children.
animal rights	Animal rights should not take priority over research experiments that fulfill human needs.
	When millions of animals die for such frivolous reasons as the testing of new cosmetics, shampoos, household cleaners, and radiator fluids when safe products already exist, we've gone too far.

Notice that in each case the thesis statement is a viewpoint about the subject or topic. The thesis deals with a narrower view of the broader subject and makes the author's position clear. You may not agree with the viewpoint, but if the essay is well written, it will support the author's opinion and cause you to evaluate your own viewpoint. A key element in reading, then, is to make certain you understand an author's thesis or viewpoint on the subject of the essay.

Below are some thesis statements. Separate the topic from the writer's viewpoint. In the space provided, write two phrases, one explaining the topic and the other explaining the point being made about the topic.

1. A college education may be important, but its value is overemphasized by many employers.

   topic: _____ college education _____

   viewpoint: _____ value is overemphasized _____

2. A good divorce is better for children than a bad marriage.

   topic: _____ divorce _____

   viewpoint: _____ children better for bad marriage _____

3. Our society seems afraid or ashamed of growing old and places too much emphasis on youth.

topic: _growing old_

viewpoint: _aging too much emphsis on youth._

4. Most of the suggestive visuals shown on MTV distract from the music and subliminally brainwash the viewer.

topic: _MTV_

viewpoint: _____

Compare the content of your phrases with the following chart:

Topic	Viewpoint Expressed
1. college education	value overemphasized by employers
2. divorce	children better off than in a bad marriage
3. aging	ashamed/afraid of aging, too much value placed on youth
4. MTV visuals	distract from music and subliminally brainwash

Thesis statements are usually clearly stated within the essay; often you can find a sentence or two that directly states the author's views. At other times, no one sentence states the thesis, but the author's viewpoint becomes clear once you have read the supporting evidence. In those cases, it's necessary to form the author's thesis in your own words.

Writing Exercise

In your reading journal or on a separate sheet, write today's date and the page numbers you just read. In a paragraph, explain the difference between an essay thesis and a topic. Provide two examples of each.

Supporting Evidence

Once a writer has his or her thesis in mind, the next step is to provide **supporting evidence.** If a thesis is controversial, such as whether or not abortion should be legal, then the writer must provide evidence that will at least cause someone who disagrees to look at abortion from a new angle. As a reader, you need to look for the reasons given to support the thesis. You may still disagree with the author when you have finished reading, but you will understand why the author feels as he or she does.

Of course, you have to be careful that your own feelings or bias on the subject don't cause you to reject or accept the author's viewpoints without thinking carefully about the evidence presented. Let's say you or family members have participated in antiabortion protests. Because of your close involvement, you immediately resent or reject the thesis that abortion should be legal. Your own bias or prejudice (feelings that keep you from seeing another view) could cause you to miss some valid points that you had never considered before, points that might help you understand another person's viewpoint. You still might not change your mind, but it's important to keep an open mind as you read supporting evidence.

In essays, support is given in the form of paragraphs. A paragraph is in some ways similar to a mini-essay. Just as every essay has an implied or stated thesis, a well-written paragraph has an implied or stated **topic sentence.** A topic sentence states the key point or idea of the paragraph. The rest of the sentences support it, just as paragraphs support a thesis.

Good writers use a variety of paragraph types to support their thesis statements. These types are sometimes called **rhetorical modes or patterns.** Because humans think in certain basic ways, we can sometimes communicate better with one another if we use these thinking patterns in our writing. Eight common patterns are presented here.

Description: When authors want to reach one or all of our five senses— sight, sound, smell, touch, and taste—they use description. See if you can visualize what's being described in this paragraph:

> Unable to pay city taxes or incapable of influencing the city to live up to its duty to serve all citizens, the poorer barrio families remain trapped in the nineteenth century and survive the best they can. The backyards have well-worn paths to the outhouses, which sit near the alley. Running water is considered a luxury in some parts of the barrio. Decent drainage is usually unknown, and when it rains, the water stands for days, an incubator of health hazards and an avoidable nuisance. Streets, costly to pave, remain rocky trails. Tires do not last long, and the constant rattling and shaking grind away a car's life and spread dust through screen windows.
>
> —Robert Ramirez, "The Barrio"

Even though there is no stated topic sentence in the paragraph, it is not difficult for us to understand the point the author wants to make about the poorer barrio communities. The city does not live up to its duty to all citizens in the barrio, resulting, we are shown, in "trapped" families using "well-worn paths to the outhouses" where "running water is a luxury." Standing rainwater becomes an "incubator of health hazards." Cars wear out fast because of the unpaved, rocky roads. The author relies on our reactions to his description to imply (suggest or hint at) his message.

Narration: Narration is often used when authors want to tell a story or relate an anecdote about something that has happened in their lives. A paragraph using narration moves from one occurrence to another, generally in chronological order. Here is an example:

> I was saved from sin when I was going on thirteen. But not really saved. It happened like this. There was a big revival at my Auntie Reed's church. Every night for weeks there had been much preaching, singing, praying, and shouting, and some very hardened sinners had been brought to Christ, and the membership of the church had grown by leaps and bounds. Then just before the revival ended, they held a special meeting for children, "to bring the young lambs to the fold." . . . That night I was escorted to the front row and placed on the mourners' bench with all the other young sinners.
>
> —Langston Hughes, "Salvation"

Here the author uses first-person narration, which means that he tells us his story from his own point of view. He takes us back to his thirteenth year and then proceeds to narrate for us the story of how he was saved, "but not really." As readers we can expect the rest of the story to be told in a chronological fashion, moving from one incident to the next. We might say that the topic sentence is the first one, but to be more accurate the main idea of the paragraph is a combination of the first three sentences.

Analysis: An author may wish to take a subject and examine its parts. For instance, a writer could analyze a poem by looking at the way it is structured, examining the number of lines and stanzas, identifying the rhyme scheme, or weighing the reasons behind the use of certain words. Another author may wish to show how a rotary engine works, which would be called a **process analysis,** a step-by-step explanation of the way the engine works. A paragraph based on an analysis pattern reads like this:

> An algorithm is a step-by-step procedure for solving a problem in a finite amount of time. When you start your car, you go through a step-by-step procedure. First, you insert the key. Second, you make sure the transmission is in neutral or park. Third, you depress the gas pedal. Fourth, you turn the key to the start position. If the engine starts within a few seconds, you then release the key to the ignition position. If the engine doesn't start, you wait ten seconds and repeat steps three through six. Finally, if the car doesn't start, you call the garage.
>
> —Nell Dale, *Programming in Pascal*

The topic sentence in this paragraph is the first one, and the subject is how to start a car engine. The paragraph begins analyzing or explaining the process in chronological order. As a reader, we can follow each of the steps. In this case, the process can be told in one paragraph. If the process were more complex, each step in the process might require a paragraph or more to elaborate.

Illustration and example: If you are explaining something to someone who doesn't quite understand, you might say, "For instance," and then proceed to give an example or two to clarify what you mean. The same technique is used in writing. Here is a paragraph that uses the illustration and example pattern:

> Dr. Wayne Dyer, in his book *Your Erroneous Zones,* claims that we have grown up in a culture which has taught us that we are not responsible for our feelings even though the truth is that we always were. He claims we have learned a "host of sayings" to defend ourselves against the fact that we control our feelings. For example, here are some of the utterances that we use over and over to take the blame off ourselves and place it on others:
>
> "You hurt my feelings."
> "You make me feel bad."
> "I can't help the way I feel."
> "He makes me sick."
> "You're embarrassing me."
> "You made me look foolish."
>
> Dyer feels that each of these sayings has a built-in message that we are not responsible for how we feel, when in fact we are in charge of how we feel.
>
> —Adam Ribb, "Responsibility at Large"

As is often the case, the topic sentence for the paragraph is the first one. Notice that the main point is to summarize for us what Dr. Wayne Dyer says in his book *Your Erroneous Zones* about growing up in our culture to think that we are not responsible for our feelings. As a reader, it's important to distinguish between what an author is saying and what someone being written about is saying. The author of the paragraph selects examples of sayings Dyer believes we use to imply that others are responsible for how we feel when, according to Dyer, we are actually in charge of our feelings. The examples are used to support Dyer's views. These are not the views of the paragraph writer. In fact, we don't know what the author thinks about Dyer's views.

Notice that the **transitional phrase** "for example" alerts us to what is coming. Transitional expressions such as *for instance, also, likewise, in addition, furthermore,* and *more than that* alert us that more examples of the same idea are about to be presented. Words such as *but, however, although,* and *rather* should make us aware that a point is about to be modified or contrasted. When we read *consequently, so, therefore, in conclusion, thus,* or *as a result,* we know that we are about to get a summary or the conclusion of a point. An author's use of transitional words is of great help when we read. Remember to use them in your own writing.

Before learning about more paragraph patterns, read the paragraphs below. Underline the topic sentence of each, and then in the spaces provided write the paragraph pattern being used and its purpose. Some paragraphs may use more than one pattern.

1. I looked around the room, and my heart sank. Cobwebs dangled from the ceiling; the once whitewashed walls were yellow with

age and streaked with dust. The single naked bulb was coated with grime and extremely dim. Patches of the cement floor were black with dampness. A strong musty smell pervaded the air. I hastened to open the only small window with its rust-pitted iron bars. When I succeeded in pulling the knob and the window swung open, flakes of peeling paint as well as a shower of dust fell to the floor. The only furniture in the room was three narrow beds of rough wooden planks, one against the wall, the other two stacked one on top of the other. A cement toilet was built into one corner.

—Nien Cheng, *Life and Death in Shanghai*

pattern used: _____ (Narration) description ____

purpose: _____

2. Americans, unlike people almost everywhere else in the world, tend to define and judge everybody in terms of the work they do, especially work performed for pay. Charlie is a doctor; Sam is a carpenter; Mary Ellen is a copywriter at a small ad agency.

—Nickie McWhirter, "What You Do Is What You Are"

pattern used: _____ example ____

purpose: _____

3. It was at Stanford, one day near the end of my senior year, that a friend told me about a summer construction job he knew was available. I was quickly alert. Desire uncoiled within me. My friend said that he knew I had been looking for summer employment. He knew I needed some money. Almost apologetically he explained: It was something I probably wouldn't be interested in, but a friend of his, a contractor, needed someone for the summer to do menial jobs. There would be lots of shoveling and raking and sweeping. Nothing too hard. But nothing more interesting either. Still, the pay would be good. Did I want it? . . . I did. Yes, I said, surprised to hear myself say it.

—Richard Rodriguez, "Workers"

pattern used: _____ narration ____

purpose: _____

4. Grasp the cone with the right hand firmly but gently between the thumb and at least one but not more than three fingers, two-thirds of the way up the cone. Then dart swiftly away to an open area, away from the jostling crowd at the stand. Now take up the classic ice-cream-cone-eating stance: feet from one to two feet apart, body bent forward from the waist at a twenty-five-degree angle,

right elbow well up, right forearm horizontal, at a level with your collarbone and about twelve inches from it. But don't start eating yet! Check first to see what emergency repairs may be necessary. Sometimes a sugar cone will be so crushed or broken or cracked that all one can do is gulp at the thing like a savage, getting what he can of it and letting the rest drop to the ground, and then evacuating the area of catastrophe as quickly as possible.

—L. Rust Hills, "How to Eat an Ice Cream Cone"

pattern used: _____*analysis*_____

purpose: _____

Paragraph 1 uses primarily description, but it is told through first-person narration. The topic sentence is the first one, with the rest of the paragraph describing why her heart sank. The purpose of the paragraph is to describe the room. Paragraph 2 uses examples to support the topic sentence, which is the first one. The purpose is to show that Americans judge people by the work they do. Paragraph 3 uses first-person narration with the purpose of telling about a summer job the author accepted. It is difficult to point to any clearly stated topic sentence, but if there is one, it's the first one. Paragraph 4 uses analysis. Its purpose is to show us the step-by-step process of eating an ice cream cone. Description is also used to help explain the process. There is no stated topic sentence. Make certain you understand these patterns before going on.

Writing Exercise

In your reading journal or on a separate sheet, write today's date and the page numbers you just read. Define "topic sentence." Then differentiate the four rhetorical modes or patterns you just read about and explain why understanding them can help you read or write better.

Division and classification: Classification is used to divide a subject into groups or parts on the basis of similarities. In the following paragraph, notice how the authors divide and classify *baby boomers,* a term applied to people born between 1946 and 1964.

Understandably, the younger half of the baby boom is much more concerned with finances. Since 1967, a UCLA questionnaire has asked incoming students why they want to go to college; among the choices provided are "to become well off financially," or "to gain a meaningful life philosophy." In 1967, as the oldest boomers were entering college, nearly 85 percent said they were going to school for philosophical reasons, and less than half went to school to get rich. By 1985, as the youngest boomers were entering school, three-fourths said, "give me the money." Only 44 percent said they wanted a meaningful life philosophy.

—Jay Olgilvy et al., "What's a Baby Boomer?"

The topic sentence, the first one, states that the younger half of the baby boom generation is more concerned with finances. The rest of the paragraph divides the baby boom generation into older and younger groups. It then classifies the younger half as more interested in attending school for financial gain and the older half as more interested in being educated for philosophical reasons. Statistical support is provided through the UCLA questionnaire.

Comparison and contrast: An author uses this pattern to show similarities (comparison) and differences (contrast) in the subjects under discussion. For instance:

> Crime as presented on television is different from what it is in reality. On television, murder, assault, and armed robbery are the most common crimes. However, in real life, quiet burglaries, clever larcenies, unspectacular auto thefts, and drunkenness are the most common. Video detectives solve 90 percent of their cases. But in reality, the figure is much lower. On TV, only 7 percent of violence occurs between relatives, while this accounts for more than 25–30 percent of interpersonal violence in real life.

Here a comparison and contrast, mostly contrast, is made between crime as portrayed on television and crime as it occurs in real life. Notice the use of the words *however* and *but* to show contrast. Key transitional words often used to show comparisons are *similarly, likewise, compared with, both/and,* and *in the same way.* The words *although, however, but, on the other hand, instead of, different from,* and *as opposed to* are used to indicate contrast.

Definition: In order to clarify words and terms by providing more explanation than a dictionary, or to explain the writer's interpretation of something, a longer definition is sometimes needed. Frequently, examples and comparison or contrast are used to help define. Notice in the following example how the author defines the term *American dream:*

> First, let us get this [American] dream business—and business it now seems to be—straight. The word *dream* is not a synonym for *reality* or *promise.* It is closer to *hope* or *possibility* or even *vision.* The original American dream had only a little to do with material possessions and a lot to do with choices, beginnings and opportunity.
>
> —Betty Anne Younglove, "The American Dream"

Here the author is defining the term *American dream* as she sees it. By comparing and contrasting, she defines what it is and is not, implying that there is a new, incorrect definition that has more to do with materialism than its original, true meaning.

Cause and effect: A cause-effect paragraph explains why something happens or happened. Some keywords that serve as clues in such paragraphs are *because of this, for this reason, as a result,* and *resulting in.* Sometimes the effects are presented first and the cause of the effects last; at other times it is the other way around.

See if you can distinguish between the cause and the effect in the following paragraph:

> Television commercials brought a lot of fun and fun-loving folks into the picture. Everything that people in those commercials did looked like fun: taking Polaroid snapshots, swilling beer, buying insurance, mopping the floor, bowling, taking aspirin. We all wished, I'm sure, that we could have half as much fun as those rough-and-ready guys around the locker room, flicking each other with towels and pouring champagne. The more commercials people watched, the more they wondered when the fun would start in their own lives.
>
> —Suzanne Britt, "Fun. Oh, Boy. Fun. You Could Die from It."

The cause here is watching fun-loving folks in television commercials. The effect is that they made everything look like fun, causing still another effect: people wondered when they would begin having fun.

To make certain you can recognize the writing patterns you just learned about, read the paragraphs below. Underline the topic sentence of each, and then in the spaces provided write the paragraph pattern being used and its purpose. Some paragraphs may use more than one pattern.

1. If you're within a few miles of a nuclear detonation, you'll be incinerated on the spot! And if you survive the blast, what does the future promise? The silent but deadly radiation, either directly or from fallout, in a dose of 400 rems could kill you within two weeks. Your hair would fall out, your skin would be covered with large ulcers, you would vomit and experience diarrhea and you would die from infection or massive bleeding as your white blood cells and platelets stopped working.

   —Ken Keyes, Jr., *The Hundredth Monkey*

   pattern used: _____

   purpose: _____

2. An inference is a statement *about* the unknown made on the basis of what *is* known. In other words, an inference is an educated guess. If a woman smiles when a man tells her she is attractive, he can infer she is pleased. If she frowns and slaps him, he can guess she is not pleased. His inferences are based on what is known: people generally smile when they are pleased and frown when displeased. However, to know for certain why she slapped him, we would have to ask her.

   pattern used: _____

   purpose: _____

3. What do L.A. [Los Angeles] women want? According to the poll, their top two goals in life are having a happy marriage, named by 37%, and helping others, 21%. Those are followed by career and a desire to be creative. Power and fame rank low on the list, with 1% each. But among women who've never been married, career takes top priority, followed by marriage and helping others. Four percent chose fame. A happy marriage appears to be the most popular goal in the Valley and Southeast areas, where it was chosen by 46% of the women—about double the number on the Westside.
   —Cathleen Decker, "The L.A. Woman"

   pattern used: _____

   purpose: _____

4. Every paragraph you write should include one sentence that's supported by everything else in that paragraph. That is the topic sentence. It can be the first sentence, the last sentence, the sixth sentence, or even a sentence that exists only in your mind. When testing your article for topic sentences, you should be able to look at each paragraph and say what the topic sentence is. Having said it, look at all the other sentences in the paragraph and test them to make sure they support it.
   —Gary Provost, "The 8 Essentials of Nonfiction That Sells"

   pattern used: _____

   purpose: _____

5. A trend that began about 10 years ago in Lincoln Heights seems to have hit a critical point now. It's similar to the ethnic tug-of-war of yesteryear, but different colors, different words are involved. Today Chinese and Vietnamese are displacing the Latinos who, by choice or circumstance, had Lincoln Heights virtually to themselves for two solid generations. . . . The bank where I opened my first meager savings account in the late 1950s has changed hands. It's now the East-West Federal Bank, an Asian-owned enterprise. The public library on Workman Street, where I checked out *Charlotte's Web* with my first library card, abounds with signs of the new times: It's called "La Biblioteca del Pueblo Heights," and on the door there's a notice that the building is closed because of the Oct. 1 earthquake; it's written in Chinese.
   —Luis Torres, "Los Chinos Discover El Barrio"

   pattern used: _____

   purpose: _____

6. Walnut Canyon offered the Sinagua more than cozy home sites. A dependable supply of water flowed along the stream bed on the floor of the canyon. Fertile volcanic-cinder soil lay within about two miles of the canyon rim. A variety of trees, for fuel and implements, grew within the canyon and on the mesa. Other wild plants, a source of food and medicines, lined the banks of the stream and blanketed the slope. Game, furred and feathered, abounded in the canyon and on the mesa top.

—"Walnut Canyon," Superintendent of Documents, U.S. Government Printing Office

pattern used: _____

purpose: _____

Compare your responses to the paragraphs with these:

1. The topic sentence is the third one. The basic pattern is cause and effect, with description of the effects of the blast provided. The cause is the nuclear bomb and the effect is death. The purpose is to show that you will die from radiation even if the initial blast doesn't kill you.

2. The first sentence is the topic sentence. The pattern is definition, with the example of the man and woman used to clarify the definition. The purpose is to define *inference.*

3. There really isn't a topic sentence. The implied topic sentence is an answer to the question that begins the paragraph, such as "Here is the result of the polls showing what L.A. women want." To show us what they want, the author uses the classification "L.A. women" and divides or groups them according to poll percentages. She further groups the women by areas: the Valley, the Southeast, and the Westside. The purpose is to reveal what L.A. women want, according to the polls.

4. The first sentence is the topic sentence. The author uses both definition and process analysis. He defines what a topic sentence is and its position in the paragraph. Then he shows how to test for an implied or directly stated topic sentence in each paragraph. The purpose is to stress the importance of the topic sentence in writing.

5. The topic sentence is the third one. The rest of the sentences contrast the differences in Lincoln Heights from the time he lived there to now. Examples such as the library and the bank are used to show the contrast. The purpose is to show that what was once a Latino neighborhood is now being shared by Asians.

6. The topic sentence is the first one, stating that Walnut Canyon offered more than "cozy home sites." The pattern used is a combination of description and examples that show why the site was a good place for the Sinagua to live—the purpose of the paragraph.

Make certain that you understand what a topic sentence is and that you can recognize all eight paragraph patterns before reading on.

Writing Exercise

In your reading journal or on a separate sheet, write today's date and the page numbers you just read. Define the four rhetorical modes or patterns you just read about, and explain why understanding them can help you read or write better.

Order of Support

The third ingredient of a well-structured essay, in addition to thesis and supporting evidence, is the **order or arrangement of the thesis and its supporting evidence.** A good writer will arrange the supporting points for the thesis in a logical, progressive order. What we see when we read an essay is the final product. What we *don't* see are the many different writing drafts the writer went through before deciding which supporting point should go where or which paragraph pattern of development worked best. As a writer, you will need to go through the same process of writing several drafts before deciding which one works best for your audience.

It would be convenient if all essays followed the same writing pattern, but it would also be boring. Part of the pleasure of reading is to experience the various ways writers work with words and ideas. Still, many essays do follow the traditional form, shown in the diagram on the next page. Keep in mind, however, that longer essays may take two or three paragraphs rather than one to introduce their topic and thesis. Most of your student essay writing assignments will probably be short enough to allow you to follow this model.

The diagram represents the basic structure of an essay. Longer essays will, of course, contain more paragraphs. Sometimes an author writes two or three paragraphs of introduction. There may be a dozen supporting paragraphs, and the conclusion may well take more than one paragraph. Sometimes an author's thesis may not be clear until the last paragraph. The typical essay form, however, is much the way it is outlined above, and the diagram probably represents the way your instructor wants you to construct essays in this course.

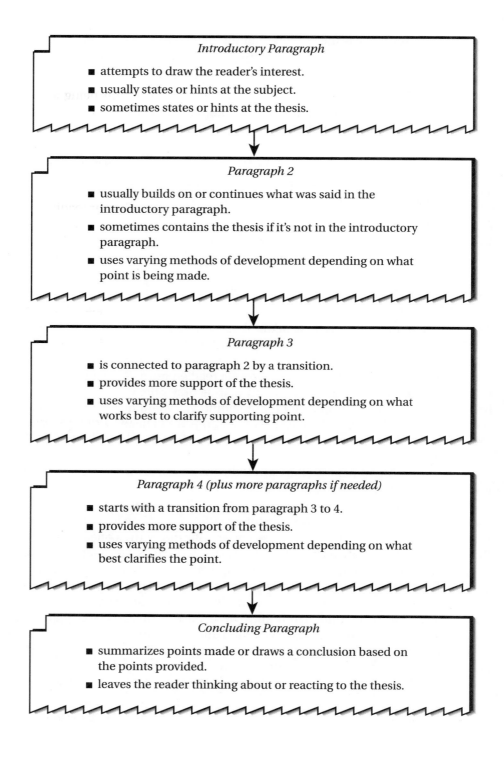

Introductory Paragraph

- attempts to draw the reader's interest.
- usually states or hints at the subject.
- sometimes states or hints at the thesis.

Paragraph 2

- usually builds on or continues what was said in the introductory paragraph.
- sometimes contains the thesis if it's not in the introductory paragraph.
- uses varying methods of development depending on what point is being made.

Paragraph 3

- is connected to paragraph 2 by a transition.
- provides more support of the thesis.
- uses varying methods of development depending on what works best to clarify supporting point.

Paragraph 4 (plus more paragraphs if needed)

- starts with a transition from paragraph 3 to 4.
- provides more support of the thesis.
- uses varying methods of development depending on what best clarifies the point.

Concluding Paragraph

- summarizes points made or draws a conclusion based on the points provided.
- leaves the reader thinking about or reacting to the thesis.

Before Going On

You have learned that three basic ingredients make up a good essay: a thesis, sufficient support of the thesis, and a logical order or arrangement of the supporting material. Good reading comprehension depends upon being able to identify an author's thesis based on the support that is provided. You have also learned eight different paragraph patterns or rhetorical modes that writers use to express their views: description, narration, analysis, illustration and example, definition, classification and division, comparison and contrast, and cause-effect relationships. Topic sentences are supported through the use of these patterns. In addition, you have learned the basic structure most essays follow to support the thesis. Applying this knowledge can enhance both your reading and writing skills.

Writing Exercise

In your journal or on a separate sheet of paper, write a paragraph that defines the three basic elements that constitute a well-structured essay. Make certain your paragraph has a topic sentence to support. Your instructor may want to see it.

Understanding the Content

Let's look now at the skills you need to better understand what you read. To get the most from your reading, you need to be able to separate main ideas from supporting details, to distinguish fact from opinion and bias, and to draw inferences from implied statements. As you read, all of these skills work together, but for clarification purposes we'll look at each skill separately.

Separating Main Ideas from Supporting Details

The main idea in an essay is the thesis, which we've already discussed on pages 5–7. As you've seen, each paragraph in an essay supports that main idea. You've also learned that each paragraph is, in a way, a mini-essay. Paragraphs, too, have a main idea, expressed through the topic sentence and supported by the rest of the sentences.

Read the following paragraph and underline what you think is the main idea. Determine what paragraph pattern is used.

> There are almost as many definitions of meditation as there are people meditating. It has been described as a fourth state of consciousness (neither waking, sleeping, nor dreaming); as a way to recharge one's inner batteries; as a state of passive awareness, of "no mind." Some teachers regard meditation as the complement to prayer: "Prayer is when you talk to God;

meditation is when you listen to God." Some say meditation teaches the conscious mind to be still.

—Diana Robinson, "Recharging Yourself Through Meditation"

The point of the paragraph is to show that there are many definitions of meditation. Each of the supporting sentences provides an example of a different definition of meditation to show just how varied they are. An outline of the paragraph might look like this:

Main idea:	"There are almost as many definitions of meditation as there are people meditating."
Support:	one definition: fourth state of consciousness (neither waking, sleeping, nor dreaming)
Support:	second definition: recharging one's batteries
Support:	third definition: state of passive awareness, no mind
Support:	fourth definition: complement to prayer
Support:	fifth definition: teaches mind to be still

What we see are five different definitions that support the statement made in the first sentence. The first sentence, then, is the topic sentence.

Looking for the main idea in the first sentence of a paragraph is a good place to begin, but as you've already seen, it doesn't always appear there. Read and then underline the main idea in the following paragraph:

In one year, about $3.5 billion is spent for television commercial time. Where does all this money come from, and where does it go? Suppose Ford Motor Company buys $1 million worth of air time from NBC to introduce its new models in the fall. First it hires an advertising agency to actually produce the commercials. Of the $1 million, 15% goes to the agency for its services, and 85% goes to the network. The network in turn uses some of its 85% to pay program costs and some to pay local stations who broadcast the shows on which Ford commercials are carried. This latter payment usually equals about one-third of the local station's base rate (the amount a station would receive for commercial time bought by a local advertiser).

In the above paragraph, the first sentence does *not* state the main idea. Most of the paragraph provides an example of what would happen to one million dollars spent by the Ford Motor Company on television advertising. The example is used to provide a breakdown of where the money spent on television advertising comes from and where it goes, providing an answer to the question in the second sentence of the paragraph: "Where does all this money [$3.5 billion spent on TV advertising] come from, and where does it go?" In a way, then, the main idea is really a combination of the first two sentences of the paragraph. An outline of the paragraph might look something like this:

Main idea:	Here's an example of where the $3.5 billion a year spent on advertising comes from and where it goes.

Support: If Ford Motor Company spent $1 million on TV ads:

1. 15% would go to an advertising agency
2. 85% would go to the network, which would pay
   a. program costs
   b. local stations that broadcast the shows on which ads appear (about one-third of the local station's base advertising rate)

In this paragraph, then, there is no one topic sentence expressing the main idea, but by combining the first two sentences, we can form a topic sentence of our own. Here is another paragraph. Underline what you think is the main idea.

> The Upjohn Company is studying anti-cholesterol therapy that would actually reverse some coronary artery injury. They are also doing some exciting research in combating hypertension. In addition, they are working on important advances against deadly heart arrhythmias, or irregular heartbeat rhythms, plus a new way to zero in on blood clots with fewer side effects. These are just a few of the research projects against heart disease that Upjohn is working on.

The main idea in the paragraph appears in the last sentence. It sums up the purpose of each of the other sentences—to provide examples of the research projects Upjohn is working on in the area of heart disease. An outline of the paragraph might look like this:

Main idea: Here are a few examples of Upjohn's research projects against heart disease.

Support: anti-cholesterol therapy to reverse coronary artery injury

Support: ways to combat hypertension

Support: advances against heartbeat irregularities (arrhythmias)

Support: ways to treat blood clots with fewer side effects

Thus, we see that it doesn't matter where a topic sentence is placed; first, last, or somewhere in between, it will always contain the main idea of the paragraph.

When you have difficulty separating main ideas from the details of a paragraph, you may need to stop and outline the passage that is giving you trouble. Remember that reading entails a combination of skills, only one of which is separating main ideas from supporting details. But identifying the main idea, whether in a paragraph or an essay, is crucial to good comprehension.

Separating Fact from Opinion

Once you have identified the main ideas from supporting details, you need to separate facts from opinions. A **fact** is usually defined as something that can be proven. We accept something as a fact only when many different people come to the same conclusion after years of observation, research, and experimentation. Evidence that supports a fact is generally arrived at objectively. An **opinion,** on the other hand, is a belief, feeling, or judgment made about something or someone that a person may hold as fact but cannot prove. Evidence that supports an opinion is usually subjective. *Beautiful/ugly, wonderful/terrible, nice/disgusting,* and *greatest/worst* are examples of subjective words writers often use to express their views. When you see them, you're reading opinions, even if you agree with the author.

But separating facts from opinions is not always easy. One reason is that facts change. At one time in history, it was a "fact" that the earth was flat (members of the Flat Earth Society still believe it); it was a "fact" that the sun revolved around the earth; it was a "fact" that the atom couldn't be split; it was a "fact" that no one would ever walk on the moon. Today, enough evidence has been gathered to prove that these and many other "facts" are wrong. Who knows what "facts" of today may be laughed at by future generations?

Another reason that separating fact from opinion is difficult is that opinion statements can be made to sound factual. We might read in one anthropology book that the first inhabitants of North America arrived "around 25,000 years ago." Another book might say North America was first inhabited "over 35,000 years ago." Which is the correct figure? Since no one who lived back then kept records, and since anthropologists disagree on the exact date the first Native Americans came, we have to be careful that we don't accept such information as actual fact. We could take the trouble to read several anthropology journals and textbooks to get an overview of what various anthropologists believe, but until there is more factual evidence, we can't accept either date as fact. In the future, there may be enough evidence gathered to prove a particular date.

Another reason for the difficulty in separating fact from opinion is our personal bias or prejudice. Frequently, we allow our feelings and beliefs to interfere with our acceptance of facts. Certain ideas and thoughts are instilled in us as we grow up. Family, friends, and people we admire all influence our thinking. Sometimes we unknowingly accept someone's opinion as fact simply because of our faith in that person.

Let's look now at some statements of fact and opinion. In the following paragraph, underline any verifiable facts (those statements that can be supported with objective evidence).

> In the U.S., 1 in 6 couples has difficulty conceiving or bearing a child. About 27 percent of women between ages 15 and 44 can't have children because of physical problems. The sperm count of U.S. males has fallen more than 30 percent in 50 years. Some 25 percent of men are considered functionally sterile. Experts suspect that environmental pollution is a cause.
>
> —Stanley N. Wellborn, "Birth"

In this case the entire paragraph should have been underlined. You may have hesitated marking the last sentence as fact. But the sentence doesn't say that environmental pollution *is* a cause; it merely says that experts suspect it is, and it can be verified that experts do suspect it is a cause. All of the paragraph can be accepted as factual. The author of the paragraph does not offer his opinion; he merely presents objective, statistical data.

Read the following paragraph and underline any statements in it that seem to be factual or that could be verified as fact:

> It's hard to believe, but in the ninth decade of the 20th Century, *The Catcher in the Rye, Of Mice and Men, Huckleberry Finn,* and *The Diary of Anne Frank,* among other books, are still the objects of censorship in the nation's public schools. And the incidence of book bannings is going up, according to a report by People for the American Way, the liberal watchdog group. In the last year, the study found, there were efforts to ban books in schools in 46 of the 50 states, including California. Many of them succeeded.
>
> —Editorial, *Los Angeles Times*

The opening four words, "It's hard to believe," constitute a statement of opinion, but the majority of the paragraph can be verified as fact. We could do research on censorship to see if the books mentioned are "still objects of censorship in the nation's public schools." We could read the study mentioned by People for the American Way to see if the numbers quoted are correct. We could investigate the group that did the study to see if it is reliable. If we disagree with the statement because we don't want to believe it, that's because of personal bias; basically, there's no reason we shouldn't accept the statement as verifiable.

Now read this paragraph and underline any statements that appear to be facts:

> The purpose of education is to teach students to think, not to instill dogma or to train them to respond in predictable ways. Far from being banned, controversial material should be welcomed in schools. Students should be taught the critical ability to evaluate different ideas and to come to their own conclusions. It is a disservice to them and to society to restrict instructional material to a single viewpoint.
>
> —Editorial, *Los Angeles Times*

If you underlined anything in the above paragraph, you didn't underline any facts. Regardless of how true or false you think the ideas in the paragraph are, they are all opinions. On a personal level, we may agree with the statements made, but that doesn't make them facts. Not everyone agrees with the purpose of education as stated above; many people do not want controversial materials presented to their children. In fact, some parents select certain schools for their children *because* only one viewpoint is taught.

Here's one more statement on censorship. Again, read it and underline any statements that seem to be factual.

> Everyone older than 50 grew up in a time when Hollywood films were strictly censored by the industry itself to exclude explicit sexual scenes, gruesome violence, and vulgar language. The Supreme Court in the 1950s struck down

movie censorship. It extended to film makers the First Amendment protection traditionally enjoyed by newspapers and book publishers. The court also redefined the anti-pornography and anti-obscenity statutes into meaninglessness.

Those decisions were praised as liberal advances, but their consequences were unforeseen and disastrous. . . . Unless they are reversed, the coarsening and corrupting of the nation's youth will continue.

—William Shannon, "Shield Our Youth with Censorship"

A mixture of fact and opinion appears here. At one time, the film industry *did* censor itself; in the 1950s, the Supreme Court *did* rule against movie censorship by expanding the interpretation of the First Amendment; some people *did* praise this as a liberal advance. This can all be verified. The last sentence, however, is opinion. There is no verifiable proof that the lack of censorship in the movies is the cause for the "coarsening and corrupting of the nation's youth," nor is there verifiable proof that unless the decisions the author cites are reversed, the corruption of youth will continue. He uses facts to make his opinions appear true.

As a careful reader, you will want to use the essays in Part 2 as a means of practicing the separation of facts from opinions.

Drawing Inferences

Another reading skill essential to effective reading is **drawing inferences.** Sometimes writers don't state directly what they mean; they imply or suggest their meaning. When that happens, we have to draw inferences from what they do say.

Drawing an inference is sometimes called "making an educated guess." Based on what an author tells us, we can often guess what other thoughts, feelings, and ideas the author may have that are not stated directly. For instance, what are some things you can tell about the writer of the following paragraph that are not directly stated?

In 1997, we commemorated the 110th anniversary of Sherlock Holmes's "birth." The great sleuth made his first appearance in 1887, and right from the start was so popular that when his creator killed him off after twenty-four adventures, followers eventually forced Conan Doyle to bring him back to life. Even today, the intrepid duo of Holmes and his stalwart companion Dr. Watson continue to delight each new generation of readers.

The author doesn't say it straight out, but we can infer from what is said that the writer is very knowledgeable about the Sherlock Holmes stories because of the facts that are presented. We also suspect that the author has probably read most or all of the stories and likes them very much; notice the use of such phrases as "great sleuth," "intrepid duo," and "continue to delight." Finally, based on the vocabulary and structural organization used, we can infer that the writer is fairly literate. These inferences help us get a sense of the person writing, a sense that goes beyond what is actually written. We may not always be right, but the more we practice, the more our inferences will be good educated guesses.

Read the following paragraph and see what inferences you can draw about the author.

> We say that it is our right to control our bodies, and this is true. But there is a distinction that needs to be made, and that distinction is this: Preventing a pregnancy is controlling a body—controlling your body. But preventing the continuance of a human life that is not your own is murder. If you attempt to control the body of another in that fashion, you become as a slave master was—controlling the lives and bodies of his slave, chopping off their feet when they ran away, or murdering them if it pleased him.
>
> —Ken Lonnquist, "Ghosts"

You probably can infer that the author of the paragraph is against abortion. While he agrees with pro-abortionists that we have a right to control our bodies, he draws the line after conception. We can infer, then, that he defines human life as beginning at the moment sperm and egg fuse. We can also infer that he is opposed to slavery. We might even suspect that his use of the unpleasant image of slave masters cutting off the feet of runaways in connection with abortion is done deliberately to win readers to his way of thinking. If we are pro-abortionists, we might still disagree with him, but we will better understand the reasons for his views.

Now let's put together all of this section on understanding content. Read the next paragraph, underline what you think is the main idea, and see what you can infer about the author:

> Controversy—the heart of politics—has gotten a bad name in the textbook business, and publishers have advised their writers to avoid it. This fear of controversy is distorting our children's education, leaving us with biology texts that neglect evolution history and texts that omit the important influence of religion. Similarly, in civics and government texts, it is treatment of such volatile events as the Vietnam war, the Watergate scandal, the civil rights movement, and the school prayer debate that is "dulled down" to the point of tedium, or minimized to the point of evasion.
>
> —Arthur J. Kropp, "Let's Put an End to Mediocre Textbooks"

If you underlined the first sentence as the main idea, you are partly right. But there are parts of the second sentence that also apply. One paragraph method used here is cause-effect: the cause, the fear of publishers to deal with controversial issues in textbooks; the effect, a distortion of children's education. Although the author mentions that publishers have advised their writers to avoid certain issues in textbooks, the paragraph does not support that point. The support statements that are provided are instead examples of issues that are either left out or watered down in textbooks, which the author believes then distorts children's education. Thus, the paragraph uses a combination of cause-effect and illustration-example. Here is a possible outline of the paragraph:

Main idea: Fear among publishers to deal with controversial issues has resulted in a distortion of children's education. (cause-effect)

Support: biology texts that neglect evolution history

Support: omission of the important influence of religion

Support: civics and government texts that "dull down" or minimize
  a. Vietnam war
  b. Watergate scandal
  c. civil rights movement
  d. school prayer debate

Though he does not directly state it, we can infer that the author is against censorship and that he believes children should be exposed to controversy. We can infer that he does not want everything in textbooks to be watered down to show only the "smooth" side of life. We can also infer that the author believes publishers are responsible for producing books that do not challenge students. This, we might guess, is from the fear that controversial subjects in textbooks might offend some people, who would then put pressure on the schools not to buy those books.

As written, most of what is stated is opinion. To prove or disprove what he says and implies, we would need to examine textbooks in many of the areas he mentions, or do further research on the subject of textbook censorship.

Use the following passage to practice all of the reading skills you have learned.

Adaptability and lifelong learning are now the cornerstones of success. What direction does a person take to prepare for a lifetime of change? The one degree which provides training which never becomes obsolete is the liberal arts degree; it teaches you how to think. It also teaches you how to read, write and speak intelligently, get along with others, and conceptualize problems. For the first time in several decades, the liberal arts degree is coming to the forefront of the employment field.

Growing ranks of corporate executives are lamenting that college students are specializing too much and too early. What corporate America really needs, according to chief executive officers of major corporations, is students soundly grounded in the liberal arts—English, especially—who then can pick up more specific business or technical skills on the job. Few students, however, seem to be listening to this message. Today's best selling courses offer evidence that students want to take the courses that provide direct job related skills rather than the most basic survival skills in the workplace: communication and thinking skills. They want courses they can parlay into jobs—and high paying ones at that.

—Debra Sikes and Barbara Murray,
"The Practicality of the Liberal Arts Major"

Writing Exercise

In your journal or on a separate sheet of paper, answer the following questions about the two paragraphs you just read. You may look back at the essay paragraphs if you need to do so.

1. What writing pattern is used in the first paragraph?
2. In your own words, write a one-sentence statement of the main idea of the first paragraph.
3. List the support provided for the main idea of the first paragraph.
4. In your own words, write a topic sentence for the second paragraph.
5. What inference can you draw regarding the authors' attitude toward a liberal arts degree?
6. Is the passage mostly fact or opinion? Explain.
7. What does the passage imply about most of today's college students?

Wording will be different, of course, but compare your answers with these:

1. Examples of the benefits of a liberal arts education make up the bulk of the paragraph; thus the illustration and example pattern is used.
2. A combination of the first three sentences is needed to cover the major point of the paragraph, so the main idea is "The one degree that provides adaptability and lifelong learning skills is the liberal arts degree."
3. The liberal arts degree (1) teaches you how to (a) think, (b) read, write, and speak intelligently, (c) get along with others, and (d) conceptualize problems; and (2) it is coming to the forefront of the employment field.
4. The basic idea is "Corporate executives feel that college students are coming into business too specialized, but students don't seem to be listening."
5. The authors seem in favor of the degree.
6. The passage is mostly opinion. (However, you should be aware that the passage is taken from an article that is based on the findings of research conducted with corporate executives.)
7. The last two sentences imply that most of today's college students are more interested in obtaining job skills that they think will land them high-paying jobs. They are more interested in making money than preparing for lifelong change and adaptability.

Make your goal the ability to read well enough to answer correctly these types of questions when you read. Part 2 will provide ample practice.

Before Going On

You have learned that reading critically requires the ability to distinguish main ideas from supporting details, to separate fact from opinion, and to draw inferences from authors' direct statements.

Writing Exercise

In your journal or on a separate sheet of paper, write a paragraph explaining what major field of study you have selected, why you selected it, and what you hope to learn. If you have not yet selected a major, write a paragraph that discusses areas of study you are considering and why. Make certain that you have a clearly stated topic sentence and adequate support. Your instructor may want to see this exercise.

Marking as You Read

To improve your comprehension and concentration, read the essays in Part 2 with a pen or pencil in hand, making notations in the margins. Marking as you read slows you down; it helps you to get engaged with the author, to catch your thoughts and put them in writing before you forget them. How you mark or take notes as you read is up to you, but you might want to consider doing all or some of the following:

1. Underline only major points or statements. Don't underline almost everything as some students do. Force yourself to read so carefully that you are sure that a statement or phrase is important before you mark it. Identifying the paragraph method used may help you see the difference between main ideas and supporting points.

2. Use numbers in the margins when a series of points is listed or discussed. This, too, will help you distinguish the main ideas from supporting points.

3. Think about and react to what you are reading. In the margins, write your reactions, such as "Good point!" or "Never thought of that" or "Where's the proof?" if you don't believe a statement.

4. If there's not much room in the margins, create your own kind of shorthand: Use an exclamation mark (!) when a statement surprises you, a question mark (?) when you don't understand a point, or abbreviations, such as "ex" for example or "prf" for proof—anything that will remind you of your reaction.

5. Write a paragraph summarizing the reading selection. If you can't, then you may need to read it again.

These are just suggestions. You or your instructor may have other methods for marking. Feel free to mark your books in any way that will help your reading concentration. Whatever the method, the reasons for marking are to gain control of concentration and to develop close, analytical reading.

Try to cultivate an interest in the assigned readings. If you don't know anything about the subject of a reading selection, keep asking questions as you read, such as "What does the author mean by this statement?" and "How do I know if this is true?" and "What's the point of this comment?" Asking questions about what you are reading will keep you involved. Don't try to read for too long a period of time. And don't try to read assignments when you are tired; you won't concentrate very well. Good reading requires a fresh mind.

Here's a reading selection typical of the kind in Part 2 of this book. Read it through once. Then read it again, marking it up as suggested above or using your own marking techniques.

The Wet Drug = booze

PETE HAMILL

1   Among the worst bores in the Western world are religious converts and reformed drunks. I have never been knocked off a horse on the way to Damascus, but I did give up drinking more than a dozen years ago. This didn't make me feel morally superior to anyone. If asked, I would talk about going dry but, from the first, I was determined to preach no sermons and stand in judgment of no human being who took pleasure in the sauce. → liquor

2   But I must confess that lately my feelings have begun to change. Drinking and drunks now fill me with loathing. Increasingly, I see close friends—human beings of intelligence, wit and style—reduced to slobbering fools by liquor. I've seen other friends ruin their marriages, brutalize their children, destroy their careers. I've also reached the age when I've had to help bury a few people who allowed booze to take them into eternity.   = liquor

3   In the past few weeks, two ghastly episodes have underlined for me the horror that goes with alcohol. In New Bedford, Mass., a 21-year-old woman was beaten and repeatedly raped by a gang of drunks in a bar called Big Dan's. There were at least 15 onlookers to her violation; they did nothing to prevent it. All of them were drunk or drinking.

4   In New York, four teen-age boys were killed when a car driven by a fifth kid smashed into a concrete wall at 90 mph. They were all under the legal drinking age of 19; nevertheless, they had managed to spend a long night drinking in a public bar, and got drunk enough to die. When it was over, and they had pried the human pieces out of the torn rubber and steel, the driver was charged with four counts of manslaughter. His worst punishment may be that he lived.

5   These are not isolated cases. This year more than 25,000 Americans will die in auto accidents caused by alcohol. And the roads are not the

only site of the horror. Studies indicate that alcohol is a factor in 86 percent of our homicides, 83 percent of our fatal fires, 72 percent of robberies, 52 percent of wife-beatings, 38 percent of cases of child abuse. We can never be certain how many on-the-job accidents are caused by drinking, how many drownings, how many suicides.

6   All of this is bizarre. We live in a culture that certifies alcohol as an acceptable drug and places marijuana smokers or coke dealers in jail. Presidents and statesmen toast each other with the wet drug. It's advertised on radio and TV. Popular music is full of references to it. But when the mellow moments, the elegant evenings are over, there are our kids, smashing themselves into eternity with the same drug.

7   I'm not suggesting here any bluenose return to Prohibition. But I wish we would begin to make it more and more clear that drinking to drunkenness is one of the more disgusting occupations of human beings.

8   For every beer commercial showing all those he-men getting ready to drink, we should show footage of destroyed teenagers, their bodies broken and bleeding, beer cans filling what's left of the back seat. For every high fashion couple toasting each other with wine, show men and women puking on their shoes, falling over tables, sliding away into violence.

9   If cigarette advertising could be banned from TV, so should commercials for the drug called alcohol. Cigarette smokers, after all, usually kill only themselves with their habit. Drunks get behind the wheels of their cars and kill strangers. *How about second hand smoke?*

10   At night now, driving along any American road, you come across these vomiting slaughterers, slowly weaving from lane to lane, or racing in confused fury to the grave at 90 mph. They don't know the rest of us exist and, what's more, they don't care. They are criminal narcissists, careening around until they kill others and themselves.

11   We Americans should begin immediately to remind ourselves that when we drink we are entering the company of killers and fools. *= we take risk.*   *opinion*

Here again is the essay you just read. Compare your markings with those below. Your markings will be different, but compare what you underlined as main ideas and what you marked as supporting points with those marked in the model. They should be similar.

The Wet Drug

PETE HAMILL

Among the worst bores in the Western world are religious converts and reformed drunks. I have never been knocked off a horse on the *ask* ? way to Damascus, but I did give up drinking more than a dozen years *instr* *what* ago. This didn't make me feel morally superior to anyone. If asked, I *mea* would talk about going dry but, from the first, I was determined to preach no sermons and stand in judgment of no human being who took pleasure in the sauce. Booze? Ah, the wet drug!

transition

changed his mind why? 1. foolish acting 2. ruined marriages 3. child beating 4. ruined careers 5. death

But I must confess that lately my feelings have begun to change. Drinking and drunks now fill me with loathing. Increasingly, I see close friends—human beings of intelligence, wit and style—reduced to slobbering fools by liquor. I've seen other friends ruin their marriages, brutalize their children, destroy their careers. I've also reached the age when I've had to help bury a few people who allowed booze to take them into eternity.

example of drunks in bar—beating/raping woman

In the past few weeks, two ghastly episodes have underlined for me the horror that goes with alcohol. In New Bedford, Mass., a 21-year-old woman was beaten and repeatedly raped by a gang of drunks in a bar called Big Dan's. There were at least 15 onlookers to her violation; they did nothing to prevent it. All of them were drunk or drinking.

example of 4 teenage deaths from drunk driving

Yuk! (Descriptive)

In New York, four teen-age boys were killed when a car driven by a fifth kid smashed into a concrete wall at 90 mph. They were all under the legal drinking age of 19; nevertheless, they had managed to spend a long night drinking in a public bar, and got drunk enough to die. When it was over, and they had pried the human pieces out of the torn rubber and steel, the driver was charged with four counts of manslaughter. His worst punishment may be that he lived.

statistics on damage from drinking problems 1. auto accidents 2. homicides 3. fires 4. robberies 5. wife beating 6. child abuse

These are not isolated cases. This year more than 25,000 Americans will die in auto accidents caused by alcohol. And the roads are notthe only site of the horror. Studies indicate that alcohol is a factor in 86 percent of our homicides, 83 percent of our fatal fires, 72 percent of robberies, 52 percent of wife-beatings, 38 percent of cases of child abuse. We can never be certain how many on-the-job accidents are caused by drinking, how many drownings, how many suicides.

good point if alcohol is so damaging why legal?

examples of acceptability contrasted with problem

All of this is bizarre. We live in a culture that certifies alcohol as an acceptable drug and places marijuana smokers or coke dealers in jail. Presidents and statesmen toast each other with the wet drug. It's advertised on radio and TV. Popular music is full of references to it. But when the mellow moments, the elegant evenings are over, there are our kids, smashing themselves into eternity with the same drug.

I'm not suggesting here any bluenose return to Prohibition. But I wish we would begin to make it more and more clear that drinking to drunkenness is one of the more disgusting occupations of human beings.

For every beer commercial showing all those he-men getting ready to drink, we should show footage of destroyed teenagers, their bodies broken and bleeding, beer cans filling what's left of the back

wants to counter all "acceptable" drinking images in media with negative, "realistic" ones

seat. For every high fashion couple toasting each other with wine, show men and <u>women puking on their shoes, falling over tables,</u> sliding away into violence.

comp cont

wants to ban alcohol ads

If cigarette advertising could be banned from TV, so should commercials for the drug called alcohol. Cigarette smokers, after all, usually kill only themselves with their habit. Drunks get behind the wheels of their cars and kill strangers.

str ima

At night now, driving along any American road, you come across these <u>vomiting slaughterers</u>, slowly weaving from lane to lane, or racing in confused fury to the grave at 90 mph. They don't know the rest of us exist and, what's more, they don't care. They are criminal <u>narcissists</u>, careening around until they kill others and themselves.

stron ima

?

We Americans should begin immediately to remind ourselves that when we drink we are entering the company of killers and fools.

force endi sound fed

—ask teacher about ". . . way to Damascus" in first ¶
—look up <u>narcissist</u>
—strong argument—uses personal appeal, emotional appeal, facts & figures
—guess booze is a wet drug—never thought about it before

If you aren't used to this type of reading, it may take one or two practices before you feel confident about what you are doing. But it's practice worth your time.

Writing Summaries

Another habit worth developing is to write a one-paragraph summary in your journal of each essay you are assigned to read. Doing so requires that you put to use all the reading skills discussed earlier. To write an accurate summary, you need to recognize the main idea of the essay (the thesis), identify its supporting points, separate fact from opinion, and draw inferences. You then use this information to write an objective summary, including only what the author says, not your opinions. When you write a summary in your journal, follow these steps:

1. Think about what you want to say first. Try writing down the author's thesis in your own words and then listing the supporting points. Use this as an outline for your summary.

2. Don't write too much, about two hundred words or less. One paragraph is usually enough, although there may be times when two paragraphs are needed. The idea of a summary is to present only the main idea and supporting points.

3. Be objective; that is, don't give your own opinions or value judgments.

4. In your first sentence, provide the author's name, the title of the work, and an indication of what the essay is about. Once you have stated the author's name, you don't need to repeat it in your summary.

5. Use your own words, except for phrases you feel are important to include for clarity of a point. These phrases should have quotation marks around them.

6. Avoid using phrases such as "the author believes" or "another interesting point is." Just state what the author says.

 ## Writing Exercise

As practice, write a one-paragraph summary in your journal or on a separate sheet of paper of the essay you just read, Pete Hamill's "The Wet Drug." You will probably want to look over your markings or reread the essay before you begin.

Naturally, your wording will be different, but see if your summary contains the same basic points as this one:

> Excessive drinking is disgusting and harmful, says Pete Hamill in his essay, "The Wet Drug." Although he had vowed not to moralize or pass judgment on those who still drank after he quit, Hamill has changed his mind after witnessing the harm he has seen from the "drinking to drunkenness" of friends and others. As support, Hamill provides examples of what excessive drinking has done to some of his friends, such as acting foolish, ruined marriages and careers, child beating, and even death. He then cites two recent news accounts of harm from excessive drinking, one regarding a woman who was beaten and raped by a gang in a bar, another of four teens killed in an auto accident. Finally, the author presents some national statistics on the effects drinking has on auto accidents, homicides, fatal fires, wife beatings, child abuse, and on-the-job accidents. Because we live in a society that "certifies alcohol as an acceptable drug," we should counter all acceptable images of drinking with more realistic images of the results of drunkenness. Commercials for alcohol, like those for cigarettes, should be banned from TV.

Notice that the summary's first sentence includes the author, title, and thesis of the essay. The summary then presents the evidence Hamill uses to support his thesis: examples of the effects drinking has had on Hamill's friends, recent "horror stories" in the news of crime and violence related to drinking, and statistics on the harm caused by drinking. The summary concludes with Hamill's suggestion for countering the "acceptable" media images of drinking with more realistic ones.

The summary is objective; the only opinions used are those of Hamill, the author of the essay. Notice, too, that when the summary uses words from the essay, those words are identified with quotation marks.

You can write a good summary only when you truly understand what you have read. Writing good summaries in your journal ensures that you have read carefully. In addition, the summaries serve as good resources if you ever need to go back to review what you've read.

Writing Reflections

Writing your reflections on what you read is another useful type of journal entry to consider. Writing summaries requires objectivity; but you also need to capture on paper your subjective reactions, ideas, and questions that arise from the reading selections assigned. For instance, following are some examples of subjective responses to Pete Hamill's thesis that commercials for alcoholic beverages should be banned. You may have had one or more of these reactions after you read it.

- I disagree with Hamill's thesis; ads don't cause drunken behavior.

- Why is alcohol legal when other drugs, such as marijuana, are not?

- Hamill's essay reminds me of my Uncle Al, killed by a drunk driver.

- I never thought of alcohol as a "wet drug," but I see it is.

- A recent Bud commercial did make drinking beer look like fun. Could such ads get people to start drinking?

- I never realized that alcohol was such a contributing factor to so much destruction.

- I doubt if Hamill's essay will stop anyone from drinking, especially college students.

None of the examples are "right or wrong." They are subjective responses to Hamill's thesis. Such reactions should be written down, even if they don't directly relate to the essay. They could become useful seeds for writing an essay of your own at some later date.

Reflection entries are also a good place to write down some examples of the way a writer works. For instance, you may have been struck by Hamill's use of language to reveal his disgust. You might want to write down some of the passages that struck you the most, such as:

- "I've had to help bury a few people who allowed booze to take them into eternity."

- ". . . these vomiting slaughterers, slowly weaving from lane to lane . . ."

- ". . . when we drink we are entering the company of killers and fools."

Or you may have found the language too dramatic. State how you feel. Such entries help you pay more attention to a writer's style and use of language. In turn, you will become more conscious of your own word choices.

Reflection entries are also a good place for questions you might want to pursue later or ask your instructor. Here are some possible questions that might come up while or after reading Hamill's essay:

- To what does "knocked off a horse on the way to Damascus" refer?

- What does the word "bluenose" in paragraph 7 mean?

- When did Prohibition occur? Why didn't it work?

- What does he mean by "criminal narcissists"?

Some of your questions can be answered by looking in a dictionary, others by asking your instructor.

Capturing your thoughts, ideas, and questions in writing while actually thinking about them keeps you from forgetting about them when you get involved in another assignment.

Collecting Words to Learn

It is a good idea to set aside a section in your journal where you keep a list of the words you know you should learn. The only way you're going to enlarge your vocabulary is to take the time to expand it. You need a strong vocabulary not only to handle sophisticated reading but also to express yourself in your own writing.

How you can best develop your vocabulary is something only you know, but just collecting a list of words is not going to help you learn them. You need to do something with the list.

As you know, words often have more than one meaning; their definitions depend on their contextual usage: that is, how they are used in a given sentence. So don't merely accumulate unknown words from the reading selections. Write down the entire sentence or at least the phrase in which the word appears. That way, when you look up the word in a dictionary, you can pick from among the various meanings the definition that fits. Once you have looked up the word to learn, write a sentence of your own using it in the proper context. Show your sentences to your instructor to make certain you are using the words correctly. Then use as many as possible in your own writing until they become as familiar as the words you already use. Yes, this takes time, but how else are you going to develop your vocabulary?

Before Going On

In order to understand better what you read, and remember it longer, be an active reader by carrying on a dialogue with the author. Make brief notations and marks in your books as you read. In addition, keep a reading journal where you can write objective summaries of the readings. Also use the journal as a place to record your reactions, ideas, and questions prompted by the reading selections. Finally, in order to enlarge your vocabulary, keep a list of new words from the readings and learn as many as you can.

Writing Exercise

In your reading journal or on a separate sheet of paper, write today's date and the page numbers you just read. Summarize the important points in Chapter 1. Use your previous journal entries as a guide.

2

Viewpoints on Writing Essays

> *"Writing is manual labor of the mind:*
> *a job, like laying pipe."*
>
> —John Gregory Dunne

Calvin and Hobbes

by Bill Watterson

Peanuts

Charles Schultz

In the previous chapter, "Viewpoints on Reading Essays," you looked at some methods and qualities of a good essay reader. Now you'll learn what it takes to be a good essay writer. What you learned about an essay's thesis, supporting paragraphs, and organization will be useful in writing essays. In fact, much of that information will sound familiar. The difference is that you will now look at the essay from a writer's point of view rather than a reader's. As a reader, you see only the final efforts of a writer; in this section, you'll see each of the various writing stages that lead to the finished product.

Three basic writing steps are presented here: how to get started, how to get your ideas in writing, and how to rewrite or polish what you write. But good writing is seldom a quick one-two-three process. It involves starting and stopping, eagerly writing away and angrily throwing away, moving along and stalling, feeling pleased and feeling frustrated, thinking you're finished and then realizing you need to start again. Sometimes a writing assignment may seem to come effortlessly; more often you will have to work very hard at it.

Writers go about writing in various ways. Hundreds of books exist on how to write, each one offering "the right way." But regardless of their differences, most of them cover at least three basic stages of writing: methods for getting started, methods for writing a first draft, and methods for revising and editing. These three stages in the writing process will be presented in that order in this section, but the order in which you follow them may vary with each essay you write. Once you increase your knowledge of what goes into writing an essay, you may modify the stages to suit yourself.

This basic three-step approach should make writing easier for you. It will give you a sense of direction and an understanding of what is expected of you as a writer. Let's look at each of these steps more closely.

Getting Started: Finding a Working Thesis (Stage 1)

As you learned in the section on reading, essays are structured around a thesis, the main idea an author wants to develop. The thesis is what the author wants to say about the topic or subject of the essay. Sometimes an instructor gives you a topic for an essay. In that case, you have to decide what you want to say about it and what thesis will guide what you want to say. Sometimes you are left on your own and must come up with both an essay topic and a thesis.

Once you've been given a writing assignment, make the topic interesting for yourself. Finding a slant that interests you will make it easier to write about the subject assigned. Also, unless the assignment requires research, think about the assignment in terms of what you already know. Depending upon the topic, that's not always easy, but here are some methods for selecting and making a topic your own.

Discovering Ideas in Your Reading Journal

Your reading journal is one of the best places to start searching for a topic and thesis. If your instructor asks you to write an essay dealing with the general topic of an assigned reading selection, you may have already written down some reactions, ideas, or questions that you can use as a starting point. So look over your journal entries. Also, look over any textbook markings you made when you read the assignment. Just by keeping in mind that you have to write on something from that particular reading selection, you might see other essay possibilities in your markings that didn't occur to you before. By using your reflections on what you read, you will have not only a possible topic and working thesis but also an essay that is based on your feelings and opinions.

Let's say you are assigned to read Pete Hamill's "The Wet Drug" from Chapter 1. The writing assignment is to agree or disagree with the author's opinion that advertisements for alcoholic beverages should be banned from television. In this case, both your topic and thesis have been given to you. By checking your journal entry for the essay, you discover that you wrote down your reaction, a notation that you agree (or disagree) with the author. You might begin by writing down a working thesis: "I agree (or disagree) with Pete Hamill in his essay 'The Wet Drug' when he says advertisements for alcoholic beverages should be banned from television." Then look again at each of Hamill's supporting points and show why you agree or disagree with his points. Such an approach at least gets you started. You may even change your mind once you begin. That's why the term *working thesis* is used at this stage. It's quite normal to discover you want to go in a different direction after writing several hundred words. Just accept that forced flexibility as part of the writing process.

At other times you may be assigned a broader topic that you must write about. Let's say that an instructor wants you to write a five-hundred-word essay on some aspect of television commercials. A review of your journal entry on Hamill's essay shows that you wrote some questions: "Where did Hamill get his statistics?" "Doesn't Hamill know that hard liquor ads are already banned on TV?" "How much of an effect do beer and wine ads on TV have on teens? adults?" "Why should such ads be banned from TV but allowed in magazines?" Looking for answers to your own questions is also a good place to find a topic and a thesis. You can see how thoughtful journal entries can stimulate your own writing.

Brainstorming

When the topic is too broad for a short essay, you have to narrow it down. How do you whittle down a topic to something you can handle if you can't even think of something to write about? **Brainstorm.** There are at least two ways to brainstorm for ideas: one way is to create a list of your ideas, and another is to cluster them. Let's look at **creating a list** first.

You've probably participated in brainstorming sessions at one time or another. If so, you know it is important to follow the rules. Done correctly, brainstorming can be used to help you select a topic. For instance, if the general writing assignment is to write about television commercials, then take a sheet of paper and start writing down whatever ideas about the topic pop into your head. The trick here is not to be critical as you jot down your thoughts; just put your ideas on paper even if you don't like them at the time. It's important not to interrupt the flow of thoughts by stopping to ask yourself if what you've written is a good idea or not; you can decide that later. Just let your brain "storm." Once you have exhausted all your thoughts about the topic, then look at your list and see which ones are useful.

Sometimes it's helpful (and fun) to work with other classmates as a team. Getting together with two or three others to brainstorm brings out ideas for the assigned topic that you might not have thought about on your own.

Here's an example of a brainstorming list a student wrote on television commercials:

TV Commercials

pretty stupid
Miller Lite bar scenes
lots of automobile ads
seem louder than program
  being watched
repetitive, get boring
some seem sexy
have you driven a Ford
  lately?
hate the interruptions
What does the ad cost?
Double Mint gum twins
Some are funny (Isuzu)
truck splashing through
  rivers, up hills

are they necessary?
music used is hot
  sometimes
one after the other
obnoxious but memorable
attractiveness of some
  makes you want to buy
causes dissatisfaction
  with what you don't
  have
Saturday morning kids'
  ads

As you can see, some of these entries provide a sense of direction for an essay on television commercials. Some are slogans and scenes from TV commercials that she remembers. Others are her opinions about commercials. A closer look at the list may reveal that some items are dated or unusable. It doesn't matter. Making the list prompted her to think about the assigned subject.

It may be that once you decide upon a topic, such as Saturday morning kids' ads, you may need to do more brainstorming. Another brainstorming session dealing with the chosen topic should provide more specific ideas on it. If few ideas come, it may be that you shouldn't use that topic. Making a brainstorming list is useful because it helps prevent writer's block and gets ideas flowing. Discovering and narrowing down a possible topic through brainstorming saves you from false starts.

Try a little brainstorming. In the following space, brainstorm for three minutes on the topic "sports." Remember to write down everything that comes to your mind, even if it doesn't seem related. Don't be critical of any ideas; just list as many as you can in the time your instructor allows.

SPORTS

Now look over your brainstorming list. Sports is obviously a broad subject, too broad to write about in an essay. Circle any items on your list that could serve as a narrower topic for an essay dealing with some aspect of sports. For instance, you might have listed the name of your favorite athlete, or the disappointing basketball game you attended last night, or a memorable moment in a game you might have played in high school, or your favorite sport.

Once you have decided on a narrower topic in your brainstorming list, place a check mark beside any other items that might help support your topic. If you can't find many, brainstorm again on the new topic you've chosen. Gradually, you will begin to narrow a topic down to a size you can handle with ideas for supporting points.

In the space following, list two topics from your final brainstorming session that you might use for an essay topic, and then create a working thesis statement for each.

topic: _____

working thesis statement: _____

_____

topic: _____

working thesis statement: _____

_____

Another method is **clustering.** In *Writing the Natural Way,* Gabriele Rico claims that we have two minds, our "Design mind" and our "Sign mind." Most of us have learned to write through our Sign mind, the part of the brain that deals with rules and logic. Our Sign mind criticizes, censors, and corrects errors. Because most of our training in writing deals with the Sign mind, our Design mind—the creative, less critical side of our brain—doesn't get developed much. This often leaves our creative side blocked and unused. A good piece of writing requires that both minds work together. Using an analogy with music, Rico says our Sign mind "attends to the notes," whereas our Design mind "attends to the melodies."

Clustering is a way to tap into the Design mind, the part of the brain that doesn't care about rules. It helps bring out our more creative side. A type of brainstorming, clustering brings to the surface our hidden thoughts. Rather than merely making a list of ideas, clustering creates a design, a pattern of thought.

Here's how clustering works. Write down a word or phrase in the center of a page (the **nucleus thought**), and then allow your mind to flow out from the center, like ripples created by a stone thrown into water. Rapidly write down and circle whatever comes to mind, connecting each new word or phrase with a line to the previous circle. When a new thought occurs, begin a new "ripple," or branch.

An example of clustering on the topic "TV commercials" appears on the facing page. Notice that there are five branches stemming from the nucleus thought: "dumb," "costly," "emotional appeal," "harmful," and "none?" Each one of these leads the writer closer to a workable subject. If one of these branches seems interesting enough to write about, that branch can become the nucleus for a new clustering to gain more specific details. A few minutes of clustering on an assigned topic frequently provides a sense of direction that is truly your own. Chances are your essay will be different from the norm because clustering has brought forth ideas in your mind that your usual approach to writing would not have touched.

Give clustering a try. In your journal or on a separate sheet of paper, use the clustering technique for three minutes on the topic "social problems." Write the nucleus thought "social problems" in the middle of the page and circle it. Then begin branching and clustering your ideas on the subject.

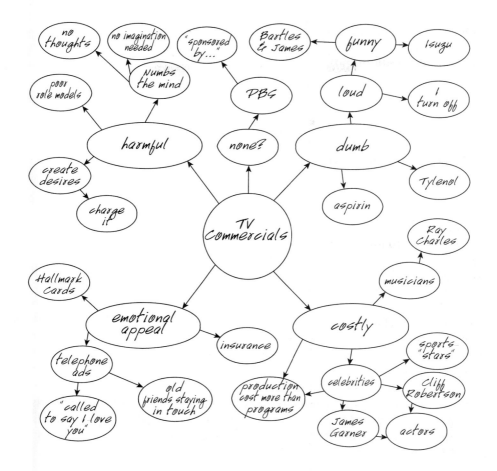

Look over your clustering. Pick two of the branches from the cluster that could serve as a narrower essay topic than "social problems." For instance, you might have a cluster branch on AIDS education, rising unemployment, inner-city gangs, racial bigotry, or police brutality. Make certain your branch contains some support for that issue. If not, you may need to take one of your branches and do some more clustering on that branch.

In the spaces following, write in two possible topics from your clustering that you could use for an essay and create a working thesis statement for each.

topic: _____

working thesis statement: _____

_____

topic: _____

working thesis statement: _____

_____

Writing Exercise

In your journal or on a separate sheet of paper, write a summary of what you just read about brainstorming and its usefulness in finding a usable topic for an essay.

Freewriting

In his book *Writing with Power,* Peter Elbow recommends freewriting as still another way to focus on a writing topic or to break writer's block. Elbow claims that practicing freewriting for ten minutes a day increases writing skills within a few weeks. Freewriting isn't polished writing, but it helps open you up to the thinking-writing process without the worrying about mechanical errors that often blocks thinking. As Elbow states in his book, what's important about freewriting is not the end product, but the process.

To freewrite, simply start writing words on a page and see what comes out. There are only two rules: don't stop to think about what you are saying, and don't stop to worry about errors in writing. Just try to write down as fast as you can exactly what's going through your mind. If you can't think of anything, write, "I can't think of anything." Repeat the phrase until you do think of something. It won't take long. You'll be surprised to see how many useful ideas for topics often emerge as you read what you've freewritten.

Following is an example of freewriting done by a student who was asked to freewrite about television commercials for a few minutes. The errors aren't important here; the ideas are.

TV commercials? I don't know anything about TV commercials. This is stupid. Don't see how writing without stopping is going to help get a topic. Any way I can't think of anything to say - can't think of anything to say - can't think - okay, enough! Maybe I could write about how much I hate commercials. I guess I do watch them cause I'm too lazy to get up and turn them off or down. Need a remote control. Even PBS stations have commercials now I've noticed. "This program brought to you buy... blah, blah, blah." Guess there'd be no TV programs without commercials, a necessary nuisance. Really the purpose of television is to sell things. We get so caught up in certain programs we forget why they are there - to sell. I guess people - me - buy the stuff they sell or they wouldn't put so much money into advertising. Super Bowl ads run into the millions just for 30 seconds. But we buy, buy, buy. I need to watch some commercials and relly look at them.

Notice that the student didn't stop to fix spelling or grammatical mistakes made during the freewriting. Such mistakes don't matter. What matters in freewriting is what thoughts you capture.

If you look carefully at the sample, you'll notice that after expressing resentment toward the freewriting idea and some spinning around, the student begins to form thoughts about television commercials. He touches on possible ideas to pursue: why he hates commercials but watches them; the need for advertisements so that programs can exist; the purpose of television; the success of television advertising; the costs of advertising. In the end, the student realizes he may need to carefully examine some television advertisements before writing about any specific commercial. All these possibilities came from a few minutes of freewriting.

A ten-minute freewriting session is also useful before you begin to write an essay. It can get you warmed up to writing, discipline you to write when you don't feel like it, and help you get ideas into words without worrying about the writing process itself. Once the words begin to flow, so do the ideas buried in your subconscious.

Some students like to freewrite for a few minutes in their journals after completing a reading assignment. It helps them capture ideas, experiences, feelings, and reactions prompted by the reading assignment and exercises. You might want to make this a part of your assignments, too.

Freewriting is an especially good technique to use if you work with a word processor. You can turn off the monitor light, and since you won't see anything on the screen, you can concern yourself only with writing your thoughts. When you're finished, turn up the monitor light and read what you have written. Chances are that you will find a topic you can handle.

Use a page in your journal to see how freewriting works. Write for just five minutes on the topic "family." Remember, keep writing the whole time. Don't stop to think about what you are saying; just write whatever comes to your mind, even if it's not about family. Don't worry about mistakes in spelling or grammar. Come back here when you have finished.

Now look over your freewriting. In your journal, write down all possible essay topics that you see in it. Then pick two possible topics you could use for an essay and write a working thesis statement for each.

topic: _____

working thesis statement: _____

_____

topic: _____

working thesis statement: _____

_____

Before Going On

You now know some approaches for finding an essay topic on your own. One way is to look over your journal entries for possible topics. Another is to brainstorm for topics, either by making a list or by clustering. Still another is to freewrite. If you experience difficulty selecting a topic for an essay, try one or all of these approaches. Feel free to modify them to fit your style of thinking and writing.

 ## Writing Exercise

In your journal or on a separate sheet of paper, write a paragraph that explains and describes one of the four methods for finding an essay topic: using journal entries, listing, clustering, or freewriting. In a second paragraph, tell which one you prefer and why. Your instructor may want you to turn this exercise in.

Getting It on Paper: Supporting Your Thesis (Stage 2)

Refining Your Thesis

Sometimes it's possible to sit down and write an essay from beginning to end. But more often than not, you'll find yourself surrounded by crumpled sheets of paper containing false starts, because you tried to write before you and your thesis were ready.

Here's a more practical and productive way to get your ideas on paper. Let's say that after clustering for ideas on the broad topic of television commercials, you narrow your subject to harmful television commercials. That branch of your cluster contains three reasons you think they are harmful: "create desires," "poor role models," and "numbs the mind." You realize now that when you wrote "numbs the mind" you were really thinking about television in general, not just commercials. So that leaves only two points.

Now you are wondering exactly what you meant about "role models" and decide it's not something you could easily write about. That leaves only one point: "create desires." You consider forgetting the whole idea, but you scribble down a possible working thesis: "Television advertisements create desires for things we don't need and often can't pay for." That, you think, is something you can write about because you have experienced those desires.

Had you gone ahead and started writing a draft on the three items of the cluster "leg," you would have eventually realized you couldn't do it, but not before you wasted a lot of time, effort, and paper. In most cases, it pays to think before you write.

Even now, with a working thesis, you still aren't ready to write a first draft. To defend your thesis as stated, you'd have to show that TV ads create a desire for things we don't need and sometimes can't pay for. Do all television ads do this? No, so you change your thesis: "*Some* television advertisements create desires for things we don't need and often can't pay for." Now, which ones do that? You remember a television advertisement you saw for the Ford Ranger truck. The ad made the truck look so appealing you bought one, even though you really couldn't afford it. In fact, you had to get your parents to cosign the loan. Further, you bought new speakers for the truck's stereo, which you didn't really need either.

As you think about your working thesis, it dawns on you: you use a brand of toothpaste and after-shave lotion because you've been influenced by commercials on television! You never used any after-shave lotion until that ad appeared. Even last night, you called an 800 number to order a collection of Eric Clapton CDs advertised on television.

Suddenly, you realize your thesis really applies to you! So you change your working thesis again: "Some television advertisements create desires *in me* for things *I* don't really need and often can't pay for." But the thesis sounds awkward, so you refine it: "Sometimes I am influenced by television advertisements and buy things I don't need and often can't afford."

Now you can see why the term *working thesis* is used at this stage of essay writing.

In the process of developing a thesis, the ideas used to form it often become part of the support, as in the example above.

Working thesis:	Sometimes I am influenced by television advertisements and buy things I don't need and often can't afford.
Support:	the Ford truck I bought
Support:	the toothpaste I use
Support:	the after-shave lotion I started using
Support:	the CDs I ordered

Rather than writing a draft at this point, it would be better to brainstorm a bit more. What other ads have given you the "wants"? You soon come up with these:

Support:	subscription to *Time* magazine (a free watch came with it)
Support:	subscription to *Sports Illustrated* (a free videotape came with it)
Support:	new speakers for the truck
Support:	Nike tennis shoes (they had to be that brand)
Support:	a survival knife I didn't need

By now, you are embarrassed by the growing list; that's enough support to prove your point.

Before going on, make certain you understand what is meant by a working thesis and support. Some of the statements below are working thesis statements; others are not. Circle the number of the thesis statements and then explain in the space provided what the topic is and what support would be needed.

1. First impressions of people can be misleading.

   _____

   _____

2. The salaries of major league sports players compared with those of teachers reflect the real attitude people have toward education.

   _____

   _____

3. The value of pets

   _____

   _____

4. Marriage, an outdated institution, is kept alive by religious advocates and
   lawyers who make money from divorces.

   _____

   _____

5. The problems of today's students

   _____

   _____

6. Affirmative action in the workplace is no longer needed.

   _____

   _____

Compare your answers with these. Item 1 could be used as a working thesis. The
essay topic is first impressions of people. The keyword requiring support is
"misleading." Examples are needed to support how first impressions can be
misleading. Item 2 is also a possible working thesis. The topic is inequities in the
salaries of teachers and major sports figures. The implied thesis is that people
don't really care about education as much as they care about sports. Item 3
should not have been circled. The value of pets is a topic, but there is no statement about the value of pets. Item 4 contains the thesis that marriage is an outdated institution. Support would attempt to show that religious advocates and
lawyers are responsible for keeping marriage a legal institution because of their
own gain. Item 5 is only a topic, not a thesis statement. What about the problems
of today's students? Are there any? If so, what are they? Item 6 should have been
circled. The subject or topic is affirmative action; the support must show there
is no need for it in the workplace.

Grouping Your Ideas
Even after deciding on a working thesis, you're not quite ready to begin your first
draft. You can't simply go down the list of supporting ideas, write a sentence

about each one, and connect the sentences into an "essay." You need to organize the list in some way. Here's one way:

Group 1	*Group 2*	*Group 3*	*Group 4*
truck	toothpaste	*Time* subscription	records
truck's speakers	after-shave	*Sports Illustrated*	knife
	tennis shoes	subscription	

Group 1 deals with the truck; Group 2, personal items; Group 3, magazine subscriptions; and Group 4, miscellaneous items.

Outlining Your Support

Using the reasoning behind your grouping, write an **informal outline** to follow when you begin your first draft.

Thesis: Sometimes I am influenced by television advertisements and buy things I don't need and often can't afford.

Major support: unnecessary truck purchase

–didn't need it; old car OK

–parents had to cosign

–didn't need new speakers

Major support: unnecessary personal items

–changed toothpaste

–started using after-shave

–bought Nike tennis shoes; already had new Pumas

Major support: unnecessary magazine subscriptions

–subscribed to *Time* for the watch; already have one

–subscribed to *Sports Illustrated* for the free videotape of sports events

Major support: unnecessary miscellaneous purchases

–Clapton CDs; could have borrowed them from friends and made tapes

–survival knife, for what?

This informal outline provides a structure for getting your ideas on paper. Following it ensures organized support of the thesis.

There may be times when an instructor requires you to attach a more **formal outline** to your essay. In that case, you should submit something along these lines:

Main idea: Sometimes I am influenced by television advertisements and buy things I don't need and often can't afford.

I. Unnecessary truck purchase

    A. didn't need it; old car fine

    B. couldn't afford it

        1. parents had to cosign

        2. stuck with payments

    C. spent even more on unnecessary new speakers

II. Unnecessary changes in personal items

    A. switched brand of toothpaste

    B. started using after-shave lotion

    C. bought Nike tennis shoes because of ad

III. Unnecessary magazine subscriptions

    A. subscribed to *Time* for the free watch

    B. subscribed to *Sports Illustrated* for the free videotape

IV. Unnecessary miscellaneous purchases

    A. Clapton CDs

    B. survival knife

Regardless of what form an outline takes, it is, like a working thesis, usually a working outline. Once you start writing, new ideas may surface and you may add, delete, or change what you have in your outline. Until the final essay draft, nothing written should be considered permanent.

For practice, pick one of the topics you got from brainstorming or clustering on pages 41–44. In the space provided, write a working thesis and list your support. If you don't have at least eight supporting points, do more brainstorming or clustering on your topic.

topic: _____

working thesis: _____

_____

support: _____

support: _____

support: _____

support: _____

support: _____

support: _____

support: _____

support: _____

Writing Exercise

In your journal or on a separate sheet of paper, group your support in the preceding activity into some type of organizational pattern you could follow to write your first draft.

Writing an Argumentative Essay

An argumentative essay contains a thesis that is debatable. Good topics for argumentative essays are controversial and can be disputed. The working thesis for the outline on pages 50–51, "Sometimes I am influenced by television advertisements and buy things I don't need and often can't afford," is not argumentative. A thesis that states, "Television advertisements use subliminal techniques to force viewers to buy goods they don't need or want" is argumentative.

Which of the following do you think would make a good argumentative thesis?

1. Atheists should not be allowed to teach elementary-school children.

2. We would all be healthier if we became vegetarians.

3. A healthy liver is vital to our bodily functions.

4. Campus parking fees should be reduced since there is currently inadequate parking space for students.

5. Many college English departments are no longer requiring students to read Shakespeare in order to graduate.

6. For population control, the United States should establish an immigration quota allowing only fifty thousand entrants a year for the next five years.

As stated, items 3 and 5 are not argumentative. They are both factual statements, and while essays could be written based on the statements, there is nothing to argue. The rest of the statements can be debated because counterarguments can be made against them. Notice that all the thesis statements are conclusions and must be supported with evidence or critical reasoning. Such support must be supplied to argue for or against each of the thesis statements.

Purpose and audience: In writing an argumentative essay, your basic purpose is to convince readers that your viewpoint or position is better than an opposing one. Depending on your subject, you need to consider your audience. Do you want to give more support to an audience that already agrees with you? Do you want to win over those opposed to your views? Do you want to inspire readers to some action? Do you want to stop your audience from acting upon some issue? These are questions you must think about before developing your thesis, since your support must reach the audience you want to convince.

Rational and emotional support: Good arguments usually combine rational appeals involving logical evidence that supports the thesis with emotional appeals to the reader's feelings and beliefs. An argument that appeals only to the reader's rational side could fail to reach a common ground between the writer and the audience. However, emotional appeal shouldn't be used alone and shouldn't be used at all when the emotional issues raised do not relate to the thesis.

A reasonable argument depends on the evidence you use. Facts, statistics, specific examples, and opinions of experts are all useful in supporting your argument. Don't distort, exaggerate, oversimplify, or misquote your evidence to fit your argument. You will probably need to do some research on your topic in order to gather the evidence you need.

Consider your opposition's viewpoints. A good argument will take on the opposing views and show why they are not as reasonable or as true as yours. Be willing to recognize the merits of your opposition, but try to show why your views or evidence is more reasonable to consider.

Logical fallacies: Logical fallacies are errors in reasoning. You need to be able to spot them in the argument of your opposition as well as avoid making them yourself in any essay you write. Here is a list of some of the more common ones you should know and their definitions:

1. **Hasty generalization:** a conclusion or an opinion based on too little evidence.

2. **Either/or fallacy:** an implication that something must be either one thing or another; giving a complicated problem only two alternatives.

3. **False analogy:** a refusal to consider key differences or overreliance on the similarities in an analogy.

4. **Bandwagon fallacy:** an appeal to the audience's desire to be part of the in-group.

5. **Non sequitur:** a false conclusion drawn from irrelevant data.

6. **Begging the question:** accepting an opinion that is open to question as if it were already proved or disproved.

7. **Argument ad hominem** (Latin for "to the man"): an attack on the opponent rather than the opponent's thesis.

8. **Argument ad populum** (Latin for "to the people"): an argument for a conclusion that is based on shared prejudices and values.

When reading or writing an argumentative essay, be aware of these common fallacies. They weaken any argument.

Checking your argument: If you write an argumentative essay, check for the following points:

1. Make certain your thesis is arguable and can be developed through rational and emotional support.

2. Consider the members of your audience and the type of information they need.

3. Make certain your evidence is accurate, relevant, and adequate.

4. Consider the opposition's viewpoint and provide logical rebuttal if needed.

5. Check for logical fallacies in your own argument.

Of course, the three organizational writing stages being discussed in this chapter apply to argumentative essays as well.

Writing Exercise

In your journal, write down three topics that lend themselves to an argumentative essay. Write a possible thesis statement for each one that you feel you could develop in an essay. Then write another thesis statement for each topic that reflects an opposing viewpoint.

Nutshell Statements

You could begin writing your first draft at this point, but first you might want to write a nutshell statement. A nutshell statement is a one-paragraph statement of the **purpose** of your essay, the **support** you will use, and the **audience** for whom you are writing. *It is not, nor should it be considered, the opening paragraph of your essay.* It is a way for you to make certain your purpose, support, and intended audience fit.

A nutshell statement for an essay based on the outline on pages 50–51 might read:

The purpose of my essay is to show how I am influenced by television commercials to buy things I don't need and often can't pay for. As support, I will reveal some of the items I have purchased recently because of ads I have seen, such as my new truck, personal items, magazine subscriptions, and other miscellaneous things. My intended audience will be other buyers like myself, who have yet to realize the power television ads have on us.

Notice that the statement of purpose contains the thesis. The statement regarding support summarizes the major groups or categories of evidence to be discussed. The statement about audience provides a picture of the real or imaginary people interested in the subject or those you want to make more aware of your subject.

Your audience is an important factor whenever you write. A quick note regarding your whereabouts using sentence fragments and no punctuation may be acceptable to your roommate, but certainly inappropriate for your boss. When planning an essay, then, it is necessary that you give thought to its purpose and audience. Suppose, for instance, your audience is not other buyers like yourself, but parents of young children. Your revised nutshell statement might read like this:

> The purpose of my essay is to show the negative influence of television commercials aimed at young children. As support, I will describe some of the advertisements that appear on children's early-morning and Saturday programming that brainwash children and turn them into would-be consumers. My intended audience will be parents who allow their children to watch television unsupervised.

Notice the changes that need to be made as a result of your new audience. Now the thesis goes beyond the personal influence of television advertising to its influence on younger children. A different set of advertisements will be necessary for support of the thesis. Since the intended audience is now parents, even the language of the essay will need to be more formal and, given your purpose, more convincing.

Here is still another nutshell statement dealing with television commercials:

> The purpose of my essay is to write an argument in rebuttal to an article that appeared in the *Boston Globe*'s editorial pages today that claims that television commercials do not influence us. As support, I will use my own experiences, as well as factual information taken from my library research. My intended audience is the author of the article with whom I disagree and other *Globe* newspaper readers.

In this case, the final piece will be an argumentative essay that explains what the article in the *Globe* says and then provides proof that those comments about television commercials are wrong. Since the audience interested in the topic will be a fairly literate group of newspaper readers, the language selected must be appropriate, the arguments persuasive, and the other author shown to be wrong.

Even though your ultimate "audience" is your instructor, who will read and grade your essay, you should write for an audience that either is interested in your thesis or needs to be made aware. Thinking about audience before you write can help you determine the type of vocabulary to use, what arguments to present, and what to assume your audience may know about the subject. For instance, if your intended audience is fifth-grade students, you will have to write at a level they can understand. The words you use, your sentence structure, and the content will have to be geared to that group. On the other hand, if you are writing to convince antiabortionists to change their minds, you will need to understand their reasoning and provide counterarguments. You will have to imagine what they might say in reaction to what you say. You will have to decide what approach will get them to even listen to your views. Should you use sarcasm? sympathy? medical terms?

A nutshell statement requires that you have your purpose, support, and audience in mind before you begin writing. If you can complete a nutshell statement, then you are ready to begin your first draft. But keep in mind that the nutshell statement is *not* your opening paragraph.

Once you have your thesis, support, and audience in mind, you're ready to start your first draft.

Writing Exercise

In your journal, write a one-paragraph nutshell statement for an essay based on the outline you completed on pages 51–52.

Patterning Your Paragraphs: The Beginning

As readers, we see only the finished product of a writer, not all the changes that went into creating it. What finally appears as a beginning or introductory paragraph may actually be the last paragraph an author writes. In other words, it is not infrequent that the opening paragraph you write in a first draft is *not* the opening paragraph in the final draft. In fact, that first paragraph may not even be used in the final draft, or it could be changed so much it no longer resembles what you started with. By the time revisions are made and the support has been established, your old introductory paragraph may be obsolete.

Most of us, however, begin writing our first drafts with what we think will be our introduction. It helps us formulate and state our thesis. Such a paragraph might help *us* get started, but it may not get our readers interested in what we have to say. What, then, are some effective ways to begin an essay?

Here are some suggestions that may work for you, depending on your essay audience and purpose. Many of the essays in this book use these methods. Check out the essays mentioned to see each strategy at work.

1. Get right to the point, stating your thesis and your general reasons for feeling or believing as you do. One drawback to this approach is that unless your

thesis is stated in such a way that your audience will be interested in reading on, it could be a boring opening. Examine the opposing points of view on the Pledge of Allegiance by Phil Donahue and Rochelle Riley (pp. 249, 253) to see how they use this direct technique.

2. Use a quotation or reference to other writings that relate to your thesis, one by someone respected by almost everyone, one that supports your point of view, or one that you disagree with and want to disprove in your essay. Rachel L. Jones does this in "What's Wrong with Black English" (p. 209).

3. Tell a brief anecdote or story that relates in some way to or introduces the point of your thesis. For examples, look at the introductory paragraphs in Roger von Oech's "To Err Is Wrong" (p. 83) or Brent Staples's "Night Walker" (p. 144).

4. Use one or more questions that cause the reader to think about your topic, questions that you intend to answer in the body of your essay. Jeanne Park's opening paragraph in "Eggs, Twinkies and Ethnic Stereotypes" (p. 235) is a question. Debra Sikes and Barbara Murray use questions in their first two opening paragraphs in "The Practicality of the Liberal Arts Major" (p. 114). See also Mary Seymour's opening paragraph in "Call Me Crazy, But I Have to Be Myself" (p. 135). Or look at David Gergen's selection, "Keeping Faith in Kids" (p. 227).

5. Provide some startling statistics or information that will get your reader's attention and that will appeal to the reader's good sense. Notice how this is done in Mary Sherry's "In Praise of the F Word" (p. 91).

6. Describe a scene that gets attention and pulls your reader into the subject. Francis Flaherty describes a troubling scene in "'The Ghetto Made Me Do It'" (p. 161) that sets the stage for the selection.

7. Be creative and use a combination of the above.

The introductory paragraph is an important one. Make certain that whatever method you use, your opening draws your reader's interest, fits into the point of your essay, and gets the reader involved in your subject. Reminder: Don't use your nutshell statement as an introductory paragraph.

Patterning Your Paragraphs: The Middle

As a means for better reading comprehension, Chapter 1 presented some paragraph methods that writers use. Now let's look at those same paragraph patterns from the writer's angle.

Recall that the **topic sentence** in a paragraph serves the same function as the thesis statement in an essay. Just as what you say in your essay depends on the point of your thesis, what you say and how you say it depend on the topic sentence of your paragraph. Here are some possible topic sentences for paragraphs. Notice that the way they are written pretty much determines the paragraph pattern.

Topic Sentence	*Best Pattern*
The Chevy Blazer commercial was very appealing.	**description** Descriptive details should be provided to create an image in the reader's mind of the commercial's appeal.
Yesterday I went from one truck dealership to the next looking for the best deal.	**narration** A narrative would take the reader from one dealership experience to the next relating what happened at each.
I now recognize three reasons why I buy many things I don't really need.	**analysis** Each of the three reasons for the buying problem needs to be examined.
I recently bought several things I don't need.	**illustration-example** Evidence needs to be provided to illustrate the unnecessary items purchased. Examples of the things not needed or a narrative about the buying of unnecessary items is required.
Pat's mother says he is the perfect example of an impulsive buyer.	**definition** The term *impulsive buyer* needs to be defined so readers understand what Pat is an example of.
The commercial showed the four basic types of auto stereo speakers.	**division-classification** The topic sentence divides the speakers into four basic types, each of which needs to be named and discussed.
The Dodge truck commercial appealed to Jim more than the one for Chevrolets.	**comparison-contrast** While some description of the two truck ads may be needed, the topic sentence calls for a comparison of the two ads to show why Jim preferred one over the other.
Because the Ford commercial was so well done, I bought one of Ford's trucks.	**cause-effect** The cause here is the ad, and the effect is the purchase; description of the well-done ad may be needed to help explain the cause.

It is important to see here that the way you state a topic sentence requires that you structure your paragraph with a pattern that supports it. Of course, all the examples above are "working" topic sentences. After you have developed your support, you may need to change the wording of the topic sentence to fit what you wrote.

You may decide that the topic sentence is best placed at the end of the paragraph or in the middle, or that it should be implied rather than stated. Remember, revision is not limited to any one particular stage. It occurs at all points during the writing process. But if writing does not come easily for you, try writing a topic sentence that you can use as the first sentence in the paragraph and work from there.

Here are some topic sentences taken from the reading selections in this book. In the space provided, write a one-sentence statement that tells what pattern or method should be used to develop the paragraph and why.

1. "Compared to the animals around us, there's no doubt we are a remarkable phenomenon."

   _____

   _____

2. "I will never forget that Sunday as long as I live."

   _____

   _____

3. "I remember going out to play tennis one day about 20 years ago and having my wife stop me in the doorway with a piece of friendly advice."

   _____

   _____

4. "There are four reasons for practicing freewriting."

   _____

   _____

5. "After the dishes have soaked in water hot enough to deform small plastic implements, I begin my attack."

   _____

   _____

6. "We humans live with contradictions in our behavior."

_____

_____

7. "Irony is not easy to explain."

_____

_____

8. "Television journalism has recently stimulated political conservatism."

_____

_____

Compare your statements with these. The wording may be different, but the explanations should contain the same ideas.

1. The **comparison-contrast** method will show why humans are a phenomenon compared with other animals.

2. A **narration** will tell us about that unforgettable Sunday.

3. The rest of the paragraph is an example of **description**—the author describes his wife's advice.

4. **Division-classification** is required to show each of the four reasons for practicing freewriting.

5. The "attack" on the dishes is a process calling for a **step-by-step analysis.**

6. **Examples and illustrations** of contradictory behavior are needed for support.

7. An extended **definition** of irony should show why it isn't easy to define.

8. If television journalism has stimulated political conservatism, some proof or support of this **cause-effect** relationship is required.

If you had trouble with these, you may want to review the section on paragraph patterns in Chapter 1.

Patterning Your Paragraphs: The Ending

As with essay introductions, there is no one way to conclude an essay. Many students tend to repeat almost verbatim in their closing paragraph what they said in their opening one. However, the concluding paragraph of an essay should not simply duplicate what has already been written. Instead, you will usually want to do one of these three things in your last paragraph, depending on what your thesis is:

1. Summarize the major points of the essay. This can be tricky. Try to summarize by using different wording to restate the points you've made in a fresh but familiar way. Don't use this method in a short essay with only three or four supporting paragraphs. This approach works best when you have written a longer piece with many points. Your summary will help your reader pull them all together.

2. Draw a conclusion based on the information you have presented. This method works best when you have been arguing for a particular viewpoint and have presented evidence that needs to be highlighted in order to draw a conclusion for the reader. Usually, you begin your paragraph with words such as "Thus, we can see from these facts that . . . ," or "For these reasons we must conclude that . . . ," and then you state your conclusion. [Note: Don't confuse the word *conclusion,* meaning "the end," with "drawing a conclusion," or making a judgment based on information provided.]

3. Emphasize the need for change or more attention on the subject. Make a pitch for what needs to be done, based on the information you have presented in your essay. Call upon your readers to think more, care more, or act more on the subject of your essay now that you have successfully made your case.

Many of the paragraph patterns already discussed can be used effectively in concluding paragraphs.

Writing Exercise

In your journal or on a separate sheet of paper, summarize the information on writing beginning, middle, and ending paragraphs. Make certain you understand pages 47–61 before going on.

First Draft

Let's say that you decide to follow the formal outline on page 51 about the effect of television commercials. The first draft might look something like this:

```
                    First Draft

        1     I have a tendency to buy things I see on television

              commercials even though I don't need them and often can't

              pay for them. The other night I was putting myself to sleep

              by watching a late movie on TV when an ad with a fast-

              talking announcer began describing a new collection of Eric

              Clapton CDs. You've probably seen the kind I mean. You get

              to hear little pieces of music with famous singers singing
```

one or two lines sung then they cut to the next song. Anyway, I like all of the songs they played, and when the announcers said, "Call this 800 number now and get these fabulous songs not sold in any record store," I called and ordered the record set. This is not unusual behavior for me.

2   I bought my Ford truck because of a TV commercial. It seemed like every time I watched TV I'd see the same ad for the truck. It showed the truck going through mud, climbing hills, and carrying heavy loads. Then it showed a guy and his girlfriend all dressed up pulling up in front of some fancy restaurant in the truck all shined up. The girl was something else and every time the ad came on I caught myself looking at her and not the truck. Anyway, the next thing I knew I had talked my folks into cosigning the loan for me even though they tried to talk me out of it. Banks don't loan money to college students to buy trucks. There wasn't anything wrong with my old car. But I came up with this crazy idea I could get some parttime work hauling or something to help make the payments. I think that's what convinced them to help out. Anyway, now I can't afford to take a girl out because I'm too busy with classes, homework, and an evening job I have to keep to make my truck payments.

3   I also have two magazine subscriptions that I don't even have time to read. When TIME showed an ad on TV for a good deal on a subscription, plus a free watch, I called their toll-free number. Then Sports Illustrated ran an ad for their magazine offering a free videocassette of famous sports plays if you subscribed to them. Of course, I called their toll-free number. Now unread magazines are stacking up around my room. ~~Not only that, they sent me a Beta videocassette and we've got VHS.~~

4   I realize now that I have even been persuaded by TV ads to buy items I never used before. My family has always used Crest. After seeing all those ads for Closeup and having kissable breath, I got my mom to buy some for me. I even use an after-shave lotion now because of ads. I use to do

like my dad and just put on a little of mom's skin cream
after I shaved. And even though I didn't need them, I
bought a new pair of Nike tennis shoes because a TV
commercial for a local shoe store had them on sale.

5   Last night there was a commercial on TV for a good deal
on a neat looking survival knife. It looked like something
the commandos use. It had a big blade, a compass in the
handle, with a fish hook and line, matches and the sheath
had a little pocket with a sharpening stone in it.
Naturally, I ordered one.

6   When my mom heard about this she called me an "impulsive
compulsive buyer." When I asked her what she meant, she
just yelled look it up. After looking it up, I realize
she's right. I need to belong to a "buyers anonymous" group
or something.

Even though the outline wasn't followed exactly, it served to get the ideas into a rough draft in essay form. Of course, this is just the first draft. There's more to be done.

This is a good place to make another pitch for word processing. If you don't know how already, you should learn to write on a word processor. Making changes, doing revisions, and producing neat essays is so much easier once you learn word processing. A recent study done by a professional organization of English teachers revealed that students who submitted typed papers usually got a letter grade higher than those who submitted handwritten papers. But more importantly, word processing enables you to make changes without having to re-type your entire essay.

Whatever you use for your first drafts—pencil, pen, typewriter, or word processor—don't worry about mistakes in punctuation, word choice, spelling, and the like. At this point, you just want to get your essay ideas into words on paper. If you stop to make too many corrections as you write, you may lose your train of thought. Worry about the nitty-gritty later. On the other hand, if there's an error you can quickly change, go ahead and do it, but never at the expense of thoughtful content.

Before Going On

Remember that a working thesis statement is open to changes based on your supporting ideas. Before writing a first draft, make certain you have sufficient support to develop your thesis. Once you are satisfied that you do, organize or outline the support as a writing guide. Writing a nutshell statement before you begin your draft helps you focus on your thesis, support, and audience. As you write your draft, be aware that all paragraphs should have an implied or directly stated topic sentence. The wording of your topic sentence can often provide a clue as to the best paragraph pattern to use. However, don't let concern over paragraph patterns or mechanical errors get in the way of getting your ideas on paper. Changes and corrections can be made during the revision and editing process.

Writing Exercise

Look again at the draft of the student essay on television commercials. Apply the information on reading essays from Chapter 1. Mark and take notes as you read. Then, in your journal or on a separate sheet of paper, write what you would tell the student about the essay, offering your suggestions for improvement and indicating errors that should be changed. Your instructor may want to see your paper.

Getting It Right: Revising and Editing (Stage 3)

It can't be said too often that good writing frequently requires many rewrites. Don't be impatient. Revision is necessary, expected, and part of the writing process. A final draft may look nothing like the first one. There's much to do before turning in your masterpiece.

Revising

Here's a checklist to guide revision of your first draft:

1. *Have you made your point?*
   Make sure your thesis is clear. Stated or implied, your purpose should be clear to the reader. Have someone read your draft; if he or she doesn't understand the point you're trying to make, rewrite until it becomes clear. It's even possible that you will need to change your entire thesis once a first draft is completed.

2. *Does your support move smoothly from one point to the next?*
   Rearrange what you have written so that the ideas flow easily from one to the next. You may need to "cut and paste," or move a sentence or paragraph from one place to another. Use scissors and literally cut up your draft, moving parts around where you want them. (Here again, word processing helps. With a word processor you can easily move whole paragraphs without having to cut or retype.) To move smoothly and logically from one point to the next, use transitional words and phrases such as these:

however	thus	in addition
although	on the other hand	first
therefore	in conclusion	next

furthermore	in other words	finally
moreover	for instance	as a result
consequently	for example	also

3. *Have you developed each paragraph fully?*
   Look closely at the topic sentence of each paragraph. Do you provide enough support to fully develop the topic sentence? You may need to add more information or to take out information that does not relate to the topic sentence. You may need to rewrite your topic sentence to fit the content of the paragraph.

4. *Will your essay interest your audience?*
   Try to make your essay interesting for your audience. Your opening paragraph should grab the readers' attention and make them want to read on. Try to get a picture in your mind of your audience and talk to them in writing. Sometimes the opening paragraph doesn't take shape until several drafts are completed.

5. *Is the tone of your essay consistent?*
   Use the same **tone of voice** throughout your essay. For instance, the tone of the student's rough draft on television commercials is personable and friendly. Using contractions (such as **don't** instead of **do not**) is acceptable in informal writing. The essay is not written for the audience of a scholarly or professional journal. If it were, it would need more formal language, less personal narrative, and a thesis that dealt more broadly with television commercials and cited sources other than personal experience.

6. *Have you said everything you want and need to say and nothing else?*
   Make certain you have said everything necessary to support your thesis. On the other hand, you may need to cut out passages that aren't relevant or that repeat what you've already said.

7. *Have you thought of a title that reflects your thesis?*
   Sometimes a title for an essay comes immediately to mind, even before it is written. But it's best to hold off until you have at least written your first draft. A title, like a thesis, should not be too general. It should reflect the purpose, the content, and the tone of your essay.

Let's apply the above checklist to the rough draft on television commercials. Here's what it might look like:

1   I have a tendency to buy things I see on television [Place at end of essay] commercials even though I don't need them and often can't pay for them. The other night I was putting myself to sleep by watching a late movie on ~~TV~~ television when ~~an ad~~ a commercial with a fast-talking announcer began describing a new collection of Eric Clapton CDs. You've probably seen the kind I mean. ~~You get to hear~~ They play little ~~pieces~~ snippets of ~~music~~ one or two lines ~~sung~~ of a song then

they cut to the next ~~song~~ one. ~~Anyway,~~ I like all of the songs

they played, ~~and~~ so when the announcer said, "Call this 800
Operators on duty.

number now and ~~get these~~ order this fabulous CD set ~~songs~~ not sold in any

~~record~~ store," I ~~called and ordered the record set~~ did. This is ¶ new ¶

not unusual behavior for me.

2   ↳ I bought my Ford truck because of a TV commercial. It

seemed like every time I watched TV I'd see the same ad for
Ford at work during the day

the truck. It showed the ~~truck~~ going through mud, climbing
the truck at night,

hills, and carrying heavy loads. Then it showed ~~a guy and~~
cleaned and polished

~~his girlfriend all dressed up~~ pulling up in front of ~~some~~ a posh

As the driver got out, a doorman helped the woman out. Both looked elegant, but
~~fancy~~ restaurant ~~in the truck all shined up. The girl was~~

she really got to me.
~~something else and~~ every time the ad came on I caught
I realize now it wasn't the truck I wanted.

myself looking at her and not the truck. ~~Anyway,~~ the next
a   new ¶

thing I knew I had talked my folks into cosigning ~~the~~ loan
a new truck since

for ~~me even though~~ they tried to talk me out of it. Banks
because

don't loan money to college students to buy trucks. There

wasn't anything wrong with my old car. But I came up with

this crazy idea I could get some part-time work hauling or
delivering

~~something~~ to help make the payments. I think that's what
I wish I hadn't been so convincing.

convinced them to help out. ~~Anyway,~~ now I can't afford to

take a girl out because I'm too busy with classes,

homework, and an evening job I have to keep to make my

truck payments.
Thanks to television commercials

3   I also have two magazine subscriptions that I don't even
I saw a commercial

have time to read. When ~~Time showed an ad on TV~~ for a ~~good~~
reduced price   for Time

~~deal~~ on a subscription, plus a free watch, I called their
offered a low-priced

toll-free number. Then Sports Illustrated ~~ran an ad for~~
subscription and

~~their magazine offering~~ a free videocassette of famous

sports plays ~~if you subscribed to them.~~ Of course, I called

their toll-free number. Now unread magazines are stacking

up around my room.

4   I realize now that I have even been persuaded by TV ads

to buy items I never used before. My family has always used
the need for

Crest. After seeing all those ads for Closeup and ~~having~~

kissable breath, I got my mom to buy some for me. I even
began using   the influence of commercials I'd

~~use~~ an after-shave lotion now because of ~~ads.~~ I use to do

> like my dad and just put on a little of mom's skin cream
> after I shaved. And even though I didn't need them, I
> bought a new pair of Nike tennis shoes because a TV
> commercial for a local shoe store had them on sale.
> 5   Last night there was a commercial on TV for a good deal
> on a~~ neat~~ *interesting* looking survival knife, ~~It looked like something~~ *similar to the ones*
> ~~the~~ commandos use. It ha*s* a big blade, a compass in the
> handle, with a fish hook and line, matches and the sheath
> had a little pocket with a sharpening stone in it.
> Naturally, I ordered one. **end here**
>
>   When my mom heard about this she called me an "impulsive
> compulsive buyer." When I asked her what she meant, she
> just yelled look it up. After looking it up, I realize
> she's right. I need to belong to a "buyers anonymous" group
> or something.

Look more closely at some of the changes being considered for the next draft. Sentences are to be moved or removed. Wording has been changed, in some cases to keep from repeating words, in others to be more descriptive or clear. New paragraphs have been started in different places, and the last paragraph has been moved. While none of the support has changed, more attention has been paid to the flow of support, with smoother transitions from one idea to the next. Attention to such details is the basis for the second draft. And even after that draft is completed, it may be necessary to write still another.

After applying the revision checklist to several different drafts, you might have a paper resembling this one. Look carefully at the changes made.

> About to doze off while watching an old movie on television
> the other night, a commercial caught my eye. The sound came up
> as a fast-talking announcer began describing a new CD col-
> lection of Eric Clapton's music. You've probably seen the kind
> I mean. They play little snippets of singers singing one or two
> seconds of a song that made them famous, cutting quickly from
> one to the next. I like all the Clapton tunes they played, so
> when the announcer urged, "Call this toll-free number now . . .
> operators are standing by . . . order this fabulous set of
> records not available in any store," I did.
>
>   This, I'm sorry to say, is not unusual behavior for me. For
> instance, when I saw a television commercial offering a free

digital watch along with a reduced price on a subscription to TIME, I called their toll-free number. Then Sports Illustrated offered a low price subscription along with a free videocassette of some famous sports plays. Of course, I had to call their toll-free number too. Now I have unread magazines stacking up around my room. Not only that, the videocassette they set me is for a Beta machine, we've got VHS.

TV commercials have influenced me so much that I even use personal items I have never used before, my family has used Crest toothpaste ever since I can remember. But after all those ads for Close-up (I think its the kissable breath idea) I had my mom buy some just for me. And, like my dad, I used to just apply a little of moms skin cream on my face after I shaved. But now, thanks to the influence of television commercials, I have tried several bands of after-shave lotion.

The biggest purchase I ever made because of a TV commercial is my truck. It seemed like every time I watched TV I'd see the same ad for a Ford pickup truck. It showed the truck at work during the day going through mud, climbing hills, and carrying heavy loads. Then it showed the truck at night, cleaned and polished, pulling up in front of a plush restaurant. As the driver got out, a doorman helped his date step out. Both of them looked elegant. But it was the woman that got me. Every time the commercial comes on, I caught myself looking at her, not the truck. Anyway, the next thing I knew I had talked my folks into cosigning a loan for a new truck, since banks don't loan money to unemployed college students to buy new trucks. They tried to talk me out of it because there wasn't anything wrong with my old one. But you know how it is when you really want something. I rationalized that I could get part-time work hauling or delivering to help make payments. I think that's what convinced my mom and dad to help out.

Now I wish I hadn't been so convincing. I can't afford to go out on a date because I'm too busy with classes, homework, and an evening job. If I don't make my truck payments, my parents

said they would sell my truck. They don't want to be stuck with
the payments. I can't blame them.

    Recently a local shoe store announced on television that
Nike tennis shoes were on sale. The next day, I bought a pair,
even though I had just bought a pair of Pumas a week before.
When my mom heard, she called me an "impulsive compulsive
buyer". When I asked her what she meant, she yelled, "Look it
up!" and mumbled something about my need to join a "buyers
anonymous" group or quit watching so much TV.

    She's right I have a tendency to buy things I see on
television even though I don't need them or can't really afford
them. Even last night, there was a commercial for a survival
knife similar to the type commandos use. The knife has a big
blade, a hollow handle with a fish hook, some line, a few
matches, a compass that screws on top of the knife handle, and
the sheath has a little pocket on the side with a sharpening
stone, I just couldn't resist calling there toll-free number.

This draft still retains the same thesis and support, but it is structured differently. The position of the thesis has been moved from the opening paragraph to
the end. The first draft opened with the thesis statement and then provided examples of "impulsive compulsive" buying. This draft opens with a narrative
anecdote that reflects the subject and thesis of the essay, rather than directly stating it. The narrative now builds on one purchase after the other and ends with the
thesis statement. This seems to work better because the thesis itself doesn't deal
with any resolution of the problem, only an awareness of the influence of television commercials on the author.

Other changes in the position of the supporting materials have been made.
The largest purchase, the truck, has been moved toward the end of the essay, with
smaller purchases leading up to it. The placement of the Nike purchase after the
truck purchase works well because it reflects the mother's exasperation with her
son's buying habits. It also serves as a transition to the last paragraph, which now
contains the thesis and an acknowledgment that the author's mother is right: another needless purchase, the survival knife, is made. The essay ends with a touch
of humor, yet leaves the reader with a feeling of pity for the author.

While the student essay is not perfect, it is an honest essay based on experience and it fits the assignment given: to write an essay on some aspect of television. Had the assignment been more specific, such as one requiring research on
the effects of television advertising, then this first-person essay would not do.

As improved as this draft is over the first, there is still more to do before the student can turn it in. The essay needs editing.

Editing

Once you are satisfied that your essay's organizational structure and thesis are clear and fully developed, you need to edit your essay for errors in punctuation and mechanics. Of course, as you do this you may also see other problems or errors that need revision. Revision is a continual process, even though you may be focusing on making specific corrections.

Here is a list of questions to ask yourself when you edit your latest draft:

1. *Have you given yourself some time off between drafts?*
   Put your essay aside for at least a couple of hours before editing. In fact, it's a good idea to do this after each draft. You need to get away from what you've written so you can come back to it with "fresh eyes."

2. *Have you read each sentence aloud to hear how it sounds?*
   Begin editing by reading aloud the *last* sentence of your essay. Once you're satisfied it is the best you can do, read aloud the next-to-last sentence and evaluate it the same way. Gradually work your way to the beginning of the essay sentence by sentence. It sounds odd, but doing so forces you to look at each sentence out of context, as a separate piece of writing. Listen to the way the sentence sounds. If it is difficult to read or sounds awkward, rewrite it. Make certain each sentence is complete, not a fragment, a piece of a sentence.

3. *Have you used proper punctuation?*
   Don't form a comma splice by putting a comma (,) between two sentences. If you aren't sure where a comma belongs, it's probably best to leave it out. Place periods (.) at the ends of sentences, not at the ends of phrases or introductory clauses. Use apostrophes (') to show possession (Tom's house, the grandparents' house). Watch for *you're* (you are) as opposed to *your* (belonging to), and *it's* (it is) as opposed to *its* (belonging to it). Use the serial comma (x, y, and z).

4. *Do your verbs agree with their subjects?*
   Watch for sentences that contain singular subjects and plural verbs. For instance, in the following sentence the subject is singular, but a plural verb is used:

   > A set of books are missing.

   Because *set* is the subject, not *books*, the verb *is* should be used. Look also for sentences that contain plural subjects but singular verbs, such as:

   > Boxes of computer software was everywhere.

   The sentence should use the verb *were* to agree with the subject *boxes*. Such mistakes are easy to make.

5. *Are your pronoun references correct?*

Look at each pronoun (*his, her, their, its,* etc.) and make sure it agrees with what it refers to. For instance, it's incorrect to write:

Everyone in the group must buy their own lunch.

Since *everyone* is singular, the plural pronoun *their* can't be used. It should read:

Everyone in the group must buy his or her own lunch.

[Note: Avoid sexist usage. Don't use *his* when the reference being made is to a group containing both men and women.] Don't confuse *there* (not here), *they're* (they are), and *their* (belonging to them).

6. *Have you repeated the same word too often?*

If you don't own a thesaurus, a dictionary of synonyms (words that mean the same thing), you should buy one. Several are published in paperback editions. A good thesaurus will not only define words for you but also provide synonyms and antonyms (words that are opposite in meaning). When you notice that you are repeating a word, look it up and use a synonym.

7. *Do you have a title that reflects your thesis?*

A title, like a thesis, should not be too general. It should reflect the purpose and the content of your paper. A title should also fit the tone of your essay. If your essay is serious in tone, it's probably best to have a title that is direct; if your essay is light or humorous, try a catchy title.

For practice in editing, apply the steps of the preceding editing checklist to the last draft of the student essay on pages 67–69. Change any errors you find and give the essay an appropriate title.

Writing Exercise

In your journal or on a separate sheet of paper, write a one-paragraph summary of the editing checklist. Make certain you have a topic sentence that allows you to discuss all the steps. Your instructor may want to see your summary.

Here is what the next draft of the essay might look like after editing and minor revisions. Compare your markings with those below.

Trouble with Toll-Free Numbers

awkward
change
opening

About to doze off while watching an old movie on television
                    the sound of   attention
the other night, a commercial caught my ~~eye~~. The sound came up

as a fast-talking announcer began describing a new CD

collection of Eric Clapton's music. You've probably seen the

kind I mean. They play little snippets of singers singing one or two seconds of a song that made them famous, cutting quickly from one to the next. I like all the Clapton tunes they played, so when the announcer urged, "Call this toll-free number now . . . operators are standing by . . . order this fabulous set of records not available in any store," I did.

This, I'm sorry to say, is not unusual behavior for me. For instance, when I saw a television commercial offering a free digital watch along with a reduced price on a subscription to *Time*, I called their toll-free number. Then *Sports Illustrated* offered a low price subscription along with a free videocassette of some famous sports plays. Of course, I had to call their toll-free number, too. Now I have unread magazines stacking up around my room.

[margin: underline magazine titles]

TV commercials have influenced me so much that I even use personal items I have never used before, my family has used Crest toothpaste ever since I can remember. But after all those ads for Close-up (I think it's the kissable breath idea) I had my mom buy some just for me. And, like my dad, I used to just apply a little of mom's skin cream on my face after I shaved. But now, thanks to the influence of television commercials, I have tried several bands of after-shave lotion.

[margin: cap m.; it's = it is; possessive]
[margin right: comma replace period; comma @ intro phr]

The biggest purchase I ever made because of a TV commercial is my truck. It seemed ~~like~~ *that* every time I watched TV I'd see the same ad for a Ford pickup truck. It showed the truck at work during the day going through mud, climbing hills, and carrying heavy loads. Then it showed the truck at night, cleaned and polished, pulling up in front of a plush *-looking* restaurant. As the driver got out, a doorman helped his date step out. Both of them looked elegant. But it was the woman ~~that~~ *who* got me. Every time the commercial ~~comes~~ *came* on, I caught myself looking at her, not the truck. Anyway, the next thing I knew I had talked my ~~folks~~ *parents* into cosigning a loan for a new truck, since banks don't loan money to unemployed college students to buy new trucks. They tried to talk me out of it because there wasn't anything wrong with my old one. But you know how it is when you really want something. I rationalized that I could get part-time work

[margin: use who to refer to people]
[margin right: the doorman's date?; past ten]

hauling or delivering to help make payments. I think that's
what convinced my mom and dad to help out.

Now I wish I hadn't been so convincing. I can't afford to go
out on a date because I'm too busy with classes, homework, and
an evening job. If I don't make my truck payments, my parents
said they would sell my truck. They don't want to be stuck with
the payments. I can't blame them. [new ¶] Recently a local shoe store
announced on television that Nike tennis shoes were on sale.
The next day, I bought ~~a pair~~ them, even though I had just bought a   *pair used twice*
pair of Pumas a week before. When my mom heard, she called me
an "impulsive compulsive buyer", When I asked her what she   *period goes inside*
meant, she yelled, "Look it up!" and mumbled something about
my need to join a "buyers anonymous" group or quit watching so
much TV.

run-on sentence needs ⊙   She's right, I have a tendency to buy things I see on
television even though I don't need them or can't really afford
them. Even last night, there was a commercial for a survival
knife similar to the type commandos use. The knife has a big
blade, a hollow handle with a fish hook, some line, a few
matches, a compass that screws on top of the knife handle, and
the sheath has a little pocket on the side with a sharpening
stone, I just couldn't resist calling ~~there~~ their toll-free number.   *ww wrong word*

You are now ready to type up the final draft to submit to your instructor.

Proofreading

Once you write, type, or print out your final draft, you should proofread your paper for typing and spelling mistakes. It's possible that even then you might notice changes that have to be made. Remember that revising and editing, even though presented here as Stage 3, can happen at any stage of the writing process.

If the final copy of your essay has many mistakes, you may need to recopy or retype it. However, if it has only a few minor errors, use the proofreading guide in Appendix A to make your corrections.

Your final copy might be marked like this after proofreading:

Trouble with Toll-Free Numbers

The other night I was about to doze off while watching an
old movie on television when the sounds of a commercial

caught my attention. A fast-talking announcer began describing
a new compact disk collection of Eric Clapton's music. You've
probably seen the kind I mean. They play little snippets of
singers singing one or two seconds of a song that made them
famous, cutting quickly from one to the next. I like all the
Clapton tunes they played, so when the announcer urged, "Call
this toll-free number now . . . operators are standing by
. . . order this fabulous set of CDs not available in any
store," I did.

   This, I'm sorry to say, is not unusual behavior for me. For
instance, when I saw a television commercial offering a free
digital watch along with a reduced price on a subscription to
Time, I called ~~their~~ its toll-free number. Then <u>Sports Illustrated</u>
offered a low-priced subscription along with a free
videocassette of famous sports plays. Of course, I had to call
~~their~~ its toll-free number, too. Now I have stacks of unread
magazines around my room.

   TV commercials have influenced me so much that I even use
personal items I never used before. My family has brushed with
Crest toothpaste ever since I can remember. But after all those
ads for Close-up (I think it's the kissable breath idea), I had
Mom buy some just for me. And, like my dad, I used to just
apply a little of Mom's skin cream on my face after I shaved.
But now, thanks to the influence of television commercials, I
have tried several brands of after-shave lotion.

   The biggest purchase I ever made because of a TV commercial
was my truck. Almost every time I watched TV, I would see the
same ad for a Ford pickup truck. It showed the truck at work
during the day going through mud, climbing trails ~~tails~~, and carrying
heavy loads. Then it showed the truck at night, cleaned and
polished. Neon signs reflected off the truck as it pulled in
front of a plush-looking restaurant. As the driver, now dressed
in his finest, got out, a doorman helped the driver's ~~his~~ elegant-looking
date step from the truck. But it was the woman who got me.
Every time the commercial came on, I caught myself looking at
her, not the truck.

Anyway, the next thing I knew I had talked my parents into cosigning a loan for a new truck, since banks don't loan money to unemployed college students to buy new trucks. They tried to discourage me because there wasn't anything wrong with my old one. But you know how it is when you ^think you^ really want something. I rationalized that I could get part-time work hauling or delivering to help make payments. I think that's what convinced my mom and dad to help out.

Now I wish I hadn't been so convincing. I can't afford to go out on a date because of my truck payments. After attending classes, doing my homework, and working an evening job, I'm too tired to do anything b~~y~~^u^t watch TV. If I don't make my truck payments, my parents said they ~~would~~ ^will^ sell my truck. They don't want to be stuck with the bill. I can't blame them.

But my buying hasn't stopped there. Recently a local shoe store announced on television that Nike tennis shoes were on sale. The next day, I bought them, even though I had just bought a pair of Pumas a week before. When my mom heard, she called me an "impulsive compulsive buyer." When I asked her what she meant, she yelled, "Look it up!" and mumbled something about my need to join a "buyers anonymous" group or quit watching so much TV.

She's right; I have a tendency to buy things I see on television even though I don't need them or can't really affrod them. Even last night, there was a commercial for a survival knife similar to the type commandos use. It has a big blade, a hollow handle with a fish hook, some line, a few matches, a compass that screws on top of the handle, and the sheath has a little pocket on the side with a sharpening stone. When the~~ir~~ toll-free number was announced, I just couldn't resist calling.

Using the proper proofreading marks relieves you of retyping or recopying your entire essay. One of the reasons for double-spacing each page is to leave room to make corrections neatly. Of course, if there are so many corrections that the paper is too messy to read, you will have to redo it.

To practice your proof-marking skill, use these standard proofreading symbols to correct the paragraph below the list.

to remove a letter	rea**lll**y
to insert a word or letter	lib**ᴀ**ry
to insert punctuation	professors book
to insert a space	the model|essay
to reverse letters	rev**r**ese ~~smaller~~
to change a word	a little ~~larger~~ smaller
to close up a space	re verse

Lets say you are assigned to do research on what critics have said abuot John Updikes novel <u>The Witches of Eastwick</u>. In such a case secondary sources will be called for in your pa per. If, on the other hand the assignment calls for your own analysis of the novel, you will neeed to stick to the primary source, the novel Reading secondarysources on the novel, however, may provide you with ideas arguments that could be useful in supporting your own analysis of the book.

Compare your markings with the following to see how well you did.

Let's say you are assigned to do research on what critics have said abuot John Updikes novel <u>The Witches of Eastwick</u>. In such a case, secondary sources will be called for in your pa per. If, on the other hand, the assignment calls for your own analysis of the novel, you will neeed to stick to the primary source, the novel. Reading secondary sources on the novel, however, may provide you with ideas, *and* arguments that could be useful in supporting your own analysis of the book.

Before submitting an essay that has this many corrections in one paragraph, you should retype it. The corrections get in the way of the content.

Your instructor may require that you follow a particular format regarding size of margins; position of name, title, and page numbers; and so on. If not, you will find information on form and style beginning on page 434.

Before Going On

Remember that revising and editing are necessary and vital to good writing. Use the revision stage to make certain that your essay makes its point, that the point is supported adequately, that each paragraph is developed fully, that your tone is consistent, and that you have done your best to make the essay interesting to your audience. When editing, look at each sentence separately. Make certain that each sentence is complete and that it sounds correct. Check for correct punctuation, subject-verb agreement, pronoun agreement, and overuse of certain words. Consult Appendix A for the proper essay format and proofreading guide.

Writing Exercise

In your journal or on a separate sheet of paper, write three paragraphs summarizing the major points of each of the three stages of writing presented in this chapter. Make certain each paragraph has a topic sentence and that each paragraph is developed fully. Apply the three writing stages to this writing exercise. Your instructor may want you to turn in this exercise.

Revising and Editing Checklists: Brief Versions

Before turning in a completed essay to your instructor, use the following check-lists to make certain you have applied the steps in the three writing stages presented in this chapter.

Revision checklist (pages 64–65): When you revise the various drafts of an essay, ask yourself the following questions:

_____ 1. Have I made my point? Is my thesis clear?

_____ 2. Does my support move smoothly from one point to the next? Is my support logically arranged? Do I use transitional words and phrases to aid the reader?

_____ 3. Have I fully developed each paragraph? Does each paragraph have a topic sentence? Have I added or cut information if necessary?

_____ 4. Will my essay interest my audience? Does my opening paragraph grab the reader's attention?

_____ 5. Is the tone of my essay consistent? Do I use the same tone throughout? Is the language appropriate for my audience?

_____ 6. Have I said everything I need to say? Is my thesis fully developed? Does everything relate to the thesis?

Editing checklist (pages 70–71): When you edit the various drafts of an essay, ask yourself the following questions:

_____ 1. Have I given myself some time off between drafts? Have I put my essay aside for at least two hours?

_____ 2. Have I read each sentence aloud to hear how it sounds? Did I read each sentence from last to first?

_____ 3. Have I used proper punctuation?

_____ 4. Do my subjects and verbs agree in tense and number?

_____ 5. Are my pronoun references correct?

_____ 6. Have I avoided repeating the same word too often?

_____ 7. Do I have a title that reflects my thesis or subject?

On the Net

There are many places on the Internet to go for help with your writing. If you need assistance, the following sites may be able to help you:

1. The On-Line Writing Lab (OWL) at Purdue University offers assistance with writing projects, help with grammar, referrals to other sources, downloadable handouts, and Internet search tools. There is a comprehensive list of other OWL sites so you can be sure to get whatever you need, whenever you need it. Online tutors will answer your questions and provide assistance. To access the site, go to _owl.english.purdue.edu_ and follow the instructions to get the help you need.

2. The University of Maine Writing Center can be found at _www.ume.maine.edu/ ~wcenter/._ This site provides a comprehensive online list of other online writing labs for you to visit. Visit a few and see if one is more appropriate for your writing research needs.

Visit either of these sites or browse the Net to find a new site using the keyword "writing."

PART 2

Readings Worth Thinking and Writing About

3 Viewpoints on Learning

FOCUS ON LEARNING

To help you focus on the subject of this chapter, answer the following questions. You may want to write the answers in your journal or be prepared to discuss them in class.

1. Read the "Doonesbury" strip on the opposite page. Why is the professor so surprised by the student's response? What type of student is the professor used to? What does he mean when he says he thought his students were all stenographers? Do most of the teachers you know hold the same attitude as the one in the cartoon strip?

2. What type of student are you? Do you speak up in class, or do you tend to be a stenographer? Do you prefer lecture classes or those that involve class discussion? Why?

3. Read the quotation above the "Doonesbury" strip. What does the statement mean? Do you agree? Why or why not? Do you know how to learn on your own?

4. Learning occurs in many places and through many forms. What is the most recent thing you have learned about yourself? How did you learn it?

> *"Most teachers would agree that the primary goal of education is to teach students how to learn on their own."*
>
> —Kenneth Graham and H. Alan Robinson

DOONESBURY

G. B. TRUDEAU

I magine what your life would be like if you woke up one morning and everything you had ever learned was gone from your head. You wouldn't be able to get out of bed, dress yourself, feed yourself, or find the bathroom, much less know how to use it. You wouldn't be able to talk, read, or write. You wouldn't know what a television was, how to drive a car, or how to use a telephone. In other words, you'd be helpless.

We all know that learning is important. But what exactly is it? A dictionary might tell you that learning is acquiring knowledge through experience or study (sounds all right); a teacher might tell you that it's memorizing what you need to know for a test (we could argue that one); your boss might tell you that it's mastery of the task you're hired to do (OK, if the pay's good); a psychology book might tell you that learning is a relatively permanent change in behavior due to past experience (that one could use some examples); your parents may tell you that learning is achieved by a "Do as I say, not as I do" approach (no comment).

Obviously, learning takes place in many ways and forms. Hardly a day goes by that we don't learn something, either directly or indirectly. For instance, from television you will "learn" that minorities are generally criminals, victims, service workers, or students (come on, now!), and you might "learn" from a friend that smoking is "cool" (but what about the surgeon general?). The tendency, however, is to link learning with school. Then, of course, we can think about the definition of school. Is it a building labeled elementary, junior high, or senior high school? Is it the ivy-walled institution called college or university? Is it the warehouse converted into an adult education center? Is it Sunday school, the synagogue, or church? Is it the media—from television to the *National Enquirer*? Is it the city streets? Some type of schooling certainly occurs in all these places.

This chapter does not provide any definitive answers to what learning and schooling are. Instead, reading selections with various viewpoints on learning are offered. As you practice your reading skills, let your reactions to the ideas and the exercises provide some ideas for essays of your own.

 ## Preparing to Read

Take a minute or two to look over the following reading selection. Note the title and author, read the opening paragraph, and check the essay's length. Make certain you have the time now to read it carefully and to do the exercises that follow it. Then, in the spaces provided, answer the following questions.

1. What does the title mean to you? _____

_____

2. What do you think this selection will have to say about making mistakes?

_____

3. How do you feel about making mistakes? _____

_____

Vocabulary

Good comprehension of what you are about to read depends upon your understanding of the words below. The number following each word refers to the paragraph where it is used.

plateau (1) an elevated, stable state *flat*

cultivates (3) fosters, nurtures

embedded (3) planted, fixed firmly

incentive (3) drive, desire, motivation (in this case, the grading system)

penalizes (4) subjects to penalty, places a disadvantage on

garners (4) acquires, gains

stigma (4) mark of shame or disgrace

adherence (8) faithful attachment, devotion

germinal phase (8) beginning or earliest stage

erroneous (9) mistaken, based on error

exemplifies (10) serves as an example

phenomenon (10) a perceivable occurrence or fact

combust (11) burn

analogous (11) alike in certain ways

Brittany (16) an area on the northern coast of France across the English Channel from England

precedence (18) the state of having prior existence, priority

innovators (18) creators or introducers of something new

diverging (24) branching out, departing from the norm

deleterious (25) damaging, harmful

amoeba (25) shapeless, microscopic, one-celled organism

atrophy (26) waste away

To Err Is Wrong

Roger von Oech

Typing

Hits and Misses

1   In the summer of 1979, Boston Red Sox first baseman Carl Yastrzemski became the fifteenth player in baseball history to reach

the three thousand hit plateau. This event drew a lot of media attention, and for about a week prior to the attainment of this goal, hundreds of reporters covered Yaz's every move. Finally, one reporter asked, "Hey Yaz, aren't you afraid all of this attention will go to your head?" Yastrzemski replied, "I look at it this way: in my career I've been up to bat over ten thousand times. That means I've been unsuccessful at the plate over seven thousand times. That fact alone keeps me from getting a swollen head."

2   Most people consider success and failure as opposites, but they are actually both products of the same process. As Yaz suggests, an activity which produces a hit may also produce a miss. It is the same with creative thinking; the same energy which generates good creative ideas also produces errors.

3   Many people, however, are not comfortable with errors. Our educational system, based on "the right answer" belief, cultivates our thinking in another, more conservative way. From an early age, we are taught that right answers are good and incorrect answers are bad. This value is deeply embedded in the incentive system used in most schools:

Right over 90% of the time = "A"

Right over 80% of the time = "B"

Right over 70% of the time = "C"

Right over 60% of the time = "D"

Less than 60% correct, you fail.

From this we learn to be right as often as possible and to keep our mistakes to a minimum. We learn, in other words, that "to err is wrong."

Playing It Safe

4   With this kind of attitude, you aren't going to be taking too many chances. If you learn that failing even a little penalizes you (e.g., being wrong only 15% of the time garners you only a "B" performance), you learn not to make mistakes. And more important, you learn not to put yourself in situations where you might fail. This leads to conservative thought patterns designed to avoid the stigma our society puts on "failure."

5   I have a friend who recently graduated from college with a Master's degree in Journalism. For the last six months, she has been trying to

find a job, but to no avail. I talked with her about her situation, and realized that her problem is that she doesn't know how to fail. She went through eighteen years of schooling without ever failing an examination, a paper, a midterm, a pop-quiz, or a final. Now, she is reluctant to try any approaches where she might fail. She has been conditioned to believe that failure is bad in and of itself, rather than a potential stepping stone to new ideas.

6   Look around. How many middle managers, housewives, administrators, teachers, and other people do you see who are afraid to try anything new because of this fear of failure? Most of us have learned not to make mistakes in public. As a result, we remove ourselves from many learning experiences except for those occurring in the most private of circumstances.

A Different Logic

7   From a practical point of view, "to err is wrong" makes sense. Our survival in the everyday world requires us to perform thousands of small tasks without failure. Think about it: you wouldn't last very long if you were to step out in front of traffic or stick your hand into a pot of boiling water. In addition, engineers whose bridges collapse, stock brokers who lose money for their clients, and copy-writers whose ad campaigns decrease sales won't keep their jobs very long.

8   Nevertheless, too great an adherence to the belief "to err is wrong" can greatly undermine your attempts to generate new ideas. If you're more concerned with producing right answers than generating original ideas, you'll probably make uncritical use of the rules, formulae, and procedures used to obtain these right answers. By doing this, you'll by-pass the germinal phase of the creative process, and thus spend little time testing assumptions, challenging the rules, asking what-if questions, or just playing around with the problem. All of these techniques will produce some incorrect answers, but in the germinal phase errors are viewed as a necessary by-product of creative thinking. As Yaz would put it, "If you want the hits, be prepared for the misses." That's the way the game of life goes.

Errors as Stepping Stones

9   Whenever an error pops up, the usual response is "Jeez, another screwup, what went wrong this time?" The creative thinker, on the other hand, will realize the potential value of errors, and perhaps say something like, "Would you look at that! Where can it lead our thinking?" And then he or she will go on to use the error as a stepping stone to a new idea. As a matter of fact, the whole history of discovery is filled with people who used erroneous assumptions and failed

ideas as stepping stones to new ideas. Columbus thought he was finding a shorter route to India. Johannes Kepler stumbled on to the idea of interplanetary gravity because of assumptions which were right for the wrong reasons. And, Thomas Edison knew 1800 ways *not* to build a light bulb.

10   The following story about the automotive genius Charles Kettering exemplifies the spirit of working through erroneous assumptions to good ideas. In 1912, when the automobile industry was just beginning to grow, Kettering was interested in improving gasoline-engine efficiency. The problem he faced was "knock," the phenomenon in which gasoline takes too long to burn in the cylinder—thereby reducing efficiency.

11   Kettering began searching for ways to eliminate the "knock." He thought to himself, "How can I get the gasoline to combust in the cylinder at an earlier time?" The key concept here is "early." Searching for analogous situations, he looked around for models of "things that happen early." He thought of historical models, physical models, and biological models. Finally, he remembered a particular plant, the trailing arbutus, which "happens early," i.e., it blooms in the snow ("earlier" than other plants). One of this plant's chief characteristics is its red leaves, which help the plant retain light at certain wavelengths. Kettering figured that it must be the red color which made the trailing arbutus bloom earlier.

12   Now came the critical step in Kettering's chain of thought. He asked himself, "How can I make the gasoline red? Perhaps I'll put red dye in the gasoline—maybe that'll make it combust earlier." He looked around his workshop, and found that he didn't have any red dye. But he did happen to have some iodine—perhaps that would do. He added the iodine to the gasoline and, lo and behold, the engine didn't "knock."

13   Several days later, Kettering wanted to make sure that it was the redness of the iodine which had in fact solved his problem. He got some red dye and added it to the gasoline. Nothing happened! Kettering then realized that it wasn't the "redness" which had solved the "knock" problem, but certain other properties of iodine. In this case, an error had proven to be a stepping stone to a better idea. Had he known that "redness" alone was not the solution, he may not have found his way to the additives in iodine.

Negative Feedback

14   Errors serve another useful purpose: they tell us when to change direction. When things are going smoothly, we generally don't think about them. To a great extent, this is because we function according to the principle of negative feedback. Often it is only when

things or people fail to do their job that they get our attention. For example, you are probably not thinking about your kneecaps right now; that's because everything is fine with them. The same goes for your elbows: they are also performing their function—no problem at all. But if you were to break a leg, you would immediately notice all of the things you could no longer do, but which you used to take for granted.

15   Negative feedback means that the current approach is not working, and it is up to you to figure out a new one. We learn by trial and error, not by trial and rightness. If we did things correctly every time, we would never have to change direction—we'd just continue the current course and end up with more of the same.

16   For example, after the supertanker *Amoco Cadiz* broke up off the coast of Brittany in the spring of 1978, thereby polluting the coast with hundreds of thousands of tons of oil, the oil industry rethought many of its safety standards regarding petroleum transport. The same thing happened after the accident at the Three Mile Island nuclear reactor in 1979—many procedures and safety standards were changed.

17   Neil Goldschmidt, former secretary of transportation, had this to say about the Bay Area Rapid Transit (BART):

> It's gotten too fashionable around the country to beat up on BART and not give credit to the vision that put this system in place. We have learned from BART around the country. The lessons were put to use in Washington, in Atlanta, in Buffalo, and other cities where we are building mass transit systems. One of the lessons is not to build a system like BART.

We learn by our failures. A person's errors are the whacks that lead him to think something different.

Trying New Things

18   Your error rate in any activity is a function of your familiarity with that activity. If you are doing things that are routine and have a high likelihood of correctness, then you will probably make very few errors. But if you are doing things that have no precedence in your experience or are trying different approaches, then you will be making your share of mistakes. Innovators may not bat a thousand—far from it—but they do get new ideas.

19   The creative director of an advertising agency told me that he isn't happy unless he is failing at least half of the time. As he puts it, "If you are going to be original, you are going to be wrong a lot."

20   One of my clients, the president of a fast-growing computer company, tells his people: "We're innovators. We're doing things nobody

has ever done before. Therefore, we are going to be making mistakes. My advice to you: make your mistakes, but make them in a hurry."

21   Another client, a division manager of a high-technology company, asked his vice president of engineering what percentage of their new products should be successful in the marketplace. The answer he received was "about 50%." The division manager replied, "That's too high. 30% is a better target; otherwise we'll be too conservative in our planning."

22   Along similar lines, in the banking industry, it is said that if the credit manager never has to default on any of his loans, it's a sure sign he's not being aggressive enough in the marketplace.

23   Thomas J. Watson, the founder of IBM, has similar words: "The way to succeed is to double your failure rate."

24   Thus errors, at the very least, are a sign that we are diverging from the main road and trying different approaches.

Nature's Errors

25   Nature serves as a good example of how trial and error can be used to make changes. Every now and then genetic mutations occur—errors in gene reproduction. Most of the time, these mutations have a deleterious effect on the species, and they drop out of the gene pool. But occasionally, a mutation provides the species with something beneficial, and that change will be passed on to future generations. The rich variety of all species is due to this trial and error process. If there had never been any mutations from the first amoeba, where would we be now?

Summary

26   There are places where errors are inappropriate, but the germinal phase of the creative process isn't one of them. Errors are a sign that you are diverging from the well-traveled path. If you're not failing every now and then, it's a sign you're not being very innovative.

Tip #1:
If you make an error, use it as a stepping stone to a new idea you might not have otherwise discovered.

Tip #2:
Differentiate between errors of "commission" and those of "omission." The latter can be more costly than the former. If you're not making many errors, you might ask yourself, "How many opportunities am I missing by not being more aggressive?"

Tip #3:
Strengthen your "risk muscle." Everyone has one, but you have to exercise it or else it will atrophy. Make it a point to take at least one risk every twenty-four hours.

Tip #4:
Remember these two benefits of failure. First, if you do fail, you
learn what doesn't work; and second, the failure gives you an
opportunity to try a new approach.

Understanding the Content

Feel free to reread all or parts of the selection to answer the following questions.

1. Does von Oech believe "to err is wrong"? Why?

2. How does von Oech feel about the traditional grading system in schools? Why?

3. According to the author, what is wrong with "playing it safe"?

4. What are some of the "useful purposes" of making mistakes?

5. Explain what von Oech means when he says in his conclusion that we should differentiate between errors of "commission" and those of "omission."

6. What two benefits of failure does the author propose?

7. To what audience do you think the author is writing? Why?

8. Is there an implied or stated thesis? What is it?

✯✯✯

Looking at Structure and Style

1. How does von Oech use the first two paragraphs to lead us into his subject and thesis?

2. What is the cause-effect relationship discussed in paragraph 4?

3. What is the function of paragraphs 5 and 6?

4. What is being compared and contrasted in paragraphs 7 and 8?

5. Is this essay mostly formal or informal? Pick out some words or phrases that support your answer.

6. For what purpose does the author use paragraphs 9–13? Are they effective?

7. What writing pattern is used in paragraphs 14, 16, and 17?

8. How would you describe the author's attitude and tone?

Evaluating the Author's Viewpoints

1. Do you agree or disagree with von Oech's comments regarding the traditional educational grading system? Why?

2. In paragraph 6, the author says, "Most of us have learned not to make mistakes in public. As a result, we remove ourselves from many learning experiences except for those occurring in the most private of circumstances." Is this true? Is it true of you?

3. Respond to paragraph 25. What does von Oech mean? Do you agree?

4. Do you agree with von Oech that we should take at least one risk every twenty-four hours? Why? What kind of risks does he have in mind?

5. Where and when are errors inappropriate?

Pursuing Possible Essay Topics

1. Make a list of von Oech's arguments for the positive side of making errors. Write an essay that agrees with his thesis, but provide examples of your own. Or write an essay that disagrees with him.

2. Write about a time when you learned from an error you made.

3. Discuss your viewpoints on the traditional grading system. What are the pros and cons? How has it affected your learning?

4. Use this statement from the essay as the thesis for your own essay: "Most people consider success and failure as opposites, but they are actually both products of the same process."

5. In his book *Escape from Childhood,* educator John Holt states:

   > Young people should have the right to control and direct their own learning, that is, to decide what they want to learn, and when, where, how, how much, how fast, and with what help they want to learn it. To be still more specific, I want them to have the right to decide if, when, how much, and by whom they want to be *taught* and the right to decide whether they want to learn in a school and if so which one and for how much of the time.

   Write an essay that supports or refutes Holt's radical statement about learning. How would his ideas work? How would such an approach change the present educational system?

6. Write an essay about your own learning style. How do you learn best? What kind of teaching seems to help you learn best?

7. Freewrite or brainstorm on one or more of the following:

   a. making mistakes   d. nature's errors

   b. famous errors   e. negative feedback

   c. grades   f. trying new things

8. Ignore these and find your own topic on some aspect of learning.

Preparing to Read

Take a minute or two to look over the following reading selection. Note the title and author, read the opening paragraph, and check the essay's length. Make certain you have the time now to read it carefully and to do the exercises that follow it. Then, in the spaces provided, answer the following questions.

1. What do you think the title means? _____

_____

_____

2. What will be the subject of this essay? _____

_____

3. What might you learn from reading it? _____

_____

Vocabulary

Good comprehension of what you are about to read depends upon your understanding of the words below. The number following each word refers to the paragraph where it is used.

semiliterate (1) having only an elementary level of reading and writing ability

impediments (4) obstacles, barriers, hindrances

trump card (4) a card from the suit in a card game that outranks all other suits for the duration of the game

composure (6) self-possession, calmness

chemical dependency (9) addiction to drugs

In Praise of the F Word

Mary Sherry

1   Tens of thousands of 18-year-olds will graduate this year and be handed meaningless diplomas. These diplomas won't look any

different from those awarded their luckier classmates. Their validity will be questioned only when their employers discover that these graduates are semiliterate.

2   Eventually a fortunate few will find their way into educational-repair shops—adult-literacy programs, such as the one where I teach basic grammar and writing. There, high-school graduates and high-school dropouts pursuing graduate-equivalency certificates will learn the skills they should have learned in school. They will also discover they have been cheated by our educational system.

3   As I teach, I learn a lot about our schools. Early in each session I ask my students to write about an unpleasant experience they had in school. No writers' block here! "I wish someone would have had made me stop doing drugs and made me study." "I liked to party and no one seemed to care." "I was a good kid and didn't cause any trouble, so they just passed me along even though I didn't read well and couldn't write." And so on.

4   I am your basic do-gooder, and prior to teaching this class I blamed the poor academic skills our kids have today on drugs, divorce and other impediments to concentration necessary for doing well in school. But, as I rediscover each time I walk into the classroom, before a teacher can expect students to concentrate, he has to get their attention, no matter what distractions may be at hand. There are many ways to do this, and they have much to do with teaching style. However, if style alone won't do it, there is another way to show who holds the winning hand in the classroom. That is to reveal the trump card of failure.

5   I will never forget a teacher who played that card to get the attention of one of my children. Our youngest, a world-class charmer, did little to develop his intellectual talents but always got by. Until Mrs. Stifter.

6   Our son was a high-school senior when he had her for English. "He sits in the back of the room talking to his friends," she told me. "Why don't you move him to the front row?" I urged, believing the embarrassment would get him to settle down. Mrs. Stifter looked at me steely-eyed over her glasses. "I don't move seniors," she said. "I flunk them." I was flustered. Our son's academic life flashed before my eyes. No teacher had ever threatened him with that before. I regained my composure and managed to say that I thought she was right. By the time I got home I was feeling pretty good about this. It was a radical approach for these times, but, well, why not? "She's going to flunk you," I told my son. I did not discuss it any further. Suddenly English became a priority in his life. He finished out the semester with an A.

7   I know one example doesn't make a case, but at night I see a parade of students who are angry and resentful for having been passed along until they could no longer even pretend to keep up. Of average

intelligence or better, they eventually quit school, concluding they were too dumb to finish. "I should have been held back," is a comment I hear frequently. Even sadder are those students who are high-school graduates who say to me after a few weeks of class, "I don't know how I ever got a high-school diploma."

8   Passing students who have not mastered the work cheats them and the employers who expect graduates to have basic skills. We excuse this dishonest behavior by saying kids can't learn if they come from terrible environments. No one seems to stop to think that—no matter what environments they come from—most kids don't put school first on their list unless they perceive something is at stake. They'd rather be sailing.

9   Many students I see at night could give expert testimony on unemployment, chemical dependency, abusive relationships. In spite of these difficulties, they have decided to make education a priority. They are motivated by the desire for a better job or the need to hang on to the one they've got. They have a healthy fear of failure.

10   People of all ages can rise above their problems, but they need to have a reason to do so. Young people generally don't have the maturity to value education in the same way my adult students value it. But fear of failure, whether economic or academic, can motivate both.

11   Flunking as a regular policy has just as much merit today as it did two generations ago. We must review the threat of flunking and see it as it really is—a positive teaching tool. It is an expression of confidence by both teachers and parents that the students have the ability to learn the material presented to them. However, making it work again would take a dedicated, caring conspiracy between teachers and parents. It would mean facing the tough reality that passing kids who haven't learned the material—while it might save them grief for the short term—dooms them to long-term illiteracy. It would mean that teachers would have to follow through on their threats, and parents would have to stand behind them, knowing their children's best interests are indeed at stake. This means no more doing Scott's assignments for him because he might fail. No more passing Jodi because she's such a nice kid.

12   This is a policy that worked in the past and can work today. A wise teacher, with the support of his parents, gave our son the opportunity to succeed—or fail. It's time we return this choice to all students.

Understanding the Content

Feel free to reread all or parts of the selection to answer the following questions.

1. What is the "F word" discussed in the essay?

2. What is Sherry's attitude toward the F word?

3. What reasons does the author give for believing that the threat of flunking students is a positive teaching tool?

4. What choice does the author want to give to students? Why is she particularly interested in the subject?

5. What is the point of this selection? What does it have to do with the subject of learning?

Looking at Structure and Style

1. How does paragraph 2 help to support paragraph 1?

2. What is the point of paragraph 3?

3. How does Sherry use paragraphs 5 and 6 to support her viewpoint?

4. What is the point of paragraphs 9 and 10?

5. What audience do you think the author had in mind when she wrote this essay?

Evaluating the Author's Viewpoints

1. Do you agree with the author that "flunking as a regular policy has just as much merit today as it did two generations ago" (11)? Why?

2. What are some good arguments for *not* flunking students?

3. The author contends that fear of failure can motivate students. Explain why you do or do not agree.

4. Explain why you would or would not like to have Sherry as a teacher.

Pursuing Possible Essay Topics

1. Recall a time when fear of failure motivated you to accomplish something.

2. Summarize the reasons why the author is in praise of the F word.

3. Write an essay that takes the opposite viewpoint regarding the F word.

4. Explore the pros and cons of withholding high school diplomas from students who lack the ability to learn, despite fear of failure.

5. Brainstorm or freewrite on one or both of the following:

   a. fear of failure

   b. flunking

Preparing to Read

Take a minute or two to look over the following reading selection. Note the title and author, read the opening paragraph, and check the essay's length. Make certain you have the time now to read it carefully and to do the exercises that follow it. Then, in the spaces provided, answer the following questions.

1. What do you think the title means? _____

   _____

   _____

2. What do you think the selection will say about cheating? _____

   _____

   _____

3. Why do you think the author uses the second person, "Your kid's going to pay for cheating," in the title? _____

   _____

Vocabulary

Good comprehension of what you are about to read depends upon your understanding the words below. The number following each word refers to the paragraph where it is used.

plagiarism (1) passing off as one's own the ideas or writings of another

expulsion (1) being thrown out of something or from somewhere

syllabus (2) an outline or a summary of the main points of a course of study

conspicuously (3) easily noticed

besieged (4) surrounded with hostile forces, harassed

crowing (5) boasting

condemnation (5) strong disapproval

amorality (8) lack of virtue

complicit (8) being involved as an accomplice to a wrongdoing or a crime

cribbing (10) copying, stealing, or cheating

Your Kid's Going to Pay for Cheating— Eventually

Leonard Pitts, Jr.

1   Last week, school officials in Piper, Kan., adopted an official policy on plagiarism—with punishments ranging from redoing an assignment to expulsion. Unfortunately, all that comes too late to help Christine Pelton.

2   She used to be a teacher. Taught biology at Piper High, to be exact. Then, last fall, she assigned her students to collect 20 leaves and write a report on them. The kids knew from the classroom syllabus— a document they and their parents both signed—that cheating would not be tolerated. Anyone who plagiarized would receive no credit for the assignment, which counted toward half their semester grade.

3   Maybe you've heard what happened next. Twenty-eight of Pelton's 118 sophomores turned in work that seemed conspicuously similar. It took only a little Web research for her to confirm that they had indeed cut-and-pasted their papers together.

4   True to her word, Pelton issued 28 zeroes. What followed was to moral integrity as the Keystone Kops are to law enforcement. Parents rose in outrage, some even making harassing, post-midnight phone calls to her home. Pelton offered the cheaters make-up assignments that would have allowed them to pass the class with D's. They refused. Besieged by angry mothers and fathers, the school board ordered the teacher to soften the punishment.

5   She went to school the next day and found the kids in a celebratory mood, cheering their victory and crowing that they no longer had to listen to teachers. By lunchtime, Pelton had quit. The school's principal and 13 of 32 teachers have also reportedly resigned. In the months since then, the cheaters have become the target of ridicule and condemnation in media around the world.

6   In spite of that, the parents of the 28 ethically challenged students continue to rally to their defense. One says it's not plagiarism if you only copy a sentence or two. Another expresses doubt the kids even know what plagiarism means.

7   To that, I can only say this: Please shut up. Haven't you already done enough damage?

8   Students have always cheated, yes. Always schemed to see the questions ahead of time, write notes on sweaty palms, peer over the shoulder of the teacher's pet. But what's most troubling here is not the amorality of adolescents, but the fact that parents are so eagerly complicit, so ready to look the other way, so willing to rationalize the

fact that their children are, in essence, liars and thieves. Lying about authorship of the work, thieving the grade that results.

9   Those students, their parents and the school board that caved in like cardboard in the rain are all emblematic of a society in which cheating has become not just epidemic but somehow, tolerated, even at the highest levels. As one senior told *CBS News,* "It probably sounds twisted, but I would say that in this day and age, cheating is almost not wrong."

10   Who can blame the kid for thinking that way when the news is full of noted historians cribbing from one another, Enron cooking the books well done, Merrill Lynch recommending garbage stock, a Notre Dame football coach falsifying his resumé. Whatever works, right? Ours is not to judge, right?

11   Wrong.

12   At the risk of being preachy, I'd like to point out the common thread between the historians, the coach, Enron and Merrill Lynch: They all got caught.

13   Cheaters almost always do. No, not necessarily in big, splashy stories that make *CBS News.* Sometimes, it's just in the small, quiet corners of inauthentic lives when they are brought up short by their own inadequacies and forced to acknowledge the hollowness of their achievements. To admit they aren't what others believe them to be.

14   Reputation, it has been said, is about who you are when people are watching. Character is about who you are when there's nobody in the room but you. Both matter, but of the two, character is far and away the most important. The former can induce others to think well of you. But only the latter allows you to think well of yourself.

15   This is the lesson of Piper High, for those who have ears to hear.

16   Turns out Christine Pelton is still teaching after all.

Understanding the Content

Feel free to reread all or parts of the selection to answer the following questions.

1. Who is Christine Pelton?

2. What did parents do after Christine Pelton issued the grades on her students' work, with twenty-eight zeroes handed out?

3. What did Christine Pelton do as a result of her students' and their parents' actions?

4. According to the author, what is the definition of reputation? of character?

5. According to the author, what do almost all cheaters have in common?

6. What was the end result of the plagiarism scandal at Piper High?

Looking at Structure and Style

1. What is the thesis of this essay? Is it implied or stated? If stated, where?

2. What is the purpose of paragraph 10?

3. What is the author's attitude about the parents of Christine Pelton's students? How can you tell? What words or phrases does he use to convey his feelings?

4. Are paragraphs 15 and 16 effective as concluding paragraphs? Why or why not?

Evaluating the Author's Viewpoints

1. Does the author agree or disagree with the parents of Christine Pelton's students, who rallied to the students' defense? How can you tell?

2. How does the author feel about Christine Pelton and the stance she took regarding cheating and plagiarism?

3. How does the author feel about the students who plagiarized? Does he think that they plagiarized knowingly, or that they didn't really understand what plagiarism was? How can you tell? What words or phrases does he use to convey his feelings?

4. What does the author mean by "Turns out Christine Pelton is still teaching after all"?

5. Based on your reading of this selection, who does the author think is most at fault here? The students? Their parents? The school officials? How can you tell?

Pursuing Possible Essay Topics

1. Write an essay about cheating, in general. Is it ever morally right to cheat? Why or why not?

2. Do you agree or disagree with the statement "Reputation is about who you are when people are watching"? Why? Give examples from either current events or your own life to support your opinion.

3. Freewrite or brainstorm on the topic of "plagiarism," "cheating," or "academic responsibility."

4. Would you have handled the situation in this selection differently? If so, how? Write an essay summarizing what you think school officials in Piper, Kansas, should have done when confronted with the issue of plagiarism, the outraged parents, and Christine Pelton's resignation.

5. Write an essay in opposition to Leonard Pitts's stance in this selection. Defend the students' actions and their right to cut and paste information from the Internet for their homework.

6. Ignore these topics and find your own topic related to cheating.

Preparing to Read

Take a minute or two to look over the following reading selection. Note the title and author, read the first two paragraphs, and check the essay's length. Make certain you have the time now to read it carefully and to do the exercises that follow it. Then, in the spaces provided, answer the following questions.

1. Judging from the title, what do you think this essay will be about? _____

_____

_____

2. How do you think the author feels about the state of education today?_____

_____

_____

3. How do you feel about "Progressive Education," as described in paragraph 2?

_____

_____

Vocabulary

Good comprehension of what you are about to read depends upon your understanding of the words below. The number following each word refers to the paragraph where it is used.

excised (4) removed as if by cutting

mandate (5) authoritative command or instruction

curriculum (5) all the courses of study offered by an educational institution

assertion (6) something declared or stated positively, often with no support or attempt at proof

systematically (8) using step-by-step procedures

dogma (8) doctrine or system of beliefs relating to matters such as morality and faith

adherent (9) supporter, as of a cause or an individual

irrespective of (9) regardless of

methodology (11) body of practices, procedures, and rules used in a discipline or an inquiry

inculcate (11) impress something upon the mind of another by frequent instruction or repetition

shackles (12) restrictions, restraints

enshrining (12) cherishing as sacred

Essence of Education

Robert W. Tracinski

1   The essence of education is the teaching of facts and reasoning skills to our children, so that they learn how to think.

2   Yet for almost a century, our schools have been under assault by an approach to education that elevates feelings over facts. Under the influence of Progressive Education, "socialization"—getting the student in touch with other children's feelings—is now more important than getting him in touch with the facts of history, mathematics or geography.

3   "Creative spelling"—in which students are encouraged to spell words in whatever way they feel is correct—is more important than the rules of language. Urging children to "feel good" about themselves is more important than ensuring that they acquire the knowledge necessary for living successfully.

4   This emotion-centered, anti-reason assault on education has found a new ally: those who believe the literal words of the Bible. The Kansas Board of Education has just excised the theory of evolution from the state's official science standards. Several other states have enacted similar anti-evolution policies, thereby elevating the feelings of religious fundamentalists over the accumulated evidence of the entire science of biology.

5   These policies do not actually ban the teaching of evolution, nor do they mandate the teaching of "Creationism"—the biblical claim that the Earth and all life on it were created in six days. They simply drop evolution from the required curriculum. The goal of the religious activists is to keep students ignorant of the theory of evolution,

or to encourage the teaching of evolution and Creationism side-by-side, as two "competing" theories.

6   Consider what this latter would mean in the classroom. On the one side, teachers would present the theory of evolution, supported by countless observations, all integrated into a comprehensive explanation of virtually every fact in its field. On the other side, teachers would present—what? All that the Creationist view offers is the assertion by would-be authorities that an ancient religious text reveals that 10,000 years ago God created the world in six days.

7   Some of these religious activists claim that they reject the teaching of evolution because it is "unproven," since it lacks "sufficient evidence."

8   Yet their arguments systematically reject the need for proof and evidence. Scientists can point to a billion-year-long fossil record of continuous changes across all species as they develop from more-primitive to present-day forms. They can point to the natural variations among members of a species, variations that change from one climate to another as species adapt to their environments. But the Creationist categorically dismisses the evidence—because it contradicts biblical dogma.

9   The central issue is not whether there is enough scientific evidence to validate a particular conclusion—but whether science as such, rather than faith, is the basis for arriving at conclusions. There can be no scientific debate between these two positions. There can be no rational argument between a view that rests on observation and reason, and one that rests on blind faith—i.e., on its adherents' desire to believe something, irrespective of logic.

10   If the Creationist approach were taken seriously, what would remain of education? If evidence and reasoning are to be "balanced" by faith or feelings—what, then, would not belong in the curriculum? Even the theory that the Earth is flat has proponents who feel it is true. More to the point, what is to stop teachers from presenting any other nonrational view of the origin of man? Why not give equal time to, say, the Nazi claim that the white race descended from the superior Aryans?

11   The most ominous implication of the Creationist position is its belief that, in judging the truth of an idea, one can simply ignore rational evidence—if it clashes with one's desire to believe otherwise. This is a disastrous methodology to inculcate in our children—and it is even more dangerous to back it up with the rulings of a government body.

12   The crucial role of education is to provide young people with the information and methods they need in order to learn how to think independently. Education has liberated mankind from the shackles

of myth, superstition and unchallenged tradition. But the prevailing trend—from both the "progressive left" and the "religious right"—is to reverse this development, by enshrining feelings over facts and faith over reason.

13   If campaigns such as the one against teaching evolution are allowed to succeed, the ultimate result will be the extinction of genuine education.

Understanding the Content

Feel free to reread all or parts of the selection to answer the following questions.

1. What is "Creationism"? What is the basic teaching of this theory?

2. How does the author define "socialization," as it is being used in schools as a teaching method?

3. What state's school board has "excised the theory of evolution from the state's official science standards"? Why has it done this?

4. Why do some religious activists reject the teaching of evolution?

5. According to the author, what is the "most ominous implication of the Creationist position" in terms of education?

Looking at Structure and Style

1. How does the author use the first two paragraphs to establish the subject of the essay?

2. What is the author's thesis? Is it stated or implied? If stated, where?

3. What is the tone and attitude of the essay? What words or phrases give you an idea of the author's tone?

4. Why does the author discuss "Progressive Education" in the second paragraph? What purpose does this discussion serve?

5. Does the author make a sound argument against "Creationism"? If so, what paragraphs support his argument?

6. How does the author refute the argument made by religious activists that (in the author's words) students should be kept "ignorant of the theory of evolution"? What facts does he present? Is he effective in refuting the argument?

7. How does the author compare the teaching of faith and feelings? What comparisons does he draw to make his point?

Evaluating the Author's Viewpoints

1. Do you agree with the author's statement that "the essence of education is the teaching of facts and reasoning skills to our children, so that they learn how to think"? Why or why not?

2. What is the author's opinion of people whom he brands "religious activists"? How can you tell?

3. Do you agree that antievolution advocates' "arguments systematically reject the need for proof and evidence"? Why or why not?

4. Do you think the author presents an unbiased view of Progressive Education? Explain.

Pursuing Possible Essay Topics

1. Do you think the Bible should be read literally? Why or why not? Write an essay defending your viewpoint.

2. Are you in support of the teaching of evolution? Write an essay arguing either for or against the teaching of evolution in schools.

3. Do you think that all references to feelings and faith should be excised from today's curriculum? Write an essay discussing your viewpoint.

4. Do you support Progressive Education? Write an essay discussing why it is important to teach children to "feel good" about themselves.

5. Brainstorm or freewrite on one or more of the following:

   a. the teaching of evolution

   b. the Creationist view

   c. Progressive Education

   d. socialization

   e. creative spelling

   f. teaching faith and feelings over fact and reason

6. You can reject these topics and choose one of your own based on something you find interesting in the essay.

Preparing to Read

Take a minute or two to look over the following reading selection. Note the title and author, read the opening paragraph, and check the essay's length. Make certain you have the time now to read it carefully and to do the exercises that follow it. Then, in the spaces provided, answer the following questions.

1. From the title and the opening paragraph, what do you think this story will be about?_____

_____

_____

2. Who is the narrator? How does the author use language to give you an impression of the narrator in the first paragraph?_____

_____

_____

Vocabulary

Good comprehension of what you are about to read depends upon your understanding of the words below. The number following each word refers to the paragraph where it is used.

nappy (1) kinky, frizzy

sachet (1) small packet of perfumed powder used to scent clothes, as in trunks or closets

gofer (1) employee who runs errands in addition to regular duties

pinafore (2) sleeveless garment similar to an apron, worn especially by girls as a dress or overdress

surly (2) ill-humored, gruff

faggot (3) disparaging term for a gay or homosexual man

fused (13) united by having been melted together

curtsy (16) gesture of respect or reverence made chiefly by women by bending the knees with one foot forward and lowering the body

fiberglass (25) material consisting of extremely fine glass fibers, used in making yarns, fabrics, insulators, and structural objects or parts

recitation (26) the act of reciting memorized materials

liable (38) apt, likely

somersaults (44) acrobatic stunts in which the body rolls in a complete circle, heels over head

The Lesson

TONI CADE BAMBARA

1   Back in the days when everyone was old and stupid or young and foolish and me and Sugar were the only ones just right, this lady moved on our block with nappy hair and proper speech and no makeup. And quite naturally we laughed at her, laughed the way we did at the junk man who went about his business like he was some big-time president and his sorry-ass horse his secretary. And we kinda hated her too, hated the way we did the winos who cluttered up our parks and pissed on our handball walls and stank up our hallways and stairs so you couldn't halfway play hide-and-seek without a goddamn gas mask. Miss Moore was her name. The only woman on the block with no first name. And she was black as hell, cept for her feet, which were fish-white and spooky. And she was always planning these boring-ass things for us to do, us being my cousin, mostly, who lived on the block cause we all moved North the same time and to the same apartment then spread out gradual to breathe. And our parents would yank our heads into some kinda shape and crisp up our clothes so we'd be presentable for travel with Miss Moore, who always looked like she was going to church, though she never did. Which is just one of the things the grownups talked about when they talked behind her back like a dog. But when she came calling with some sachet she'd sewed up or some gingerbread she'd made or some book, why then they'd all be too embarrassed to turn her down and we'd get handed over all spruced up. She'd been to college and said it was only right that she should take responsibility for the young ones' education, and she not even related by marriage or blood. So they'd go for it. Specially Aunt Gretchen. She was the main gofer in the family. You got some ole dumb shit foolishness you want somebody to go for, you send for Aunt Gretchen. She been screwed into the go-along for so long, it's a blood-deep natural thing with her. Which is how she got saddled with me and Sugar and Junior in the first place while our mothers were in a la-de-da apartment up the block having a good ole time.

2   So this one day Miss Moore rounds us all up at the mailbox and it's puredee hot and she's knockin herself out about arithmetic. And school suppose to let up in summer I heard, but she don't

never let up. And the starch in my pinafore scratching the shit outta me and I'm really hating this nappy-head bitch and her god-damn college degree. I'd much rather go to the pool or to the show where it's cool. So me and Sugar leaning on the mailbox being surly, which is a Miss Moore word. And Flyboy checking out what everybody brought for lunch. And Fat Butt already wasting his peanut-butter-and-jelly sandwich like the pig he is. And Junebug punchin on Q.T.'s arm for potato chips. And Rosie Giraffe shifting from one hip to the other waiting for somebody to step on her foot or ask her if she from Georgia so she can kick ass, preferably Mercedes'. And Miss Moore asking us do we know what money is, like we a bunch of retards. I mean real money, she say, like it's only poker chips or monopoly papers we lay on the grocer. So right away I'm tired of this and say so. And would much rather snatch Sugar and go to the Sunset and terrorize the West Indian kids and take their hair ribbons and their money too. And Miss Moore files that remark away for next week's lesson on brotherhood, I can tell. And finally I say we oughta get to the subway cause it's cooler and besides we might meet some cute boys. Sugar done swiped her mama's lipstick, so we ready.

3   So we heading down the street and she's boring us silly about what things cost and what our parents make and how much goes for rent and how money ain't divided up right in this country. And then she gets to the part about we all poor and live in the slums, which I don't feature. And I'm ready to speak on that, but she steps out in the street and hails two cabs just like that. Then she hustles half the crew in with her and hands me a five-dollar bill and tells me to calculate 10 percent tip for the driver. And we're off. Me and Sugar and Junebug and Flyboy hangin out the window and hollering to everybody, putting lipstick on each other cause Flyboy a faggot anyway, and making farts with our sweaty armpits. But I'm mostly trying to figure how to spend this money. But they all fascinated with the meter tick-ing and Junebug starts laying bets as to how much it'll read when Flyboy can't hold his breath no more. Then Sugar lays bets as to how much it'll be when we get there. So I'm stuck. Don't nobody want to go for my plan, which is to jump out at the next light and run off to the first bar-b-que we can find. Then the driver tells us to get the hell out cause we there already. And the meter reads eighty-five cents. And I'm stalling to figure out the tip and Sugar say give him a dime. And I decide he don't need it bad as I do, so later for him. But then he tries to take off with Junebug foot still in the door so we talk about his mama something ferocious. Then we check out that we on Fifth Avenue and everybody dressed up in stockings. One lady in a fur coat, hot as it is. White folks crazy.

4   "This is the place," Miss Moore say, presenting it to us in the voice she uses at the museum. "Let's look in the windows before we go in."

5   "Can we steal?" Sugar asks very serious like she's getting the ground rules squared away before she plays. "I beg your pardon," say Miss Moore, and we fall out. So she leads us around the windows of the toy store and me and Sugar screamin, "This is mine, that's mine, I gotta have that, that was made for me, I was born for that," till Big Butt drowns us out.

6   "Hey, I'm goin to buy that there."

7   "That there? You don't even know what it is, stupid."

8   "I do so," he say punchin on Rosie Giraffe. "It's a microscope."

9   "Whatcha gonna do with a microscope, fool?"

10   "Look at things."

11   "Like what, Ronald?" ask Miss Moore. And Big Butt ain't got the first notion. So here go Miss Moore gabbing about the thousands of bacteria in a drop of water and the somethinorother in a speck of blood and the million and one living things in the air around us is invisible to the naked eye. And what she say that for? Junebug go to town on that "naked" and we rolling. Then Miss Moore ask what it cost. So we all jam into the window smudgin it up and the price tag say $300. So then she ask how long'd take for Big Butt and Junebug to save up their allowances. "Too long," I say. "Yeh," adds Sugar, "outgrown it by that time." And Miss Moore say no, you never outgrow learning instruments. "Why, even medical students and interns and," blah, blah, blah. And we ready to choke Big Butt for bringing it up in the first damn place.

12   "This here costs four hundred eighty dollars," say Rosie Giraffe. So we pile up all over her to see what she pointin out. My eyes tell me it's a chunk of glass cracked with something heavy, and different-color inks dripped into the splits, then the whole thing put into a oven or something. But for $480 it don't make sense.

13   "That's a paperweight made of semi-precious stones fused together under tremendous pressure," she explains slowly, with her hands doing the mining and all the factory work.

14   "So what's a paperweight?" asks Rosie Giraffe.

15   "To weigh paper with, dumbbell," say Flyboy, the wise man from the East.

16   "Not exactly," say Miss Moore, which is what she say when you warm or way off too. "It's to weigh paper down so it won't scatter and make your desk untidy." So right away me and Sugar curtsy to each other and then to Mercedes who is more the tidy type.

17   "We don't keep paper on top of the desk in my class," say Junebug, figuring Miss Moore crazy or lyin one.

18   "At home, then," she say. "Don't you have a calendar and a pencil case and a blotter and a letter-opener on your desk at home where you do your homework?" And she know damn well what our homes look like cause she nosys around in them every chance she gets.

19   "I don't even have a desk," say Junebug. "Do we?"

20   "No. And I don't get no homework neither," say Big Butt.

21   "And I don't even have a home," say Flyboy like he do at school to keep the white folks off his back and sorry for him. Send this poor kid to camp posters, is his specialty.

22   "I do," says Mercedes. "I have a box of stationery on my desk and a picture of my cat. My godmother bought the stationery and the desk. There's a big rose on each sheet and the envelopes smell like roses."

23   "Who wants to know about your smelly-ass stationery," say Rosie Giraffe fore I can get my two cents in.

24   "It's important to have a work area all your own so that . . ."

25   "Will you look at this sailboat, please," say Flyboy, cuttin her off and pointin to the thing like it was his. So once again we tumble all over each other to gaze at this magnificent thing in the toy store which is just big enough to maybe sail two kittens across the pond if you strap them to the posts tight. We all start reciting the price tag like we in assembly. "Handcrafted sailboat of fiberglass at one thousand one hundred ninety-five dollars."

26   "Unbelievable," I hear myself say and am really stunned. I read it again for myself just in case the group recitation put me in a trance. Same thing. For some reason this pisses me off. We look at Miss Moore and she lookin at us, waiting for I dunno what.

27   "Who'd pay all that when you can buy a sailboat set for a quarter at Pop's, a tube of glue for a dime, and a ball of string for eight cents? It must have a motor and a whole lot else besides," I say. "My sailboat cost me about fifty cents."

28   "But will it take water?" say Mercedes with her smart ass.

29   "Took mine to Alley Pond Park once," say Flyboy. "String broke. Lost it. Pity."

30   "Sailed mine in Central Park and it keeled over and sank. Had to ask my father for another dollar."

31   "And you got the strap," laugh Big Butt. "The jerk didn't even have a string on it. My old man wailed on his behind."

32   Little Q.T. was staring hard at the sailboat and you could see he wanted it bad. But he too little and somebody'd just take it from him. So what the hell. "This boat for kids, Miss Moore?"

33   "Parents silly to buy something like that just to get all broke up," say Rosie Giraffe.

34   "That much money it should last forever," I figure.

35   "My father'd buy it for me if I wanted it."

36   "Your father, my ass," say Rosie Giraffe getting a chance to finally push Mercedes.

37   "Must be rich people shop here," say Q.T.

38   "You are a very bright boy," say Flyboy. "What was your first clue?" And he rap him on the head with the back of his knuckles, since Q.T. the only one he could get away with. Though Q.T. liable to come up behind you years later and get his licks in when you half expect it.

39   "What I want to know is," I says to Miss Moore though I never talk to her, I wouldn't give the bitch that satisfaction, "is how much a real boat costs? I figure a thousand'd get you a yacht any day."

40   "Why don't you check that out," she says, "and report back to the group?" Which really pains my ass. If you gonna mess up a perfectly good swim day least you could do is have some answers. "Let's go in," she say like she got something up her sleeve. Only she don't lead the way. So me and Sugar turn the corner to where the entrance is, but when we get there I kinda hang back. Not that I'm scared, what's there to be afraid of, just a toy store. But I feel funny, shame. But what I got to be shamed about? Got as much right to go in as anybody. But somehow I can't seem to get hold of the door, so I step away for Sugar to lead. But she hangs back too. And I look at her and she looks at me and this is ridiculous. I mean, damn, I have never ever been shy about doing nothing or going nowhere. But then Mercedes steps up and then Rosie Giraffe and Big Butt crowd in behind and shove, and next thing we all stuffed into the doorway with only Mercedes squeezing past us, smoothing out her jumper and walking right down the aisle. Then the rest of us tumble in like a glued-together jigsaw done all wrong. And people lookin at us. And it's like the time me and Sugar crashed into the Catholic church on a dare. But once we got in there and everything so hushed and holy and the candles and the bowin and the handkerchiefs on all the drooping heads, I just couldn't go through with the plan. Which was for me to run up to the altar and do a tap dance while Sugar played the nose flute and messed around in the holy water. And Sugar kept givin me the elbow. Then later teased me so bad I tied her up in the shower and turned it on and locked her in. And she'd be there till this day if Aunt Gretchen hadn't finally figured I was lyin about the boarder takin a shower.

41   Same thing in the store. We all walkin on tiptoe and hardly touchin the games and puzzles and things. And I watched Miss Moore who is steady watchin us like she waitin for a sign. Like Mama Drewery watches the sky and sniffs the air and takes note of just how much slant is in the bird formation. Then me and Sugar bump smack into each other, so busy gazing at the toys, 'specially the sailboat. But we don't laugh and go into our fat-lady bump-stomach routine. We just

stare at that price tag. Then Sugar run a finger over the whole boat. And I'm jealous and want to hit her. Maybe not her, but I sure want to punch somebody in the mouth.

42   "Watcha bring us here for, Miss Moore?"

43   "You sound angry, Sylvia. Are you mad about something?" Givin me one of them grins like she tellin a grown-up joke that never turns out to be funny. And she's lookin very closely at me like maybe she plannin to do my portrait from memory. I'm mad, but I won't give her that satisfaction. So I slouch around the store bein very bored and say, "Let's go."

44   Me and Sugar at the back of the train watchin the tracks whizzin by large then small then gettin gobbled up in the dark. I'm thinkin about this tricky toy I saw in the store. A clown that somersaults on a bar then does chin-ups just cause you yank lightly at his leg. Cost $35. I could see me askin my mother for a $35 birthday clown. "You wanna who that costs what?" she'd say, cocking her head to the side to get a better view of the hole in my head. Thirty-five dollars could buy new bunk beds for Junior and Gretchen's boy. Thirty-five dollars and the whole household could go visit Granddaddy Nelson in the country. Thirty-five dollars would pay for the rent and the piano bill too. Who are these people that spend that much for performing clowns and $1,000 for toy sailboats? What kinda work they do and how they live and how come we ain't in on it? Where we are is who we are, Miss Moore always pointin out. But it don't necessarily have to be that way, she always adds then waits for somebody to say that poor people have to wake up and demand their share of the pie and don't none of us know what kind of pie she talkin about in the first damn place. But she ain't so smart cause I still got her four dollars from the taxi and she sure ain't gettin it. Messin up my day with this shit. Sugar nudges me in my pocket and winks.

45   Miss Moore lines us up in front of the mailbox where we started from, seem like years ago, and I got a headache for thinkin so hard. And we lean all over each other so we can hold up under the draggy-ass lecture she always finishes us off with at the end before we thank her for borin us to tears. But she just looks at us like she readin tea leaves. Finally she say, "Well, what did you think of F.A.O. Schwartz?"

46   Rosie Giraffe mumbles, "White folks crazy."

47   "I'd like to go there again when I get my birthday money," says Mercedes, and we shove her out the pack so she has to lean on the mailbox by herself.

48   "I'd like a shower. Tiring day," say Flyboy.

49   Then Sugar surprises me by sayin, "You know, Miss Moore, I don't think all of us here put together eat in a year what that sailboat costs." And Miss Moore lights up like somebody goosed her. "And?" she say, urging Sugar on. Only I'm standin on her foot so she don't continue.

50   "Imagine for a minute what kind of society it is in which some people can spend on a toy what it would cost to feed a family of six or seven. What do you think?"

51   "I think," say Sugar pushing me off her feet like she never done before, cause I whip her ass in a minute, "that this is not much of a democracy if you ask me. Equal chance to pursue happiness means an equal crack at the dough, don't it?" Miss Moore is besides herself and I am disgusted with Sugar's treachery. So I stand on her foot one more time to see if she'll shove me. She shuts up, and Miss Moore looks at me, sorrowfully I'm thinkin. And somethin weird is goin on, I can feel it in my chest.

52   "Anybody else learn anything today?" lookin dead at me. I walk away and Sugar has to run to catch up and don't even seem to notice when I shrug her arm off my shoulder.

53   "Well, we got four dollars anyway," she says.

54   "Uh hunh."

55   "We could go to Hascombs and get half a chocolate layer and then go to the Sunset and still have plenty money for potato chips and ice-cream sodas."

56   "Uh hunh."

57   "Race you to Hascombs," she say.

58   We start down the block and she gets ahead which is O.K. by me cause I'm goin to the West End and then over to the Drive to think this day through. She can run if she want to and even run faster. But ain't nobody gonna beat me at nuthin.

Understanding the Content

Feel free to reread all or parts of the selection to answer the following questions.

1. How do the children in the story feel about Miss Moore?

2. What does the narrator want to do with the five dollars Miss Moore gives her for cab fare?

3. Where does Miss Moore take the children when they arrive in New York City?

4. What does Mercedes keep on her desk at home?

5. Why do you think the narrator is ashamed to enter the toy store?

6. What does Miss Moore hope the children will learn by visiting the toy store?

7. Do you think Sylvia learns anything from her day with Miss Moore? Why or why not?

Looking at Structure and Style

1. What adjectives does the author use to describe Miss Moore and her appearance? What do those words tell you about how the narrator feels about Miss Moore?

2. Why do you think the author tells the story using Sylvia as the narrator in the first person?

3. The author begins many sentences with the words *and* and *but.* Why do you think she does that? What effect does it have on the narration?

4. What is the function of paragraph 3? How does this paragraph relate to the one where Miss Moore asks, "Imagine for a minute what kind of society it is in which some people can spend on a toy what it would cost to feed a family of six or seven. What do you think?"

5. What words and phrases does the author use to give you an idea of Miss Moore's attitude and feelings toward the children?

6. Write a paragraph following the concluding sentence, "But ain't nobody gonna beat me at nuthin," to detail what you think happens to Sylvia in later years. Do you think she achieves her goals?

Evaluating the Author's Viewpoints

1. Which child in the story do you think the author most closely relates to? Why?

2. Do you think the author grew up in the same kind of economic circumstances that she describes? Why or why not?

3. What is the author's attitude toward people who "can spend on a toy what it would cost to feed a family of six or seven"?

4. Why do you think the author sets the story in F.A.O. Schwartz?

5. How do you think the author feels about the children in the story? How does she feel about Miss Moore?

Pursuing Possible Essay Topics

1. Write an essay describing an influential person in your life or someone who has taught you more than you could have learned in school.

2. When did you first become aware of class differences in society? Is there an incident or situation that stands out in your mind? If so, write an essay describing the event and your reaction to it.

3. Have you ever wanted something that you could not afford? Did you get it anyway? Describe the experience of wanting something and either getting it anyway or living without it. What, if anything, did you learn from the experience?

4. How important do you think it is to have someone like Miss Moore in your life? Write an essay convincing Sylvia of the importance of having a mentor.

5. Brainstorm or freewrite on one or more of the following:
   a. poverty
   b. class differences in America
   c. the value of education
   d. learning a lesson
   e. having a mentor

6. Don't like these topics? Think about the story and write your reactions to it.

Preparing to Read

Take a minute or two to look over the following reading selection. Note the title and author, read the opening paragraph, and check the essay's length. Make certain you have the time now to read it carefully and to do the exercises that follow it. Then, in the spaces provided, answer the following questions.

1. What do you think the title means? What is a liberal arts major? _____

_____

_____

2. What is the difference between the way our fathers prepared for their careers

and the way entering college freshmen will prepare? _____

_____

_____

3. What might you learn about preparing for your own career? _____

_____

_____

Vocabulary

Good comprehension of what you are about to read depends upon your understanding of the words below. The number following each word refers to the paragraph where it is used.

trends (1) movements, tendencies to go in a certain direction

apprenticed (1) placed under a skilled craftsman to learn a trade

obsolete (2) no longer useful

lamenting (3) complaining, regretting, showing sorrow

grounded (3) based

parlay (3) use an asset to its greatest advantage (from gambling lingo)

ivory tower (4) a place or attitude of retreat from the practical world where one is more occupied with intellectual considerations

extolling (4) praising highly

diversity (5) variety

validate (5) verify, prove

plethora (5) an excessive amount, more than enough

all encompassing (5) all inclusive, touching all bases

augment (5) supplement, add to

vehicle (7) means *(to do something)*

steeped (8) saturated, subjected thoroughly

voluminous (9) of great size

alluded (9) referred *to*

smorgasbord (9) a wide variety

The Practicality of the Liberal Arts Major

DEBRA SIKES AND BARBARA MURRAY

1   Current trends indicate that by the year 2000 the average person will change careers at least twice during a lifetime. How does the entering college student prepare for career mobility which has never before been necessary? Our fathers decided what they wanted to do in life, which was very often what their fathers had done—went to college or apprenticed themselves, and pursued the same career until retirement. Our mothers assumed one of the nurturing roles in society, if they assumed a role outside of the home at all. Things have certainly changed. No longer is life so simple.

2   Adaptability and lifelong learning are now the cornerstones of success. What direction does a person take to prepare for a lifetime

of change? The one degree which provides training which never becomes obsolete is the liberal arts degree; it teaches you how to think. It also teaches you how to read, write and speak intelligently, get along with others, and conceptualize problems. For the first time in several decades, the liberal arts degree is coming to the forefront of the employment field.

3   Growing ranks of corporate executives are lamenting that college students are specializing too much and too early. What corporate America really needs, according to chief executive officers of major corporations, is students soundly grounded in the liberal arts—English, especially—who then can pick up more specific business or technical skills on the job. Few students, however, seem to be listening to this message. Today's best selling courses offer evidence that students want to take courses that provide direct job related skills rather than the most basic survival skills in the workplace: communication and thinking skills. They want courses they can parlay into jobs—and high paying ones at that. Certainly, we can understand this mentality when we consider trends indicating that this generation will be the first who will not be able to do better economically than their parents. They don't want to leave anything to chance. Historically, the liberal arts degree was good insurance for a poverty level existence. Students are looking to history to provide some answers it simply cannot give. They would do well to examine the present.

4   One of the big problems in the liberal arts community is that we do not market what we have to offer. Students very often fail to see the practicality of studying Shakespeare as preparation for a career in the business community. Perhaps some of us have locked ourselves in the ivory tower a little too long extolling the virtues of a liberal education as preparation for citizenship and life only to the neglect of it as preparation for career or careers. Education for education's sake is noble but impractical to today's college student who is facing a competitive and rapidly changing job market. They want and deserve to know how their courses will help them get a job. We as educators owe them some answers; we must be accountable not only for learning but also for providing information regarding the transferability of classroom skills into the workplace.

5   In an attempt to provide answers, we conducted a research project in the Dallas metroplex last year, assuming the role of the liberal arts graduate seeking employment in the fields of government, banking, business, and industry. Using informational interviewing as our method of job hunting and obtaining data, we conducted twenty-five interviews with a diversity of executive officers, ranging from personnel directors to the chairman of the board of an exclusive department store and the state governor. We wished to validate, through practical and current research, that not only does the liberal arts degree provide the best preparation for a lifetime of change, but it also

provides a plethora of employment opportunities. We do not claim our research to be all encompassing, but we do feel its practicality was rewarding. We gathered data as to how the liberal arts major should present himself on paper and in person, where her best chances for employment are, and what he can do to augment the liberal arts degree. We were able to draw several conclusions as to how the liberal arts community could better prepare students for professional mobility.

The Liberal Arts Degree Is Marketable

6   Ninety percent of those interviewed responded they would hire a liberal arts major for an entry level position which could lead to the executive suite if the position itself were not executive level. The chairman of the board of a major department store in Dallas responded to the question, "For what position would you hire a liberal arts graduate?" with a direct, "Any position in the company." When asked if a buyer wouldn't need to have special skills, he replied, "Taste is acquired or learned, and the liberal arts major could certainly learn this skill on the job." This interview is typical of the responses.

Skills Acquired with a Liberal Arts Background Are Most Desired by Employers

7   We were not at all surprised to learn that the skills cited as the most desirable in an employee are those skills acquired from a liberal arts background. The cited skills are listed below in order of importance.

1. Oral communication

2. Written communication

3. Interpersonal

4. Analytical thinking

5. Critical thinking

6. Leadership

Although these skills are not solely acquired through the mastery of an academic discipline, the discipline serves as a vehicle for developing or refining these skills.

Liberal Arts Majors Can Enhance Their Credentials

8   Adaptability and lifelong learning are the cornerstones of success in today's complex and rapidly changing society. No longer can the person who is steeped in one academic discipline, but knows nothing

about anything else, meet today's demands. Based on the data we accumulated, our recommendations for the liberal arts major are the following:

1. A basic knowledge of accounting

2. Computer literacy

3. Second major in a business field

4. Multiple minors

5. Advanced degree in another field

The key here is adaptability and diversity. Contrary to what most people believe, the higher a skill level an individual can claim, the more marketable he is. About those individuals who complain that they are "overeducated" we can only assume that they are marketing themselves on the wrong level. "Overeducation" is a term whose time will not come in the foreseeable future. The problem many individuals will face is a narrowness of education rather than "overeducation."

9   Unlike Aristotle who is believed to have known everything there was to know at the time he lived, it is impossible for us to deal with the voluminous amounts of information which are produced daily. The lifelong learning which we have alluded to will not always be acquired through the traditional sixteen-week college course. We in the community college need to provide a smorgasbord of opportunities for individuals who wish to increase their mobility and options.

10   The time has come to rethink what education really is and how it relates to the functions of society. Perhaps what a liberal education does for an individual, which is more important than anything else, is to prepare him for more learning. The liberal arts background equips one with thinking skills; and those, coupled with the desire to learn, are the best preparation for career and life that any of us can possess.

Understanding the Content

Feel free to reread all or parts of the selection to answer the following questions.

1. Judging from current trends, how many times will the average person change careers during a lifetime? How does this differ from past generations?

2. The authors claim that lifelong learning and adaptability are now the cornerstones of success. What do they mean? What degree provides training that is never obsolete?

3. According to the authors, what does corporate America want and need from its college graduates?

4. Upon what evidence have the authors based their information? Are their sources reliable? objective?

5. What skills are cited as the most desirable in an employee?

6. Based on their findings, what recommendations do the authors make for the liberal arts major to consider?

7. Do the authors believe it is possible to be "overeducated"? Explain.

Looking at Structure and Style

1. How do paragraphs 1 and 2 work together to establish the subject and thesis of the essay?

2. What is the basic function of paragraphs 3 and 4? How do they support the essay's thesis?

3. Why are paragraphs 5 and 6 important for thesis support? How strong would the essay be without these two paragraphs?

4. Paragraphs 7 and 8 both use lists. Is this effective? Explain.

5. To what audience do you think the authors direct their essay? How do paragraphs 4, 9, and 10 help reveal the audience?

6. How would you describe the essay's tone and attitude toward the subject? What words or phrases reveal tone and attitude?

Evaluating the Authors' Viewpoints

1. Do the authors convince you that a liberal arts education is important to your future career? Explain.

2. In paragraph 3, the authors state that the most basic survival skills in the workplace are communication and thinking skills. Why would these be more important than, say, learning how to program a computer if your goal is to be a computer programmer?

3. Look again at the skills listed in paragraph 7. Do these skills seem important to you? Evaluate your skills in those areas. In which skill do you need the most improvement?

4. Look again at the list in paragraph 8 of the basic knowledge the authors urge for enhancing a liberal arts major. Discuss the importance of each item.

5. The authors conclude by stating that perhaps the best thing a liberal arts education can do is to prepare one for more learning. How does such a statement fit your definition of what you think education is all about?

Pursuing Possible Essay Topics

1. Argue for or against the need for a liberal arts education.

2. Discuss what you think are the most important job skills necessary for the career you have chosen or are thinking of entering. Explain why you think each is important.

3. Define what is meant by a "liberal arts major." You may want to consult your college catalog for information on the course work required or talk with a counselor on campus.

4. Explain your reasons for wanting to attend college.

5. Discuss some aspect of yourself as a student: your study skills, your attitude, your self-image, your best learning style, your needs, your expectations, and so on.

6. Explain what you consider "the best preparation for career and life that any of us can possess."

7. Brainstorm or freewrite on one or more of the following:

   a. college life   d. a good teacher

   b. your favorite class   e. student responsibility

   c. high school vs. college   f. lifelong learning

8. Ignore these and find a topic of your own related to learning.

Preparing to Read

Take a minute or two to look over the following reading selection. Note the title and the author, read the opening paragraph, and check the essay's length. Make certain you have the time now to read it carefully and to do the exercises that follow it. Then, in the spaces provided, answer the following questions.

1. What is the subject of this essay? _____

   _____

2. What do you think the author's opinion is of the subject of this essay?

   _____

   _____

3. What is segregation?_____

_____

Vocabulary

Good comprehension of what you are about to read depends upon your understanding of the words below. The number following each word refers to the paragraph where it is used.

debilitating (2) sapping energy or strength

divisive (2) creating dissension or discord

vilified (3) made to appear evil

castigated (3) severely punished

unanimous (6) sharing the same opinion or views

integrate (7) to make whole by bringing all parts together

disparity (13) the condition of being unequal

rectify (14) to set right or correct

repugnant (19) arousing disgust or aversion

Vouchers Answer New Segregation in Our Schools

Paul Goldman

1   From busing to vouchers, two U.S. Supreme Courts—one liberal, one conservative—have now both come to the same conclusion: Our public schools are unacceptably segregated.

2   Fifty years after the Brown vs. Board of Education decision, our poorest kids face a modern educational segregation as debilitating and socially divisive as the older version. It is a harsh judgment, bitterly resisted by the education establishment.

3   In his time, Chief Justice Earl Warren was vilified by the right for busing. With last week's decision, we can now expect Chief Justice William Rehnquist to be castigated by the left for suggesting that vouchers may be a possible new remedy.

4   Democrats particularly need to heed this message, even if we object to the messenger, especially after the Gore-versus-Bush decision of 2000.

5   We need to be honest and understand the reason five justices felt it was necessary to give our public education system this jolt of judicial electricity.

6   Fifty years ago, the political elite in the U.S. Senate were still refusing to give black children an equal education. So, led by Chief Justice Warren, a unanimous court decided to take matters into its own hands.

7   The justices ruled that state and local governments must integrate their public school systems. The doctrine of "separate but equal" was rejected. Or so we hoped.

8   Not surprisingly, such a sweeping social intervention by an appointed court met with massive resistance. But over time, educational systems across the nation began to integrate through busing.

9   Given our segregated housing patterns, there was no way to achieve meaningful public school integration without busing.

10   Did public school integration work? It did for me and most of the nation. It changed us, redeeming a country and sending forth a new burst of freedom.

11   But last week, the Supreme Court took a look at nearly half a century of post-Brown social statistics and came to this conclusion: For too many of the Americans who need it most, the revolution started by Warren and implemented by busing was a total failure.

12   Sadly, no thoughtful and objective person can disagree with this conclusion. As Bob Dylan's protest song against segregation asked: How many times can a man turn his head and pretend that he just doesn't see?

13   Our most needy children are far too frequently suffering under the type of educational disparity that helped lead to the Brown decision.

14   For purposes of argument, let me accept the proposition that the current leaders of public education could rectify the situation if given all the tax money they want. The reality is they are never going to get that money. They can call it a lack of will on the part of the elected elite or a lack of compassion on the part of the people, the overwhelming majority of whom have sufficient educational choice for their children.

15   To repeat: Our poorest kids are trapped in their current educational segregation. Enter, then, a split Supreme Court.

16   Those opposing the legality of the Ohio voucher plan are good and honorable men and women. They believe passionately in public education. But at the same time, they and the political elite have the luxury of not feeling the pain of their principles.

17   At this juncture in our history, this is not a situation we can continue to tolerate. In so many walks of life the elite live under one standard, while the poorest Americans are forced to live under a harsher standard of morality and social conduct.

18   To me, the voucher decision must be seen as a wake-up call, drawn from the great observation of Oliver Wendell Holmes: The law ultimately must reflect the common sense of the human condition.

19   Our educational system has again forced our poorest children to endure an unacceptable modern segregation, something that

should have been as repugnant to us today as the older segregation was 50 years ago. But we, as a people, failed to act. This cannot continue.

20   So the Supreme Court decided, again, to pull the fire alarm. I would have preferred that the court take a different approach. Still, men and women of goodwill can do some fine-tuning. But this cannot happen unless we all recognize the terrible social injustice this conservative court declared unacceptable.

21   If this opinion spurs us to finally make good on the promise of Brown to society's most vulnerable children—if it forces conservatives and liberal pontificators out of their limousines and pushes them to honestly work for a more level playing field—then our system of laws will be better for it.

Understanding the Content

Feel free to reread all or parts of the selection to answer the following questions.

1. What are school vouchers? What is their purpose?

2. According to the author, why did the Supreme Court feel that it should rule in favor of school vouchers?

3. Fifty years ago, what did the Supreme Court, led by Chief Justice Warren, do to ensure that all children got a decent education?

4. Was busing a success or a failure, according to the author?

5. How does the author view the voucher decision?

Looking at Structure and Style

1. What is the purpose of paragraphs 6–9?

2. When the author refers, in paragraph 4, to the "messenger," to whom is he referring? Why does he use the "Gore-versus-Bush decision of 2000" reference?

3. What is the thesis of this selection? Pick one sentence from the selection that effectively conveys the overall thesis.

4. In paragraph 5, "judicial electricity" is a metaphor for what?

5. Rewrite paragraph 21, the concluding paragraph, so that it effectively summarizes the author's viewpoint on school vouchers.

6. In your opinion, which paragraph most effectively supports Goldman's thesis? Why?

Evaluating the Author's Viewpoints

1. The author believes in the school voucher plan. Does he give enough evidence to support his opinion? Why or why not?

2. How does the author view the opponents of the Ohio voucher plan? What words or phrases does he use to convey how he feels?

3. According to the author, was the public school integration plan, begun fifty years ago, a success? Why or why not?

4. What is the author's tone throughout this selection? Does it remain the same throughout or change? If so, how?

5. Based on your reading of paragraphs 1–5, would you say that the author is a Democrat, Republican, or independent? Why?

Pursuing Possible Essay Topics

Wait until you have read the following essay, "School Vouchers Don't Seem the Answer" by Larry Eichel, before you write your next essay.

Preparing to Read

Take a minute or two to look over the following reading selection. Note the title and the author, read the opening paragraph, and check the essay's length. Make certain you have the time now to read it carefully and to do the exercises that follow it. Then, in the spaces provided, answer the following questions.

1. What do you think is the author's viewpoint toward school vouchers?____

   _____

   _____

   _____

2. Do you think you will agree or disagree with the author's thesis? Why?___

   _____

   _____

   _____

Vocabulary

Good comprehension of what you are about to read depends upon your understanding of the words below. The number following each word refers to the paragraph where it is used.

constitutional (1) consistent with or permissible according to the Constitution

parochial (2) relating to, or supported by, a parish; Catholic in orientation

threshold (5) the place or point of beginning, the outset

concurring (10) agreeing, being of the same opinion

resonates (10) has a profound emotional impact

cognoscenti (10) people with superior knowledge or highly refined taste

chit (12) the amount owed, a check

School Vouchers Don't Seem the Answer

LARRY EICHEL

1   No one should have been surprised by the Supreme Court's 5-4 ruling that school vouchers are constitutional. You could see it coming.

2   The controlling logic was laid out two years ago by Clarence Thomas, when the court permitted the spending of taxpayers' money to provide computers for all schools—public, private and parochial.

3   On that occasion, and again Thursday in the case of the Cleveland voucher plan, the winning argument was that programs are constitutionally acceptable—meaning they don't run afoul of the First Amendment ban on governmental action "respecting an establishment of religion"—so long as they treat religious and non-religious institutions the same.

4   Writing for the majority in the voucher case, Chief Justice William Rehnquist found that the Cleveland program is "entirely neutral with respect to religion," provides "genuine choice" and therefore "does not offend the Establishment Clause."

5   But on vouchers, constitutionality is only the threshold question. The larger issue, still to be engaged nationally, is whether vouchers make for good public policy.

6   My view is that they don't, at least as practiced thus far.

7   For me, vouchers make more sense in theory than in reality.

8   There is, I must say, something extraordinarily attractive about the concept, this idea of government's giving a poor child trapped in a failing school district a ticket out.

9   At first glance, that option sounds far better than making the kid lose years waiting, perhaps in vain, for changes in funding formulas, reductions in class size, and the arrival of new textbooks.

10   Mr. Thomas captured that sentiment in his concurring opinion Thursday, proclaiming: "While the romanticized ideal of universal public education resonates with the cognoscenti who oppose vouchers, poor urban families just want the best education for their children, who will certainly need it . . ."

11   As I read that, it struck me that vouchers have been far more "romanticized" than public education, whose warts we know. Voucher systems have problems all their own.

12   Let's start with the size of the chit. In Cleveland, it's $2,250, more in Milwaukee and in Florida, the only other jurisdictions that currently have such programs. But in no case is it enough to provide students and parents with a wide range of choices, in those few locales where a big number of alternative schools actually exist.

13   About the only place where $2,250 gets you in the door is the parochial school system.

14   In Cleveland, 82 percent of the schools that accept vouchers are religion-based, and those schools have attracted 97 percent of voucher students.

15   The numbers reflect financial reality more than free will; nearly two-thirds of those attending a religious school on vouchers do not embrace the religion.

16   There is one benefit to such modest vouchers: They do relatively little financial damage to the public school system.

17   If and when vouchers become big enough to provide genuine choice, though, they will do real harm to public education—and the millions of children who'll remain there.

18   Again, it's a matter of theory versus practice. In theory, when you take one child out of a public school—and take away the dollars spent educating him—the system is whole. In practice, it doesn't work that way. Remove one child from a school, and you've saved almost nothing; you still need the teacher, the classroom, the heating, etc.

19   Yes, as voucher advocates claim, the competitive pressure caused by giving parents more choices might push the public schools to get better, but not in ways that require money. In fact, vouchers would likely provide officials with an excuse to shortchange low-performing schools.

20   Finally, there's the question of accountability. If we as a society use dollars from the public treasury to start sending students to private and parochial schools, don't we then have the right to make some of

the same demands on them that we now make on public schools? Won't that raise a whole new set of church-state issues?

21   I'm not opposed to pilot programs. I'm not closed to the idea that there might be a way for vouchers to help the some without hurting the many. But I haven't heard it yet.

22   At this point, I can't see how vouchers are the primary answer to what ails American education. Even now that they're constitutional.

Understanding the Content

Feel free to reread all or parts of the selection to answer the following questions.

1. Which Supreme Court Justice does Eichel site in his essay and why?

2. Why is Eichel against school vouchers? Why, to him, do they "make more sense in theory than in reality."

3. What does Eichel mean by the size of the "chit"? Why does he refer to the chit in his argument against school vouchers? What examples does he give regarding dollars spent and why?

4. Why does Eichel think that "school vouchers . . . will do real harm to public education"?

5. Why does Eichel think that vouchers have been "far more 'romanticized' than public education"?

Looking at Structure and Style

1. What is Eichel's tone throughout the selection? Does it change? If so, how?

2. What is the thesis of this selection? Is it stated directly or indirectly? If directly, where?

3. How does Eichel's thesis differ from Goldman's in "Vouchers Answer New Segregation in Our Schools"?

4. How does Eichel support his statement that "vouchers make more sense in theory than in reality"? Does he effectively support this claim? How?

5. Rewrite paragraph 22, the concluding paragraph, to effectively summarize Eichel's opinion regarding school vouchers.

Evaluating the Author's Viewpoints

1. Is Eichel entirely against school vouchers? Why or why not? How can you tell?

2. Is Eichel in favor of the Supreme Court ruling?

3. Do you think you would have gotten a better education if you had been able to take advantage of school vouchers? Why or why not?

4. Do you agree or disagree with Eichel's statement "There is . . . something extraordinarily attractive about the concept [of school vouchers]"? Why or why not?

5. Based on your reading of the selection, how do you think Eichel feels about children who take advantage of school vouchers to go to parochial schools but who don't embrace the religion?

6. Do you agree or disagree with Eichel that school vouchers will do real harm to public education?

Pursuing Possible Essay Topics

1. Argue against either Goldman's thesis in "Vouchers Answer New Segregation in Our Schools" or Eichel's thesis. Whichever you choose, make sure you consider each of the main arguments and provide argumentative support for your views.

2. Pretend you are Goldman and write an argument against Eichel's thesis against school vouchers. Or pretend you are Eichel and write an argument against Goldman's thesis.

3. Write an essay expressing your own viewpoints regarding school vouchers. Do you think school vouchers should be a part of the American education system? Why or why not? Do you think they will result in the downfall of the public school system? Why or why not?

4. Discuss why you do or do not think that children who are of a different religion than that of their school should not use vouchers to go to parochial schools.

5. You are a Supreme Court justice and have just ruled in favor of the constitutionality of school vouchers. Summarize your thoughts as to why you voted as you did.

Student Essay

Read the following narrative essay written by a student at the University of Southern California and published in the *Los Angeles Times*. As you read, look for answers to these questions:

1. Would this essay satisfy a writing assignment on some aspect of learning?

2. Why do you think the student wrote it?

3. Does the student follow the basic writing suggestions provided in Chapter 2, "Viewpoints on Writing Essays"?

4. What grade would you give this essay and why?

College Brings Alienation

John Gonzales

1   My decision to chase a dream, return to college at age 24, and take the liberal arts courses that will help me become a journalist has forced me to be two people. One face is for family and longtime friends, another is for my classes and college friends.

2   My homeboys have not read Marx, Nietzsche, or Freud. They do not care to probe the economics behind their being paid less, despite working more, than their fathers. They don't want to hear about the Oedipus complex or the nature of good and evil. For them, intellectual theories are elaborate, unnecessary attempts to explain the inexplicable. Ideas do not feed their families and only seem to highlight the fact that I have begun to change. "That's enough. Don't read any more. I don't understand a word you're saying," Fidel, my *compadre*, said after I responded to his request to read him a paragraph from one of my textbooks. He had telephoned while I was doing homework and jibed, "What the hell are you studying now?"

3   I also stumble to explain my studies to my parents. My father had a sixth-grade education. My mother earned her GED 15 years after leaving high school. I often reluctantly hand them my term papers they ask to see, knowing they won't truly comprehend them. After a careful reading, my mother's usual response: "You write so beautifully, *mijo*, I didn't really understand all the words you used but we can just tell how educated you are."

4   A senior at the University of Southern California, receiving a bachelor's degree in journalism and political science this May, I painfully realize the downside to education, a subtle alienation from friends and loved ones. I understand more clearly why Latinos approach higher learning with trepidation. For beyond the barriers of low income and racism lies another fight, the struggle to blend old and new identities.

5   It is not that education is discouraged; my family is proud of me and would be crushed if I were to quit. But disproportionately few Latinos acquire higher learning and those who do often must balance an incompatible past and future.

6   I envision my old friends and new friends at my graduation party: Would they eat, drink, and laugh together or huddle in separate groups? Which group would I join? Who am I?

7   That is why many promising Latinos I know who attend college choose to major in business or other fields with more easily identifiable rewards for their parents and themselves. "I'm learning how to start and manage a restaurant," is certainly something my father, a part-time contractor, would grasp more clearly than the abstract knowledge I've obtained.

8   Noble careers that require no college sometimes seem even more attractive. My aunt, mother of an army sergeant, beams with pride at family gatherings when she recalls my cousin's boot-camp graduation. Yet my mother struggles to explain the value of my work as a journalist. Amid the music, food, and drink of the get-together, a reporter is not a craftsman with words, not a guardian of democracy, not a voice against society's ills. Instead, journalists are perceived as the intrusive talking heads on the 11 o'clock news, the Latino ones pretentiously pronouncing their surnames with forced accents.

9   For other Latinos I know studying philosophy, sociology,
and literature, the struggle to retain identity is similar.
In this political climate of Proposition 187, the demise of
the Great Society and threats to affirmative action,
analytical, creative Latino minds are needed more than
ever. But the sacrifices are great indeed.

Reaction

In your journal or on a separate sheet of paper, write your reaction to the student essay. What would you tell this student about his essay? Compare your comments with those of your classmates.

On the Net

Learning and education are such broad topics that there are thousands of Internet sites devoted to various aspects of each. If you want to do your own research, do a search on one or more of the popular search engines such as Excite, Google, or Yahoo! by typing in the keyword "learning" or "education." You will then be presented with thousands of sites related to the word you chose; you can choose the sites you would like to explore or the subjects about which you would like to learn more.

However, as you probably know from "surfing the Web," you need to be as specific as possible to get the kind of information you need. One thing you can do is choose any topic of interest related to these two areas or one related to the readings in this chapter, such as "distance learning," "plagiarism," "bilingual education," or "school vouchers," and you will get specific sites devoted to this subject.

If you want to learn more about any of the authors included in this chapter, you can search by typing in the author's name or the title of one of the selections. Try typing in "Toni Cade Bambara" and explore the many sites devoted to this author and her work.

If you would like to try your hand at researching on the Web, do one or more of the following exercises.

1. Find one site that is for school vouchers and one that is against school vouchers. Compare the information on each site. Summarize your findings.

2. Take a paper you have written and submit it to *turnitin.com* (click on "free trial" for an introduction to this site and to register to submit a paper) to see if your methods of research stand up to the scrutiny of an antiplagiarism site.

3. Look at the Piper, Kansas, education website to see if their policies on plagiarism exist on their high school's site. The site address is *www.piperschools.com.*

4. Go to your school's website and see if a stated plagiarism and/or cheating policy exists.

5. Go to three sites dedicated to the life and work of Toni Cade Bambara and evaluate their content. Which one is best, and why?

4 Viewpoints on Human Behavior

FOCUS ON BEHAVIOR

To help you focus on the subject of this chapter, answer the following questions. You may want to write the answers in your journal or be prepared to discuss them in class.

1. Read the quotation by William Shakespeare on the opposite page. What do you think it means? What does it mean to you?

2. How might the meaning of Shakespeare's quotation apply to both photographs on the opposite page?

3. What behaviors are suggested by the photographs? What do the two people in the photographs have in common? What are their differences?

4. Think of ten words or phrases that describe good or positive behavior.

5. Think of ten words or phrases that describe bad or negative behavior.

6. Think of ten words or phrases that describe your general behavior.

"What a piece of work is man!"

—William Shakespeare

Jerry Berndt/Stock Boston

Jean Delmas/Woodfin Camp

133

What makes us behave the way we do? Sociologists and psychologists, among others, are still trying to find an answer to this question. Some answers have been found. It's clear that we humans have the ability to reason and make choices. But many aspects of our physical and social environment limit the choices available to us. Still, sociologists claim that given our options and our preferences, we choose to do what we expect will be most rewarding. Whether the rewards are candy, fame, money, a better life in the future, or affection, we act or choose primarily for self-interest.

The idea of self-interest as a motive for human behavior is one that many social scientists use to try to explain our actions. Economists, observing that we seek a variety of goods for ourselves, developed their theories of supply and demand. And the success of advertising certainly depends on the self-interest of the consumer. Psychologists believe that behavior is shaped by reinforcement. That is, we repeat actions or behaviors that produce the results we desire. If our parents praise us for certain actions, we continue to act to please. Our reward is the praise we get. Sociologists believe that we seek what we expect will reward us and avoid what we perceive will cost us. Making our parents angry "costs" us; touching a hot fire "costs" us. If we are "normal," then we learn to behave according to these norms.

According to social scientists, we learn to see ourselves as others see us. In a sense, we look at ourselves from the outside. As infants and young children, we are not able to understand the meaning of the behavior of those around us. As we grow, we learn to know what we are like by seeing ourselves in others. We form an idea of what others want and expect and how they react to us. We settle into a pattern of behavior through interactions with others; we learn the "rules" of behavior for our particular environment. And even though we have choices, our behavior is frequently influenced by what those around us want or expect us to do.

Of course, we don't always follow the norm. Those who regularly don't follow the rules are considered abnormal. Some abnormal behavior is funny, some sad, some self-destructive, and some dangerous to others. The essays in this chapter deal with a variety of behavior: the good and the bad, the misunderstood, the so-called abnormal, the funny, and the unexplainable. You will recognize some of the actions described and wonder at others, but they are all part of the complex creatures called humans. It is hoped that you will both learn from the variety of readings and be stimulated by them to write your viewpoints on the subject.

Preparing to Read

Take a minute or two to look over the following reading selection. Note the title and the author, read the opening paragraph, and check the essay's length. Make certain you have the time now to read it carefully and to do the exercises that follow it. Then, in the spaces provided, answer the following questions.

1. What do you think is the subject of the essay?_____

_____

2. How do you think the author feels about the mentally ill? Why?_____

_____

_____

3. What is the author's tone toward her subject in the first paragraph?_____

_____

Vocabulary

Good comprehension of what you are about to read depends upon your understanding of the words below. The number following each word refers to the paragraph where it is used.

psychotic (3) relating to mental illness

calibration (4) adjustment or correction

keel (4) balance

vigilance (4) watchfulness

stint (5) a period of time

schisms (8) divisions

stigmatized (9) characterized as disgraceful, discredited

Call Me Crazy, But I Have to Be Myself

MARY SEYMOUR

1   Nearly every day, without thinking, I say things like "So-and-so is driving me crazy" or "That's nuts!" Sometimes I catch myself and realize that I'm not being sensitive toward people with mental illness. Then I remember I'm one of the mentally ill. If I can't throw those words around, who can?

2   Being a functional member of society and having a mental disorder is an intricate balancing act. Every morning I send my son to junior high school, put on professional garb and drive off to my job as alumni-magazine editor at a prep school, where I've worked for six years. Only a few people at work know I'm manic-depressive, or bipolar, as it's sometimes called.

3   Sometimes I'm not sure myself what I am. I blend in easily with "normal" people. You'd never know that seven years ago, fueled by the stress of a failing marriage and fanned by the genetic inheritance of a manic-depressive grandfather, I had a psychotic break. To look at me, you'd never guess I once ran naked through my yard or shuffled down the hallways of a psychiatric ward. To hear me, you'd never guess God channeled messages to me through my computer. After my breakdown at 36, I as diagnosed as bipolar, a condition marked by moods that swing between elation and despair.

4   It took a second, less-severe psychotic episode in 1997, followed by a period of deep depression, to convince me I truly was bipolar. Admitting I had a disorder that I'd have to manage for life was the hardest thing I've ever done. Since then, a combination of therapy, visits to a psychiatrist, medication, and inner calibration have helped me find an even keel. Now I manage my moods with the vigilance of a mother hen, nudging them back to center whenever they wander too far. Eating wisely, sleeping well, and exercising regularly keep me balanced from day to day. Ironically, my disorder has taught me to be healthier and happier than I was before.

5   Most of the time, I feel lucky to blend in with the crowd. Things that most people grumble about—paying bills, maintaining a car, working 9 to 5—strike me as incredible privileges. I'll never forget gazing through the barred windows of the psychiatric ward into the parking lot, watching people come and go effortlessly, wondering if I'd ever be like them again. There's nothing like a stint in a locked ward to make one grateful for the freedoms and burdens of full citizenship.

6   Yet sometimes I feel like an impostor. Sometimes I wish I could sit at the lunch table and talk about lithium and Celexa instead of "Will & Grace." While everyone talks about her fitness routine, I want to brag how it took five orderlies to hold me down and shoot me full of sedatives when I was admitted to the hospital, and how for a brief moment I knew the answers to every infinite mystery of the blazingly bright universe. I yearn for people to know me—the real me—in all my complexity, but I'm afraid it would scare the bejesus out of them.

7   Every now and then, I feel like I'm truly being myself. Like the time the school chaplain, in whom I'd confided my past, asked me to help counsel a severely bipolar student. This young woman had tried to commit suicide, had been hospitalized many times and sometimes locked herself in her dorm room to keep the "voices" from overwhelming her. I walked and talked with her, sharing stories about medication and psychosis. I hoped to show by example that manic-depression did not necessarily mean a diminished life. At commencement, I watched her proudly accept her diploma; despite ongoing struggles with her illness, she's continuing her education.

8   I'm able to be fully myself with my closest friends, all of whom have similar schisms between private and public selves. We didn't set out to befriend each other—we just all speak the same language, of hardship and spiritual discovery and psychological awareness.

9   What I yearn for most is to integrate both sides of myself. I want to be part of the normal world but I also want to own my identity as bipolar. I want people to know what I've been through so I can help those traveling a similar path. Fear has kept me from telling my story: fear of being stigmatized, of making people uncomfortable, of being reduced to a label. But hiding the truth has become more uncomfortable than letting it out. It's time for me to own up to who I am, complicated psychiatric history and all. Call me crazy, but I think it's the right thing to do.

Understanding the Content

Feel free to reread all or parts of the selection to answer the following questions.

1. From what disorder or illness does the author suffer? What does it mean to have this condition?

2. What does the author do for a living? Has she shared her past with her co-workers? Why or why not?

3. What does the author do to control her mental illness?

4. Why is the author reluctant for "people to know me—the real me"?

5. With whom is the author the most open about her mental illness, and why?

Looking at Structure and Style

1. What is the author's thesis? Is it stated or implied? If stated, where?

2. What is the purpose of paragraph 3?

3. What is the author's tone and attitude toward the subject of mental illness?

4. What message is the author trying to convey about mental illness? In what paragraph is this best expressed, and why?

5. What examples does the author give to illustrate why she feels like an "impostor"?

6. How effective is paragraph 9 as a concluding paragraph? Does this paragraph adequately convey the author's conflicted feelings about her life? Why or why not?

Evaluating the Author's Viewpoints

1. Seymour doesn't think that she should share with most people the fact that she is bipolar. Although she years "for people to know me—the real me," she fears they will be afraid of her once they learn the truth. Do you agree or disagree with her, and why?

2. Based on your reading of the selection, do you think that the author thinks her mental illness is just a case of bad luck, heredity, or a combination of both? How can you tell?

3. Discuss the author's statement "Ironically, my disorder has taught me to be healthier and happier than I was before." Does the author think she is lucky to have a mental illness? What does she mean by this statement?

4. Why do you think the author wants people to know of her "identity as bipolar"? What would she gain by revealing that to the people in her life?

Pursuing Possible Essay Topics

1. Write an essay describing how you might feel to learn that someone in your life was mentally ill or suffering from bipolar disorder. Would you feel the same way toward that person?

2. Write an essay about how you think society treats people with mental illness. Do you think that people with mental illness are stigmatized? Why or why not?

3. Do you think the author should tell the people she works with about her mental illness? Why or why not? Write an essay urging the author to either tell the people she works with or to keep her secret.

4. Write an essay from the point of view of the author's son. What do you think his life is like, imagining that he is fully aware of his mother's bipolar disorder?

5. Do you think mental illness is hereditary or just a random occurrence? Why?

6. Find your own topic related to mental illness and write an essay.

Preparing to Read

Take a minute or two to look over the following reading selection. Note the title and author, read the opening paragraph, and check the essay's length. Make certain you have the time now to read it carefully and to do the exercises that follow it. Then, in the spaces provided, answer the following questions.

1. What do you think is the subject of this essay?_____

   _____

2. Based on just the title, what do you think the author's tone will be?_____

   _____

3. Does the opening paragraph make you want to continue reading? Why?_____

   _____

Vocabulary

Good comprehension of what you are about to read depends upon your under-standing of the words below. The number following each word refers to the paragraph where it is used.

dork (title) nerd

visionary (3) one who has foresight or imagination

physique (3) the form or structure of a person's body

biorhythm (6) an inherent rhythm that appears to control or initiate various biological processes

prudishness (7) attention to decorum

plausible (8) superficially fair or reasonable

aesthetic (9) pleasing in appearance, relating to beauty

sensual (9) relating to the gratification of the senses

indolence (13) inclination to laziness

I'm Not a Dork; I'm Ahead of Today's Fashions

ALAN EHRENHALT

1   I remember going out to play tennis one day about 20 years ago and having my wife stop me in the doorway with a piece of friendly advice. "You need to get a new pair of shorts," she said. "Why?" I asked. "Do they look really stupid?" "Yes," she said. "Really stupid."

2   They did, too. They were long, covering the knee and part of the calf, and they were extremely loose and baggy everywhere. Very few people dressed like that in those days outside of Honolulu and Miami Beach.

3   I've thought about those shorts quite a bit the past few years, but until now, I've resisted the temptation to tell my wife what I've been

thinking: I wasn't badly dressed that day in the 1970s; I was just a visionary. At some point in the early 1990s, that exact kind of clothing suddenly came to be perceived as highly flattering to the ordinary male physique.

4   It all strikes me as perverse. But it serves as a reminder of the mysterious power that fashion and its conventions hold over the human brain. In the days when I was a baggy-shorts pioneer, I also had sideburns 2 or 3 inches long. Everybody I knew had them. When you come across any photograph from the 1970s, the first thing you notice is that the males all look like they're trying out for bit parts in a Western.

5   By the end of the Carter administration, long sideburns were out of style. Worse than that: They looked stupid. Ugly, in fact. As they have to most of us ever since. Now, that perception may be changing as well.

6   But that's what intrigues me about fashion. We've come to perceive yesterday's styles as not only inappropriate, but also physically repulsive. Then the process reverses itself, and we change the rules. The ugly becomes flattering, and vice versa. It's as if there's a biorhythm for dorkiness, repeating itself every 15 years or so.

7   The Dork Cycle is powerful enough to overcome what would seem to be much larger societal trends and values. Skirt length is a good example of its power. When miniskirts became fashionable in the mid-1960s, my assumption was that a permanent change in female costume had taken place. The sexual revolution had encouraged women to display their legs to the world, and they would never dream of concealing them again. A return to the prudishness of the '50s would be unthinkable.

8   It was a plausible theory, but it was wrong. By 1975, skirts were back down to the knee—not because the sexual revolution had stalled, but because the cycle had simply overpowered it. What is short must become long—and then short once more. Now skirts are up to the thigh again. That shouldn't be treated as much of a moral statement, either. The cycle is a law unto itself.

9   Or if you want an even more dramatic example, think about shaved heads for men. The aesthetic and sensual appeal of human hair has never really been in dispute for either males or females in Western civilization. It has been a given that everyone looks better with hair of some kind. Making bald heads fashionable requires a suspension of natural human preference dating back to Samson and Delilah. It isn't exactly a case of the emperor's new clothes, but it's in that category. And yet baldness became fashionable this decade, at least for a significant percentage of American men.

10   In the year 2020, we will look at old pictures of Michael Jordan and Jesse Ventura and laugh at them the way we laugh now at goofy '70s sideburns. God knows what cool guys will be wearing then: maybe a crew cut on one side and a ponytail on the other.

11   But the most intriguing question of all about the Dork Cycle is this: What causes certain people to defy it? Walk along a downtown street in any big city, and you will find a few slick, well-tailored, middle-aged professional men wearing high-water suit trousers that end a few inches above their ankles. By the standards of the moment, they look stupid. These are men smart enough to know what's fashionable, and affluent enough to afford whatever clothes they want. So why do they dress that way?

12   It could be, of course, that they're just too busy or too cheap to trade in the clothes they bought 30 years ago for something more current. But there's another possibility that's more intriguing: They understand the Dork Cycle better than the rest of us do, and they have the patience to wait it out.

13   I didn't put much stock in this last theory until a few days ago, when I read a newspaper article about the exciting new men's fashions for spring 2000. Three very hip-looking young guys were pictured in the article. And guess what they were wearing? That's right: pants that didn't even reach the ankles. Pants so short they look as if somebody left them tumbling in the dryer all weekend and they shrank. "They look profoundly comfortable," one fashion expert exulted. "They evoke a carefree youth filled with joyous indolence."

14   I read the article with interest. It's too late for me to have a carefree youth, but joyous indolence sounds pretty good. On the other hand, it took me a decade to get used to wearing pants that practically reach the ground. Now I'm supposed to change again.

15   But that's just the point: The Dork Cycle is a force too overwhelming for ordinary humans to tame. You can't outsmart it. The only sensible thing to do is keep your pants on and wait.

Understanding the Content

Feel free to reread all or parts of the selection to answer the following questions.

1. What is the "Dork Cycle"? How does it manifest itself in terms of fashion?

2. Why does the author think he is a fashion "visionary"?

3. What intrigues the author about fashion?

4. What is the author's theory as to why people defy the Dork Cycle?

5. What are some of the fashion trends that have reappeared in recent years?

Looking at Structure and Style

1. How does the author use comparison and contrast to illustrate his point about fashion trends?

2. What is the author's thesis? Is it stated or implied?

3. What is the purpose of paragraph 6? How does it support the author's thesis?

4. How does the author use humor to make his point? Give specific examples of words or phrases that the author uses that are humorous in nature but that help to convey the author's point.

5. What is the tone and attitude of the essay? Would the essay be as effective with a different tone? Why or why not?

Evaluating the Author's Viewpoints

1. How do you think the author feels about change in general?

2. What is the author saying about human nature in terms of how we are influenced by fashion?

3. Do you think the author sees himself as a "visionary"? Why or why not?

4. What is the author's opinion of fashion trends? What paragraphs support his opinion?

5. Do you think the author is influenced by fashion trends? Why or why not?

Pursuing Possible Essay Topics

1. Write a paper persuading someone that a certain fashion trend—for example, long sideburns, bell-bottom pants, or short skirts—will come back into style. Give examples of other trends that have resurfaced over the years.

2. Write a paper about what trends you will look back on in ten or fifteen years and think were silly.

3. Write about a time you wore something that was out of style at the time but has since become trendy and stylish.

4. Brainstorm or freewrite about one or more of the following:

   a. fashion

   b. trends

   c. peer pressure

   d. the Dork Cycle

5. Write on some aspect of fashion and how "we've come to perceive yesterday's styles as not only inappropriate, but also physically repulsive."

6. Write a paper discussing your feelings about change.

7. Choose a topic of your own if you don't like any of these topics.

Preparing to Read

Take a minute or two to look over the following reading selection. Note the title and author, read the opening paragraph, and check the essay's length. Make certain you have the time now to read it carefully and to do the exercises that follow it. Then, in the spaces provided, answer the following questions.

1. What is suggested by the title? _____

   _____

2. What do you think the essay will be about? _____

   _____

3. Does the opening paragraph make you want to read on? Why? _____

   _____

Vocabulary

Good comprehension of what you are about to read depends upon your understanding of the words below. The number following each word refers to the paragraph where it is used.

affluent (1) wealthy, well-to-do

impoverished (1) drained of wealth, poor

discreet (1) cautious, careful

uninflammatory (1) not arousing anger or emotion

unwieldy (2) difficult to handle

quarry (2) a hunted animal, prey

dismayed (2) unnerved, rattled, taken aback

accomplice (2) one who aids a criminal

tyranny (2) absolute power, usually unjust and cruel; here, the power muggers have to terrorize women

elicit (3) bring out or cause

avid (4) enthusiastic, eager

taut (4) strained, tense

warrenlike (5) like a *warren,* a place where small animals live, but also referring to places overcrowded with people

bandolier-style (5) the way a soldier wears an ammunition belt

perpetrators (5) those who commit crimes

solace (5) comfort

in retrospect (6) looking back on the past

bravado (6) false bravery

perilous (7) dangerous

ad hoc posse (7) a group formed for a special purpose (in this case, to chase
him); *ad hoc* is Latin for "for this"

skittish (9) nervous

congenial (9) friendly, cooperative

constitutionals (10) healthy walks

Night Walker

BRENT STAPLES

1   My first victim was a woman—white, well dressed, probably in her
early 20s. I came upon her late one evening on a deserted street in
Hyde Park, a relatively affluent neighborhood in an otherwise mean,
impoverished section of Chicago. As I swung onto the avenue behind her, there seemed to be a discreet, uninflammatory distance
between us. Not so. She cast back a worried glance. To her, the
youngish black man—a broad six feet two inches with a beard and
billowing hair, both hands shoved into the pockets of a bulky military jacket—seemed menacingly close. She picked up her pace and
was soon running in earnest. Within seconds she disappeared into a
cross street.

2   That was more than a decade ago. I was 22 years old, a graduate
student newly arrived at the University of Chicago. It was in the echo
of that terrified woman's footfalls that I first began to know the unwieldy inheritance I'd come into—the ability to alter public space in
ugly ways. It was clear that she thought herself the quarry of a mugger, a rapist, or worse. Suffering a bout of insomnia, however, I was
stalking sleep, not defenseless wayfarers. As a softy who is scarcely
able to take a knife to a raw chicken—let alone hold one to a person's
throat—I was surprised, embarrassed, and dismayed all at once. Her
flight made me feel like an accomplice in tyranny. It also made it
clear that I was indistinguishable from the muggers who occasionally seeped into the area from the surrounding ghetto. I soon gathered that being perceived as dangerous is a hazard in itself: Where
fear and weapons meet—and they often do in urban America—there
is always the possibility of death.

3   In that first year, my first away from my hometown, I was to become thoroughly familiar with the language of fear. At dark, shadowy intersections, I could cross in front of a car stopped at a traffic light and elicit the *thunk, thunk, thunk, thunk* of the driver—black, white, male, female—hammering down the door locks. On less traveled streets after dark, I grew accustomed to but never comfortable with people crossing to the other side of the street rather than pass me. Then there were the standard unpleasantries with policemen, doormen, bouncers, cabdrivers, and others whose business it is to screen out troublesome individuals *before* there is any nastiness.

4   I moved to New York nearly two years ago and I have remained an avid night walker. In central Manhattan, the near-constant crowd covers the tense one-on-one street encounters. Elsewhere, things can get very taut indeed.

5   After dark, on the warrenlike streets of Brooklyn where I live, I often see women who fear the worst from me. They seem to have set their faces on neutral, and with their purse straps strung across their chests bandolier-style, they forge ahead as though bracing themselves against being tackled. I understand, of course, that the danger they perceive is not a hallucination. Women are particularly vulnerable to street violence, and young black males are drastically overrepresented among the perpetrators of that violence. Yet these truths are no solace against the alienation that comes of being ever the suspect, an entity with whom pedestrians avoid making eye contact.

6   It is not altogether clear to me how I reached the ripe old age of 22 without being conscious of the lethality nighttime pedestrians attributed to me. Perhaps it was because in Chester, Pa., the small, angry industrial town where I came of age in the 1960s, I was scarcely noticeable against a backdrop of gang warfare, street knifings, and murders. I grew up one of the good boys, had perhaps a half-dozen fistfights. In retrospect, my shyness of combat has clear sources. As a boy, I saw countless tough guys locked away; I have since buried several, too. They were babies, really—a teen-age cousin, a brother of 22, a childhood friend in his mid-20s—all gone down in episodes of bravado played out in the streets. I chose, perhaps unconsciously, to remain a shadow—timid, but a survivor.

7   The fearsomeness mistakenly attributed to me in public places often has a perilous flavor. The most frightening of these confusions occurred in the late 1970s and early 1980s, when I worked as a journalist in Chicago. One day, rushing into the office of a magazine I was writing for with a deadline story in hand, I was mistaken for a burglar. The office manager called security and, with an ad hoc posse, pursued me through the labyrinthine halls, nearly to my editor's door. I had no way of proving who I was. I could only move briskly toward the company of someone who knew me.

8   Relatively speaking, however, I never fared as badly as another black male journalist. He went to nearby Waukegan, Ill., a couple of summers ago to work on a story about a murderer who was born there. Mistaking the reporter for the killer, police officers hauled him from his car at gunpoint and but for his press credentials would probably have tried to book him. Such episodes are not uncommon. Black men trade tales like this all the time.

9   Over the years, I learned to smother the rage I felt at so often being mistaken for a criminal. Not to do so would surely have led to madness. I now take precautions to make myself less threatening. I move about with care, particularly late in the evening. I give a wide berth to nervous people on subway platforms during the wee hours. If I happen to be entering a building behind some people who appear skittish, I may walk by, letting them clear the lobby before I return, so as not to seem to be following them. I have been calm and extremely congenial on those rare occasions when I've been pulled over by the police.

10   And on late-evening constitutionals I employ what has proved to be an excellent tension-reducing measure: I whistle melodies from Beethoven and Vivaldi and the more popular classical composers. Even steely New Yorkers hunching toward nighttime destinations seem to relax, and occasionally they even join in the tune. Virtually everybody seems to sense that a mugger wouldn't be warbling bright, sunny selections from Vivaldi's "Four Seasons." It is my equivalent of the cowbell that hikers wear when they are in bear country.

Understanding the Content

Feel free to reread all or parts of the selection to answer the following questions.

1. What point is Staples making in his essay? Is his thesis implied or stated?

2. What event caused Staples to learn that "being perceived as dangerous is a hazard in itself" (2)? What does he mean?

3. How old was the author at the time? What was his reaction?

4. What other events have made him "thoroughly familiar with the language of fear" (3)?

5. Why does Staples feel that he is "often being mistaken for a criminal" (9)?

6. What tactics or precautions does he take to avoid being mistaken for a potential criminal?

Looking at Structure and Style

1. How effective is the author's first paragraph? Does it create an interest in the essay? Why?

2. Why does Staples wait until the middle of paragraph 2 to explain what was actually happening, that he was merely taking a walk?

3. What is the function of paragraph 3? What paragraph pattern is used there?

4. What attitude do you think is expressed in paragraph 9? What inferences can you draw from the author's statements?

5. Rewrite or explain the following passages from the essay:

   a. "It was in the echo of that terrified woman's footfalls that I first began to know the unwieldy inheritance I'd come into." (2)

   b. "Where fear and weapons meet—and they often do in urban America—there is always the possibility of death." (2)

   c. "I could cross in front of a car stopped at a traffic light and elicit the *thunk, thunk, thunk, thunk* of the driver—black, white, male, female—hammering down the door locks." (3)

   d. "They seem to have set their faces on neutral, and with their purse straps strung across their chests bandolier-style, they forge ahead as though bracing themselves against being tackled." (5)

   e. "It is my equivalent of the cowbell that hikers wear when they are in bear country." (10)

6. How effective is the title? Explain.

7. What suggestions for revision, if any, would you offer the author?

Evaluating the Author's Viewpoints

1. In paragraph 2, Staples says that he learned at twenty-two that he had "the ability to alter public space in ugly ways." Explain what he means. Might the woman he describes in the opening paragraph be just as afraid of a white man in the same situation?

2. Reread the last sentence in paragraph 3. What attitude does the author reflect when he alludes to "standard unpleasantries" with people in authority? Is he exaggerating?

3. In paragraph 5, Staples says that "young black males are drastically overrepresented among the perpetrators of . . . violence." Where do you think he believes this overrepresentation takes place? Do you agree?

4. Staples reveals to his audience negative attitudes toward black males that he has experienced firsthand and does not deserve. What is your reaction to the way he has responded?

Pursuing Possible Essay Topics

1. Write about a time when your identity was questioned or you were mistakenly accused of something. How were you made to feel? How did you react?

2. Write about a time when you were frightened or felt threatened by someone. Was the fear or threat real or imagined? What led up to the situation or incident? How was it resolved?

3. Brainstorm or freewrite on one or more of the following:
   a. fear   d. gangs
   b. anger   e. danger
   c. prejudice   f. tension

4. Skim through a newspaper for two or three days to see how many episodes of street violence are reported. What effect do these reports have on people's behavior? Is street violence exaggerated?

5. Staples is a victim of stereotyping. Write an essay about the way you may knowingly or unknowingly stereotype a certain ethnic or racial group. Examine the cause or basis for your doing so.

6. Examine a behavioral characteristic—of yourself or of someone you know—that you don't like. How did the trait or attitude develop? What harm has it caused? What can you do about it?

7. Ignore these and come up with your own topic on some aspect of human behavior.

Preparing to Read

Take a minute or two to look over the following reading selection. Note the title and author, read the opening paragraph, and check the essay's length. Make certain you have the time now to read it carefully and to do the exercises that follow it. Then, in the spaces provided, answer the following questions.

1. What is suggested by the title? _____

_____

_____

2. What do you think the essay will be about? _____

_____

_____

3. Does the opening paragraph make you want to read on? Why? _____

_____

_____

Vocabulary

Good comprehension of what you are about to read depends upon your understanding of the words below. The number following each word refers to the paragraph where it is used.

devalued (1) lowered, reduced

pshaw (1) pronounced *shaw;* used to indicate disapproval

fatal (3) deadly

patrons (3) customers

Federated (3) associated, joined together; here, the name of a department store chain

accorded (3) given, granted

MLK Day (3) Martin Luther King, Jr., Day

On Holidays and How to Make Them Work

Nikki Giovanni

1 A proper holiday, coming from the medieval "holy day," is supposed to be a time of reflection on great men, great deeds, great people. Things like that. Somehow in America this didn't quite catch on.

Take Labor Day. On Labor Day you take the day off, then go to the Labor Day sales and spend your devalued money with a clerk who is working. And organized labor doesn't understand why it suffers declining membership? Pshaw. Who wants to join an organization that makes you work on the day it designates as a day off? Plus, no matter how hidden the agenda, who wants a day off if they make you march in a parade and listen to some politicians talk on and on about nothing.

2   Hey. I'm a laborer. I used to work in Walgreen's on Linn Street. We were open every holiday and I, being among the junior people, always "got" to work the time-and-a-half holidays. I hated those people who came in. Every fool in the Western world, and probably in this universe, knows that Christmas is December 25. Has been that way for over a thousand years, yet there they'd be, standing outside the door, cold, bleary-eyed, waiting for us to open so they could purchase a present. Memorial Day, which used to be Armistice Day until we got into this situation of continuous war, was the official start of summer. We would want to be out with our boyfriends barbecuing . . . or something, but there we were behind the counter waiting to see who forgot that in order to barbecue you need: (1) a grill, (2) charcoal, (3) charcoal starter. My heart goes out to the twenty-four-hour grocery people, who are probably selling meat!

3   But hey. It's the American way. The big Fourth of July sales probably reduced the number of fatal injuries as people spent the entire day sober in malls, fighting over markdowns. Minor cuts and bruises were way up, though, I'll bet. And forget the great nonholiday, Presidents' Day. The damned thing could at least have a real name. What does that mean—Presidents' Day? Mostly that we don't care enough to take the time to say to Washington and Lincoln: Well done. But for sure, as a Black American I've got to go for it. Martin Luther King, Jr.,'s birthday has come up for the first time as a national holiday. If we are serious about celebrating it, Steinberg's will be our first indication: GHETTO BLASTERS 30% OFF! FREE TAPE OF "I HAVE A DREAM" WITH EVERY VCR PURCHASED AT THE ALL-NEW GIGANTIC MARTY'S BIRTHDAY SALE. Then Wendy's will, just maybe, for Black patrons (and their liberal sympathizers) Burn-A-Burger to celebrate the special day. Procter & Gamble will withhold Clorox for the day, respectfully requesting that those Black spots be examined for their liberating influence. But what we really want, where we can know we have succeeded, is that every Federated department store offers 50 percent off to every colored patron who can prove he or she is black in recognition of the days when colored citizens who were black were not accorded all the privileges of other shoppers. That will be a big help because everybody will want to be Black for a Day. Sun tanneries

will make fortunes during the week preceding MLK Day. Wig Salons will reap great benefits. Dentists will have to hire extra help to put that distinctive gap between the middle front teeth. MLK Day will be accepted. And isn't that the heart of the American dream?

4   I really love a good holiday—it takes the people off the streets and puts them safely in the shopping malls. Now think about it. Aren't you proud to be with Uncle Sam?

Understanding the Content

Feel free to reread all or parts of the selection to answer the following questions.

1. How does Giovanni define a "proper holiday"? What does she feel is wrong with the way Americans celebrate national holidays?

2. What holidays does Giovanni specifically mention, and how does she describe the way some people spend them?

3. Was this essay written before or after Martin Luther King, Jr.'s birthday became a national holiday? How do you know? Is she for or against making Martin Luther King, Jr.'s birthday a holiday? How do you know?

4. In the last sentence of paragraph 3, Giovanni says, "And isn't that the heart of the American dream?" What does she mean?

5. How does Giovanni think people should behave on holidays? How does this differ from the behavior she describes?

Looking at Structure and Style

1. Is Giovanni's thesis stated or implied? If stated, where?

2. Giovanni uses one-word sentences, such as "Pshaw" (1), "Hey" (2), and "But hey" (3). How do these contribute to her tone? How would you describe her tone? What are some other examples of words or phrases that develop tone?

3. What is the function of paragraph 2? Is it important that Giovanni identify herself as a "laborer"? Explain.

4. How effective is the last paragraph? How does it reflect her attitude toward her subject? What other passages reflect her attitude? How would you describe her attitude?

Evaluating the Author's Viewpoints

1. Giovanni feels that people should not have to work on national holidays. Do you agree with her? Why or why not?

2. If you were offered time and a half for working on a holiday, would you be willing to do so? Why? On what holidays would you not work? Why?

3. Do you think Giovanni believes Martin Luther King, Jr.'s birthday should be a national holiday? Explain why you agree or disagree with her.

4. Giovanni seems to blame the holiday shoppers for stores staying open on holidays. Why do you think she doesn't blame those who work on holidays? Should she?

Pursuing Possible Essay Topics

1. Write an essay rebutting Giovanni's thesis or a particular viewpoint she expresses in her essay.

2. Write an essay about your favorite holiday. Why is it your favorite? How do you spend it? What does it mean to you?

3. How might shopping patterns change if people refused to work on holidays or Sundays? Would this be for the better? Do stores need to remain open on holidays? Explain.

4. Brainstorm or freewrite on one or more of the following:
   a. holiday shopping   d. shopping malls
   b. overtime   e. shopping behavior
   c. holidays   f. work

5. Ignore these and write on some aspect of behavior at work or at play.

Preparing to Read

Take a minute or two to look over the following reading selection. Note the title and author, read the opening paragraph, and check the story's length. Make certain you have the time now to read it carefully and to do the exercises that follow it. Then, in the spaces provided, answer the following questions.

1. Based on the title, what do you think the story might be about? _____

_____

2. During what time of year does the story take place? _____

_____

3. What do you think is going to happen? _____

_____

_____

Vocabulary

Good comprehension of what you are about to read depends upon your understanding of the words below. The number following each word refers to the paragraph where it is used.

diligently (1) busily, in a hard-working manner

deftly (2) easily, agilely

insolent (10) rude, bold, insulting

suffused (11) filled, overflowed

impotent (11) weak, helpless

rapt (18) absorbed, engrossed

despicable (25) mean, worthless, bad

Sunday in the Park

BEL KAUFMAN

1   It was still warm in the late-afternoon sun, and the city noises came muffled through the trees in the park. She put her book down on the bench, removed her sunglasses, and sighed contentedly. Morton was reading the *Times Magazine* section, one arm flung around her shoulder; their three-year-old son, Larry, was playing in the sandbox; a faint breeze fanned her hair softly against her cheek. It was five-thirty of a Sunday afternoon, and the small playground, tucked away in a corner of the park, was all but deserted. The swings and seesaws stood motionless and abandoned, the slides were empty, and only in the sandbox two little boys squatted diligently side by side. *How good this is*, she thought, and almost smiled at her sense of well-being. They must go out in the sun more often; Morton was so city-pale, cooped up all week inside the gray factorylike university. She squeezed his arm affectionately and glanced at Larry, delighting in the pointed little face frowning in concentration over the tunnel he was digging. The other boy suddenly stood up and with a quick, deliberate swing of his chubby arm threw a spadeful of sand at Larry. It just missed his head. Larry continued digging; the boy remained standing, shovel raised, stolid and impassive.

2   "No, no, little boy." She shook her finger at him, her eyes searching for the child's mother or nurse. "We mustn't throw sand. It may get in someone's eyes and hurt. We must play nicely in the nice sandbox." The boy looked at her in unblinking expectancy. He was about Larry's age but perhaps ten pounds heavier, a husky little boy with none of Larry's quickness and sensitivity in his face. Where was his mother? The only other people left in the playground were two women and a little girl on roller skates leaving now through the gate, and a man on a bench a few feet away. He was a big man, and he seemed to be taking up the whole bench as he held the Sunday comics close to his face. She supposed he was the child's father. He did not look up from his comics, but spat once deftly out of the corner of his mouth. She turned her eyes away.

3   At that moment, as swiftly as before, the fat little boy threw another spadeful of sand at Larry. This time some of it landed on his hair and forehead. Larry looked up at his mother, his mouth tentative; her expression would tell him whether to cry or not.

4   Her first instinct was to rush to her son, brush the sand out of his hair, and punish the other child, but she controlled it. She always said that she wanted Larry to learn to fight his own battles.

5   "Don't *do* that, little boy," she said sharply, leaning forward on the bench. "You mustn't throw sand!"

6   The man on the bench moved his mouth as if to spit again, but instead he spoke. He did not look at her, but at the boy only.

7   "You go right ahead, Joe," he said loudly. "Throw all you want. This here is a *public* sandbox."

8   She felt a sudden weakness in her knees as she glanced at Morton. He had become aware of what was happening. He put his *Times* down carefully on his lap and turned his fine, lean face toward the man, smiling the shy, apologetic smile he might have offered a student in pointing out an error in his thinking. When he spoke to the man, it was with his usual reasonableness.

9   "You're quite right," he said pleasantly, "but just because this is a public place. . . ."

10   The man lowered his funnies and looked at Morton. He looked at him from head to foot, slowly and deliberately. "Yeah?" His insolent voice was edged with menace. "My kid's got just as good right here as yours, and if he feels like throwing sand, he'll throw it, and if you don't like it, you can take your kid the hell out of here."

11   The children were listening, their eyes and mouths wide open, their spades forgotten in small fists. She noticed the muscle in Morton's jaw tighten. He was rarely angry; he seldom lost his temper. She was suffused with a tenderness for her husband and an impotent rage against the man for involving him in a situation so alien and so distasteful to him.

12   "Now, just a minute," Morton said courteously, "you must realize. . . ."

13   "Aw, shut up," said the man.

14   Her heart began to pound. Morton half rose; the *Times* slid to the ground. Slowly the other man stood up. He took a couple of steps toward Morton, then stopped. He flexed his great arms, waiting. She pressed her trembling knees together. Would there be violence, fighting? How dreadful, how incredible. . . . She must do something, stop them, call for help. She wanted to put her hand on her husband's sleeve, to pull him down, but for some reason she didn't.

15   Morton adjusted his glasses. He was very pale. "This is ridiculous," he said unevenly. "I must ask you. . . ."

16   "Oh, yeah?" said the man. He stood with his legs spread apart, rocking a little, looking at Morton with utter scorn. "You and who else?"

17   For a moment the two men looked at each other nakedly. Then Morton turned his back on the man and said quietly, "Come on, let's get out of here." He walked awkwardly, almost limping with self-consciousness, to the sandbox. He stooped and lifted Larry and his shovel out.

18   At once Larry came to life; his face lost its rapt expression and he began to kick and cry. "I don't *want* to go home, I want to play better, I don't want any supper, I don't *like* supper. . . ." It became a chant as they walked, pulling their child between them, his feet dragging on the ground. In order to get to the exit gate they had to pass the bench where the man sat sprawling again. She was careful not to look at him. With all the dignity she could summon, she pulled Larry's sandy, perspiring little hand, while Morton pulled the other. Slowly and with head high she walked with her husband and child out of the playground.

19   Her first feeling was one of relief that a fight had been avoided, that no one was hurt. Yet beneath it there was a layer of something else, something heavy and inescapable. She sensed that it was more than just an unpleasant incident, more than defeat of reason by force. She felt dimly it had something to do with her and Morton, something acutely personal, familiar, and important.

20   Suddenly Morton spoke. "It wouldn't have proved anything."

21   "What?" she asked.

22   "A fight. It wouldn't have proved anything beyond the fact that he's bigger than I am."

23   "Of course," she said.

24   "The only possible outcome," he continued reasonably, "would have been—what? My glasses broken, perhaps a tooth or two replaced, a couple of days' work missed—and for what? For justice? For truth?"

25   "Of course," she repeated. She quickened her step. She wanted only to get home and to busy herself with her familiar tasks; perhaps then the feeling, glued like heavy plaster on her heart, would be

gone. *Of all the stupid, despicable bullies,* she thought, pulling harder on Larry's hand. The child was still crying. Always before she had felt a tender pity for his defenseless little body, the frail arms, the narrow shoulders with sharp, winglike shoulder blades, the thin legs, unsure, but now her mouth tightened in resentment.

26   "Stop crying," she said sharply. "I'm ashamed of you!" She felt as if all three of them were tracking mud along the street. The child cried louder.

27   *If there had been an issue involved,* she thought, *if there had been something to fight for. . . . But what else could he possibly have done? Allow himself to be beaten? Attempt to educate the man? Call a policeman? "Officer, there's a man in the park who won't stop his child from throwing sand on mine. . . ."* The whole thing was as silly as that, and not worth thinking about.

28   "Can't you keep him quiet, for Pete's sake?" Morton asked irritably.

29   "What do you suppose I've been trying to do?" she said. Larry pulled back, dragging his feet.

30   "If you can't discipline this child, I will," Morton snapped, making a move toward the boy.

31   But her voice stopped him. She was shocked to hear it, thin and cold and penetrating with contempt. "Indeed?" she heard herself say. "You and who else?"

Understanding the Content

Feel free to reread all or parts of the selection to answer the following questions.

1. The story opens with the unnamed mother feeling happy and content. What behavior causes a change in her mood?

2. Reread paragraph 19. What do you think the mother sensed that "was more than just an unpleasant incident, more than defeat of reason by force"?

3. In paragraph 26, the mother tells her son she is ashamed of him for crying and feels that "all three of them were tracking mud along the street." What is the mother feeling at this point in the story?

4. What does the story have to say about human behavior?

Looking at Structure and Style

1. Find some words that describe the mother's feelings toward her husband, Morton, and their child, Larry, early in the story. How does the author show us that these feelings are different by the end of the story?

2. The story is told through the eyes of the mother. How does the author provide us with an image of the mother through her descriptions of Joe and his father?

3. Why do you think the author has Joe's father reading the comics and Morton reading the *Times Magazine* section? What other devices does the author use to contrast the two men?

4. What do the mother's words in the last paragraph imply? How does this contrast with her earlier feelings for her husband when he has one arm around her as he reads?

Evaluating the Author's Viewpoints

1. What do you think the author is revealing about human behavior? Is the author siding with the mother? with Morton? with Joe's father?

2. Are the behaviors of Morton, his wife, and Larry depicted realistically? Explain.

3. Reread paragraph 27. Was there "an issue involved . . . something to fight for"? Explain.

4. Morton believes that a fight wouldn't have proved anything. Do you think his wife really agrees? Does the author? Explain.

Pursuing Possible Essay Topics

1. Write about a time when you engaged in a fight or a shouting match with someone. What was the reason for the disagreement? Was the incident or issue worth fighting about? Was reason lost to temper?

2. Retell the story from Morton's point of view, or explain what Morton might have done differently and why.

3. Explain in an essay how you would behave if another person's child picked on your child in some fashion while the parent looked on and did nothing to stop it.

4. Write an essay that explains the behavior of Morton and his wife at the end of the story. Why are both of them upset with each other? What did they really want to happen? What does Larry have to do with their anger?

5. Brainstorm or freewrite on one or more of the following:

   a. bullies
   b. fighting
   c. Sunday in the park
   d. temper
   e. alien situation
   f. crying

6. Ignore these and write on some other aspect of human behavior.

Preparing to Read

Read aloud the poem shown below. Then answer the following questions.

1. What is your first reaction to the poem? _____

   _____

   _____

2. What kind of behavior is portrayed? _____

   _____

Now read the poem again and answer the questions that follow it.

We Real Cool
   —GWENDOLYN BROOKS

The Pool Players.
Seven at the Golden Shovel.

> We real cool. We
> Left school. We
>
> Lurk late. We
> Strike straight. We
>
> Sing sin. We
> Thin gin. We
>
> Jazz June. We
> Die soon.

Understanding the Content

1. What is the poem about? Is there a "thesis"? If so, is it implied or stated?

2. Who is the "We" in the poem?

3. What is the "Golden Shovel"? What might the words imply beyond the name of the pool hall?

4. What are some possible meanings of the following lines?
   a. "Strike straight."
   b. "Sing sin."
   c. "Jazz June."

Looking at Structure and Style

1. Why do you think Brooks ends all but the last line with the pronoun "We"? What difference would it make in the way the poem reads if the pronoun were placed at the beginning of each line?

2. How much information does Brooks impart in each short line about the "Seven at the Golden Shovel"?

3. Brooks intended the poem to be read aloud. How does the way she structured the poem reveal that intention?

Evaluating the Author's Viewpoints

1. Does Brooks feel the pool players in the poem are "cool"? What is her attitude toward them?

2. What does the absence of "We" in the last line prophesy?

3. What can you infer about Brooks's attitude toward education? Explain.

Pursuing Possible Essay Topics

1. Write an essay to the "We" in the poem, convincing them they should stay in school.

2. Discuss what the "We" in the poem have learned. Why do they think their behavior is "cool"?

3. Teachers in an urban school were criticized for assigning "We Real Cool" to be read by their students because the poem was considered to be immoral and to promote bad behavior. Take a stand and explain why the poem should or should not be taught in high schools. What behaviors does it encourage?

4. "Translate" the poem into an essay, writing as one of the "We" in the poem. Make certain you elaborate on each line.

5. Brainstorm or freewrite on one or more of the following:

   a. behavior   d. hanging out
   b. being cool   e. dropping out
   c. nerds   f. teasing

6. If none of the above suits you, find your own topic on some aspect of behavior.

Preparing to Read

Take a minute or two to look over the following reading selection. Note the title and author, read the first three paragraphs, and check the essay's length. Make certain you have the time now to read it carefully and to do the exercises that follow it. Then, in the spaces provided, answer the following questions.

1. What do you think is the subject of this essay? _____

   _____

   _____

2. What kind of behavior do you think will be discussed? _____

   _____

   _____

3. How do you define *ghetto*? _____

   _____

   _____

Vocabulary

Good comprehension of what you are about to read depends upon your understanding of the words below. The number following each word refers to the paragraph where it is used.

starkly (3) unmistakably, clearly

rendered (6) made, caused

fruitless (7) ineffectual, useless

eliciting (8) drawing out, causing

abhors (10) detests, offends

malady (10) ailment, disorder

exculpation (11) pardon, acquittal

sustained (14) endured, carried

debilitatingly (15) in a harmfully crippling manner

disparate (18) different, dissimilar

tacit (20) silent, unspoken

eradicate (20) abolish, destroy

propriety (30) appropriateness

"The Ghetto Made Me Do It"

FRANCIS FLAHERTY

1   When Felicia "Lisa" Morgan was growing up, her parents would sit down to meals with guns next to their plates. They were defending themselves—against each other.

2   "This was Lisa's dinner," explains attorney Robin Shellow. "She was seven at the time."

3   If nothing else, Lisa Morgan's childhood in a poor, inner-city Milwaukee neighborhood starkly illustrates the tragic effects of urban violence. "Mom shot dad," Shellow says. "And Mom shot boyfriend. . . . [Lisa's] uncle, who was actually her age, was murdered. Two days later, her other uncle was murdered. Her sister's boyfriend was paralyzed from the neck down by gunfire. Her brother was shot at and injured. Her mother once had set her father on fire."

4   If this weren't enough tragedy in one young life, Lisa Morgan's mother was a drug addict and Lisa was raped at age 12.

The "Ghetto Defense"

5   So perhaps it's not too surprising that Morgan, as a teenager, committed six armed robberies and one intentional homicide in the space of 17 minutes in October 1991. The victims were girls; the stolen objects were jewelry, shoes and a coat. The dead girl was shot at point-blank range.

6   What *is* surprising—to the legal establishment, at least—is the approach Robin Shellow used in defending Morgan. In the girl's neighborhood and in her family, Shellow argued, violence is a *norm,* an occurrence so routine that Morgan's 17 years of exposure to it have rendered her not responsible for her actions.

7   This "ghetto defense" proved fruitless in Morgan's case. In court, the young woman was found both sane and guilty. Unless Shellow wins on appeal, Morgan will be behind bars well into the next century.

8   But despite its failure for Morgan, Shellow's "cultural psychosis" or "psychosocial history" strategy has taken hold. "I've gotten hundreds of calls from interested attorneys," Shellow says. Already, the defense is being floated in courtrooms around the nation. It's eliciting both enthusiasm and outrage.

The Defense Is a Medical One

9   Technically, Shellow's defense is a medical one. She believes that Morgan suffers from post traumatic stress disorder (PTSD) and other psychological ailments stemming from her lifelong exposure to violence.

10   Like other good lawyers, Shellow knows that the law abhors broadly applicable excuses, so she emphasizes the narrowness of her claim. Morgan belongs to a very small group of inner-city residents with "tremendous intra-familial violence," only some of whom might experience PTSD. She also stresses the unrevolutionary nature of the defense, medically and legally. PTSD has been recognized as a malady in standard diagnostic texts since 1980, she says, and it has been employed as a criminal defense for Vietnam veterans, battered wives and many other trauma victims.

11   Despite Shellow's attempts to show that her defense is neither new nor broad, the case is ringing loud alarms. For, however viewed, her strategy sets up an inflammatory equation between inner-city conditions and criminal exculpation. The implication is that if you grew up in a poor, violent neighborhood and you commit a crime, you may go scot-free.

12   Yet why not a ghetto defense? After all, if a Vietnam veteran can claim PTSD from the shock of war, why shouldn't a similar defense be available for a young black reared in the embattled precincts of Bed-Stuy [Bedford-Stuyvesant neighborhood of New York City]? Sounds sensible, no? Isn't a ghetto like a battlefield?

Compare These Neighborhoods to War Zones

13   Alex Kotlowitz, who chronicled the lives of two Chicago black boys in *There Are No Children Here*, goes even further. He says the inner city can be worse than war. "You hear constant comparisons of these neighborhoods to war zones, but I think there are some pretty significant differences," he says. "In war, there's at least a sense that someday there will be a resolution, some vision that things could be different. That is not the case in the inner cities. There is no vision. And there's no sense of who's friend and who's foe."

14   There are other analogies that make the ghetto defense seem very legitimate. For instance, despite traditional self-defense principles, a battered wife in some jurisdictions can kill her sleeping husband and be legally excused for the homicide. The reason is the psychological harm she has sustained from her life of fear and violence.

15   Why not Lisa Morgan? Hasn't her life been debilitatingly violent and fearful?

16   These arguments make some lawyers hopeful about the future of Shellow's pioneering strategy. But most observers are pessimistic. "We'll get nowhere with it," says famous defense lawyer William Kunstler.

The Poor Instead of the Powerful

17   Why? One reason is that the American justice system often favors the powerful over the poor. For generations, for instance, the bloodiest crime in the nation—drunk driving—was punished with a relative wrist slap. By contrast, a recent federal law mandates that those convicted of the new crime of carjacking get socked with a minimum and mandatory 15-year sentence.

18   What explains these disparate approaches? Simple: protection of the affluent classes. Light penalties for drunk driving protect the affluent because they often drive drunk. Harsh carjacking penalties protect the affluent because they are the usual carjacking victims. "The middle class sees carjacking [laws] as protecting them from people coming out of some poor neighborhood and just showing up in *their* neighborhood and committing a crime in which they are at risk of dying," says Professor James Liebman of Columbia University School of Law.

19   Because the ghetto defense protects the poor instead of the powerful, Kunstler and others doubt it has a bright future. Other factors further dim the strategy's chances. Fear is a main one, says Professor Liebman. The ghetto defense brings a gulp from jurors because "their first thought is, 'If he's not responsible, then none of those people are,' " he reasons. And we all know what that means: riots, mayhem, Los Angeles.

20   Social guilt raises even higher the hurdles for the ghetto defense. To allow such a defense is a tacit admission that we—society—tolerate a situation so hobbling that its victims have become unaccountable for their actions. "If it ain't them who's guilty, it's us," says Michael Dowd, director of the Pace University Battered Women's Justice Center in New York. And "it's just too horrific for us to accept responsibility, too horrific to say, 'I'm responsible for what happened in L.A.' We will be able to accept the [ghetto] defense at the same moment that we are seriously moved to eradicate the realities behindthat defense."

21   What are the biggest criticisms of the ghetto defense? One focuses on the victim's identity. Battered spouses and battered children are accused of killing precisely those who hurt them. This endows the crime with a certain rough justice. But in a ghetto defense case, the victim is usually an innocent stranger.

22   Others, like Kotlowitz, worry that the ghetto defense might dislodge the cornerstone of our justice system: personal responsibility. "We have to be careful not to view people growing up in neighborhoods completely as victims; they are both victims and actors," he warns. "We can't absolve them from responsibility."

23   Lisa Morgan "went up to someone she didn't know, stole a jacket from her, and then just blew her away," he says. "There's no way as a society that we can excuse that. We can understand it, but we can't excuse it."

24   He raises a fundamental question. Everyone can point to scars from the past—alcoholic parents, tragic love, etc.—and claim exculpation. And if all are excused, who is responsible?

25   Another worry is diminished standards. "[The ghetto defense] lowers expectations," Kotlowitz continues. "It says, 'OK, I understand what you've been through, so it's OK to go out and hurt somebody.' And once you lower your expectations, particularly with kids, they will meet only those lower expectations."

A Disease Is a Disease

26   It's only fair to note that other criminal defenses also have these weaknesses. For instance, the victim of a PTSD-afflicted veteran is often an innocent passerby, and the battered-spouse doctrine certainly raises questions about personal responsibility and lowered expectations.

27   And if, as seems likely, some ghetto residents do have PTSD largely as a result of their living conditions, it's hard to see why this ailment should be exculpatory for veterans, say, but not for ghetto residents. After all, a disease is a disease, and how you got it is irrelevant.

28   How deep go the wounds from the ghetto? Here are two incidents in Morgan's life: "When Felicia was about 11, her mother put a knife to her throat and threatened to kill her," according to a psychologist's report in the case. "Felicia escaped by running into the basement, where she 'busted the lights out with my hand' so that her mother could not see her." Then, when she was 12, the landlord attacked her. "Felicia fought him off by throwing hot grease onto him, but he finally subdued her, tied her hands to the bed, stuffed her mouth with a sock and raped her."

29   How does one live like this? Morgan gives a hint. "My ears be open," she told the psychologist, "even when I'm asleep."

30   This was a *child*. Society did nothing to stop these daily depredations upon her. While the legal propriety of the ghetto defense is an important question, the biggest question of all in this story has nothing to do with personal responsibility. It has to do with society's responsibility to poor children like Morgan. What does it say about our society that such a defense was conceived? How can things have come to this pass?

Understanding the Content

Feel free to reread all or parts of the selection to answer the following questions.

1. What is meant by the "ghetto defense"? Define it in your own words.

2. Reread paragraph 8. Define what Shellow means by the "'cultural psychosis' or 'psychosocial history' strategy." What does it have to do with the ghetto defense?

3. What is post-traumatic stress disorder (PTSD)? What causes it?

4. Why do legal experts worry about the ghetto defense being used and accepted in court cases? What would be the implications? How would it affect the poor instead of the powerful?

5. What are the biggest criticisms of the ghetto defense?

6. Does Flaherty's thesis favor the ghetto defense? Why or why not?

Looking at Structure and Style

1. The first four paragraphs of the essay deal with Felicia "Lisa" Morgan. Why? How effective is this as an introduction to the author's subject?

2. Flaherty frequently uses transitional words or phrases to move from one paragraph or idea to another. Find some examples of them. How effective are they?

3. In paragraphs 13 and 14, what pattern is primarily used?

4. In paragraphs such as 12, 15, 17, 18, and 21, Flaherty uses questions. For what purpose? Is this a good technique in this case? Explain.

5. Is Flaherty's thesis stated or implied? If stated, where?

Evaluating the Author's Viewpoints

1. Robin Shellow, Felicia Morgan's attorney, believes in the ghetto defense. Do you? Explain your reasoning.

2. Flaherty raises the question that if a Vietnam veteran can claim PTSD from the shock of the war, why shouldn't a similar defense be made for a young black reared in an embattled ghetto? How do you respond to the idea?

3. Flaherty believes the American justice system often favors the powerful over the poor (17). Is her support sufficient for the reader to accept her viewpoint? Do you agree? Support your views.

4. The ghetto defense suggests that society "tolerates a situation so hobbling that its victims have become unaccountable for their actions," implying that each of us is responsible for such things as the Los Angeles riots and the living conditions in the ghettos. Do you accept such responsibility? Explain.

5. Reread the last paragraph. Does society have a responsibility to poor children like Morgan? How do you answer Flaherty's questions?

Pursuing Possible Essay Topics

Wait until after you have read the following essay, "Seeking the Roots of Violence" by Anastasia Toufexis, before attempting to write an essay on violence and its causes.

Preparing to Read

Take a minute or two to look over the following reading selection. Note the title and author, read the first two paragraphs, and check the essay's length. Make certain you have the time now to read it carefully and to do the exercises that follow it. Then, in the spaces provided, answer the following questions.

1. What do you think is the subject of this essay?_____

   _____

2. What kind of behavior do you think will be discussed? _____

   _____

3. What do you think may be the roots of violence? _____

   _____

Vocabulary

Good comprehension of what you are about to read depends upon your understanding of the words below. The number following each word refers to the paragraph where it is used.

predisposed (1) inclined, prone, liable

inflammatory (2) inciting anger, concern, or disagreement

genetics (2) the study of heredity, especially inherited characteristics

muster (3) assemble, gather, collect

incensed (3) furious, angry

tawdry (5) gaudy and cheap

disparity (7) difference, contrast
impulsive (10) acting without much thought
premeditated (10) deliberate, thought out
anomalies (14) oddities, peculiarities

Seeking the Roots of Violence
ANASTASIA TOUFEXIS

1   It's tempting to make excuses for violence. The mugger came from a broken home and was trying to lift himself out of poverty. The wife beater was himself abused as a child. The juvenile murderer was exposed to Motley Crue records and *Terminator* movies. But do environmental factors wholly account for the seven-year-old child who tortures frogs? The teenager who knifes a teacher? The employee who slaughters workmates with an AK-47? Can society's ills really be responsible for all the savagery that is sweeping America? Or could some people be predisposed to violence by their genes?

2   Until recently, scientists had no good way to explore such questions—and little incentive: the issue was seen as so politically inflammatory that it was best left alone. But advances in genetics and biochemistry have given researchers new tools to search for biological clues to criminality. Though answers remain a long way off, advocates of the work believe science could help shed light on the roots of violence and offer new solutions for society.

3   But not if the research is suppressed. Investigators of the link between biology and crime find themselves caught in one of the most bitter controversies to hit the scientific community in years. The subject has become so politically incorrect that even raising it requires more bravery than many scientists can muster. Critics from the social sciences have denounced biological research efforts as intellectually unjustified and politically motivated. African-American scholars and politicians are particularly incensed; they fear that because of the high crime rates in inner cities, blacks will be wrongly branded as a group programmed for violence.

4   The backlash has taken a toll. In the past year, a proposed federal research initiative that would have included biological studies has been assailed, and a scheduled conference on genetics and crime has been canceled. A session on heredity and violence at February's meeting of the American Association for the Advancement of Science turned into a politically correct critique of the research; no defenders of such studies showed up on the panel. "One is basically under

attack in this field," observes one federal researcher, who like many is increasingly hesitant to talk about his work publicly.

5   Some of the distrust is understandable, given the tawdry history of earlier efforts to link biology and crime. A century ago, Italian physician Cesare Lombroso claimed that sloping foreheads, jutting chins and long arms were signs of born criminals. In the 1960s, scientists advanced the now discounted notion that men who carry an XYY chromosome pattern, rather than the normal XY pattern, were predisposed to becoming violent criminals.

6   Fresh interest in the field reflects a recognition that violence has become one of the country's worst public-health threats. The U.S. is the most violent nation in the industrialized world. Homicide is the second most frequent cause of death among Americans between the ages of 15 and 24 (after accidents) and the most common among young black men and women. More than 2 million people are beaten, knifed, shot or otherwise assaulted each year, 23,000 of them fatally. No other industrialized nation comes close: Scotland, which ranked second in homicides, has less than one-fourth the U.S. rate.

7   This cultural disparity indicates that there are factors in American society—such as the availability of guns, economic inequity and a violence-saturated culture—that are not rooted in human biology. Nevertheless, a susceptibility to violence might partly be genetic. Errant genes play a role in many behavioral disorders, including schizophrenia and manic depression. "In virtually every behavior we look at, genes have an influence—one person will behave one way, another person will behave another way," observes Gregory Carey, assistant professor at the University of Colorado's Institute for Behavioral Genetics. It stands to reason that genes might contribute to violent activity as well.

8   Some studies of identical twins who have been reared apart suggest that when one twin has a criminal conviction, the other twin is more likely to have committed a crime than is the case with fraternal twins. Other research with adopted children indicates that those whose biological parents broke the law are more likely to become criminals than are adoptees whose natural parents were law-abiding.

9   No one believes there is a single "criminal gene" that programs people to maim or murder. Rather, a person's genetic makeup may give a subtle nudge toward violent actions. For one thing, genes help control production of behavior-regulating chemicals. One suspect substance is the neurotransmitter serotonin. Experiments at the Bowman Gray School of Medicine in North Carolina suggest that extremely aggressive monkeys have lower levels of serotonin than do more passive peers. Animals with low serotonin are more likely to bite, slap or chase other monkeys. Such animals also seem less social: they spend more time alone and less in close body contact with peers.

10   A similar chemical variation appears to exist in humans. Studies at the National Institute on Alcohol Abuse and Alcoholism conclude that men who commit impulsive crimes, such as murdering strangers, have low amounts of serotonin. Men convicted of premeditated violence, however, show normal levels. As for aggressive behavior in women, some researchers speculate that it might be tied to a drop in serotonin level that normally occurs just before the menstrual period. Drugs that increase serotonin, researchers suggest, may make people less violent.

11   Scientists are also trying to find inborn personality traits that might make people more physically aggressive. The tendency to be a thrill seeker may be one such characteristic. So might "a restless impulsiveness, an inability to defer gratification," says psychologist Richard Herrnstein of Harvard, whose theories about the hereditary nature of intelligence stirred up a political storm in the 1970s. A high threshold for anxiety or fear may be another key trait. According to psychologist Jerome Kagan, also of Harvard, such people tend to have a "special biology," with lower-than-average heart rates and blood pressures.

12   Findings like these may be essential to understanding—and perhaps eventually controlling—chronic wrongdoers, argue proponents of this research. "Most youth or adults who commit a violent crime will not commit a second," observes Kagan. "The group we are concerned with are the recidivists—those who have been arrested many times. This is the group for whom there might be some biological contribution." Kagan predicts that within 25 years, biological and genetic tests will be able to pick out about 15 children of every thousand who may have violent tendencies. But only one of those 15 children will actually *become* violent, he notes. "Do we tell the mothers of all 15 kids that their kids might be violent? How are the mothers going to react to their children if we do that?"

13   It is just such dilemmas that have so alarmed critics. How will the information be used? Some opponents believe the research runs the danger of making women seem to be "prisoners of their hormones." Many black scholars are especially concerned. "Seeking the biological and genetic aspects of violence is dangerous to African-American youth," maintains Ronald Walters, a political science professor at Howard University. "When you consider the perception that black people have always been the violent people in this society, it is a short step from this stereotype to using this kind of research for social control."

14   The controversy began simmering more than a year ago, when Louis Sullivan, then Secretary of Health and Human Services, proposed a $400 million federal research program on violence; 5 percent of the budget would have been devoted to the study of biochemical anomalies linked to aggressive behavior. The program was shelved before being submitted to Congress, and one reason may have been the

reaction to an unfortunate statement by Dr. Federick Goodwin, then director of the Alcohol, Drug Abuse and Mental Health Administration. Commenting about research on violence in monkeys, Goodwin said, "Maybe it isn't just the careless use of the word when people call certain areas of certain cities 'jungles.'" African-Americans were outraged. The ensuing furor forced Goodwin to resign, though Secretary Sullivan then appointed him to head the National Institute of Mental Health, a job he still holds.

15   Soon after that episode, the federally endowed Human Genome Project agreed to provide the University of Maryland with $78,000 for a conference on violence. When the program's organizers announced that the session would look at genetic factors in crime, opponents torpedoed the meeting. "A scandalous episode," charges Harvard's Herrnstein. "It is beneath contempt for the National Institutes of Health to be running for cover when scholars are trying to share their views."

16   Dr. Peter Breggin, director of the Center for the Study of Psychiatry in Bethesda, Maryland, who led the opposition that scuttled the conference, has no apologies. "The primary problems that afflict human beings are not due to their bodies or brains, they are due to the environment," he declares. "Redefining social problems as public health problems is exactly what was done in Nazi Germany."

17   Some critics see the current interest in heredity as part of an ugly political trend. "In socially conservative times," argues political scientist Diane Paul of the University of Massachusetts at Boston, "we tend to say crime and poverty are not our fault and put the blame not on society but on genes."

18   Even staunch believers in heredity's influence do not discount environment. In fact, the two are intimately entwined, and separating cause and effect is not easy. Biology may affect behavior, but behavior and experience also influence biology. Serotonin levels, for example, are not only controlled by genes but, according to research in monkeys, they can be lowered by regular exposure to alcohol. By the same token, says Kagan, a child with a fearless personality may turn into a criminal if reared in a chaotic home, but given a stable upbringing, "he could well become a CEO, test pilot, entrpreneur or the next Bill Clinton."

19   No one thinks that discovering the roots of violence will be simple. There may be as many causes as there are crimes. The issue is whether to explore all possibilities—to search for clues in both society and biology.

Understanding the Content

Feel free to reread all or parts of the selection to answer the following questions.

1. What are the arguments for conducting genetic research for clues to violent behavior? What are the arguments against such research?

2. Compared with other industrialized countries, the United States ranks highest in violent crime rates. What factors are often given as causes?

3. According to some scientists, what effect does the neurotransmitter serotonin have on behavior? What is serotonin?

4. What role does environment play in the cause and effect of violent behavior?

5. What is the author's thesis? Is she for or against genetic research dealing with violent behavior?

Looking at Structure and Style

1. What is the basic paragraph pattern(s) used in the opening paragraph? Is it effective here? Explain.

2. What is the function of paragraph 6? How does paragraph 7 build on the content of paragraph 6?

3. How well balanced are the pro and con arguments for genetic research into criminal behavior? Does the author present information fairly? Explain.

4. Describe the author's tone and attitude toward her subject. What words or phrases develop tone and attitude?

5. Does the concluding paragraph draw a conclusion or summarize the content? Is it effective as a closing paragraph? Explain.

Evaluating the Author's Viewpoints

1. In paragraph 15, Richard Herrnstein is quoted as saying, "It is beneath contempt for the National Institutes of Health to be running for cover when scholars are trying to share their views." Do you think the author agrees? Do you? Why or why not?

2. Dr. Peter Breggin helped "scuttle" a proposed conference on genetic factors and violence, believing that "redefining social problems as public health problems is exactly what was done in Nazi Germany" (16). Do you agree? Why or why not?

3. The author believes that there may be as many causes as there are crimes. Do you agree? Explain.

Pursuing Possible Essay Topics

1. Write an essay explaining your views on genetic research into violence. Should the government fund such research? Is it important research?

2. Write an essay that compares and contrasts the causes for violence as discussed in Francis Flaherty's "The Ghetto Made Me Do It" and Toufexis's essay. Explain why you think environment and heredity are the major causes of violence.

3. Write an argument that supports or refutes Dr. Peter Breggin's statement in paragraph 16.

4. Write an essay on what effect you feel your environment has had on your behavior patterns.

5. Brainstorm or freewrite on one or more of the following:

   a. chronic wrongdoers   d. aggression

   b. violent behavior   e. drugs

   c. heredity   f. impulsiveness

6. If you don't like these ideas, be aggressive and find your own topic on some aspect of behavior.

Student Essay

Read the following narrative essay written by a student. As you read, look for answers to these questions:

1. Does the essay fulfill an assignment to write about some aspect of behavior?

2. How well does the narrative hold your interest?

3. Is the thesis clear and supported well?

Teen Sex: "Too Scary Out There for Me"

Mari Kinney

1   Everyone who is anyone seems to be having sex. I'm not saying that every single person is having sex, but having sex is just as common as smoking weed. Pretty much everyone has tried it at least once.

2   It's too scary out there for me. Even safe sex doesn't seem that safe. But I think the thing that scares me most about sex is how much it hurts when your relationship doesn't work out. This happened to my friend and it broke my heart—hers too, I guess.

3   When I was 12, I hooked up two friends of mine. I knew they would be a great couple. They were both sweet and thoughtful

and had great personalities. At school everyone envied them. They were always holding hands, totally lovey-dovey. He got her rings and bracelets for her birthday. One time at school he hired some guys to come and sing her favorite song, "Always and Forever," then later took her and her family out to the Red Lobster. She once got him an autographed Cowboys jersey, his favorite team.

4   He'd carry her books for her, and one Christmas, gave her all his hard-earned Christmas money so she could visit her family in Guatemala for the holidays.

5   But two years later, things took a turn for the worse. The spark was fading. They didn't go out much. The couple that everyone had once envied seemed just like any other couple. He wanted to do more than just make out. To be honest, so did she, but her family was Catholic. Her mom always said, "Your virginity is everything. Don't ever give it away. Only to the man that you marry and love."

6   The more she wouldn't put out, the more aggravated and distant he got. It was, "Sorry, I forgot about the date." "I forgot about your birthday." "I forgot to call you back—I was busy." They were breaking up and getting back together every other day.

7   One day she told me she had the solution—to have sex. She said, "This will make everything better." I said, "No, this is what he wants." I tried to convince both of them it was just going to make everything worse. But they were like, tonight's the night. They shut me out. She was fighting to save a relationship that wasn't meant to be.

8   The next day they were all happy, holding hands again. Then two weeks later, she came to me. "What am I going to do? My period hasn't come."

9   She called me the next day. She was pregnant. She had to tell her boyfriend and her parents.

10   She invited me over to be there when she told him. His response was: "Are you sure it's mine?" She gave away her treasure to this guy, and he was basically saying she was a tramp.

11   The next day, he wanted to know why she didn't get an abortion. She told him she could never do that because it was

against the teachings of the Catholic church. Meanwhile, her parents were upset. They wanted to know how she was going to take care of a baby.

12   She was a smart, college-bound girl with good grades. So they looked into adoption. I think this was the right decision, because she couldn't excel in school and take care of a baby.

13   The months went by. Everybody at school could tell she was pregnant. But her relationship with her boyfriend got worse. He wouldn't take her calls, he wasn't there. When my friend was six months pregnant, he wanted to see other people. She reminded him that it was his kid, too. He said, I'm too young to be taking care of a kid. So she was on her own.

14   In her seventh month she stayed home because of complications. She had her baby in her eighth month and gave it away for adoption. I haven't seen her since then because her parents sent her away to Guatemala so she could learn some values.

15   So in the end, they split up and I lost both their friendships. Sex messed everything up. I think teens should think about the love and friendship they are putting at risk when they have sex, not to mention the risk of pregnancy and AIDS. These days, the only person you can trust is yourself. That's why I have better things to do than go out there and lose my virginity.

16   I think we all feel lonely and want to feel loved, but sex won't fix that. It's just a temporary physical act. I don't know exactly how you find love, but I know you can't fix things instantly by having sex.

Reaction

In your journal or on a separate sheet of paper, write your reaction to the student essay. How well does the essay fit the assignment to write on some aspect of behavior? Does the narrative hold your interest? Why or why not? Is the thesis well supported? What grade would you give the essay? Why?

weird

On the Net

Like education, human behavior is a broad topic that encompasses many different subject areas. You can search the Internet to find out more about any topics that interest you from the chapter or look up additional information about an author. Here are a couple of interesting sites that you might like to look at—after you have finished writing all of your essays for the chapter.

1. By going to *www.queendom.com,* you will have access to a number of interesting and fun personality tests that may give you some insight into your own behavior. Test topics range from general knowledge to personality tests, nutrition and eating habits to career choice and preparation tests. This site, called Test Junkie, is mostly for fun. The site developers run a disclaimer that the tests may give you insight into your personality, but they also may not. The developers advise you to "go on this journey with your mind . . . and your eyes . . . wide open."

2. The Kaplan Minds games site, at *www1.kaplan.com,* has a more academic focus. Visit this site if you are interested in learning more about the standardized tests that will be given to you during your academic career (visit the "college" link on the site) and how to excel at them. This site also includes interesting information for those entering college and those already enrolled. If you want to continue with your academic career, you can visit the "graduate" section or visit sites geared toward specific careers, like "education" or "nursing." You can take practice tests and assess where you need to spend time to pass and do well on specific tests.

If you'd like to explore some of the topics in the chapter, do a keyword search. Or, think about doing one or more of the following activities.

1. Find a website devoted to people with bipolar disorder. Based on your examination of this site, is the information presented in Mary Seymour's article "Call Me Crazy . . ." accurate? Does this site give any information about possible treatments, living with bipolar, or telling loved ones about the condition? Summarize your findings.

2. Look at websites devoted to Brent Staples and learn more about this author. See if there are any links to additional readings by Staples, and read another one of his essays.

3. Visit two or three sites devoted to Gwendolyn Brooks and learn more about her life and other writings.

5 Viewpoints on Cultural Heritage

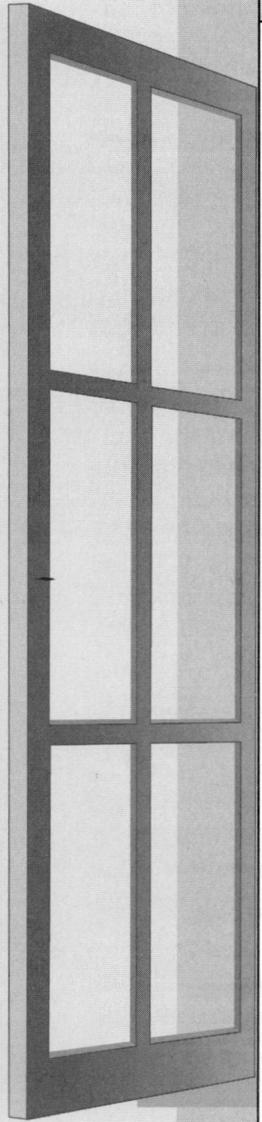

FOCUS ON CULTURAL HERITAGE

[handwritten: 10/21 Home work → MO]

To help you focus on the subject of this chapter, answer the following questions. You may want to write the answers in your journal or be prepared to discuss them in class.

1. Read the quotation by Emma Lazarus on the opposite page. It is part of a poem inscribed on the Statue of Liberty. What do you think she means? Does the inscription fit today's public mood toward immigrants? Explain.

2. What meaning does the Statue of Liberty hold for you? What do you think Liberty is holding in her left hand?

3. For millions of European immigrants, the first view of the United States after a long ocean voyage was the Statue of Liberty. How do you think they might have responded to the sight of the statue?

4. On the opposite page, the bottom photo captures an immigrant family of the early 1900s arriving at Ellis Island, where they had to await processing for legal admission. From where might they have come? Why might they have been willing to leave their homeland to come to America? What might America have gained by their coming here?

5. For what reasons might you give up your homeland to emigrate to another country? What difficulties would you face?

6. What is your own cultural heritage? From where did your ancestors originally come? Why did they come here?

"Give me your tired, your poor
Your huddled masses yearning to breathe free,
The wretched refuse of your teeming shore.
Send these, the homeless, tempest-tost to me,
I lift my lamp beside the golden door!"

—Emma Lazarus

Use your viewpoint to answer the questions using good sentence structure and paragraphing.

Frederick Bodin/Stock Boston

Brown Brothers

The history of the United States is filled with accounts of people who came from all over the world to settle here. Many came willingly to find a better life, some were forced to come as slaves or to be used as cheap labor, some were driven from their homelands for political reasons, some fled from war, and still others came hoping to get rich quickly and then go back home. Immigration, especially of people from western and southern Europe, was high between 1870 and 1920. Between the years 1880 and 1900 alone, a half million people came to this country *each year.* During the next fourteen years, over a million people immigrated to America *each year.* Whether born here or an immigrant, everyone living in America felt widespread cultural and institutional changes. The rise of an urban-industrial way of life that attracted thousands of people to cities, the growing interest in scientific knowledge and research, and the variety of new cultures that the immigrants brought with them all had an effect on education, science, fashion, food, music, art, literature, publishing, and politics. People referred to America as a "melting pot," a place where people of all types could blend together.

Immigration was somewhat restricted during the 1940s and 1950s, but another surge in immigration occurred in the 1970s, although not always through normal channels. According to Charles M. Dollar's *America: Changing Times,* estimates of illegal aliens arriving during this ten-year period matched the number of legal aliens, four million.

> Most of the "new" immigration of the seventies came from the Western hemisphere and Asian nations. Statistics showed Mexico to be the leading source, with over 550,000 legal entrants from 1970–1978; the Philippines and Korea each accounted for about 300,000 in the same period, and Cuba, over 250,000. Other sources of more than 100,000 immigrants (1970–1978) included China (Taiwan), India, the Dominican Republic, Jamaica, and Vietnam. These immigrants, as well as hundreds of thousands of illegal newcomers every year . . . put great strains on the ability of the American Government to cope with such numbers.

Because it is difficult to determine the number of illegal entries to the United States, these figures are probably low.

What will be the makeup of America's population by the year 2010? By the mid-1980s, it was estimated that there were between twelve and fifteen million people of Spanish origin here. The United States is now the fifth-largest Spanish-speaking country in the world, following Mexico, Spain, Argentina, and Colombia. Hispanics, three out of every five from Mexico, are the second-largest and fastest-growing minority group in this country. In addition, Asian immigration is also on the rise. It is estimated that as many as twelve million Asians have immigrated here.

Some sociologists are concerned that America is no longer a "melting pot" but a "salad bowl." Unlike most earlier immigrants who were willing to learn

English and wanted to "melt" into American life, many of today's immigrants don't see the need to assimilate, or blend in. How will all this affect America's future?

Preparing to Read

Take a minute or two to look over the following reading selection. Note the title and author, read the opening paragraph, and check the essay's length. Make certain you have the time now to read it carefully and to do the exercises that follow it. Then, in the spaces provided, answer the following questions.

1. What do you think the title means? _____

_____

2. After reading the first paragraph, what do you think the theme of the essay

   will be?_____

_____

3. What do you think the author means by "the United States of the 21st century

   will be undeniably ours. Again"? _____

_____

Vocabulary

Good comprehension of what you are about to read depends upon your understanding of the words below. The number following each word refers to the paragraph where it is used.

managerial (1) of or relating to a manager or management

compounded (1) formed by a union of separate elements, ingredients, or parts

assimilate (3) make similar

revolución (4) Spanish word for revolution

shilling (4) luring a person to sell or deceive

icon (4) pictorial representation

loca (4) Spanish word for crazy

constituency (5) group or body that patronizes or supports

median (5) in the middle

demographic (5) group with specific statistical characteristics

pivotal (7) vitally important

anorexia (8) loss of appetite

senescence (8) the process of becoming old

The Legacy of Generation Ñ

Christy Haubegger

1   About 20 years ago, some mainstream observers declared the 1980s the "decade of the Hispanic." The Latino population was nearing 15 million! (It's since doubled.) However, our decade was postponed—a managerial oversight, no doubt—and eventually rescheduled for the '90s. What happens to a decade deferred? It earns compounded interest and becomes the next hundred years. The United States of the 21st century will be undeniably ours. Again.

2   It's Manifest *Destino*. After all, Latinos are true Americans, some of the original residents of the *Américas*. Spanish was the first European language spoken on this continent. Which is why we live in places like *Los Angeles, Colorado* and *Florida* rather than The Angels, Colored and Flowered. Now my generation is about to put a Latin stamp on the rest of the culture—and that will ultimately be the Ñ legacy.

3   We are not only numerous, we are also growing at a rate seven times that of the general population. Conservative political ads notwithstanding, this growth is driven by natural increase (births over deaths) rather than immigration. At 30, I may be the oldest childless Latina in the United States. More important, however, while our preceding generation felt pressure to assimilate, America has now generously agreed to meet us in the middle. Just as we become more American, America is simultaneously becoming more Latino.

4   This quiet *revolución* can perhaps be traced back to the bloodless coup of 1992, when salsa outsold ketchup for the first time. Having toppled the leadership in the condiment category, we set our sights even higher. Fairly soon, there was a congresswoman named Sanchez representing Orange County, a taco-shilling Chihuahua became a national icon, and now everyone is *loca* for Ricky Martin.

5   We are just getting started. Our geographic concentration and reputation for family values are making us every politician's dream constituency. How long can New Hampshire, with just four Electoral
College votes—and probably an equal number of Hispanic residents—continue to get so much attention from presidential candidates? Advertisers will also soon be begging for our attention. With a
median age of 26 (eight years younger than the general market),
Latinos hardly exist outside their coveted 18–34 demographic.
Remember, we may only be 11 percent of the country, but we buy 16
percent of the lipliner.

6   The media will change as well, especially television, where we
now appear to be rapidly approaching extinction. Of the 26 new
comedies and dramas appearing this fall [1999] on the four major
networks, not one has a Latino in a leading role. The Screen Actors
Guild released employment statistics for 1998 showing that the
percentage of roles going to Hispanic actors actually declined from
the previous year. But, pretty soon, the cast of "Friends" will need
to find some *amigos*. Seeing as they live in New York City, and
there's almost 2 million of us in the metropolitan area, this
shouldn't prove too difficult.

7   Face it: this is going to be a bilingual country. Back in 1849, the
California Constitution was written in both Spanish and English,
and we're headed that way again. If our children speak two languages
instead of just one, how can that not be a benefit to us all? The re-
Latinization of this country will pay off in other ways as well. I, for
one, look forward to that pivotal moment in our history when all
American men finally know how to dance. Latin music will no longer
be found in record stores under foreign and romance will bloom
again. Our children will ask us what it was like to dance without a
partner.

8   "American food" will mean low-fat enchiladas and hamburgers
served with rice and beans. As a result, the American standard of
beauty will necessarily expand to include a female size 12, and
anorexia will be found only in medical-history books. Finally, just
in time for the baby boomers' senescence, living with extended
family will become hip again. "Simpsons" fans of the next decade
will see Grandpa moving back home. We'll all go back to church
together.

9   At the dawn of a new millennium, America knows Latinos as en-
tertainers and athletes. But, someday very soon, all American
children can dream of growing up to be writers like Sandra Cisneros,
astronauts like Ellen Ochoa, or judges like Jose Cabranes of the
Second Circuit Court of Appeals. To put a Latin spin on a famous
Anglo phrase: It is truly *mañana* in America. For those of you who
don't know it (yet), that word doesn't just mean tomorrow; *mañana*
also means morning.

Understanding the Content

Feel free to reread all or parts of the selection to answer the following questions.

1. What is the Ñ legacy as described by the author?

2. What makes the Latino population "every politician's dream constituency"?

3. What does the author say has contributed to the "quiet *revolución*" in America?

4. What has accounted for the growth of the Latino population in American society?

5. According to the author, how will the media change to reflect the influence of Latinos in American society?

6. In a society in which Latino influences are numerous, how will the following things change, according to the author: American food, the American standard of beauty, Latin music availability, how people dance?

7. What examples does the author give of successful Latinos in America?

Looking at Structure and Style

1. What is the author's thesis? Is it stated or implied? If stated, where?

2. Is the first paragraph effective in setting the tone for the essay?

3. How does the author use statistics to support her thesis? Give specific examples.

4. What is the purpose of the last paragraph? Is it effective in providing a solid conclusion? Why or why not?

5. How does the author use current cultural icons to support her theory about the influence of Latinos in American society and culture? Give specific examples from the essay. Are these examples effective? Why or why not?

Evaluating the Author's Viewpoints

1. What do you think is the author's opinion of a bilingual society? Where in the essay does she allude to how she feels about this issue?

2. After reading the selection, do you agree that the 1980s were the "decade of the Hispanic"? Why or why not?

3. Do you agree with the author that "Latinos are true Americans"? Why or why not?

4. Why do you think the author feels compelled to explain that the growth of Latinos in the general population is due to "natural increase (births over deaths) rather than immigration"?

5. What contributions have Latinos made in American history, according to the author?

Pursuing Possible Essay Topics

1. What contributions has your culture made to American society? Write an essay, giving specific examples.

2. Write about how you would feel about living in a completely bilingual society.

3. Write a paper either in support of or in opposition to bilingual education.

4. Are you as proud of your cultural heritage as the author is of hers? Write an essay describing your pride or lack of pride in your heritage and why you have this feeling.

5. What do you think the new millennium holds for people of different ethnic backgrounds in the United States? Do you think that cultural diversity will have a more positive or a more negative influence on society? Why?

6. Find your own topic on some aspect of cultural heritage and write an essay.

Preparing to Read

Take a minute or two to look over the following reading selection. Note the title and author, read the opening paragraph, and check the essay's length. Make certain you have the time now to read it carefully and to do the exercises that follow it. Then, in the spaces provided, answer the following questions.

1. What do you think the essay will say about Latinos and Mexican immigrants?

_____

2. What do you think the author means by the title?_____

_____

_____

3. What might you learn from reading this essay?_____

_____

_____

Vocabulary

Good comprehension of what you are about to read depends upon your understanding of the words below. The number following each word refers to the paragraph where it is used.

embodies (7) represents, gives form to

plagues (7) disturbs, annoys, bothers

coupled (8) combined, joined

naive (15) innocent, gullible

acculturated (17) changed as a result of contact with another culture

remote (18) distant, far off

disaffection (25) alienation, separation

The Great Divide

MICHAEL QUINTANILLA

1   Virginia Gomez wanted to share a story.

2   The 13-year-old eighth-grader and her friends—all American-born Latinas—were walking past three Mexican immigrant sixth-graders after school recently. One of the younger children was sipping from a soda can. Suddenly, one of Virginia's friends bopped the bottom of the can.

3   "Wham! The soda spilled all over the little girl," Virginia recalled. As she and her friends walked away, the immigrant student muttered a Spanish obscenity.

4   "What? You want to start something?" Virginia's friend asked the now-frightened girl. "Tell me to my face . . . Wetback!"

5   "We're all proud of being Mexican," said Virginia—who was born in Los Angeles to immigrant parents—as she talked about the on-campus incident the day after it occurred at Nimitz Middle School in Huntington Park.

6   "But the thing is we see ourselves as different even though we have the same culture," she said. "We're American and they're not."

7   Virginia's story embodies all the elements of a conflict that plagues many Latino students today: the alienation and prejudice that divide American-born Latino kids and their immigrant classmates. The students often segregate themselves during lunchtime, on the basketball court, at school dances, and while hanging out on campus before and after school.

8   A language barrier coupled with an unfamiliar teen culture—the culture of the popular American Latino kids who wear baggy clothes with Doc Martens or Nikes and listen to deep-house and hip-hop—adds to the problem of assimilation for immigrant students.

9   In most cases, students agree, it's the American-born Latinos who ridicule the immigrants.

10   They make fun of the immigrant boys who dress in white buttoned shirts instead of T-shirts and high-water cotton trousers instead of oversized jeans. They ridicule the immigrant girls in their ruffled starched blouses and pleated skirts and braids tied with bows. They make fun of the immigrant children's shyness, respectfulness and dedication to academics.

11   The U.S.-born Latinos call the Mexican kids "*quebradita* people" because of their banda music and *quebradita* dances. They make fun of the immigrants' "nerdy" Mickey Mouse–adorned backpacks and have even coined a term for them: "Wetpacks."

12   They call the immigrant students other names—"beaner," "Wehac" (a derogatory term for a Mexican immigrant of Indian descent) and tell them to "go back where you come from." Immigrant students at Nimitz reported that when they run around the track in gym class, American-born teens shout "Corrale! Corrale! La Migra! La Migra!" ("Run! Immigration!")

13   Brad Pilon, a bilingual school psychologist with the Los Angeles Unified School District, works with about 70 schools—most with a majority Latino enrollment—in the mid-city area, including Belmont High School's Newcomer Center, which helps hundreds of recent non-English speaking immigrants adjust in school.

14   "These kids feel the segregation, they live it," Pilon said. "They get beat up, get lunches stolen, are laughed at in their faces" by U.S.-born Latinos, he said. Often the immigrant student is too scared to report the harassment. Also, Pilon said, students soon learn that if they were to report such incidents, "nothing would be done" because overloaded teachers and administrators often aren't aware the problem exists.

15   "The immigrant kids, especially the newest arrivals, are naive, open and most of all vulnerable when they come to school," Pilon said. "When they first come here, like anybody who moves anywhere, they are faced with the problem of fitting in."

16   For most, fitting in is their dream even though they often view American kids as lazy, unmotivated and disrespectful to their parents and teachers.

17   Ramon A. Gutierrez, director of the Center for the Study of Race and Ethnicity at the University of California, San Diego, said this Latino rift is not something new. He cited a 10-year-old study conducted in the San Jose area, where a researcher found four Latino groups that segregated themselves from each other in one school— "the recent lower-income Mexican immigrant; the middle-class Mexican immigrant; the acculturated Chicano kids and the cholo kids; lower-income Mexican Americans."

18   "There have always been tensions and stresses between individuals of a remote immigrant past and recent immigrants," he said. "What it boils down to is discrimination based not only on immigrant status," Gutierrez said, but also on language and social class.

19   "If you went to Beverly Hills High, you'd find lower-class white kids segregated from the wealthier kids. It's segregation based on social standing," he said.

20   Rene Estrella, a leadership class adviser and biology teacher at Belmont High School, where 90% of the 4,500 enrollment is Latino, said immigrant Latino students "take the brunt of discrimination" from American-born students because "the people who are privileged to be born here think that they are superior to the person who was not.

21   "I think most kids who come to Belmont don't have too much to feel good about, growing up in the area. They don't get out of this area very much and anything they can hold onto to get a better identity, even if it means making others feel lower, makes them feel important."

22   Estrella said storytelling sessions in his classes helped bring students together last semester, and he probably will continue them. For several minutes at the start of each class, students shared their lives with other classmates. Immigrant students spoke about their homelands, family members killed in their war-torn countries and their adjustment to life in the United States.

23   "Hearing each other's stories united the students. It made the American-born kids understand the struggle so many of the newcomers have experienced and the struggle they still face, especially when they are segregated," Estrella said.

24   "We are oppressing each other and that bothers me," said Lupe Simpson, principal of Nimitz, the second-largest middle school in the country. The school has an enrollment of 3,200 students—97% Latino, one-fifth of that number recent immigrants.

25   Simpson said she is deeply concerned about the "anti-Mexican" feelings of some of her students as well as the isolation and disaffection immigrant children deal with daily. "But I don't see this as a defeat," she said. "It's a challenge."

26   She hopes students will embrace her plan for a buddy program that would pair native and immigrant Latinos so they could help and learn from each other. Another idea she is exploring is to have award assemblies for the whole student body, instead of the English as a Second Language students having their assemblies separately, as they do now. And she wants to speak to teachers and administrators about integrating students in classrooms, during sporting events and at school dances.

27   "We have to do something so the kids can see that that kind of thinking prevails in their lives and where does it end? We have to start ending it with ourselves. We have to show our kids that we are more alike than we are different," she said after listening to some of the students express their feelings in recent interviews at the school.

28   Gabriela Rico, 13, a Nimitz eighth-grader from Mexico, said she is mocked in gym class because she doesn't always understand the games.

29   "The Chicanos don't speak to us at all. They don't try to teach us. That's what we want most of all—to learn the games, to learn English, to be like them," she said, as other immigrant children nodded.

30   "I know they make fun of me," Gabriela said, her eyes on a book on her lap. "I tell my mother and she tells me not to be like them and show off, not to place value on materialistic things like clothes or shoes or to care too much about appearances."

31   Julio Bejarano, an 11-year-old sixth-grader also from Mexico, said he gets along fine with kids in his neighborhood, many of them American-born. But at school, it's a different world. He said he is not accepted "as a friend by the Latino Americanos," never invited to join in a game of basketball or to sit with them at lunchtime "because they think we are inferior to them because we were not born here." His eyes water. The room is silent for a few seconds.

32   Language is the biggest obstacle, he said, even though it should be the key to bridging the communications gap because an overwhelming majority of the American Latinos are bilingual.

33   "We talk to them in Spanish because we don't know English and even though they know how to speak Spanish, they talk to us in English. Why don't they want to communicate with us?" Julio said.

34   Nancy Garcia, also 11, said she has an American Latina "good friend," but still there's no escaping the prejudice. "My friend tells me that she *is* superior to me," Nancy said, even though Nancy's grades are better.

35   "I don't know why she says that," Nancy paused. "I think she might be envious of us because we are so proud of our culture."

36   Still, she said she yearns to one day be accepted by her American-born Latino classmates because "I love the get-togethers they have at school, the way they dress, the way they dance, their music."

37   Image, said American-born classmate Lisa Moreno, 13, plays a big role in the self-imposed segregation at her school. "You have to know

how to dress so you can be in the 'in-crowd.' Immigrant girls wear Payless shoes."

38   Peer pressure keeps them from befriending the immigrants, students said. "If I were to hang around with them, then I wouldn't be in the in-crowd anymore," explained Lisa.

39   Said Virginia Gomez: "Straight out, we haven't welcomed the Mexicans with open arms. We're like, 'You want to be with us? I don't think so.' "

40   "It shouldn't be this way—two groups," said Virginia, who is student body president at Nimitz. "But what can you do to stop it? Some people are not going to change no matter what you do."

41   Rudy Lopez, a Los Angeles–born 13-year-old Latino at Nimitz, agreed that both groups should be united, especially "when they haven't done anything to us to treat them bad."

42   That's a sentiment shared by several students at Belmont.

43   Sandra Flores, 16, a 10th-grader born in Los Angeles, said, "I have newcomer friends and it's very hard for them. I think they are afraid to talk to U.S. Latinos because they are expecting us to put them aside, you know, ignore them. That's why they come to their own little groups."

44   "It's sad to see us segregated like that, especially when the immigrant students have such a big enthusiasm for learning, for having better futures. They are really smarter than us," she said.

45   Ernesto, a 16-year-old Guatemalan (who preferred not to use his surname), said he chooses to remain a loner because he doesn't want to be rejected as he was last year in junior high school.

46   "We get rejected because of the way we dress, talk, the way we are," he said. So he and his immigrant friends hang out together, encourage each other, lift each other's spirits. As a group, they are secure and safe. It's what gets them through the day.

47   Still, it's unfathomable sometimes to Ernesto and other immigrant young people that they have left one war to face another.

48   "We come from war-torn countries," he said. "Our families have struggled to come here for a better future and then we still have to struggle with people who are from our own race."

Understanding the Content

Feel free to reread all or parts of the selection to answer the following questions.

1. To what does the title refer? What is the main reason for the divide?

2. What are some of the problems that prevent the assimilation of Mexican immigrants with American-born Latinos?

3. What types of segregation and harassment are some Mexican immigrants faced with?

4. What are some of the actions schools are taking to close the divide?

Looking at Structure and Style

1. Because this selection originally appeared in a newspaper, paragraphs are short. If you were to edit the article, where might you combine paragraphs?

2. The opening uses an anecdote to draw reader interest. How effective is it? Would another method work just as well? Explain.

3. Quintanilla quotes from several sources. How helpful are these in supporting his story? Are the sources credible?

4. How would you describe the author's tone and attitude? What words or phrases help develop tone and attitude?

5. How effective is the last paragraph?

Evaluating the Author's Viewpoints

1. Is Quintanilla mostly objective or subjective in his reporting? Explain.

2. Ramon Gutierrez explains the "great divide" in paragraph 19 by stating, "If you went to Beverly Hills High, you'd find lower-class white kids segregated from the wealthier kids. It's segregation based on social standing." Do you agree with his viewpoint? Explain.

3. Storytelling sessions and buddy programs are cited as two initiatives intended to stop the prejudice toward Mexican immigrants. Do you think these methods can be helpful in eliminating prejudice? Explain.

Pursuing Possible Essay Topics

1. Write about a time when you felt segregated from a group or felt prejudice against you. What was the cause? How did you feel? How did it affect your own prejudices?

2. Interview your parents or grandparents. What is their heritage? Have they ever experienced segregation or prejudice based on their heritage? How did it affect them?

3. What cultural groups in your neighborhood bear the brunt of segregation or prejudice? What is the cause? How might things be changed? Are you part of the problem?

4. Brainstorm or freewrite on one or more of the following:
   a. your heritage   d. immigrants
   b. language barriers   e. American
   c. prejudice   f. foreign

5. Ignore these and write on some other aspect of culture or heritage.

Preparing to Read

Take a minute or two to look over the following reading selection. Note the title and author, read the opening paragraph, and check the essay's length. Make certain you have the time now to read it carefully and to do the exercises that follow it. Then, in the spaces provided, answer the following questions.

1. What does the title tell you about the essay? What do you think when you see

   the term "cultural baggage"?_____

   _____

2. What does the term "cultural heritage" mean to you?_____

   _____

3. Is your cultural heritage important to you? If so, how? _____

   _____

Vocabulary

Good comprehension of what you are about to read depends upon your understanding of the words below. The number following each word refers to the paragraph where it is used.

  chauvinism (2) partiality to a group or place to which one belongs or has belonged

  venerable (3) impressive by reason of age

  militant (4) aggressive

  ecumenism (4) a movement promoting unity among religious groups

  tartans (5) garments with a plaid design, patterned to designate distinctive clans

seder (7) Jewish ceremonial dinner held on the first evening or first and second evenings of Passover

secular (8) not specifically religious

progenitors (9) ancestors in a direct line

epiphany (10) an illuminating discovery

spewed (11) came forth in a flood or gush

maxim (11) general truth, fundamental principle, rule of conduct

Cultural Baggage

Barbara Ehrenreich

1   An acquaintance was telling me about the joys of rediscovering her ethnic and religious heritage. "I know exactly what my ancestors were doing 2,000 years ago," she said, eyes gleaming with enthusiasm, "and *I can do the same things now.*" Then she leaned forward and inquired politely, "And what is your ethnic background, if I may ask?"

2   "None," I said, that being the first word in line to get out of my mouth. Well, not "none," I backtracked. Scottish, English, Irish—that was something, I supposed. Too much Irish to qualify as a WASP; too much of the hated English to warrant a "Kiss Me, I'm Irish" button; plus there are a number of dead ends in the family tree due to adoptions, missing records, failing memories and the like. I was blushing by this time. Did "none" mean I was rejecting my heritage out of Anglo-Celtic self-hate? Or was I revealing a hidden ethnic chauvinism in which the Britannically derived served as a kind of neutral standard compared with the ethnic "others"?

3   Throughout the 60's and 70's, I watched one group after another—African-Americans, Latinos, Native Americans—stand up and proudly reclaim their roots while I just sank back ever deeper into my seat. All this excitement over ethnicity stemmed, I uneasily sensed, from a past in which *their* ancestors had been trampled upon by *my* ancestors, or at least by people who looked very much like them. In addition, it had begun to seem almost un-American not to have some sort of hyphen at hand, linking one to more venerable times and locales.

4   But the truth is, I was raised with none. We'd eaten ethnic foods in my childhood home, but these were all borrowed, like the pasties, or Cornish meat pies, my father had picked up from his fellow miners in Butte, Montana. If my mother had one rule, it was militant ecumenism in all matters of food and experience. "Try new things,"

she would say, meaning anything from sweetbreads to clams, with an emphasis on the "new."

5   As a child, I briefly nourished a craving for tradition and roots. I immersed myself in the works of Sir Walter Scott. I pretended to believe that the bagpipe was a musical instrument. I was fascinated to learn from a grandmother that we were descended from certain Highland clans and longed for a pleated skirt in one of their distinctive tartans.

6   But in *Ivanhoe,* it was the dark-eyed "Jewess" Rebecca I identified with, not the flaxen-haired bimbo Rowena. As for clans: Why not call them "tribes," those bands of half-clad peasants and warriors whose idea of cuisine was stuffed sheep gut washed down with whisky? And then there was the sting of Disraeli's remark—which I came across in my early teens—to the effect that his ancestors had been leading orderly, literate lives when my ancestors were still rampaging through the Highlands daubing themselves with blue paint.

7   Motherhood put the screws on me, ethnicity-wise. I had hoped that by marrying a man of Eastern European–Jewish ancestry I would acquire for my descendants the ethnic genes that my own forebears so sadly lacked. At one point, I even subjected the children to a seder of my own design, including a little talk about the flight from Egypt and its relevance to modern social issues. But the kids insisted on buttering their matzohs and snickering through my talk. "Give me a break, Mom," the older one said. "You don't even believe in God."

8   After the tiny pagans had been put to bed, I sat down to brood over Elijah's wine. What had I been thinking? The kids knew that their Jewish grandparents were secular folks who didn't hold seders themselves. And if ethnicity eluded me, how could I expect it to take root in my children, who are not only Scottish-English-Irish, but Hungarian-Polish-Russian to boot?

9   But, then, on the fumes of Manischewitz, a great insight took form in my mind. It was true, as the kids said, that I didn't "believe in God." But this could be taken as something very different from an accusation—a reminder of a genuine heritage. My parents had not believed in God either, nor had my grandparents or any other progenitors going back to the great-great level. They had become disillusioned with Christianity generations ago—just as, on the in-law side, my children's other ancestors had shaken off their Orthodox Judaism. This insight did not exactly furnish me with an "identity," but it was at least something to work with: we are the kind of people, I realized—whatever our distant ancestors' religions—who do *not* believe, who do not carry on traditions, who do not do things just because someone has done them before.

10   The epiphany went on: I recalled that my mother never introduced a procedure for cooking or cleaning by telling me, "Grandma

did it this way." What did Grandma know, living in the days before vacuum cleaners and disposable toilet mops? In my parents' general view, new things were better than old, and the very fact that some ritual had been performed in the past was a good reason for abandoning it now. Because what was the past, as our forebears knew it? Nothing but poverty, superstition and grief. "Think for yourself," Dad used to say. "Always ask why."

11   In fact, this may have been the ideal cultural heritage for my particular ethnic strain—bounced as it was from the Highlands of Scotland across the sea, out to the Rockies, down into the mines and finally spewed out into high-tech, suburban America. What better philosophy, for a race of migrants, than "Think for yourself"? What better maxim, for people whose whole world was rudely inverted every 30 years or so, than "Try new things"?

12   The more tradition-minded, the newly enthusiastic celebrants of Purim and Kwanzaa and Solstice, may see little point to survival if the survivors carry no cultural freight—religion, for example, or ethnic tradition. To which I would say that skepticism, curiosity and wide-eyed ecumenical tolerance are also worthy elements of the human tradition and are at least as old as such notions as "Serbian" or "Croatian," "Scottish" or "Jewish." I make no claims for my personal line of progenitors except that they remained loyal to the values that may have induced all of our ancestors, long, long ago, to climb down from the trees and make their way into the open plains.

13   A few weeks ago, I cleared my throat and asked the children, now mostly grown and fearsomely smart, whether they felt any stirrings of ethnic or religious identity, etc., which might have been, ahem, insufficiently nourished at home. "None," they said, adding firmly, "and the world would be a better place if nobody else did, either." My chest swelled with pride, as would my mother's, to know that the race of "none" marches on.

Understanding the Content

Feel free to reread all or parts of the selection to answer the following questions.

1. What is the author's cultural heritage?

2. Why did certain groups proclaiming their heritage in the 1960s and 1970s make the author uncomfortable?

3. How did the author strive for a cultural heritage as a child? What did she do to identify and acknowledge her roots?

4. What did the author hope to gain for her children by marrying a man with an Eastern European–Jewish background?

5. What did the author do to try to introduce tradition and religious identity into her children's lives? How did her children react to her attempts?

6. How did the author's parents feel about tradition? What did her father tell her as a child that the author classifies as a "better philosophy, for a race of migrants"?

7. How do the author's children feel about the way they were raised in terms of their ethnic and religious identity?

Looking at Structure and Style

1. What is the main function of paragraphs 1 and 2? Are these two paragraphs effective as an opening to the essay?

2. The author quotes her parents in several paragraphs. What is the purpose of these quotations?

3. How does paragraph 4 explain the author's viewpoint on cultural heritage and support her thesis? How does paragraph 10 help support what the author states in paragraph 4?

4. What is the function of paragraph 6?

5. Is paragraph 13 an effective conclusion? Why or why not?

6. The essay details the author's coming to terms with her cultural heritage. What stages of her life does she use to illustrate her journey?

Evaluating the Author's Viewpoints

1. What does the author think of people who embrace a strong cultural heritage?

2. How has the author's attitude toward cultural heritage changed throughout her life?

3. What is the author's religious background? How has this helped shape her views on cultural heritage?

4. Does the author feel a need to pass on traditions and rituals to her children? Explain.

5. Is the author proud of her Scottish-English-Irish background? Why or why not? What examples from history does the author give to support your conclusion?

Pursuing Possible Essay Topics

1. How important do you think it is that children grow up with a strong sense of their cultural heritage? Write an essay discussing your viewpoint.

2. What is your cultural background? Write an essay discussing how your ethnicity has defined who you are and who you will become.

3. Discuss some aspect of your culture of which you are particularly proud. What contributions has your culture made to society that make it stand out from other cultures?

4. Do you think the advice "Think for yourself; always ask why" would be helpful to a child growing up in today's society? Why or why not?

5. Brainstorm or freewrite on one or more of the following:

   a. cultural heritage
   b. ethnicity
   c. diversity
   d. religious tradition
   e. rituals

6. Ignore these and find a topic of your own related to culture or cultural heritage.

Preparing to Read

Take a minute or two to look over the following reading selection. Note the title and the author, read the opening paragraph, and check the essay's length. Make certain you have the time now to read it carefully and to do the exercises that follow it. Then, in the spaces provided, answer the following questions.

1. On the basis of the title, what do you think this essay will be about?_____

_____

2. How do you think the author feels about the subject of the essay?_____

_____

3. From reading the first paragraph of this essay, describe the author._____

_____

Vocabulary

Good comprehension of what you are about to read depends upon your understanding of the words below. The number following each word refers to the paragraph where it is used.

mortified (1) shamed or humiliated

reputed (3) generally considered, assumed

dubious (4) doubtful

infamous (7) having an extremely bad reputation

interminable (8) seeming to be without end

hues (9) colors

ancestry (10) family tree, lineage

contorted (11) twisted or strained out of shape

brouhaha (12) commotion, racket

Why Must Everything Be Black or White?

E.R. Shipp

1   When I was in seventh or eighth grade at the "Negro" school in Conyers, Ga., another girl and I were mortified to think that one of us might be the darkest member of our class. So we went around asking people to look at the two of us and tell us.

2   Being black was not exactly hip in Georgia in the mid-1960s. Indeed, to call someone "black" was still considered something of an insult. So now comes word that "white" Staten Islanders—the Westerinens—are in a way crossing the color line from the opposite direction.

3   Not many "whites" have reclaimed their "black" identity as the Westerinens have in trying to be officially declared the descendants of Thomas Jefferson and his reputed "black" mistress, Sally Hemings.

4   The dubious reward for acceptance into the Monticello Association, the 700-member organization composed of descendants of the two daughters of Jefferson and his wife, is the right to be buried at Jefferson's estate, Monticello. The Westerinens, who are descendants of Sally Hemings' youngest son, Eston Hemings, have been at this for

several years. This month, as in the past, their attempt to be accepted failed.

5   All this is an illustration of just how wacky is our fascination with categorizing people in this country according to race—a concept that social scientists say has no biological basis.

6   When Halle Berry won an Academy Award for Best Actress, blacks took pride as she accepted on behalf of "every nameless, faceless woman of color that now has a chance because this door tonight has been opened." But one couldn't help notice that while she is considered "black" and apparently considers herself to be, she was seated next to her "white" mother.

7   So what—besides the history of race in this country—makes her more black than white? Sort of like Homer Plessy, the Louisianan who by all accounts was more "white" than "black"—but just black enough that those who knew him knew that he should not sit in the "white" passenger car on a train in 1892. The lawsuit that ensued led to the now-infamous "separate but equal" Supreme Court decision that was not overturned until 1954.

8   During NBC's interminable commemoration of its 75th anniversary, members of "The Cosby Show" cast were reunited to reflect on the significance of that sitcom. Some viewers thought it an impossibility that a very fair-skinned actress, Sabrina LeBeauf, could have been taken seriously as the daughter of dark-skinned Bill Cosby.

9   "Up until 'The Cosby Show,' I don't think people realized that African-Americans came in all different hues, all different colors from the rainbow," LeBeauf said in a "Today" show interview.

10   That's largely a factor of their non-black ancestry. I know blacks with Irish ancestry and Italian ancestry and Jewish ancestry. But no matter how recent that lineage, they are deemed to be black.

11   The contorted thinking that persuades the Monticello Association to deny the evidence that has swayed a number of scholars—including some involved with the Thomas Jefferson Foundation that runs Monticello—is rather entertaining from a distance.

12   But this whole brouhaha is even more ridiculous if, as historian J. A. Rogers proclaimed in the early 1960s in "The Five Negro Presidents," Jefferson himself was part black.

Understanding the Content

Feel free to reread all or parts of the selection to answer the following questions.

1. Where did the author grow up, and during what era?

2. Who are the Westerinens, and what are they trying to accomplish?

3. What is the Monticello Association, and what is the reward for being accepted into it?

4. According to the author, how do social scientists feel about categorizing people by race?

5. What claim does historian J. A. Rogers make about Jefferson?

Looking at Structure and Style

1. What is the author's thesis? Is it stated or implied? If stated, where?

2. What support does Shipp provide for her thesis, if any? Is the support effective?

3. What is the purpose of paragraphs 5–9?

4. What is the purpose of paragraph 10?

5. How effective is paragraph 12 as a concluding paragraph? Rewrite paragraph 12 so that it summarizes the author's key points and her thesis.

6. How effective is the opening paragraph in conveying how the author feels about race and her black heritage?

Evaluating the Author's Viewpoints

1. E.R. Shipp states that "our fascination with categorizing people in this country according to race" is "wacky." Do you agree or disagree? Why?

2. Based on your reading of paragraph 6, what do you think E.R. Shipp thinks about Halle Berry considering herself "black"? How can you tell?

3. How does Shipp feel about the Westerinens and the Monticello Association? What words or phrases does she use to convey her feelings?

Pursuing Possible Essay Topics

1. Brainstorm or freewrite on the topic of race.

2. Write an essay in which you defend the rights of the Westerinens to join the Monticello Association.

3. Write an essay either agreeing or disagreeing with the author that growing up in the South in the mid-1960s was a time when "to call someone 'black' was still considered something of an insult" (paragraph 2).

4. What is your racial and cultural background? Write an essay describing how you identify with one part of your background over another and why.

5. How do you think people should be identified? By race? By land of origin? Write an essay exploring your thoughts on this topic.

6. Ignore these possible topics and find a topic of your own related to race.

Preparing to Read

Take a minute or two to look over the following reading selection. Note the title and author, read the opening paragraph, and check the essay's length. Make certain you have the time now to read it carefully and to do the exercises that follow it. Then, in the spaces provided, answer the following questions.

1. Is the author from the United States?_____

_____

_____

2. Why did the author's parents come to the United States? _____

_____

_____

3. What do you think the author is going to say about her cultural heritage?

_____

_____

Vocabulary

Good comprehension of what you are about to read depends upon your understanding of the words below. The number following each word refers to the paragraph where it is used.

incompatible (2) opposite, contrary, unsuitable to each other

taunted (3) insulted, ridiculed, jeered

mocked (7) treated with ridicule or scorn

nuances (8) shades, gradations

Time to Look and Listen

Magdoline Asfahani

1   I love my country as many who have been here for generations cannot. Perhaps that's because I'm the child of immigrants, raised with a conscious respect for America that many people take for granted. My parents chose this country because it offered them a new life, freedom and possibilities. But I learned at a young age that the country we loved so much did not feel the same way about us.

2   Discrimination is not unique to America. It occurs in any country that allows immigration. Anyone who is unlike the majority is looked at a little suspiciously, dealt with a little differently. The fact that I wasn't part of the majority never occurred to me. I knew that I was an Arab and a Muslim. This meant nothing to me. At school I stood up to say the Pledge of Allegiance every day. These things did not seem incompatible at all. Then everything changed for me, suddenly and permanently, in 1985. I was only in seventh grade, but that was the beginning of my political education.

3   That year a TWA plane originating in Athens was diverted to Beirut. Two years earlier the U.S. Marine barracks in Beirut had been bombed. That seemed to start a chain of events that would forever link Arabs with terrorism. After the hijacking, I faced classmates who taunted me with cruel names, attacking my heritage and my religion. I became an outcast and had to apologize for myself constantly.

4   After a while, I tried to forget my heritage. No matter what race, religion, or ethnicity, a child who is attacked often retreats. I was the only Arab I knew of in my class, so I had no one in my peer group as an ally. No matter what my parents tried to tell me about my proud cultural history, I would ignore it. My classmates told me I came from an uncivilized, brutal place, that Arabs were by nature anti-American, and I believed them. They did not know the hours my parents spent studying, working, trying to preserve part of their old lives while embracing, willingly, the new.

5   I tried to forget the Arabic I knew, because if I didn't I'd be forever linked to murderers. I stopped inviting friends over for dinner, because I thought the food we ate was "weird." I lied about where my parents had come from. Their accents (although they spoke English perfectly) humiliated me. Though Islam is a major monotheistic religion with many similarities to Judaism and Christianity, there were no holidays near Chanukah or Christmas, nothing to tie me to the "Judeo-Christian" tradition. I felt more excluded. I slowly began to turn into someone without a past.

6   Civil war was raging in Lebanon, and all that Americans saw of that country was destruction and violence. Every other movie seemed to feature Arab terrorists. The most common questions I was asked

were if I had ever ridden a camel or if my family lived in tents. I felt burdened with responsibility. Why should an adolescent be asked questions like "Is it true you hate Jews and you want Israel destroyed?" I didn't hate anybody. My parents had never said anything even alluding to such sentiments. I was confused and hurt.

7   As I grew older and began to form my own opinions, my embarrassment lessened and my anger grew. The turning point came in high school. My grandmother had become very ill, and it was necessary for me to leave school a few days before Christmas vacation. My chemistry teacher was very sympathetic until I said I was going to the Middle East. "Don't come back in a body bag," he said cheerfully. The class laughed. Suddenly, those years of watching movies that mocked me and listening to others who knew nothing about Arabs and Muslims except what they saw on television seemed like a bad dream. I knew then that I would never be silent again.

8   I've tried to reclaim those lost years. I realize now that I come from a culture that has a rich history. The Arab world is a medley of people of different religions; not every Arab is a Muslim, and vice versa. The Arabs brought tremendous advances in the sciences and mathematics, as well as creating a literary tradition that has never been surpassed. The language itself is flexible and beautiful, with nuances and shades of meaning unparalleled in any language. Though many find it hard to believe, Islam has made progress in women's rights. There is a specific provision in the Koran that permits women to own property and ensures that their inheritance is protected— although recent events have shown that interpretation of these laws can vary.

9   My youngest brother, who is 12, is now at the crossroads I faced. When initial reports of the Oklahoma City bombing pointed to "Arab-looking individuals" as the culprits, he came home from school crying. "Mom, why do Muslims kill people? Why are the Arabs so bad?" She was angry and brokenhearted, but tried to handle the situation in the best way possible: through education. She went to his class, armed with Arabic music, pictures, traditional dress and cookies. She brought a chapter of the social-studies book to life, and the children asked intelligent, thoughtful questions, even after the class was over. Some even asked if she was coming back. When my brother came home, he was excited and proud instead of ashamed.

10   I only recently told my mother about my past experience. Maybe if I had told her then, I would have been better equipped to deal with the thoughtless teasing. But, fortunately, the world is changing. Although discrimination and stereotyping still exist, many people are trying to lessen and end it. Teachers, schools, and the media are showing greater sensitivity to cultural issues. However, there is still much that needs to be done, not for the sake of any particular ethnic or cultural group but for the sake of our country.

11   The America that I love is one that values freedom and the differences of its people. Education is the key to understanding. As Americans we need to take a little time to look and listen carefully to what is around us and not rush to judgment without knowing all the facts. And we must never be ashamed of our pasts. It is our collective differences that unite us and make us unique as a nation. It's what determines our present and our future.

Understanding the Content

Feel free to reread all or parts of the selection to answer the following questions.

1. How did Asfahani react to the prejudice toward Arabs she discovered among her classmates? What does she feel was the source or reason for her classmates' attitude?

2. What attitude does Asfahani have toward her heritage now? What brought about the change?

3. How did Asfahani's mother help her son face the prejudice toward Arabs among his classmates?

4. What does Asfahani feel is the key to overcoming the kind of teasing and prejudice felt toward unfamiliar cultures?

5. What is the subject of the essay and its thesis?

Looking at Structure and Style

1. Is the thesis stated or implied? If stated, where?

2. How effective is the opening paragraph? Does it establish a subject and thesis? Does it engage your interest? Explain.

3. What is the function of paragraph 7?

4. How effective is the last paragraph? Does it summarize the essay, or does it draw a conclusion regarding the author's subject? Explain.

5. Describe the author's tone and attitude. What words or phrases develop both?

6. Explain the meaning of the title. What connection does it have with the author's thesis?

Evaluating the Author's Viewpoints

1. Asfahani, American born, says that she loves this country "as many who have been here for generations cannot" (1). Why does she say this? Is she right?

2. Regarding prejudice toward various cultural heritages, Asfahani says "there is still much that needs to be done, not for the sake of any particular ethnic or cultural group but for the sake of our country" (10). Do you agree? Explain.

3. Asfahani believes that "it is our collective differences that unite us and make us unique as a nation" (11). Do you agree? Do you hold prejudicial feelings toward certain ethnic groups? Why?

Pursuing Possible Essay Topics

1. Write about a time when you felt prejudice or were teased because of your ethnic background. How did you respond? Did it make you ashamed of your heritage or prouder?

2. Write about a time when you participated in teasing or hurting someone because of his or her ethnic background. Why did you do it? What was gained by it? What made you feel superior?

3. Pick one of the following statements and respond:

   a. "The America that I love is one that values freedom and the differences of its people." (11)

   b. Education is the key to understanding ethnic differences.

4. Write an essay about the contributions that your own (or another) cultural heritage has made to American culture.

5. Freewrite or brainstorm on one or more of the following:

   a. Arabs   d. stereotyping

   b. civilized   e. ethnic discrimination

   c. cultural melting pot   f. language

6. Find your own topic for an essay on cultural heritage.

Preparing to Read

Take a minute or two to look over the following reading selection. Note the title and author, read the opening paragraph, and check the essay's length. Make certain you have the time now to read it carefully and to do the exercises that follow it. Then, in the spaces provided, answer the following questions.

1. What do you think Baldwin will say about black English? _____

_____

_____

2. Do you think there is such a language as "black English"? Explain.

_____

_____

_____

Vocabulary

Good comprehension of what you are about to read depends upon your understanding of the words below. The number following each word refers to the paragraph where it is used.

incontestably (1) without a doubt

dubiously (1) doubtfully, suspiciously

articulate (2) express well

temporal (3) brief, short-lived, temporary

antecedents (4) those who came before

qualms (5) misgivings, uneasiness

diaspora (7) the exile or dispersal of a homogeneous group

repudiate (11) disclaim, refuse

If Black English Isn't a Language, Then Tell Me, What Is?

JAMES BALDWIN

1   The argument concerning the use, or the status, or the reality, of black English is rooted in American history and has absolutely nothing to do with the question the argument supposes itself to be posing. The argument has nothing to do with language itself but with the *role* of language. Language, incontestably, reveals the speaker. Language, also, far more dubiously, is meant to define the other— and, in this case, the other is refusing to be defined by a language that has never been able to recognize him.

2   People evolve a language in order to describe and thus control their circumstances, or in order not to be submerged by a reality that they cannot articulate. (And, if they cannot articulate it, they *are* submerged.) A Frenchman living in Paris speaks a subtly and crucially different language from that of the man living in Marseilles; neither sounds very much like a man living in Quebec; and they would all have great difficulty in apprehending what the man from Guadeloupe, or Martinique, is saying, to say nothing of the man from Senegal—although the "common" language of all these areas is French. But each has paid, and is paying, a different price for this "common" language, in which, as it turns out, they are not saying, and cannot be saying, the same things: They each have very different realities to articulate, or control.

3   What joins all languages, and all men, is the necessity to confront life, in order, not inconceivably, to outwit death: The price for this is the acceptance, and achievement, of one's temporal identity. So that, for example, though it is not taught in the schools (and this has the potential of becoming a political issue) the south of France still clings to its ancient and musical Provençal, which resists being described as a "dialect." And much of the tension in the Basque countries, and in Wales, is due to the Basque and Welsh determination not to allow their languages to be destroyed. This determination also feeds the flames in Ireland for among the many indignities the Irish have been forced to undergo at English hands is the English contempt for their language.

4   It goes without saying, then, that language is also a political instrument, means, and proof of power. It is the most vivid and crucial key to identity: it reveals the private identity, and connects one with, or divorces one from, the larger, public, or communal identity. There have been, and are, times, and places, when to speak a certain language could be dangerous, even fatal. Or, one may speak the same language, but in such a way that one's antecedents are revealed, or (one hopes) hidden. This is true in France, and is absolutely true in England: The range (and reign) of accents on that damp little island make England coherent for the English and totally incomprehensible for everyone else. To open your mouth in England is (if I may use black English) to "put your business in the street": You have confessed your parents, your youth, your school, your salary, your self-esteem, and alas, your future.

5   Now, I do not know what white Americans would sound like if there had never been any black people in the United States, but they would not sound the way they sound. *Jazz,* for example, is a very specific sexual term, as in *jazz me, baby,* but white people purified it into the Jazz Age. *Sock it to me,* which means, roughly, the same thing, has been adopted by Nathaniel Hawthorne's descendants with no qualms or hesitations at all, along with *let it all hang out* and *right on!*

Beat to his socks, which was once the black's most total and despair-ing image of poverty, was transformed into a thing called the Beat Generation, which phenomenon was, largely, composed of *uptight,* middle-class white people, imitating poverty, trying to *get down,* to get *with it,* doing their *thing,* doing their despairing best to be *funky,* which we, the blacks, never dreamed of doing—we *were* funky, baby, like *funk* was going out of style.

6   Now, no one can eat his cake, and have it, too, and it is late in the day to attempt to penalize black people for having created a lan-guage that permits the nation its only glimpse of reality, a language without which the nation would be even more *whipped* than it is.

7   I say that this present skirmish is rooted in American history, and it is. Black English is the creation of the black diaspora. Blacks came to the United States chained to each other, but from different tribes: Neither could speak the other's language. If two black people, at that bitter hour of the world's history, had been able to speak to each other, the institution of chattel slavery could never have lasted as long as it did. Subsequently, the slave was given, under the eye, and the gun, of his master, Congo Square, and the Bible—or, in other words, and under these conditions, the slave began the formation of the black church, and it is within this unprecedented tabernacle that black English began to be formed. This was not, merely, as in the European example, the adoption of a foreign tongue, but an alchemy that transformed ancient elements into a new language: *A language comes into existence by means of brutal necessity, and the rules of the language are dictated by what the language must convey.*

8   There was a moment, in time, and in this place, when my brother, or my mother, or my father, or my sister, had to convey to me, for ex-ample, the danger in which I was standing from the white man standing just behind me, and to convey this with a speed, and in a language, that the white man could not possibly understand, and that, indeed, he cannot understand, until today. He cannot afford to understand it. This understanding would reveal to him too much about himself, and smash that mirror before which he has been frozen for so long.

9   Now, if this passion, this skill, this (to quote Toni Morrison) "sheer intelligence," this incredible music, the mighty achievement of having brought a people utterly unknown to, or despised by "history"—to have brought this people to their present, troubled, troubling, and unassailable and unanswerable place—if this absolutely unprecedented journey does not indicate that black English is a language, I am curious to know what definition of language is to be trusted.

10   A people at the center of the Western world, and in the midst of so hostile a population, has not endured and transcended by means of

what is patronizingly called a "dialect." We, the blacks, are in trouble, certainly, but we are not doomed, and we are not inarticulate because we are not compelled to defend a morality that we know to be a lie.

11   The brutal truth is that the bulk of the white people in America never had any interest in educating black people, except as this could serve white purposes. It is not the black child's language that is in question, it is not his language that is despised: It is his experience. A child cannot be taught by anyone who despises him, and a child cannot afford to be fooled. A child cannot be taught by anyone whose demand, essentially, is that the child repudiate his experience, and all that gives him sustenance, and enter a limbo in which he will no longer be black, and in which he knows that he can never become white. Black people have lost too many black children that way.

12   And, after all, finally, in a country with standards so untrustworthy, a country that makes heroes of so many criminal mediocrities, a country unable to face why so many of the nonwhite are in prison, or on the needle, or standing, futureless, in the streets—it may very well be that both the child, and his elder, have concluded that they have nothing whatever to learn from the people of a country that has managed to learn so little.

Understanding the Content

Feel free to reread all or parts of the selection to answer the following questions.

1. What reasons does Baldwin give for calling black English a language?

2. Baldwin says that "language is also a political instrument, means, and proof of power" (4). What does he mean?

3. What are some of the words Baldwin claims Americans would not speak if it were not for black English?

4. What is Baldwin's definition of language?

Looking at Structure and Style

1. Describe Baldwin's tone and attitude. What words, phrases, or passages help develop both?

2. What is the function of paragraphs 2 and 3? What paragraph patterns are used?

3. What is the purpose of paragraph 8? How does it help develop Baldwin's viewpoint and attitude?

4. How does Baldwin's title reflect his thesis? What is his thesis?

Evaluating the Author's Viewpoints

1. Reread paragraph 6. What does Baldwin mean by penalizing "black people for having created a language that permits the nation its only glimpse of reality"? Do you agree? Explain.

2. Do you agree with Baldwin's definition of language? Explain.

3. Reread paragraph 12. Do you agree with Baldwin's final comments? Why or why not?

Pursuing Possible Essay Topics

Before writing an essay in response to any ideas you may have after reading James Baldwin's essay, wait until you have read the following essay by Rachel Jones, "What's Wrong with Black English."

Preparing to Read

Take a minute or two to look over the following reading selection. Note the title and author, read the opening paragraph, and check the essay's length. Make certain you have the time now to read it carefully and to do the exercises that follow it. Then, in the spaces provided, answer the following questions.

1. What do you think the author means by "black English"? _____

_____

2. Do you think the essay will deal with what is "wrong" with black English?

Explain. _____

_____

3. What do you think the essay has to do with cultural heritage, the subject of

this chapter? _____

_____

Vocabulary

Good comprehension of what you are about to read depends upon your understanding of the words below. The number following each word refers to the paragraph where it is used.

linguist (1) a specialist in the study of the nature and structure of human speech

patois (1) regional dialect, substandard speech

peers (2) equals

L. Frank Baum (3) author of *The Wonderful Wizard of Oz*

Ray Bradbury (3) author of numerous science fiction stories and novels, among them *Fahrenheit 451* and *The Martian Chronicles*

doggedly (4) stubbornly, relentlessly

Valley Girl jargon (5) slang and speech pattern attributed to teenage girls living in the San Fernando Valley

articulate (6) clear and expressive in speech

staples (6) major parts

academic abstractions (6) intellectual, theoretical discussions

Malcolm X, Martin Luther King, Jr. (7) black civil rights leaders, both victims of assassination

Toni Morrison, Alice Walker, James Baldwin (7) famous contemporary black authors (Morrison, *Beloved*; Walker, *The Color Purple*; Baldwin, *Go Tell It on the Mountain*)

ethnic dialects (8) speech patterns of a particular cultural group

What's Wrong with Black English

Rachel L. Jones

1   William Labov, a noted linguist, once said about the use of black English, "It is the goal of most black Americans to acquire full control of the standard language without giving up their own culture." He also suggested that there are certain advantages to having two ways to express one's feelings. I wonder if the good doctor might also consider the goals of those black Americans who have full control of standard English but who are every now and then troubled by that colorful, grammar-to-the-winds patois that is black English. Case in point—me.

2   I'm a 21-year-old black born to a family that would probably be considered lower-middle class—which in my mind is a polite way of describing a condition only slightly better than poverty. Let's just say we rarely if ever did the winter-vacation thing in the Caribbean. I've often had to defend my humble beginnings to a most unlikely group

of people for an even less likely reason. Because of the way I look at me sideways and ask, "Why do you talk like you're white?"

3   The first time it happened to me I was nine years old. Cornered in the school bathroom by the class bully and her sidekick, I was offered the opportunity to swallow a few of my teeth unless I satisfactorily explained why I always got good grades, why I talked "proper" or "white." I had no ready answer for her, save the fact that my mother had from the time I was old enough to talk stressed the importance of reading and learning, or that L. Frank Baum and Ray Bradbury were my closest companions. I read all my older brothers' and sisters' literature textbooks more faithfully than they did, and even lightweights like the Bobbsey Twins and Trixie Belden were allowed into my bookish inner circle. I don't remember exactly what I told those girls, but I somehow talked my way out of a beating.

4   I was reminded once again of my "white pipes" problem while apartment hunting in Evanston, Illinois, last winter. I doggedly made out lists of available places and called all around. I would immediately be invited over—and immediately turned down. The thinly concealed looks of shock when the front door opened clued me in, along with the flustered instances of "just getting off the phone with the girl who was ahead of you and she wants the rooms." When I finally found a place to live, my roommate stirred up old memories when she remarked a few months later, "You know, I was surprised when I first saw you. You sounded white over the phone." Tell me another one, sister.

5   I should've asked her a question I've wanted an answer to for years: how does one "talk white"? The silly side of me pictures a rabid white foam spewing forth when I speak. I don't use Valley Girl jargon, so that's not what's meant in my case. Actually, I've pretty much deduced what people mean when they say that to me, and the implications are really frightening.

6   It means that I'm articulate and well-versed. It means that I can talk as freely about John Steinbeck as I can about Rick James. It means that "ain't" and "he be" are not staples of my vocabulary and are only used around family and friends. (It is almost Jekyll and Hydeish the way I can slip out of academic abstractions into a long, lean, double-negative-filled dialogue, but I've come to terms with that aspect of my personality.) As a child, I found it hard to believe that's what people meant by "talking proper"; that would've meant that good grades and standard English were equated with white skin, and that went against everything I'd ever been taught. Running into the same type of mentality as an adult has confirmed the depressing reality that for many blacks, standard English is not only unfamiliar, it is socially unacceptable.

7   James Baldwin once defended black English by saying it had added "vitality to the language," and even went so far as to label it a language

in its own right, saying, "Language [i.e., black English] is a political instrument" and a "vivid and crucial key to identity." But did Malcolm X urge blacks to take power in this country "any way y'all can"? Did Martin Luther King, Jr. say to blacks, "I has been to the mountaintop, and I done seed the Promised Land"? Toni Morrison, Alice Walker and James Baldwin did not achieve their eloquence, grace and stature by using only black English in their writing. Andrew Young, Tom Bradley and Barbara Jordan did not acquire political power by saying, "Y'all crazy if you ain't gon vote for me." They all have full command of standard English, and I don't think that knowledge takes away from their blackness or commitment to black people.

8   I know from experience that it's important for black people, stripped of culture and heritage, to have something they can point to and say, "This is ours, *we* can comprehend it, *we* alone can speak it with a soulful flourish." I'd be lying if I said that the rhythms of my people caught up in "some serious rap" don't sound natural and right to me sometimes. But how heartwarming is it for those same brothers when they hit the pavement searching for employment? Studies have proven that the use of ethnic dialects decreases power in the marketplace. "I be" is acceptable on the corner, but not with the boss.

9   Am I letting capitalistic, European-oriented thinking fog the issue? Am I selling out blacks to an ideal of assimilating, being as much like whites as possible? I have not formed a personal political ideology, but I do know this: it hurts me to hear black children use black English, knowing that they will be at yet another disadvantage in an educational system already full of stumbling blocks. It hurts me to sit in lecture halls and hear fellow black students complain that the professor "be tripping dem out using big words dey can't understand." And what hurts most is to be stripped of my own blackness simply because I know my way around the English language.

10   I would have to disagree with Labov in one respect. My goal is not so much to acquire full control of both standard and black English, but to one day see more black people less dependent on a dialect that excludes them from full participation in the world we live in. I don't think I talk white, I think I talk right.

Understanding the Content

Feel free to reread all or parts of the selection to answer the following questions.

1. What is Jones's position toward "black English"?

2. What reasons or support does Jones give for her argument? Are they valid reasons?

3. What do people mean when they accuse Jones of "talking white"?

4. What is Jones's rebuttal to James Baldwin's defense of black English as being a "political instrument" and a "crucial key to identity" (7)?

5. Does Jones have anything positive to say about black English?

6. Does Jones agree or disagree with the linguist Labov?

Looking at Structure and Style

1. Is the thesis stated or implied? If stated, where?

2. For what reasons does Jones begin and end her essay with a quote from and reference to William Labov, "a noted linguist"? Is this an effective writing method? Explain.

3. What is the importance of paragraph 2 to Jones's argument? Is it important that she provides this information? Why?

4. What is the function of paragraphs 3 and 4?

5. In paragraph 9, Jones asks two rhetorical questions. How well does she answer them?

6. For what reason does Jones begin paragraph 9 with questions? To what audience is she directing the questions?

7. Even if you were not familiar with Andrew Young, Tom Bradley, or Barbara Jordan, mentioned in paragraph 7, what can you infer about them from the context?

8. Describe Jones's tone.

Evaluating the Author's Viewpoints

1. Jones says, "Studies have proven that the use of ethnic dialects decreases power in the marketplace" (8). Do you agree? Should Jones have provided the names of the studies to verify her statement?

2. James Baldwin disagrees with Jones regarding black English. Whose argument is more convincing to you? Explain.

3. Jones asks in paragraph 9, "Am I letting capitalistic, European-oriented thinking fog the issue?" What does she mean? How do you answer her question?

4. Jones says her goal is "to one day see more black people less dependent on a dialect that excludes them from full participation in the world we live in" (10). Do you think that not speaking standard English excludes people from full participation in the world we live in? Does this apply only to blacks? Explain your views.

Pursuing Possible Essay Topics

1. Pick either Jones's or Baldwin's position on black English and support or refute it.

2. Discuss the need for everyone in the United States to know standard English, regardless of his or her cultural heritage. If you disagree, take the opposite viewpoint.

3. React to the idea that knowing one's ethnic language is a "vivid and crucial key to identity."

4. Because of the large Hispanic and Asian population now in the United States, many states provide voter information, driver's license applications and tests, and public transportation information in other languages. Argue for or against this practice. What effect will expanding or abolishing such a practice have on our society?

5. Should people who immigrate to the United States be required to learn English before being admitted? Support your viewpoint.

6. It's predicted that large cities, such as Los Angeles, Miami, and New York, will soon have more Spanish speakers than English speakers. Write an essay on what effects this will have or already is having in such areas.

7. Brainstorm or freewrite on one or more of the following:
   a. black English
   b. ethnic dialects
   c. rapping
   d. language and culture
   e. your own speech
   f. bilingualism

8. If these lack appeal, find your own topic on some aspect of cultural heritage.

Student Essay

Read the following narrative essay written by a student who is in the process of learning English as a second language. As you read, look for answers to these questions:

1. Does the essay's subject fit the assignment to write about some aspect of cultural heritage?

2. How well does the narrative hold your interest?

3. Is the thesis clear and supported well?

Coming to America

Hieu Huynh

1   My coming to America in 1979 was not very pleasant. When
I was twelve, my parents had to leave my homeland, Vietnam.
We lived near My Tho all my years and I did not want to
leave, but they said we must. My two sisters were younger,
four and seven, and they did not know what it meant to
leave. My mother said that we must not tell any of our
friends, that our going was a secret. It was hard for me to
think I would never see my home or some of my family again.
Some of my story I tell here I remember well, but some is
not clear and is from stories my family tells.

2   I was very sad the day we left my house. We could not
take many things with us because we did not want the
authorities to know we were trying to leave Vietnam. So we
pretended that we were visiting my mother's sister and
husband who lived in a fishing village in the Mekong
Delta. Many times we were stopped by soldiers and
officials who wanted to know where we were going. My
sisters and I were afraid often. Finally, we reached their
village.

3   We stayed there for several days. Our four cousins
played with us and we did not really know what the family
was planning. But after a few days, we were awakened one
night and told to be quiet. My family, along with my uncle
and aunt and cousins, all boarded a smelly fishing boat.
The children were all told to go inside and sleep. There
were already other people I did not know on the boat, but I
found room for my sisters and they were tired and went to
sleep. I couldn't because of all the hushed talking and I
sensed fear.

4   Soon the boat started moving. It was still night and I
wondered how anyone could see where the boat was going.
Everyone was very quiet. I remember feeling sick from the
smell of the boat and the smell of fear. When light broke,

I felt the boat stop and many loud voices up above. Soon, my mother and two other women came down in the boat and went through our things, taking out gold and silver pieces. They whispered to be still and went back up. Soon we were moving again. I learned later that my parents had to pay much gold and silver to the harbor authorities in order to let us continue.

5   I forget how many days we tossed about on the ocean. Almost everyone got sick. There was not much water so we had to drink sparingly. The boat leaked because it was old and the water was sometimes very rough. We could not always cook food. Sometimes we only ate uncooked rice. The younger children cried a lot. I wanted to but did not. My parents said I must be brave for my sisters.

6   The next part of the story I do not like to tell. A large boat with Thai men who had guns and knives stopped us and made us all go on their ship. They were very mean to everybody. They ripped at our clothes thinking that we might be hiding money and jewelry, which we were. When they found some gold in one woman's blouse, they made all of us take off our clothes. When my father and other men tried to stop them, they shot a man I didn't know. They hit my father with a gun and made us all get on our knees. The evil men were shouting and my sisters were screaming and crying for my mother, but she told us to do as the men say. I could not believe all this was happening. It was so terrible it did not seem real. But it was.

7   After they ripped up our clothes and took our valuables, they told all the men and children to go back to our boat. They threw the man they shot into the water and we never saw him again. They kept my mother and two other women on their boat. We could hear them weeping and we called to her, afraid we would never see her again. My father made all the children go down into the boat. He put his arms

around us and he cried silently. Later, the women were put back on our boat and we were happy to see her alive. But she was never the same after that happened.

8   One or two days later one of the women died and it was decided to throw the body overboard. Her children cried and wanted to be thrown overboard too, but their father held them tight.

9   We all thought we would die soon on the ocean. But a Malaysian police boat found us. They were not nice, but they didn't harm us. Of course we had nothing left to be taken, and I think my mother no longer cared what happened. But they took us to Bidong Island where thousands of other refugees like us had already been taken.

10   We spent many months there. It was not easy and food was scarce. There was not much water to go around. People were sick and dying. I got sick myself and often did not know what was happening.

11   Finally, our family was interviewed by authorities. Fortunately, my father's older brother was already in the United States. Somehow things worked out, and our family finally arrived in America. But getting here was not easy. We are all some happier, but there is a part of our lives we would like to never remember again.

Reaction

In your journal or on a separate sheet of paper, write your reaction to the student essay. What would you tell this student about his essay?

On the Net

By just typing in the keywords "cultural heritage," you will be given a comprehensive list of sites related to just about every culture in the world. The search we did generated a list of more than one million sites.

Explore your own cultural heritage or a heritage about which you would like to learn more. Do your research exclusively on the

Internet by finding articles and looking at various sites that offer good information about that particular culture. Keep a list of the sites and take notes on new things that you learn.

Answer the following questions:

1. How many sites did you visit?

2. Do you think the information on the sites was reliable? Why or why not?

3. Of the sites you visited, which ones were the most helpful? Why?

4. Which sites would you not visit again? Why?

5. What are three new things that you discovered while surfing the Web?

Or, gather additional information on Thomas Jefferson, Sally Hemings, the Westerinens, or the Monticello Association. Look at different sites and write a short essay either defending the right of the Westerinens to join the Monticello Association or against their bid to join. Use facts and details culled from the sites you visit.

6

Viewpoints on Some Social Concerns

FOCUS ON SOME SOCIAL CONCERNS

To help you focus on the subject of this chapter, answer the following questions. You may want to write the answers in your journal or be prepared to discuss them in class.

1. Read the quotation by Karl Menninger on the opposite page. What do you think he means? Do you feel responsibility for all your actions, or do you tend to place blame on others or on circumstances? Explain.

2. Look at the photograph on the opposite page. What do you think is happening? What is your reaction? Explain.

3. What is it about the photo that leads you to believe it illustrates a social concern or problem?

4. What are some concerns and problems that society seems to be facing today? What can you do about them? What is your responsibility as a citizen?

*"My proposal is for the revival or reasser-
tion of personal responsibility in all human
acts, good and bad."*

—Karl Menninger

opinion

Steven Rubin/The Image Works

Voca Quiz
P 222   p 227   p231

BEIJING, CHINA   A farmer who stole the head of a 3rd-century B.C. terra-
cotta warrior and tried to sell it for $81,000 has been sentenced to death, an
official Chinese newspaper reported Saturday.

SAN FRANCISCO   A man convicted and sentenced to prison for raping a
young girl, then cutting off her arms and leaving her to die, was released today after serving three years of a twenty-year sentence.

In our society most of us probably feel that a death sentence for stealing the head
of a statue is too severe, while letting a man free after serving only a three-year
term for raping and mutilating a child seems an outrage. But regardless of our reactions, the newspaper items reflect the social values of two different cultures.

As we live and grow, we learn the culture of the society in which we live.
Sociologist Rodney Stark, in his book *Sociology,* tells us that the most significant
elements of culture that we must learn are values, norms, and roles. Stark defines
values thus: "The values of a culture identify its ideals—its ultimate aims and
most general standards for assessing good and bad or desirable and undesirable.
When we say people need self-respect, dignity, and freedom . . . we are invoking
values." While values are rather general, **norms** are quite specific. "They are rules
of governing behavior," Stark says. "Norms define what behavior is required, acceptable, or prohibited in particular circumstances. Norms indicate that a person
should, ought, or must act (or not act) in a certain way." A collection of these
norms connected with a particular position in a society is called a **role.** For instance, each of us has "a relatively clearly defined role to fulfill: student, friend,
woman, husband, shopper, pedestrian, cop, nun, bartender, wife, and so on."
Thus, values, norms, and roles are connected.

How we think and act in the various roles we play is based on our society's values and norms. For instance, we generally expect a minister's behavior to follow
certain norms: no smoking, no sexually deviant behavior, no using bad language,
no wearing swim trunks while delivering a Sunday sermon. At the same time,
your role while attending a church service is composed of certain norms: no playing your Walkman during the service, no shouting at friends across the aisle, no
removing money from the collection plate.

History shows us that Americans have always been concerned with moral values. Chapters in textbooks are devoted to issues of right and wrong. Today we
wonder how belief systems could ever have permitted the hanging of people as
witches in Salem, the once widespread acceptance of slavery, the disregard for
the rights of Native Americans, the long denial of voting rights and working privileges for women, the overt discrimination toward Jews and other religious
groups, the racial segregation from drinking fountains to schoolrooms, and the
"blacklisting" and labeling as communists those who spoke out against government policies in the 1950s. Yet, at various times in our society, such norms were
considered acceptable social behavior.

More recently, our society has had to deal with the social clashes caused by
our involvement in Vietnam, the Watergate and Iran-Contra scandals, our

presence in the Persian Gulf and Central America, attitudes toward gay rights, prayer in public schools, AIDS, abortion, and definitions of pornography and censorship, just to name a few. Disagreements over issues such as these create conflicts within our society that force us to re-examine our social values, norms, and roles. Doing so often brings about a change in attitudes and values from generation to generation. What was acceptable and valued in society yesterday may not be today. What is acceptable today may not be tomorrow. And vice versa.

The following reading selections reflect some viewpoints and reactions to some current social concerns. Use them to practice your critical reading skills and to stimulate your own thinking regarding social issues and values.

Preparing to Read

Take a minute or two to look over the following reading selection. Note the title and the author, read the opening paragraph, and check the essay's length. Make certain you have the time now to read it carefully and to do the exercises that follow it. Then, in the spaces provided, answer the following questions.

1. What do you think the title means?_____

_____

2. What is the subject of this essay?_____

_____

3. What is the author's attitude toward the subject of the essay?_____

_____

Vocabulary

Good comprehension of what you are about to read depends upon your understanding of the words below. The number following each word refers to the paragraph where it is used.

speculated (4) contemplated, theorized

fudged (6) embellished, overstated

accountability (10) answerability, responsibility

endeavor (18) try earnestly

cynicism (18) scornful attitude or quality

expediency (19) suitability, desirability
negotiate (26) settle, arrange for, haggle
ideology (32) beliefs, philosophy

Ethical Tightrope

JIM LICHTMAN

1   It started with a question.

2   I had just finished speaking to a group of businessmen about the need for a greater commitment to ethical standards in our lives. According to the Josephson Institute of Ethics, there have been more ethics scandals in the last five years than in the previous five decades combined.

3   At the end of the talk, one man raised his hand and asked: "How did we get in this mess?"

4   "Maybe," I speculated, "we lost our sense of purpose. Maybe we've forgotten what we once stood for." Our idealism, our spirit seemed to be centered in our collective purpose. We were a nation of people, who pulled together, supported one another and overcame any obstacle.

5   "Americanism," Teddy Roosevelt once said, "means the virtues of courage, honor, justice, truth, sincerity and hardihood." Those are strong words, proud words, words that define a country—its people and its purpose. But where is that purpose today? We seem to be more focused on obtaining rock-hard abs than rock-hard ethical standards.

6   Somewhere in our search for the good life, for our families and ourselves, we compromised. Not all at once, but in little ways and over many years. We fudged the numbers. Not a lot. Just a little bit because we had a deadline to meet. Or we took advantage of information, not for ourselves perhaps but for a worthy organization. We told lies of convenience that we thought wouldn't hurt anybody until slowly, little by little, we justified, rationalized and compromised what we once stood for.

7   If Mr. Roosevelt's words seemed to define us as a country, the rest of his quote may appear surprisingly prophetic. "The things that will destroy America are prosperity-at-any-price, peace-at-any-price, safety-first instead of duty first, the love of soft living and the get-rich-quick theory of life."

8   If we are ever going to return to the standards we once had, we're going to have to stop the relentless need to finger-point and blame and begin to take a good look in the mirror and ask ourselves what we stand for.

9   Then, we need to take action.

10   First, we need to commit to a set of standards that we know to be right. The Ten Commandments and Golden Rule are a good start but they should also reflect a commitment to accountability and a sincere desire to strive to do our best in all circumstances.

11   Second, we need to raise our awareness of ethics in the decisions we make on a daily basis: are we treating people honestly, fairly, with respect and consideration? Ben Franklin said, "The noblest question in the world is, what good may I do in it?" Ethics is not about what we say or what we intend. It's about what we do. And how we utilize our principles in small ways, as well as those that challenge the courage of our convictions, will determine the purpose and course of our lives.

12   Third, we need to cultivate a culture of cooperation. We need to focus less on rights and more on the responsibilities we have to each other. So many times people fail to take into account the effect their decisions have on others. In an interview about the 1996 Everest tragedy, climber Jon Krakauer observed, ". . . we were a bunch of individuals who liked each other . . . and got along well enough, but we never had this feeling that we were all in it together. . . . We were all in it for ourselves when we should have been in it for each other."

13   But we can change that. And that change begins when we are willing to stand up and stand for our highest aspirations.

14   Does this sound unrealistic; too idealistic?

15   Speaking to a group of executives from a large retail industry, the president of one company came up to me afterwards and said, "Sitting out there listening to you, I was wondering—is this guy living in the real world? Does he have any clue about the competitive pressures we face? Then I thought, what if I caught one of my own people fudging the numbers, deceiving me about our business in order to meet a goal? That's when I realized how important my example and the example set forth by my managers is to our long-term success."

16   I'm not saying this is easy. Good character is formed by living under conditions that demand good conduct. But let's try this—

17   Let's try working together in a truly cooperative way with others.

18   Let's endeavor to look, as Lincoln said, "to the better angles of our nature" without the cynicism of "waiting for the other shoe to drop."

19   Let's strive to demonstrate the courage of our convictions instead of giving in to the expediency of short-term gains.

20   Let's try to become a little more heroic in our own lives instead of looking to others.

21   Let's criticize less and inspire more.

22   Let's understand that we may not get all the business that we might want, but that the people we do work with will get the highest level of talent, performance and integrity possible.

23   Let's recognize that we can be honest and fair and still be tough.

24   Let's try to take responsibility more seriously than we take ourselves.

25   Let's try elevating a reputation for honor as much as we honor elevating the bottom line.

26   And let's understand that we may be able to negotiate many things, but we will never negotiate our integrity.

27   We can achieve all these things and get the job done, if we think before we act; treat others as we want to be treated.

28   We can, if we remember that it's okay to be skeptical but destructive to be relentlessly cynical because it damages the long-term ideal that we can always be better than we are.

29   We can, if we remember that we are all in this together and that "This country," as Teddy Roosevelt reminds us, "will not be a good place for any of us to live in, unless we make it a good place for all of us to live in."

30   We can, if we embrace compassion not as a catch phrase but as the universal truth that it is and the individual value of seeing ourselves in another that is so critical to our progress.

31   And when we get tired and feel swallowed-up by the endless details of our lives, believing that nothing we do will ever make a difference, we need to consider Mother Teresa's reminder that, "We are not called to do great things, only little things with great love."

32   Ethical principles such as honesty, fairness, loyalty, responsibility, compassion and moral courage are global in their application and universal in their truth. They do not belong to any political, ethnic, or religious ideology; they belong to all of us. And they need to be embraced by all of us if we are ever to find meaningful solutions to the challenges we face to our convictions. But how to do this seems to be the tough question.

33   One way is to follow the words of the ancient Greek philosopher, Socrates. "The greatest way to live with honor is to be what we pretend to be."

Understanding the Content

Feel free to reread all or parts of the selection to answer the following questions.

1. Summarize the author's response to the question "How did we get in this mess?"

2. How does the author feel that we, as Americans, have "compromised," or "fudged the numbers"?

3. How did Teddy Roosevelt define "Americanism"? What did he think would "destroy America"?

4. According to the author, what are the three things we need to do to return to the "standards we once had"?

5. How does the author think that good character is formed?

6. According to the author, what are "global in their application and universal in their truth"?

Looking at Structure and Style

1. The author uses four sources to support his views. Are they valid sources? Are all of the sources suitable examples to support his thesis? Why or why not?

2. What is the author's thesis? Is it stated or implied? If stated, where?

3. How effective is paragraph 33 as a concluding paragraph? Does it accurately summarize the main point of this essay? Why or why not?

4. Why does the author use two examples from speeches given to business executives? How do these examples help to bring the message of this essay to light?

5. What is Lichtman's attitude toward the subject of ethics? What is his tone?

6. Summarize, in your own words, the advice given by the author in paragraphs 17–26.

7. What is the purpose of paragraph 6?

Evaluating the Author's Viewpoints

1. Do you disagree or agree with the author's statement in paragraph 8? Why or why not?

2. What does the statement included in paragraph 33 mean: "The greatest way to live with honor is to be what we pretend to be"? Do you agree or disagree?

3. What piece of advice given by Lichtman in this selection resonates with you the most? Why?

4. Is this essay by Lichtman written in a subjective or objective way? Why?

5. Why do you think this selection is entitled "Ethical Tightrope"?

Pursuing Possible Essay Topics

1. Brainstorm or freewrite on one or more of the following topics:

   a. ethical principles   d. idealism   g. loyalty
   b. morality   e. honesty
   c. immorality   f. fairness

2. Of the following ethical principles listed by Lichtman in the selection—honesty, fairness, loyalty, responsibility, compassion, and moral courage—which do you value most and why? Write an essay discussing why you value this ethical principle over all others.

3. What sort of ethical standards do you look for in friends? Why? Write an essay describing your best friend and his or her moral code.

4. What kind of ethical standard have you set for yourself? How easy is it to live to a high moral standard?

5. Write an essay reacting to Mother Teresa's statement "We are not called to do great things, only little things with great love."

6. Do you think, like Lichtman, that ethical principles "need to be embraced by all of us if we are ever to find meaningful solutions to the challenges we face to our convictions"? Why or why not? Write an essay defending your viewpoint.

7. How important do you think it is to "see ourselves in another"?

8. Ignore these possible topics and write your own essay on ethics or ethical principles.

 ## Preparing to Read

Take a minute or two to look over the following reading selection. Note the title and author, read the first two paragraphs, and check the essay's length. Make certain you have the time now to read it carefully and to do the exercises that follow it. Then, in the spaces provided, answer the following questions.

1. What is your opinion of the "Y generation"? _____

_____

_____

2. Based on the title, what do you think this essay will be about? _____

_____

_____

3. Why do you think the author uses the results of a survey in the opening paragraph? Is this an effective way to get the reader's attention? _____

_____

_____

Vocabulary

Good comprehension of what you are about to read depends upon your understanding of the words below. The number following each word refers to the paragraph where it is used.

rattled (1) upset

hellions (2) troublesome or mischievous people

crusade (5) something undertaken with enthusiasm and zeal

estranged (7) removed from associations

solace (7) relief, consolation

arsenals (8) collections of weapons

[Fri. Dec 16th
11:30 AM - 1:30 PM]

Final

Keeping Faith in Kids

DAVID GERGEN

1   All across the country, people are rattled about teenagers. A national survey by Public Agenda, published early this month, found that 74 percent of parents described kids these days as "rude," "irresponsible," and "wild." Only 40 percent said these children will grow up to make America a better place. And this survey was taken even before kids began cutting down their classmates at Littleton and Conyers.

2   Are we really raising a nation of hellions? What's wrong with the Y generation?

3   The truth is that most kids these days are not the problem we think. If anything, they will one day prove to be the answer—because this generation is much healthier than the gloomy headlines in recent weeks would suggest.

4   In the *New Republic* earlier this year, Gregg Easterbrook pointed out some encouraging trends. In 1980, 72 percent of high school seniors said they had been drinking alcohol recently; by 1998, that

figure had dropped to 52 percent. Drug usage, especially marijuana, is down as well. Teen pregnancy rates have been falling since 1991 and most recently were at the same level as in 1980. Homicides remain historically high among teens, but striking improvements have come in big cities like New York, Boston, and Los Angeles.

Creating a Crusade

5   Meanwhile, young people by the droves are signing up as volunteers in their communities. In the past five years alone, 100,000 have enlisted in AmeriCorps—more than the Peace Corps had in its first 20 years. Last week, in his annual report on "America's Promise," Gen. Colin Powell spoke glowingly about the number of teenagers as well as adults who are volunteering to work with children. He thinks the country can create not just a movement but a crusade.

6   Eric Harris and Dylan Klebold may have seared their images into our imagination after killing classmates at Columbine High. But the more representative member of their generation, now hailed by churches everywhere, was Cassie Bernall. She was the young lady sought out by one of the killers, who put a gun to her head while she was praying and asked if she still believed in God. "Yes," said Cassie, knowing she would die for her answer.

7   America does have a serious problem, but it's not the younger generation. It's the sickness that has crept into our soul. We have a culture that leaves many people feeling estranged, their dignity destroyed, and this can lead to extreme antisocial behavior by those who can't find solace in their friends or family.

8   Every generation, no matter how good, has had its share of loners, misfits, and plain old wackos. When many of us were growing up, these social outcasts vented their frustrations with fists or knives. Now they can break into gun arsenals their folks keep at home; their heads are filled with violent pictures they have seen on television and in movies; their hard drives are filled with pornography that floods across the Internet.

9   If there is a silver lining in Littleton and Conyers, maybe it will come because we change our minds about the way we should live together. Congress, at least, finally seems to understand that guns are like cars: Adults should have a right to them, but society has a right to protect itself against their dangers and to keep them strictly out of the hands of kids. With luck, we will apply the same kind of common sense to the violence and pornography that pollute our popular entertainment.

10   Three quarters of teenagers say they don't belong to outside clubs and just "hang around" after school. That, too, should change. Powell said last week about the killers at Columbine: "If only we had gotten them involved in something else where their talent and their energy could have been directed to helping others, perhaps this tragedy could have been avoided." Right on.

11   It's time to see our kids for who they truly are. Most of them are not rude, wild, and irresponsible; in fact, most of them could one day make this country an immensely better place. But all of them still need a caring, compassionate adult in daily life, helping them grow up to become all they can be.

Understanding the Content

Feel free to reread all or parts of the selection to answer the following questions.

1. Who is the "Y generation"? How are they viewed by the majority of parents in America?

2. What are some of the trends that the author lists as evidence that the Y generation is not as bad as some people think?

3. The author states that "America does have a serious problem." What is it?

4. What, according to the author, is the "silver lining" of the incidents that took place in Littleton, Colorado, and Conyers, Georgia?

5. What do three-quarters of American teenagers do after school?

6. What does the author think teenagers need to "grow up to become all they can be"?

Looking at Structure and Style

1. What is the author's thesis? Is it stated or implied?

2. How does the author use statistics to support his thesis?

3. What is the function of paragraph 2? Is it effective in setting the tone for the essay?

4. How do paragraphs 5 and 6 support the author's thesis?

5. Does the author effectively support the conclusion that he states in paragraph 11? How?

Evaluating the Author's Viewpoints

1. The author does not think that the future of our teens is as grim as some people would have us think. Do you agree? Why or why not?

2. Do you agree with the author that "America does have a serious problem, but it's not the younger generation"? Why or why not? If you agree, what is the serious problem that America has, in your own words?

3. Why does the author have faith in the Y generation? Do you agree with him in his assessment of today's youth?

4. How do you think the author feels about gun control?

5. Do you think the author agrees or disagrees with the opinions held by General Colin Powell? Why or why not?

6. What does the author think contributes to society's "share of loners, misfits, and plain old wackos"?

Pursuing Possible Essay Topics

1. Write an essay about your hopes for the future of the Y generation and how you think they as a group can contribute to society.

2. Write a paper outlining steps that we as a society can take to ensure the success and growth of future generations.

3. Write a paper persuading someone that gun control is

   a. the solution to the problems in our society.

   b. not the answer to the problems in our society.

4. Make a case that parents should have a device for controlling

   a. what their children see on television.

   b. what their children look at on the Internet.

5. Write a paper outlining what you think would be a good way for students to use their time after school so that they are not just "hanging around."

6. Write a paper persuading a student to volunteer his or her time at a homeless shelter after school. Discuss the rewards of volunteering.

7. Pick your own topic related to a social concern and write an essay about it.

Preparing to Read

Take a minute or two to look over the following reading selection. Note the title and author, read the opening paragraph, and check the essay's length. Make certain you have the time now to read it carefully and to do the exercises that follow it. Then, in the spaces provided, answer the following questions.

1. What do you think this essay will be about?_____

_____

2. What are the three things the author thinks we can do to make more young people vote in elections? _____

_____

3. Do you think the author agrees with the sentence "Young people aren't interested in politics and don't care enough to vote"? Why or why not? _____

_____

Vocabulary

Good comprehension of what you are about to read depends upon your understanding of the words below. The number following each word refers to the paragraph where it is used.

relevant (1) having a bearing on or connection with the matter at hand

initiative (3) the first step; the opening move

tabulated (4) condensed, listed

anonymity (6) the quality or state of being unknown or unacknowledged

coercing (6) forcing to act or think in a certain way by use of pressure, threats, or intimidation

Big Ideas for a Better America

JOHN F. KENNEDY, JR.

1   It's become an all-too familiar refrain: Young people aren't interested in politics and don't care enough to vote. Just over 30% of those under age 25 voted in the 1996 elections. But history has clearly shown—as recently as Bill Clinton's first campaign in 1992—that if young people are engaged in the political process, they will vote. So the important question is how we might make voting more convenient, appealing and relevant.

2   One way to start is to make voting more convenient. Stories from foreign lands where lines of voters wait patiently for days to vote are inspiring, but it's not going to happen here. Last year, Oregon voters approved a measure requiring that all voting be done by mail as of next year. But the downside is that the long lead time required to process all the responses requires that voters make their decision long before the campaign ends.

3   A better idea is to start an initiative to let Americans vote over the Internet. You can do about everything else over the Internet, so why not vote? In fact, California already is considering the idea, and AT&T is researching the technology to make it possible.

4   Here's how it might work: At whatever time of day they like, voters could go to a computer wherever they like—at home, at the office or in a public space such as a library. At a Web site, voters would enter a secure password and see an electronic ballot, including perhaps pictures of and information on the candidates. The votes could be tabulated instantaneously, so that once the polls close, a final count would be immediately available.

5   Such ease and efficiency would appeal most to the group that now votes least: young people, who are generally well-skilled in and have access to computers. The election last fall of Jesse Ventura as governor of Minnesota showed that young people learn about politics over the Internet. Think how many more would vote if they could do so online.

6   The major stumbling block is guaranteeing safeguards against fraud. Critics say a voter's identity cannot be verified over the Internet. It would be easy, however, to establish the same level of security used when voting in person (most locales require only a signature). Ensuring anonymity is another obstacle. AT&T says it can make it impossible to trace a ballot to the voter. And while experts say technological advances can take care of those questions, there are some problems no computer can fix. For example, there is no way to know whether an online voter has someone looking over his or her shoulder or even coercing the voter. As with Oregon's mail-in voting, new laws must prohibit such coercion.

7   Some opponents argue that online voting will take away one more civic experience Americans share. It's hard to kiss rituals goodbye, but if the result is greater participation, it's a worthwhile sacrifice. We need to develop dramatic steps to revitalize our democracy for the next century.

Understanding the Content

Feel free to reread all or parts of the selection to answer the following questions.

1. What is the author's main suggestion for making the voting process easier?

2. What are some of the problems inherent in online voting?

3. What do some opponents of online voting think is a potential shortcoming of adopting this approach?

4. What example does the author give as evidence that young people learn about politics over the Internet?

5. Which communications company says that it can ensure anonymity in the voting process?

Looking at Structure and Style

1. Is the author's thesis stated or implied? If stated, where?

2. How does paragraph 4 support paragraph 3?

3. What is the function of paragraph 5?

4. What is the function of paragraph 6?

5. Is paragraph 7 an effective concluding paragraph? Why or why not?

Evaluating the Author's Viewpoints

1. What is the author's opinion of online voting?

2. Does the author think that young people are interested in politics?

3. Does the author think that the problems inherent in online voting are insurmountable? What passages in the essay support your answer?

4. What is one of the problems the author sees with Oregon's mail-in voting?

Pursuing Possible Essay Topics

1. Write an essay either defending or arguing against the possibility of online voting.

2. Write an essay discussing whether you would ever vote online in a presidential election.

3. Write an essay encouraging young people to vote, whether it is in the traditional sense or online.

4. Write an essay persuading someone that it is his or her civic responsibility to vote.

5. Write an essay outlining some of the problems you see in the adoption of an online voting plan.

6. What ideas do you have that you think would make America a better place? Write an essay discussing some of your ideas.

7. Freewrite or brainstorm on one or more of the following:

   a. civic duty and responsibility

   b. democracy

   c. online voting

   d. young people and politics

8. Come up with your own topic on civic duty and write an essay.

Preparing to Read

Take a minute or two to look over the following reading selection. Note the title and author, read the first two paragraphs, and check the essay's length. Make certain you have the time now to read it carefully and to do the exercises that follow it. Then, in the spaces provided, answer the following questions.

1. What questions does the title raise in your mind? _____

_____

_____

2. What is an ethnic stereotype? _____

_____

_____

3. What is an overachiever? _____

_____

_____

Vocabulary

Good comprehension of what you are about to read depends upon your understanding of the words below. The number following each word refers to the paragraph where it is used.

basking (4) enjoying, thriving on the pleasure of something

limelight (4) the focus of public attention

condescending (5) snobbish, arrogant, haughty

elitist (6) pertaining to a small and privileged group

abounds (9) multiplies, appears everywhere

culinary (11) pertaining to the kitchen or cooking

metamorphose (12) change, transform, alter

bigotry (14) intolerance of others' beliefs, race, or politics

Eggs, Twinkies and Ethnic Stereotypes

JEANNE PARK

1   Who am I?

2   For Asian-American students, the answer is a diligent, hardworking and intelligent young person. But living up to this reputation has secretly haunted me.

3   The labeling starts in elementary school. It's not uncommon for a teacher to remark, "You're Asian, you're supposed to do well in math." The underlying message is, "You're Asian and you're supposed to be smarter."

4   Not to say being labeled intelligent isn't flattering, because it is, or not to deny that basking in the limelight of being top of my class isn't ego-boosting, because frankly it is. But at a certain point, the pressure became crushing. I felt as if doing poorly on my next spelling quiz would stain the exalted reputation of all Asian students forever.

5   So I continued to be an academic overachiever, as were my friends. By junior high school I started to believe I was indeed smarter. I became condescending toward non-Asians. I was a bigot; all my friends were Asians. The thought of intermingling occurred rarely if ever.

6   My elitist opinion of Asian students changed, however, in high school. As a student at what is considered one of the nation's most competitive science and math schools, I found that being on top is no longer an easy feat.

7   I quickly learned that Asian students were not smarter. How could I ever have believed such a thing? All around me are intelligent, ambitious people who are not only Asian but white, black and Hispanic.

8   Superiority complexes aside, the problem of social segregation still exists in the schools. With few exceptions, each race socializes only with its "own kind." Students see one another in the classroom, but outside the classroom there remains distinct segregation.

9   Racist lingo abounds. An Asian student who socializes only with other Asians is believed to be an Asian Supremacist or, at the very least, arrogant and closed off. Yet an Asian student who socializes

only with whites is called a "twinkie," one who is yellow on the outside but white on the inside.

10   A white teen-ager who socializes only with whites is thought of as prejudiced, yet one who socializes with Asians is considered an "egg," white on the outside and yellow on the inside.

11   These culinary classifications go on endlessly, needless to say, leaving many confused, and leaving many more fearful than ever of social experimentation. Because the stereotypes are accepted almost unanimously, they are rarely challenged. Many develop harmful stereotypes of entire races. We label people before we even know them.

12   Labels learned at a young age later metamorphose into more visible acts of racism. For example, my parents once accused and ultimately fired a Puerto Rican cashier, believing she had stolen $200 from the register at their grocery store. They later learned it was a mistake. An Asian shopkeeper nearby once beat a young Hispanic youth who worked there with a baseball bat because he believed the boy to be lazy and dishonest.

13   We all hold misleading stereotypes of people that limit us as individuals in that we cheat ourselves out of the benefits different cultures can contribute. We can grow and learn from each culture whether it be Chinese, Korean or African-American.

14   Just recently some Asian boys in my neighborhood were attacked by a group of young white boys who have christened themselves the Master Race. Rather than being angered by this act, I feel pity for this generation that lives in a state of bigotry.

15   It may be too late for our parents' generation to accept that each person can only be judged for the characteristics that set him or her apart as an individual. We, however, can do better.

Understanding the Content

Feel free to reread all or parts of the selection to answer the following questions.

1. Explain what the title means.

2. Why did Park become an overachiever?

3. What has Park's becoming an overachiever to do with her thesis? What is her thesis?

4. Why is the author against what she calls "culinary classifications"?

5. Does Park believe that Asian students are smarter than most others? Why?

6. Explain Park's comment "Labels learned at a young age later metamorphose into more visible acts of racism" (12).

Looking at Structure and Style

1. How effective is the one-sentence opening paragraph? Does the author answer her own question?

2. What is the function of paragraphs 3–5?

3. What is the function of paragraphs 6 and 7?

4. In what paragraph does Park move from discussing her dilemma to discussing a larger problem? Is the transition smooth? Explain.

5. How does Park support her statement that begins paragraph 9, "Racist lingo abounds"?

6. Explain how Park supports her topic sentence in paragraph 12.

7. To what audience does Park seem to be writing? Explain why you think so.

Evaluating the Author's Viewpoints

1. Park believes that learning ethnic stereotypes at a young age can create "more visible acts of racism." What does she mean? Do you agree? Why?

2. Do you agree with the author that we all hold misleading stereotypes of people that limit us from learning about other cultures? What stereotypes of other cultures do you have?

3. Reread the last paragraph. Is Park being too idealistic? Why?

4. What advice, if any, would you give the author if she asked for your help in revising this essay?

Pursuing Possible Essay Topics

1. Discuss any stereotypes you have of others. Where did you get these opinions? What would it take to change your mind?

2. Write an essay revealing some of the current ethnic slurs and name-calling ("racist lingo") that you have heard, similar to what Park calls "culinary classifications."

3. Pick one foreign culture, such as Chinese or Mexican, and discuss what immigrants from that culture have brought to this country that we now take for granted as "American."

4. Discuss your own social circle and explain why it is composed of the people in it.

5. Begin an essay as Park does with the question "Who am I?" and answer your question.

6. Write an essay about the stereotype most people have of your ethnic background.

7. Brainstorm or freewrite on one or more of the following:

   a. prejudice   d. skinheads

   b. stereotypes   e. intolerance

   c. bigotry   f. your neighborhood

8. If you are prejudiced against these suggestions, come up with one of your own that deals with a social issue you want to explore.

 ## Preparing to Read

Take a minute to two to look over the following reading selection. Note the title and the author, read the opening paragraph, and check the essay's length. Make certain you have the time now to read it carefully and to do the exercises that follow it. Then, in the spaces provided, answer the following questions.

1. From the title, what do you think this essay will be about?_____

   _____

2. After reading the first paragraph, is the essay about what you thought?_____

   _____

3. How does the author feel about her subject matter?_____

   _____

Vocabulary

Good comprehension of what you are about to read depends upon your understanding of the words below. The number following each word refers to the paragraph where it is used.

flourished (2) prospered, thrived, benefited

argot (3) slang, jargon

supplicants (4) beggars

dovetailed (5) combined or connected into a unified whole

contingent (6) an assembled, representative group

bureaucratic (6) managerial, central

Our Tired, Our Poor, Our Kids

ANNA QUINDLEN

1   Six people live here, in a room the size of the master bedroom in a modest suburban house. Trundles, bunk beds, dressers side by side stacked with toys, clothes, boxes, in tidy claustrophobic clutter. One woman, five children. The baby was born in a shelter. The older kids can't wait to get out of this one. Everyone gets up at 6 a.m., the little ones to go to day care, the others to school. Their mother goes out to look for an apartment when she's not going to drug-treatment meetings. "For what they pay for me to stay in a shelter I could have lived in the Hamptons," Sharanda says.

2   Here is the parallel universe that has flourished while the more fortunate were rewarding themselves for the stock split with SUVs and home additions. There is a boom market in homelessness. But these are not the men on the streets of San Francisco holding out cardboard signs to the tourists. They are children, hundreds of thousands of them, twice as likely to repeat a grade or be hospitalized and four times as likely to go hungry as the kids with a roof over their heads. Twenty years ago New York City provided emergency shelter for just under a thousand families a day; last month it had to find spaces for 10,000 children on a given night. Not since the Great Depression have this many babies, toddlers and kids had no place like home.

3   Three mothers sit in the living room of a temporary residence called Casa Rita in the Bronx and speak of this in the argot of poverty. "The landlord don't call back when they hear you got EARP," says Rosie, EARP being the Emergency Assistance Rehousing Program. "You get priority for Section 8 if you're in a shelter," says Edna, which means federal housing programs will put you higher on the list. Edna has four kids, three in foster care; she arrived at Casa Rita, she says, "with two bags and a baby." Rosie has three, they share a bathroom down the hall with two other families. Sharanda's five range in age from 13 to just over a year. Her eldest was put in the wrong grade when he changed schools. "He's humiliated, living here," his mother says.

4   All three women are anxious to move on, although they appreciate this place, where they can get shelter, get sober and keep their kids at the same time. They remember the Emergency Assistance Unit, the

city office that is the gateway to the system, where hundreds of families sit every day surrounded by their bags, where children sleep on benches until they are shuffled off dull-eyed for one night in a shelter or a motel, only to return as supplicants again the next day.

5   In another world middle-class Americans have embraced new-home starts, the stock market and the Gap. But in the world of these displaced families, problems ignored or fumbled or unforeseen during this great period of prosperity have dovetailed into an enormous subculture of children who think that only rich people have their own bedrooms. Twenty years ago, when the story of the homeless in American became a staple of news reporting, the solution was presented as a simple one: affordable housing. That's still true, now more than ever. Two years ago the National Low Income Housing Coalition calculated that the hourly income necessary to afford the average two-bedroom apartment was around $12. That's more than twice the minimum wage.

6   The result is that in many cities police officers and teachers cannot afford to live where they work, that in Las Vegas old motels provide housing for casino employees, that in shelters now there is a contingent of working poor who get up off their cots and go off to their jobs. The result is that if you are evicted for falling behind on your rent, if there is a bureaucratic foul-up in your welfare check or the factory in which you work shuts down, the chances of finding another place to live are very small indeed. You're one understanding relative, one paycheck, one second chance from the street. And so are your kids.

7   So-called welfare reform, which emphasizes cutbacks and make-work, has played a part in all this. A study done in San Diego in 1998 found that a third of homeless families had recently had benefits terminated or reduced, and that most said that was how they had wound up on the street. Drugs, alcohol and domestic abuse also land mothers with kids in the shelter system or lead them to hand their children over to relatives or foster homes. Today the average homeless woman is younger than ever before, may have been in foster care or in shelters herself and so considers a chaotic childhood the norm. Many never finished high school, and have never held a job.

8   Ralth Nunez, who runs the organization Homes for the Homeless, says that all this calls for new attitudes. "People don't like to hear it, but shelters are going to be the low-income housing of the future," he says. "So how do we enrich the experience and use the system to provide job training and education?" Bonnie Stone of Women in Need, which has eight other residences along with Casa Rita, says, "We're pouring everything we've got into the nine months most of

them are here—nutrition, treatment, budgeting. By the time they leave, they have a subsidized apartment, day care and, hopefully, some life skills they didn't have before."

9   But these organizations are rafts in a rising river of need that has roared through this country without most of us ever even knowing. So now you know. There are hundreds of thousands of little nomads in America, sleeping in the back of cars, on floors in welfare offices or in shelters five to a room. What would it mean, to spend your childhood drifting from one strange bed to another, waking in the morning to try to figure out where you'd landed today, without those things that confer security and happiness: a familiar picture on the wall, a certain slant of light through a curtained window? "Give me your tired, your poor," it says on the base of the Statue of Liberty, to welcome foreigners. Oh, but they are already here, the small refugees from the ruin of the American dream, even if you cannot see them.

Understanding the Content

Feel free to reread all or parts of the selection to answer the following questions.

1. What is the "parallel universe" that Quindlen refers to in paragraph 2?

2. According to Quindlen, when was the last time in American history that so many "babies, toddlers and kids had no place like home"?

3. According to the author, what is the result of the high cost of housing in this country?

4. Why does Anna Quindlen refer to shelters as "rafts in a rising river of need"?

5. How long do women generally stay at Casa Rita, according to Bonnie Stone? What does the shelter hope to provide during that time?

Looking at Structure and Style

1. What is Quindlen's thesis? Is it stated or implied? If stated, where?

2. What sources does Anna Quindlen use to support her thesis? Are they sound sources? Why or why not?

3. How does the author compare and contrast middle-class Americans with the homeless? What examples of how both sides live in society does she use to show the disparity between the two groups?

4. What is the purpose of paragraph 1?

5. What is the purpose of paragraphs 5 and 6?

6. What reasons does the author give to explain how mothers with kids end up in the shelter system?

7. What effect does homelessness have on children, according to Anna Quindlen? List the effects she mentions in her essay.

Evaluating the Author's Viewpoints

1. How does the author view welfare reform? How can you tell?

2. What is Anna Quindlen's attitude toward homelessness?

3. What does the author want you to know about homeless people, and especially homeless children, in America? Which paragraph best summarizes the information that Quindlen wants you to take away from this essay?

4. How does the author describe the typical homeless woman?

Pursuing Possible Essay Topics

1. Write an essay discussing how you feel about the problem of homelessness in America.

2. What, if anything, do you think the government should do to help homeless people in America? Write an essay discussing your viewpoint.

3. Write an essay outlining what you think the women living in the shelter, as described by Anna Quindlen, need to do to avoid becoming homeless again.

4. What effects do you think homelessness has on children? What do you think is the worst lasting effect homelessness has on an individual child?

5. Did this essay make you feel more sympathetic, less sympathetic, or about the same about the problem of homelessness? Write an essay discussing your reaction to this selection by Anna Quindlen.

6. Brainstorm or freewrite on the topic of homelessness.

7. Ignore these topics and find your own topic about homelessness or homeless children.

Preparing to Read

Take a minute or two to look over the following reading selection. Note the title and author, read the opening paragraph, and check the essay's length. Make certain you have the time now to read it carefully and to do the exercises that follow it. Then, in the spaces provided, answer the following questions.

1. Judging by the title, what do you think will be the subject of the essay? _____

   _____

   _____

2. Why do you think the author opens his essay with the incident he describes?

   _____

   _____

3. What connection do you make between the title and the opening paragraph?

   _____

   _____

Vocabulary

Good comprehension of what you are about to read depends upon your understanding of the words below. The number following each word refers to the paragraph where it is used.

severing (title) cutting, removing from

sullen (1) gloomy, showing no humor

skulk (1) creep around, move sneakily

striped overalls . . . pocket (1) prisoner's uniform

John Dillinger (3) a bank robber listed by the FBI as one of the ten most wanted criminals, shot to death by G-men in 1934

deadbeat (3) a person who doesn't pay his or her debts

Mace (4) an irritating aerosol spray used to ward off an attacker

12-gauges (4) shotguns

Armageddon (4) the final decisive conflict

impenetrable (4) not capable of being entered or invaded

depleting (4) using up

surveillance devices (4) pieces of equipment, such as closed-circuit TV cameras and electronic sensors, that observe your actions while you shop

gas chiselers (4) those who drive away without paying for their gasoline

incorrigibly (5) in the manner of one who cannot be corrected or changed

integrity (5) personal honesty

collective paranoia (5) society's developing fear that no one can be trusted and "everyone is out to get me"

.38 (6) pistol

habitable (7) suitable for living in

punitive (7) punishing

Severing the Human Connection

H. Bruce Miller

1   Went down to the local self-serve gas station the other morning to fill up. The sullen cashier was sitting inside a dark, glassed-in, burglar-proof, bullet-proof, probably grenade-proof cubicle covered with cheerful notices. "NO CHECKS." "NO CREDIT." "NO BILLS OVER $50 ACCEPTED." "CASHIER HAS NO SMALL CHANGE." And the biggest one of all: "PAY BEFORE PUMPING GAS." A gleaming steel box slid out of the wall and gaped open. I dropped in a $20 bill. "Going to fill 'er up with no-lead on Number 6," I said. The cashier nodded. The steel box swallowed my money and retracted into the cubicle. I walked back to the car to pump the gas, trying not to slink or skulk. I felt like I ought to be wearing striped overalls with a number on the breast pocket.

2   The pay-before-you-pump gas station (those in the trade call it a "pre-pay") is a response to a real problem in these days of expensive gas and cut-rate ethics: people who fill their tanks and then tear out of the station without paying. Those in the business call them "drive-offs." The head of one area gasoline dealers' association says drive-offs cost some dealers $500 to $600 a month. With a profit margin of only about a nickel a gallon, a dealer has to sell a lot of gallons to make up that kind of loss. The police aren't much help. Even if the attendant manages to get a license plate number and description of the car, the cops have better things to do than tracking down a guy who stole $15 worth of gas. So the dealers adopt the pre-pay system.

3   Intellectually, I understand all of this, yet I am angry and resentful. Emotionally I cannot accept the situation. I understand the dealers' position, I understand the cops' position. But I cannot understand why I should be made to feel like John Dillinger every time I buy a tank of gasoline. It's the same story everywhere. You go to a department store

and try to pay for a $10.99 item with a check and you have to pull out a driver's license, two or three credit cards and a character reference from the pope—and then stand around for 15 minutes to get the manager's approval. Try to pay with a credit card and you have to wait while the cashier phones the central computer bank to make sure you're not a deadbeat or the Son of Sam or something. It's not that we don't trust you, they smile. It's just that we have to protect ourselves.

4   Right. We all have to protect ourselves these days. Little old ladies with attack dogs and Mace and 12-gauges, shopkeepers with closed-circuit TVs and electronic sensors to nab shoplifters, survivalists storing up ammo and dehydrated foods in hope of riding out Armageddon, gas station owners with pay-before-you-pump signs and impenetrable cashiers' cages—all protecting themselves. From what? From each other. It strikes me that we are expending so much time, energy and anguish on protecting ourselves that we are depleting our stock of mental and emotional capital for living. It also strikes me that the harder we try to protect ourselves, the less we succeed. With all the home burglar alarms and guard dogs and heavy armament, the crime rate keeps going up. With all the electronic surveillance devices, the shoplifters' take keeps climbing. The gas chiselers haven't figured out a way to beat the pre-pay system yet, but they will.

5   Is it that the people are simply incorrigibly dishonest, that the glue of integrity and mutual respect that holds society together is finally dissolving? I don't know, but I suspect that if something like this really is going on, our collective paranoia contributes to the process. People, after all, tend to behave pretty much the way other people expect them to behave. If the prevailing assumption of a society is that people are honest, by and large they will be honest. If the prevailing assumption is that people are crooks, more and more of them will be crooks.

6   What kind of message does a kid get from an environment where uniformed guards stand at the entrance of every store, where every piece of merchandise has an anti-shoplifting tag stapled to it, where every house has a burglar alarm and a .38, where the gas station cashiers huddle in glass cages and pass your change out through a metal chute? What can he conclude but that thievery and violence are normal, common, expected behaviors?

7   A society which assumes its members are honest is humane, comfortable, habitable. A society which treats everyone like a criminal becomes harsh, unfeeling, punitive, paranoid. The human connection is severed; fear of detection and punishment becomes the only deterrent to crime, and it's a very ineffective one. Somehow, sometime—I don't know when, but it was within my lifetime—we changed from the first type of society to the second. Maybe it's too late to go back again, but the road we are now on is a dark and descending one.

Understanding the Content

Feel free to reread all or parts of the selection to answer the following questions.

1. What does Miller mean by his title, "Severing the Human Connection"? How does it relate to his thesis?

2. What is a "pre-pay" station and why, according to the author, were these stations started?

3. Circle the letters of the following statements from the essay that are facts:
   a. "The cops have better things to do than tracking down a guy who stole $15 worth of gas." (2)
   b. "The gas chiselers haven't figured out a way to beat the pre-pay system yet, but they will." (4)
   c. "People, after all, tend to behave pretty much the way other people expect them to behave." (5)
   d. "The head of one area gasoline dealers' association says drive-offs cost some dealers $500 to $600 a month." (2)
   e. "A society which assumes its members are honest is humane, comfortable, habitable." (7)

4. In paragraph 3, Miller mentions the Son of Sam. Even if you don't know to whom this refers, what conclusions can you draw about the character of the Son of Sam based on this reference?

5. Can we infer that the author believes our society was more honest and humane when he was younger than it is today?

6. Can we infer that Miller believes that the more we surround ourselves with devices to protect us from crime, the more young people will assume that crime is a common way of life?

7. Do you think Miller himself has succumbed to "our collective paranoia"? Why?

8. Does Miller conclude his essay with any hope for a better society?

Looking at Structure and Style

1. What experience caused Miller to think about the subject of his essay? How does he use that experience in his introduction?

2. What other examples besides the "pre-pay" gas station does the author use to help support his viewpoint?

3. What image does the author want us to see in the last sentence of paragraph 1?

4. Rewrite or explain the following passages from the essay in your own words:

   a. "The steel box swallowed my money and retracted into the cubicle." (1)

   b. "It strikes me that we are expending so much time, energy and anguish on protecting ourselves that we are depleting our stock of mental and emotional capital for living." (4)

   c. "The road we are now on is a dark and descending one." (7)

   d. ". . . survivalists storing up ammo and dehydrated foods in hope of riding out Armageddon . . ."(4)

5. Reread the opening paragraph. How would you describe Miller's tone? What particular words or phrases help establish this tone?

6. Is this essay written mostly from an objective or a subjective viewpoint? Explain.

7. Discuss your response to Miller's writing style. What techniques does he use that you like or dislike? What suggestions would you offer him for revision?

Evaluating the Author's Viewpoints

1. Miller says that people tend to behave pretty much the way other people expect them to behave. Do you agree? Why? Is your own behavior based on what other people expect of you? How does your behavior change when you are around certain people, such as friends, parents, teachers, etc.?

2. Miller believes our society is "on a dark and descending road." Explain why you agree or disagree.

Pursuing Possible Essay Topics

1. Agree or disagree with Miller's statement in question 4b above.

2. Write an essay describing a time in your life when you were treated or made to feel like a criminal.

3. Write an essay that answers the opening question in paragraph 5.

4. Do some research in the library on crime statistics over the last few years to see if Miller's statement that "the crime rate keeps going up" is true. Use the statistics to support or refute Miller. You might begin your research by using the *Reader's Guide to Periodical Literature* or the card catalog. Look for current publication dates.

5. Miller suggests that the effect of seemingly everyone protecting themselves with "attack dogs and Mace and 12-gauges . . . closed-circuit TVs . . . impenetrable cashiers' cages . . . burglar alarms and. . . electronic surveillance devices" is that young people get the message that thievery and violence are normal behaviors. Argue for or against his viewpoint.

6. Look through your local newspapers for some stories that show not the severing of the human connection, but a linking of the human connection. Write about them.

7. Brainstorm or freewrite on one or more of the following:

   a. crime
   b. pay before you pump
   c. mutual respect

   d. collective paranoia
   e. honesty is the best policy
   f. expected social behaviors

8. Ignore these and come up with your own topic on some aspect of a social issue that concerns you.

Preparing to Read

Take a minute or two to look over the following reading selection. Note the title and author, read the opening paragraph, and check the essay's length. Make certain you have the time now to read it carefully and to do the exercises that follow it. Then, in the spaces provided, answer the following questions.

1. What do you think is the subject of this essay? _____

   _____

   _____

2. What opinion do you think Phil Donahue holds on this issue?_____

   _____

3. What is your reaction to the opening paragraph?_____

   _____

Vocabulary

Good comprehension of what you are about to read depends upon your understanding of the words below. The number following each word refers to the paragraph where it is used.

admonition (3) warning, caution

evangelical (6) crusading, orthodox

recitation (12) narration, performance, monologue

atheists (14) nonbelievers, skeptics

obliges (15) forces, compels

constellation (19) configuration, arrangement, group of stars

My God, My Constitution

PHIL DONAHUE

1   The "Donahue" show on MSNBC premieres at a time when scores of Congressmen followed Speaker Dennis Hastert to the steps of the Capitol to pledge their allegiance to the American flag. When their united voices reached *"under God"* . . . they shouted the sacred words. Shouted. I was embarrassed.

2   Religion and devotion to God should, like St. Paul's charity, not be puffed up. God does not reward the loudest voice. Moreover, the "under God" inclusion in the pledge is, as the much-maligned majority in the Ninth Federal Circuit ruled, unconstitutional.

3   Let us revisit the framers' purpose in creating a wall between church and state. The First Amendment admonition is intended to ensure that no state official will be able to claim God's endorsement in the creation of law and public policy.

4   No teacher in a public school will be able to legally fool with a child's mind.

5   No Jewish child in a public school will be recruited to play a shepherd in a holiday Nativity pageant ("Oh Divine Savior, thank you for dying for my sins").

6   No public money will be used to the benefit of religious institutions or the evangelical promotion of any faith.

7   The Separation clause ensures the continued vitality of the state and of religion. It ensures that religion will remain a private choice free of state promotion or interference.

8   And it is working.

9   America is the most religious society in history. We sing in more church choirs, attend more church services, throw more holy water and burn more incense than any other national community in the history of civilization.

10   God bless us for that.

11   But please, keep worship out of the government's hands. Calling on God in public ceremonies requires that we choose a certain God, whose God? (". . . one nation UNDER ALLAH?")

12   It is true that God appears on our currency, and prayer recitation opens our sessions of Congress. God is so popular in the U.S., so woven into the lives of so many American citizens; that the task of keeping the First Amendment wall strong is often difficult, complex.

13   But it is worth the effort; its purpose is noble. It is to ensure that Americans remain free to worship a God of their choice, free to pray in one's home and at one's privately funded place of worship. It ensures that no money from other Americans will benefit someone else's religion. That's no small issue due to the billions in tax exemptions offered to religious institutions. This raises the tax bite of all our citizens.

14   The First Amendment also affirms the right of citizens to be without any faith at all. To be atheists. The late Madalyn Murray O'Hair used to say on the daytime DONAHUE show, "Your religious deductions are raising my taxes. Worship anything or anyone you please, but don't make me pay for it!"

15   Our constitution obliges no one to worship, pledge allegiance, or believe in anything, not the flag, not even the United States itself.

16   In 1943 The Jehovah's Witnesses won a Supreme Court decision that challenged Pennsylvania's law requiring public school students to recite the pledge.

17   Witnesses argued that their faith disallowed the salute even without the "under God" reference which did not become the standard text until the early '50s. Jehovah's Witnesses were being abused everywhere, stones were thrown at their children, a Kingdom Hall in Kennebunk, Maine, was burned to the ground, over one thousand assaults were reported. America was at war and these kids would not salute the flag. There was no overstating the loathing for them.

18   I continue to marvel today at the courage of those first graders who, accepting the instruction of Mom and Dad, stood mute while the "good" American children, like the Congress on the Capitol steps, proudly pronounced their allegiance.

19   In one of the most important decisions in the history of the Supremes, U.S. Justice Robert Jackson wrote, famously . . ."If there is any fixed star in the Constitutional constellation it is that no official, high or petty, can prescribe what shall be orthodox, in nationalism, religion, politics or any other matters of opinion."

20   Justice Jackson concluded for the majority by pronouncing that neither can any official "force by word or deed" a citizen to believe a certain way in such matters of opinion.

21   Thus, eight of the nine old white men looked out from their elevated mahogany bench and (in the majority view) said to those Witness children, "You obey your parents!"

22   Yes. Yes. Yes. For this remarkable defense of individual and unpopular liberty, I am pleased to say from my own heart, on my own time, and in my own opinion, God Bless America!

23   The plea for the intervention of the almighty is more meaningful to me because no official, high or petty, can force me to say it or to believe it.

Understanding the Content

Feel free to reread all or parts of the selection to answer the following questions.

1. According to Donahue, what is the purpose of the First Amendment?

2. What event or situation "embarrassed" Donahue?

3. What is one example that Donahue gives to illustrate why the First Amendment became part of the Constitution?

4. Which religious organization or group won a Supreme Court decision that challenged Pennsylvania's law requiring public school students to recite the pledge? Why did they bring their case to court?

5. What is Donahue's thesis? Is it stated or implied? If stated, where?

Looking at Structure and Style

1. What do paragraphs 2–7 have to do with the essay's thesis?

2. What is the purpose of paragraphs 13–15?

3. To whom does Donahue compare the "Congress on the Capital steps" and why?

4. How does paragraph 2 support paragraph 1?

Evaluating the Author's Viewpoints

1. Why, according to Donahue in paragraph 12, is "the task of keeping the First Amendment wall strong . . . often difficult, complex"?

2. Do you agree with the quote from Madalyn Murray O'Hair, "Worship anything or anyone you please, but don't make me pay for it"? Why or why not?

3. Do you agree with Donahue that we should "keep worship out of the government's hands"? Why or why not?

4. How does Donahue feel about the Supreme Court, as described in paragraphs 19–21? How can you tell?

5. Why was Donahue "embarrassed" by the actions of the Congress on the steps of the Capitol building? What did their actions represent to him?

Pursuing Possible Essay Topics

Wait until after you have read the following essay, "Pledge Words Do No Harm to Nonbelievers" by Rochelle Riley, before attempting to write an essay related to the issue surrounding the Pledge of Allegiance.

Preparing to Read

Take a minute or two to look over the following reading selection. Note the title and the author, read the opening paragraph, and check the essay's length. Make certain you have the time now to read it carefully and to do the exercises that follow it. Then, in the spaces provided, answer the following questions.

1. What do you think is the subject of this essay?_____

_____

2. What opinion does Rochelle Riley hold on this issue?_____

_____

3. What is your reaction to the opening paragraph?_____

_____

Vocabulary

Good comprehension of what you are about to read depends upon your understanding of the words below. The number following each word refers to the paragraph where it is used.

lingual (2) related to language

populace (3) the general public

fallible (12) capable of error

Pledge Words Do No Harm to Nonbelievers

ROCHELLE RILEY

1   The things that America lets sneak up on it.

2   First, we become so comfortable in our world superiority that we discount the Davids out there who want to slay our Goliath, the financial, cultural and lingual giant we've created so thoroughly that we don't even learn about other countries.

3   Then we are shocked to learn that the borders that we've kept open almost continuously for centuries have resulted in a monumental change in the U.S. populace, one that requires us to not only recognize, but also develop ways to plan for the fact that we don't all speak the same language or worship the same God.

4   So it's no wonder that many were shocked recently by a father's fight to take the words "under God" from the Pledge of Allegiance.

5   Some people thought that all the atheists had died with Madalyn Murray O'Hair, the Texas housewife who won a Supreme Court case banning public school prayer.

6   But that's not the case. And that's the amazing thing about America. Its government will never please all of the people all of the time, and that's how it's supposed to be.

Number of Nonbelievers Growing

7   Now that we've had a chance to think about it, what is the Pledge of Allegiance, really? It's just words honoring a flag that has represented a country founded "under God."

8   The words "under God" were added to the pledge by Congress in 1954. But the number of nonbelievers in America is growing.

9   Gallup polls say that the number who believe in God fell from 98 percent in 1967 to 90 percent last year.

10   Those two little words, "under God," are from a time when a single God was the one in whom most of a new country put its trust. He remains the one to whom millions pray.

11   So no one complained when America imprinted its money with "In God We Trust" and courts required the telling of truth, "so help me God."

Church and State Inseparable

12   Now, there are two choices that the country and its courts face: Judges and justices can wipe God from everything the way they've attempted to wipe Him from schools. Or we can stop pretending that the Constitution wasn't written by men—judgmental, fallible,

political, sometimes dishonest men, but religious men, who knew when they asserted a separation of church and state, it merely meant that they didn't want a church to run the government.

13   Church and state in America have always been, and will always be, inseparable. We'll just continue to hide it, on walls and in meaningful moments of silence.

14   What America must be bold enough to say is that a country founded on God is strong enough to give its citizens the freedom to choose otherwise.

15   And having a pledge that honors God doesn't harm those who don't believe. In America, you can take a pass.

16   A country founded in God's name gives you the right to fight pledges that carry His name. Our country has laws that protect those who do not have faith in God or in government. Which is why

> *I pledge allegiance*
> *To the flag*
> *Of the United States of America*
> *And to the Republic for which it stands*
> *One nation, under God, indivisible*
> *With liberty and justice for all.*

Understanding the Content

Feel free to reread all or parts of the selection to answer the following questions.

1. What is the point of Riley's essay? Is it stated anywhere? If so, where?

2. Now that you've read both selections, who is Madalyn Murray O'Hair, and for what is she famous?

3. When were the words "under God" added to the Constitution?

4. What were the results of the Gallup poll conducted in 2001 that Riley sites in her essay?

Looking at Structure and Style

1. What is the purpose of paragraphs 2 and 3? Why has Riley included these paragraphs in this selection?

2. Why does the author mention Madalyn Murray O'Hair in her selection? Does mention of this woman support the author's thesis? Why or why not?

3. What is the purpose of paragraphs 9–11?

4. Do you think that ending the selection with the Pledge of Allegiance is effective? Why or why not?

Evaluating the Author's Viewpoints

1. What is Riley's opinion regarding the removal of "under God" from the Pledge? Why does she feel that way?

2. Do you agree or disagree with Riley's statement that "government will never please all of the people all of the time, and that's how it's supposed to be"? Why?

3. Based on your reading of paragraphs 1–3, what do you think Riley's opinion of America, and of Americans in general, is? How can you tell?

4. Do you agree or disagree with Rochelle Riley that "what America must be bold enough to say is that a country founded on God is strong enough to give its citizens the freedom to choose otherwise"? Why?

5. Respond to the statement "A country founded in God's name gives you the right to fight pledges that carry His name." Do you agree? Why?

Pursuing Possible Essay Topics

1. Compare and contrast the two selections and their thesis statements. Which author—Donahue or Riley—makes a more persuasive argument? Why? Write a short essay discussing how the author who did not make as good a case could strengthen his or her argument.

2. Write an essay exploring your viewpoint on the topic of "separation of church and state." Is this a concept that Americans should take literally and defend to the end? Why or why not?

3. Do you think that the words "under God" should remain in the Pledge? Why or why not?

4. Should the words "In God We Trust" remain on American money? Why or why not?

5. Do some research and find out why the words "under God" were added to the Pledge in 1954. Do the reasons it was added still resonate today? Why or why not? Does this change your opinion on whether the words should stay in the Pledge? Write an essay summarizing your findings and your opinion.

6. Ignore these and find your own topic on some other social issue.

Student Essay

Read the following narrative essay written by a student. As you read, look for answers to these questions:

1. Does the essay deal with a social concern? If so, what?

2. Does the student have a clearly stated or implied thesis? What is the thesis?

3. Does the student sound genuinely concerned about the issue discussed? Explain.

Should I Believe in God?

Amy Kimoto

1   I do not believe in God.

2   From this point on, will I receive utter close-mindedness from you? Are my views immoral and blasphemous? Will you listen to my beliefs, my ideas, me as a person?

3   I cannot believe in something that does not exist to me. I cannot believe in God just because everybody does.

4   I was not raised in an "abnormal" household. I even went to Bible studies and prayed to God when I was younger. I know many of the stories and I have read the Bible. As I grew older, my faith faded as my many questions about God and religion grew. Now, I believe not in God but the morals he represents—the Ten Commandments: You shall not murder, you shall not commit adultery, you shall not steal, honor your father and your mother, you shall not bear false witness and so on. I must believe in these morals for they are the basis of our society. To cast down these morals is to cast down our way of governing and therefore, our nation. But believing in the morals of God isn't the same as believing in God.

5   The Constitution also represents our rights, our beliefs, what is right, and what is wrong. I do not worship Thomas Jefferson and beg him to forgive me. I do not pray to Benjamin Franklin. I admire what they wrote, for they are certainly brilliant, but I in no way idolize them.

6   Religion may bring sanctuary and guidance to some people, but I object to some of the ideas preached by many religions, like the concept that one religion is right and the rest are wrong. This close-mindedness has led to many wars and disputes. I think it is absurd that all of the religions are not united, since they are derived from the same or similar basic concepts. Even though it is human nature to believe that one religion is better than another, if all religions were united, they could serve a common cause—the betterment of humankind.

7   Another instance of close-mindedness is the intolerance of homosexuals. Daily I hear and see degradation of homosexuality. Many religions teach that this lifestyle is morally wrong and that it goes against normal society.

8   This same close-mindedness leads society to label me as a pagan or an atheist, as society needs to put a tag on everyone. I do not call myself antireligious but I am a realist. "How do you prove that God doesn't exist?" you ask. "How do you prove that Santa Claus doesn't exist?" I counter.

9   I will believe realistically and when the existence of God is proven, I will gladly convert.

Reaction

In your journal or on a separate sheet of paper, write your reaction to the student essay. What would you tell this student about her essay?

On the Net

Are you walking an ethical tightrope, as discussed in the selection of the same name in this chapter? Many companies are under fire these days for questionable practices. Look at the activities below and do one or more to further your knowledge of ethics in business situations.

1. Research the scandals dogging one of the following companies: Enron, Worldcom, or Tyco. Read a few articles on the Web and write an essay summarizing your findings. What did these companies do that necessitated government intervention and investigation?

2. Visit the BellSouth website at *http://ethics.bellsouth.com/index.html*, which includes games and scenarios that will help their employees make ethical decisions and conduct business in an ethical way. Look at the advice they give and the questions they pose.

Spend some time thinking about the pro/con selections presented at the end of this chapter by Phil Donahue and Rochelle Riley.

1. Do more research on the topic of separation of church and state, democracy, or the issues surrounding the Pledge of Allegiance. Visit *http://www.house.gov/Constitution/Constitution.html* for a full text of the United States Constitution.

2. Visit sites that are dedicated to the subject of free speech, such as *http://www.geocities.com/louisworthjones/essays.html*, which has different essays by Louis Worth Jones that take one side of the argument and explore its different facets.

3. Find three relevant and effective sites that take an opposing view to that of Jones.

4. Think about your own feelings about United States politics and the government in general, and learn what other scholars and students think by going to *http://www.usconstitution.net*. Depending on how you feel about the topic being presented, post your opinion on the "monthly poll" section.

7 Viewpoints on Family and Relationships

FOCUS ON FAMILY AND RELATIONSHIPS

To help you focus on the subject of this chapter, answer the following questions. You may want to write the answers in your journal or be prepared to discuss them in class.

1. Read the quotation by Johann Goethe on the opposite page. What do you think he means? Do you agree? Do you want to be treated that way?

2. Look at the photograph on the opposite page. What do you think is happening? What is your reaction? Explain.

3. What are the relationships like in your family? Do family members tend to treat each other "as if they were what they ought to be" and help each other "become what they are capable of being"?

4. How do you define *family?*

5. What do you think are the qualities that make up a good relationship?

"Treat people as if they were what they ought to be and you help them become what they are capable of being."

—Johann Goethe

Michael Weisbot/Stock Boston

America is made up of family groups of many diverse cultures: the Asian-American family, the Hispanic family, the black family, the European family, the Middle Eastern family, and so on. Still, despite this wide range of backgrounds, some research* suggests there are six major qualities shared by healthy families of all races and cultures:

1. a high degree of commitment to the family group and to promoting each other's happiness and welfare

2. an appreciation of one another; making the other person feel good about himself or herself

3. good communication patterns developed through spending time talking with and listening to each other

4. a desire to spend time together in active interaction

5. a strong value system, such as that found in a religious orientation

6. an ability to deal with crises and stress in a positive manner

Few families can live up to these ideals all the time. Just as an individual must work to keep mentally and physically fit, so must family members work to keep the family mentally and physically fit. Like individuals, even strong families have problems. Sometimes families break up. And just as there are no perfect parents, so there are no perfect children. But we have the option of changing our imperfect family relationships by working to develop those six characteristics of a strong family.

The subject of family relationships is one that concerns us all no matter what our backgrounds. The following essays reveal some varied viewpoints on this broad subject, covering such aspects as gender differences, mother love, and the effects family breakups can have. Read them to understand how others feel about family and relationships, as well as to stimulate ideas for an essay of your own.

Preparing to Read

Take a minute or two to look over the following reading selection. Note the title and the author, read the opening paragraph, and check the essay's length. Make certain you have the time now to read it carefully and to do the exercises that follow it. Then, in the spaces provided, answer the following questions.

*N. Stinnet and J. DeFrain, *Secrets of Strong Families* (Boston: Little, Brown, 1985).

1. Based on your reading of the title and the first paragraph, what do you think the subject of this essay will be?_____

   _____

   _____

2. What do you think the author's tone will be throughout the essay?_____

   _____

   _____

3. What do you think the title of this essay means?_____

   _____

   _____

   _____

Vocabulary

Good comprehension of what you are about to read depends upon your understanding of the words below. The number following each word refers to the paragraph where it is used.

galvanize (1) excite to action

decimates (1) devastates, wipes out

languishing (1) weak, ailing

dissertation (5) commentary, thesis

catheter (6) tube, funnel

albeit (7) even though, notwithstanding

inarticulate (8) not talkative, tongue-tied

Silent Bond

DAVID BIRO

1   There is nothing like a crisis to galvanize a family, to set its silent wheels in motion. Two years ago I found out I had PNH, a rare disease that decimates the bone marrow. I was 31, the oldest of four and the only son, about to join my father's dermatology practice. The

doctors told me my only hope was a bone-marrow transplant; they would fill my languishing marrow with healthy stem cells from a suitable donor.

2   News traveled swiftly. The next day, my three sisters converged on Memorial Sloan-Kettering Hospital. Much as certain cells in the human body rush to repair damage from an injury, my sisters gathered to take the test of marrow. Each had a 25 percent chance of being a match. Each yearned to be the donor. Each was terrified of failing.

3   Like a winning spin on a slot machine, an ideal match must correspond at six distinct genetic sites. Lisa, my oldest sister, went first: she matched at only three. Debbie, the second sister, followed with four. Michele, the youngest, went last. And in that final trembling pull of the lever, the third spin found purchase. Michele matched on all six fronts. In the genetic lottery, she was my jackpot.

4   My day-to-day knowledge of Michele was curiously incomplete. She was six years younger than I was, and recklessly pretty. We rarely talked about anything deeper than a movie or a meal. The family adventurer, she might call one day from Guatemala, where she was helping disabled children, the next from British Columbia on her way back from a trek across the Yukon. Certainly, I loved her, in the way you love a person whose external data are familiar but whose internal workings are a pleasant mystery. I knew she was a vegetarian, played the flute and had pierced ears—that was enough.

5   Now I needed her. We both knew this, although we never spoke of it. Perhaps she was too polite or embarrassed to mention my sudden reassignment from older-and-wiser to sick-and-desperate. Instead, she curtailed her activities and began to eat red meat, even to sing its praises. One night I asked her, "Are you sure you're O.K. with this?" She dismissed me with a wave of her hand, barely pausing in her dissertation on the merits of Canadian bacon. It was the best we could do.

6   The transplant took place on Feb. 15, 1996, just as a blizzard was about to blanket the city. That morning Michele was taken to the O.R., where she was jabbed 20 times in the hip-bone with a large-bore needle. Six hours later, a small syringe filled with her stem cells was injected into a catheter in my chest. Weeks passed—weeks of fevers, transfusions and tentative touching across the barrier of latex gloves, masks and gowns. Finally, good news; Michele's marrow had taken root in my bones. It had begun to produce blood cells. I was cured.

7   With the crisis over, my family was once again free to return to their respective worlds, reluctantly at first, only gradually willing to believe the danger had passed. We continued to see each other regularly, albeit on a pre-transplant schedule—for birthdays and holidays. And, in time, the experience faded to a wisp of memory. I went back to not knowing Michele and she to not knowing me.

8   Nothing had changed. At least not in the sphere of the everyday. But in that stubbornly inarticulate sphere of family, something had shifted. The bonds that joined me to my sister were redefined. She had literally become a part of me.

9   Nor was her role of donor necessarily over. In the event of a relapse, I would require more of her marrow. And so in the ensuing months, I listened to Michele's plans for far-flung journeys with fear, worry, resentment. Once I even vetoed a trip to Alaska, not telling her why, only that she couldn't go. Michele canceled her plans without a word of protest. Was I being selfish? Unreasonable? Maybe. But I couldn't ignore the fact that I was dependent on her in a way that no one person should have to depend on another.

10   "It's nice how everything worked out for you," said a young man I met at the clinic one morning while waiting to see my doctor. He, too, had undergone a transplant, and because he had no siblings, he was forced to go through a national registry where donors remain anonymous. "I know she's a woman and she's from Seattle," he explained. "I'd like to find out more so that I could thank her. She saved my life."

11   She saved his life. Just as Michele saved mine. When a stranger saves your life, she deserves whole fields of appreciation. But Michele was family and that's what families are supposed to do. I never thanked Michele—that is, not in the words we use with our friends and colleagues, in the words we use to get things done in the world. To do so would have violated the pact of silence that brothers and sisters feel compelled to uphold. But she had to know. Somehow, in that sign language of family, she had to know, and with and without each other, we moved on.

Understanding the Content

Feel free to reread all or parts of the selection to answer the following questions.

1. What is the "crisis" that galvanized the author's family, that "set its silent wheels in motion"?

2. How do Biro's sisters react to the news that he needs a bone-marrow transplant?

3. Which of Biro's sisters was a bone-marrow donor match? Describe David Biro's relationship with her prior to this occurrence.

4. What was the result of Biro's bone-marrow transplant operation? Was it successful?

5. Did David Biro's relationship with his sister change after the operation? If so, how?

6. Why didn't Biro thank his sister for donating her bone marrow?

Looking at Structure and Style

1. What is the thesis of this selection? Is it stated or implied? If stated, where?

2. How does Biro describe his sister? What kind of mental image do you get of her from his early description of her?

3. Why do you think Biro titled the selection "Silent Bond," and uses the word *silent* again in the first sentence, "There is nothing like a crisis to galvanize a family, to set its silent wheels in motion"?

4. What is the author's tone throughout the essay? Do you think that his being a physician affected the tone used? Why or why not?

5. What is the purpose of paragraphs 10 and 11?

Evaluating the Author's Viewpoints

1. How do you think the author felt about Michele before the operation? after? Did his feelings change, or did they stay the same?

2. Why do you think Biro's sister "curtailed her activities and began to eat red meat" (even though she was a vegetarian) prior to the operation? Do you think the author expected her to make that type of commitment to his cause? Why or why not?

3. What was your reaction to Biro's description of himself listening "to Michele's plans for far-flung journeys with fear, worry, resentment"? Was he justified in those feelings? Why or why not?

4. Do you agree with Biro's statement, "When a stranger saves your life, she deserves whole fields of appreciation. But Michele was family and that's what families are supposed to do"? Why or why not?

Pursuing Possible Essay Topics

1. Brainstorm or freewrite on one or more of the following topics:

   a. family relationships

   b. responsibility to family

   c. dependence on family

   d. siblings

2. Look again at Biro's statement, "But Michele was family and that's what families are supposed to do." Do you think you should do whatever is required for a family member? Why or why not? Write an essay either in support of that statement or in opposition to it.

3. What changes, if any, would you make in your lifestyle if you knew it would better someone in your family? For instance, would you stop smoking if a member of your family requested it or if his or her health was compromised by your smoking?

4. Visit the National Bone Marrow Donor Program site at *http://www.marrow.org* and read the information presented on it. Did you learn anything new? If so, summarize your findings or one or two of the personal stories on the site.

5. If none of the previously mentioned topics interests you, find your own topic related to family relationships and write about it.

Preparing to Read

Take a minute or two to look over the following reading selection. Note the title and author, read the opening paragraph (including the footnote), and check the essay's length. Make certain you have the time now to read it carefully and to do the exercises that follow it. Then, in the spaces provided, answer the following questions.

1. What will the author probably say about family? _____

_____

2. Is your family "the perfect family"? Explain. _____

_____

_____

3. How would you define "family values"? _____

_____

_____

Vocabulary

Good comprehension of what you are about to read depends upon your understanding of the words below. The number following each word refers to the paragraph where it is used.

incriminating (4) accusing, indicating fault

ministered (4) attended, took care of

welts (5) bruises, discoloration or abrasions of the skin

encrusted (7) caked, covered over

factoring out (8) excluding

deprived (11) kept from having or enjoying

The Perfect Family

ALICE HOFFMAN

1   When I was growing up in the 50's, there was only one sort of family, the one we watched on television every day. Right in front of us, in black and white, was everything we needed to know about family values: the neat patch of lawn, the apple tree, the mother who never once raised her voice, the three lovely children: a Princess, a Kitten, a Bud[1] and, always, the father who knew best.

2   People stayed married forever back then, and roses grew by the front door. We had glass bottles filled with lightning bugs and brand-new swing sets in the backyard, and softball games at dusk. We had summer nights that lasted forever and well-balanced meals, three times a day, in our identical houses, on our identical streets. There was only one small bargain we had to make to exist in this world: we were never to ask questions, never to think about people who didn't have as much or who were different in any way. We ignored desperate marriages and piercing loneliness. And we were never, ever, to wonder what might be hidden from view, behind the unlocked doors, in the privacy of our neighbors' bedrooms and knotty-pine-paneled dens.

3   This was a bargain my own mother could not make. Having once believed that her life would sort itself out to be like the television shows we watched, only real and in color, she'd been left to care for her children on her own, at a time when divorce was so uncommon I did not meet another child of divorced parents until 10 years later, when I went off to college.

4   Back then, it almost made sense when one of my best friends was not allowed to come to my house; her parents did not approve of divorce or my mother's life style. My mother, after all, had a job and a boyfriend and, perhaps even more incriminating, she was the one who took the silver-colored trash cans out to the curb on Monday nights. She did so faithfully, on evenings when she had already balanced the checkbook and paid the bills and ministered to sore throats and made certain we'd had dinner; but all up and down the street everybody knew the truth: taking out the trash was clearly a job for fathers.

1. Nicknames of characters in a popular 1954–62 television show, *Father Knows Best.*

5   When I was 10, my mother began to work for the Department of Social Services, a world in which the simple rules of the suburbs did not apply. She counseled young unwed mothers, girls and women who were not allowed to make their own choices, most of whom had not been allowed to finish high school or stay in their own homes, none of whom had been allowed to decide not to continue their pregnancies. Later, my mother placed most of these babies in foster care, and still later, she moved to the protective-services department, investigating charges of abuse and neglect, often having to search a child's back and legs for bruises or welts.

6   She would have found some on my friend, left there by her righteous father, the one who wouldn't allow her to visit our home but blackened her eye when, a few years later, he discovered that she was dating a boy he didn't approve of. But none of his neighbors had dared to report him. They would never have imagined that someone like my friend's father, whose trash cans were always tidily placed at the curb, whose lawn was always well cared for, might need watching.

7   To my mother, abuse was a clear-cut issue, if reported and found, but neglect was more of a judgment call. It was, in effect, passing judgment on the nature of love. If my father had not sent the child-support checks on time, if my mother hadn't been white and college-educated, it could have easily been us in one of those apartments she visited, where the heat didn't work on the coldest days, and the dirt was so encrusted you could mop all day and still be called a poor housekeeper, and there was often nothing more for dinner than Frosted Flakes and milk, or, if it was toward the end of the month, the cereal might be served with tap water. Would that have meant my mother loved her children any less, that we were less of a family?

8   My mother never once judged who was a fit mother on the basis of a clean floor, or an unbalanced meal, or a boyfriend who sometimes spent the night. But back then, there were good citizens who were only too ready to set their standards for women and children, factoring out poverty or exhaustion or simply a different set of beliefs.

9   There are always those who are ready to deal out judgment with the ready fist of the righteous. I know this because before the age of 10 I was one of the righteous, too. I believed that mothers were meant to stay home and fathers should carry out the trash on Monday nights. I believed that parents could create a domestic life that was the next best thing to heaven, if they just tried. That is what I'd been told, that in the best of all worlds we would live identical lives in identical houses.

10   It's a simple view of the world, too simple even for childhood. Certainly, it's a vision that is much too limited for the lives we live now, when only one in 19 families are made up of a wage-earner father, a mother who doesn't work outside the home and two or more children. And even long ago, when I was growing up, we paid too high a price when we cut ourselves off from the rest of the world. We ourselves did not dare to be different. In the safety we created, we became trapped.

11   There are still places where softball games are played at dusk and roses grow by the front door. There are families with sons named Bud, with kind and generous fathers, and mothers who put up strawberry preserves every June and always have time to sing lullabies. But do these families love their children any more than the single mother who works all day? Are their lullabies any sweeter? If I felt deprived as a child, it was only when our family was measured against some notion of what we were supposed to be. The truth of it was, we lacked for little.

12   And now that I have children of my own, and am exhausted at the end of the day in which I've probably failed in a hundred different ways, I am amazed that women alone can manage. That they do, in spite of everything, is a simple fact. They rise from sleep in the middle of the night when their children call out to them. They rush for the cough syrup and cold washcloths and keep watch till dawn. These are real family values, the same ones we knew when we were children. As far as we were concerned our mother could cure a fever with a kiss. This may be the only thing we ever need to know about love. The rest, no one can judge.

Understanding the Content

Feel free to reread all or parts of the selection to answer the following questions.

1. What type of family was typical when Hoffman was growing up? How similar or different were real-life families from those on television?

2. What was the "bargain" Hoffman's mother could not make? (3)

3. Hoffman says it "almost made sense when one of my best friends was not allowed to come to my house" (4). Why?

4. Hoffman contrasts suburban families with the families her mother worked with. What is the basic difference?

5. Reread the last sentence in paragraph 10. What does the author mean?

6. What is it that Hoffman feels is "the only thing we ever need to know about love" (12)?

Looking at Structure and Style

1. Is Hoffman's thesis stated or implied? If stated, where? Make a one-sentence statement of her thesis.

2. Hoffman uses comparison and contrast throughout her essay. What are some examples of this? Are they effective? Explain.

3. Hoffman uses several images throughout, such as silver-colored trash cans, neat lawns, and so forth. What is her purpose in doing this? Is her method effective? Explain.

4. To whom do you think Hoffman is writing? Why do you think so?

5. How would you describe Hoffman's tone? What words or phrases help develop that tone?

Evaluating the Author's Viewpoints

1. How does Hoffman define "family values"? Do you agree with her? Explain.

2. Is Hoffman's idea of "family" more the norm today than the so-called ideal norm of the 1950s?

3. What place do fathers seem to take in Hoffman's definition of "family values"?

4. How do you define "family"? "family values"?

Pursuing Possible Essay Topics

1. Write an essay that discusses erroneous concepts of family and family values. Who holds these concepts? From where do they come?

2. Interview some older people to discover what a "traditional" family lifestyle was like forty years ago. Compare it to today's lifestyle.

3. Write an essay that supports or refutes the idea of the father taking care of the family while the mother works.

4. Talk to some immigrants to this country to discover what their traditional family lifestyle was like before and after coming to this country. How much has it changed, if at all?

5. What other trends in our society are changing the traditional family unit as many people have known it? Write an essay on the forces in society that are changing the family unit.

6. Freewrite or brainstorm on one or more of the following:

   a. motherhood/fatherhood   d. the perfect parent

   b. perfect love   e. divorce

   c. maternal instincts   f. single parenting

7. If none of the above suits you, find your own topic on family or relationships.

Preparing to Read

Read aloud the poem that begins below. Then answer the following questions.

1. What is your first reaction to the poem?_____

   _____

   _____

2. What is your reaction to the grandmother? _____

   _____

   _____

Now read the poem again and answer the questions that follow it.

My Grandmother

—LINDA PASTAN

My grandmother
of the bitter mouth
and the capable hands
taught us how long you can live
without love
and be forgiven
and never forgive.
She married knowingly,
at her father's bidding,
the wrong man.
And though she called
each granddaughter "shaneh madeleh"
which means "lovely girl,"

when my cousin married
a gentile boy for love
she covered her mirrors
as for death:
for seven days
she didn't see
her once beautiful face
wasted in the glass.

Understanding the Content

1. What is the poem about?

2. What religion is the grandmother? How do we know?

3. What customs or traditions does the grandmother hold?

4. What are some possible meanings of the following phrases:
   a. "bitter mouth"
   b. "capable hands"
   c. "her father's bidding"
   d. "wasted in the glass"

Looking at Structure and Style

1. Reread the poem aloud and notice the placement of punctuation. How does this placement help you read and understand the poem?

2. How do lines 4–7 develop the grandmother's character?

3. Would the information in the poem be better expressed in prose, or does the poem allow much to be said in a few lines? Explain.

Evaluating the Author's Viewpoints

1. What is Pastan's opinion of her grandmother? Based on what we are given in the poem, would you want to meet the grandmother? Explain.

2. Do you think Pastan feels that her grandmother's life was wasted because "she married knowingly, at her father's bidding"? Explain.

3. Do you think Pastan finds it ironic that her grandmother would marry someone she didn't love, yet mourned the author's cousin when she married out of her faith for love? Explain your reaction.

Pursuing Possible Essay Topics

1. Write a descriptive essay about one of your grandparents.

2. Write an essay about a family tradition that you or one of your family members has abandoned or feels should be abandoned.

3. Argue for or against marriages arranged by parents or through mail order.

4. Argue for or against marriage as a legal necessity in our society. Has it outgrown its usefulness?

5. Brainstorm or freewrite on one or more of the following:

   a. marriage rituals   d. my family

   b. engagement rings   e. my parents

   c. elopement   f. grandparenting

6. Find a topic of your own on family relationships.

Preparing to Read

Take a minute or two to look over the following reading selection. Note the title and the author, read the opening paragraph, and check the essay's length. Make certain you have the time now to read it carefully and to do the exercises that follow it. Then, in the spaces provided, answer the following questions.

1. What do you think the author will have to say about modern-day parents and their children?_____

   _____

2. What is the author's tone toward her subject?_____

   _____

Vocabulary

Good comprehension of what you are about to read depends upon your understanding the words below. The number following each word refers to the paragraph where it is used.

deprivation (2) the condition of being deprived or denied

robust (2) healthy, strong

swaddling (2) tucking in or around

cashmere (2) a kind of luxurious wool

clique (3) private club, clan

Spoiling Our Kids

Amy Dickinson

1   My desires are pretty basic. They run along the lines of world peace, good health and an Easy Bake Oven—an item I have coveted since childhood. Don't get me wrong: I had plenty as a child, but I never possessed the light-bulb-powered "amazing toy oven that really bakes!" I ought to be over it. (We did, after all, own a pony.) But the fact is, I can't forget the toy I never got.

2   Childish feelings of mini-deprivation like this are, I suspect, helping fuel a run on luxury products for kids by parents who feel that their darlings should never go without. The robust economy and stock market have created a lot of new prosperity, and parents are increasingly swaddling their children in cashmere crib bedding, bespoke baby ball gowns and tuxedos for toddlers. At the same time, they are worried that their kids take wealth for granted, and struggle to prepare their teens for a less lavish life once they get out on their own. Inevitably, some Wall Street investment advisers are now recommending shrinks to help children of the super-rich work through their money issues.

3   In most cases, though, it seems that the ones who need help are the parents. Some think that buying little Jake the new Dreamcast game console will assure that classmates are eager to come over for play dates, or that outfitting teenaged Tammy in the fashions favored by her wealthiest classmates will win her acceptance into their clique. Others, especially among busy two-career couples, try to substitute newfound money for their still scarce time. Some executive dads think they can more easily afford to hire junior a private pitching coach than make time for an early evening game of catch.

4   That calculation might make business sense, but it grossly undervalues what kids want and need most: our time and attention. One of the favorite play dates in my circle is at a home where there are few fancy toys but where things are noisy and fun and the mom is always ready to take everyone to the skating rink or the zoo.

When a child begs for something—whether a $500 electric-powered baby Jaguar or a $7 bottle of lime-green nail polish—she's often just begging for a conversation with you. "Spoiling" is overindulgence combined with neglect, and kids can be spoiled at WalMart just as at FAO Schwartz.

5   I think parents shouldn't discuss with children the precise cost of expensive items. But by teaching your child about value, you can also demonstrate your family's values. One of my friends used a recent shoe-shopping trip with his kids to show why you might spend more for something well made that will last, but should not spend more just for a trendy name or style.

6   Kids, of course, are less impressed by words than by the example of parents who don't spoil themselves: who admire a pearl necklace or bamboo fly rod—and could easily afford them—but decide instead to give more to the church, or add to the childrens' college fund, or send grandma on that trip she's always wanted to take.

7   We can also teach our kids the quiet pleasure of waiting. This year my daughter got an Easy Bake Oven for Christmas. She opened it. She watched my face light up. And she gave it to me. "You finally got your oven!" she said. What a kid! Next year I think I'll get her a Barbie Dream House—I've wanted one since I was eight.

Understanding the Content

Feel free to reread all or parts of the selection to answer the following questions.

1. What is the one item that Dickinson always wanted since she was a child?

2. According to Amy Dickinson, what is the reason that parents spend so much money lavishing gifts on their children?

3. In Dickinson's opinion, when a child begs for something, what is he or she really looking for?

4. How does the author define "spoiling"?

5. In the author's "circle," or group of friends, whose house is the favorite location for a play date and why?

Looking at Structure and Style

1. Is Dickinson's thesis stated or implied? If stated, where?

2. What is the purpose of paragraph 1? How does it support the thesis of the essay?

3. Is the last paragraph effective as a concluding paragraph? Why or why not? If not, rewrite the paragraph to effectively summarize the point the author is trying to make.

4. What is the purpose of the example used in paragraph 4 of the mother who is "always ready to take everyone to the skating rink or the zoo"?

5. What can you infer about how the author feels about the parents she describes in paragraphs 2 and 3?

Evaluating the Author's Viewpoints

1. Do you agree or disagree with the author's statement that "you might spend more for something well made that will last, but should not spend more just for a trendy name or style"? Why?

2. What do you think Amy Dickinson thinks about today's kids in general? Does she feel that there is any hope for them to not be spoiled?

3. Do you agree or disagree with Amy Dickinson's statement, "In most cases, though, it seems that the ones who need help are the parents"? Why?

4. Do you think that if you have the money to do so, you should treat your children to as many items as they would like to have? Why or why not?

5. How do you think that "we can also teach our kids the quiet pleasure of waiting"?

Pursuing Possible Essay Topics

1. Write an essay describing what it was like to grow up in your family. Do you think you were "spoiled"? Why or why not?

2. Write an essay describing, from a financial point of view, what you would like to do differently from your parents when it comes to raising—and indulging—your own children.

3. Is there ever a time when it is appropriate to spoil a child? If so, when would that be and why?

4. If you had enough money to buy an expensive toy that your child felt he or she couldn't live without, would you spend the money to buy it? Why or why not? Write an essay defending your viewpoint.

5. Write an essay outlining how you would teach your child or children the value of a dollar.

6. Brainstorm or freewrite on one or more of the following:

   a. spoiled children

   b. parenting

   c. family values

7. Find a topic of your own on family, relationships, or parenting.

Preparing to Read

Take a minute or two to look over the following reading selection. Note the title and the author, read the opening paragraph, and check the essay's length. Make certain you have the time now to read it carefully and to do the exercises that follow it. Then, in the spaces provided, answer the following questions.

1. What do you think the title means?_____

   _____

   _____

2. Based on your reading of the first paragraph, what is one shortcoming of his family, in the author's opinion?_____

   _____

   _____

3. What do you think the rest of the essay is going to be about?_____

   _____

   _____

Vocabulary

Good comprehension of what you are about to read depends upon your understanding the words below. The number following each word refers to the paragraph where it is used.

eulogy (2) speech given at a funeral or memorial

disintegrated (5) fell apart

aneurysm (5) a blood-filled dilation or swelling of a blood vessel

House of Cards

KEVIN GRAY

1   Any excuse for a reunion and my family holds one. They lay out
the ziti in 20-pound trays. They park their cars on the neighbor's
grass. Dads with their pale legs showing sip vodka tonics and admire
the grill. Elderly aunts wave tissues against the heat. So it was at my
cousin's 30th-birthday party, held deep in the work-boot suburbs of
Connecticut. I'm not a fan of these functions, though I feel compelled to add that it's not because I don't love my family. It's my family's secrets that trouble me, the way we bury our mistakes in silence,
rewrite our private shames through public denial.

2   Midway through the day, I sat down next to Chris, a round-faced
11-year-old boy with a black bowl cut. I hadn't seen him in a couple
of years, since the funeral of his father, Anthony. He'd been like an
older brother to me when I was young, and then, at 36, he died of
heart failure. I delivered the eulogy.

3   Two years hadn't changed Chris much. Shy and freckled, with long
lashes and a polite smile, he avoided his rowdy cousins, who were
tossing footballs and whacking badminton birdies at their sisters. As
his mother and I talked over plates of ziti, Chris tried to interest us in
some dime-store magic tricks—pulling silk hankies from his chubby
fist, or asking me to pick a card from an outstretched deck.

4   Chris had never lived with his father; in fact, he'd barely even
known him. So a week after Anthony's funeral, his mother told me,
she decided to give Chris a keepsake from his father's closet. Not
just any keepsake, though. She gave him Anthony's baseball bat. As
she told me this a sly look passed over her face, and we shared a
dark laugh.

5   I don't know what stories Chris may have constructed about his
dad, but Anthony didn't play baseball. He owned the bat for other
reasons. The hero of my adolescence, the fast-talking, good-look-
ing charmer with David Cassidy hair and black outlaw eyes,
Anthony disintegrated in adulthood, turning, sadly, into a criminal
and a crackhead. Ten years before his death, a jailhouse beating
triggered an aneurysm, which paralyzed half his body. After that,
he slept with the bat by his side, to defend himself from drug dealers, who had twice broken into his home and beaten him up for unpaid debts.

6   The bat his son now owned carried powerful secrets: its secret life
as a weapon, the secret history of his father's addiction, even the
secret of how we, as a family, may have failed Anthony. I began to
wonder if these truths would come out, at what age, and what they
might mean to Chris. Meanwhile, Chris took a pen from his pocket.
He told me to write my name on the card, then slip it back in the

deck. He shuffled it behind his back. Then he handed me a card face down and asked triumphantly, "Is that the one?" I hesitated. "No," I said, feeling disappointed for him.

7   He produced three more cards and grew increasingly frustrated each time he was wrong. His mother only smiled. As it wore on, the exercise made me nervous. I wanted it to stop. I wanted to lie and say brightly, "Yup, that's it." But, of course, I couldn't. My name was on the card.

8   Standing there next to Chris and his mother, I remembered what it was like when, late in his life, Anthony showed up at these picnics. He'd be nervous and pasty, but we'd pretend not to notice, chatting desperately about the weather, sports, whatever. And we're still chatting past truths. It wasn't long ago that the woman over by the barbecue—self-starved, alcoholic and depressed—had lain down in the middle of an Interstate. (A motorist spotted her in time and rescued her.) She's been sober for two years now, but as I greeted her that afternoon, I didn't mention the transformation. Instead, I hugged her and said, "You look great." Best to act as if it never happened.

9   But, then what choice was there, really? And what was there to tell Chris about his father that would be of any help to the boy? I had always figured there'd be time for that later, but as Chris flipped card after card, I realized the time to tell secrets had passed. It would most likely be a couple more years until I saw him again. Who knows what he will learn by then. I pictured him, on a schoolyard play field somewhere in Connecticut, facing down a fastball with a crack bat. It was an odd little secret I could live with.

10   Chris's trick, meanwhile, was winding down, and not in a good way. He hadn't been able to produce the card with my name on it. And my cheery attempts to distract him from this fact were wearing thin. "Hang on a minute," Chris said, fishing in his pocket. "I usually carry a spare." He pulled out a little wooden box, slid the top along its grooves and removed a card, folded in four squares. "That it?" he said.

11   I opened it and found my name, just as I'd written it. Chris grinned, satisfied with his trick, and moved on to try it on another relative.

Understanding the Content

Feel free to reread all or parts of the selection to answer the following questions.

1. Where does the reunion take place?

2. What is Kevin Gray's relationship to Chris?

3. What is the real reason that Anthony owned the bat that Chris now has?

4. What did Anthony die from?

5. Does the author tell Chris about his father? Why or why not?

6. Is Chris successful at executing the card trick?

Looking at Structure and Style

1. Does the author's description of Anthony paint a very clear picture of who he was? of how the author felt about him? Why or why not?

2. Why does the author describe the events in the life of his female cousin in paragraph 8?

3. What is the thesis of this selection? Is it stated or implied? If stated, where?

4. What is the significance of the title? of the card trick described in the story?

5. What is the significance of the baseball bat? What does it represent to the author as a symbol?

Evaluating the Author's Viewpoints

1. Do you agree or disagree with the way Gray dealt with the secrets about Anthony? Do you think he should have told Chris? Why or why not?

2. How does Kevin Gray feel about his family in general? How can you tell?

3. Why is Gray so uncomfortable when it seems that the card trick isn't going to work? Do you think Chris's mother is uncomfortable, too? Why or why not?

4. Do you agree or disagree with Gray's statement regarding his female cousin, as described in paragraph 8, "Best to act as if it never happened"? Do you think he should have acknowledged what she went through? Why or why not?

5. Do you think Chris will ever learn the truth about his father? Why or why not?

6. How does the author feel about Anthony? How can you tell?

7. Do you think the author enjoys going to his family's reunions? How can you tell?

8. Does Gray give any indication of how he thinks Chris's life will turn out? If so, what does he think will happen? What do you think will happen to Chris?

Pursuing Possible Essay Topics

1. Write an essay in which you react to the essay by Kevin Gray. What do you think about his family and how they deal with their private issues?

2. How does your family deal with secrets or with their private issues? Do you agree with the way they handle these issues? Why or why not? Describe.

3. How does your family behave when they are all together? Write an essay describing a typical family get-together.

4. Write an essay describing some of the family members one would be likely to encounter at one of your family reunions.

5. Do you think the tradition of a family reunion is important to an extended family? Why or why not? Write an essay supporting your opinion.

6. Don't like these? Pick your own topic on family and write an essay.

 ## Preparing to Read

Take a minute or two to look over the following reading selection. Note the title and author, read the opening paragraph, and check the essay's length. Make certain you have the time now to read it carefully and to do the exercises that follow it. Then, in the spaces provided, answer the following questions.

1. What do you think is meant by the title, "Black Unlike Me"?_____

_____

_____

2. What do you think the selection is going to be about? _____

_____

3. Why do you think the author uses the incident in the first paragraph to open

the essay? _____

_____

_____

Vocabulary

Good comprehension of what you are about to read depends upon your understanding of the words below. The number following each word refers to the paragraph where it is used.

sermon (2) speech on conduct or duty

muffled (3) wrapped or padded to deaden the sound

diatribe (3) prolonged discourse

anonymous (3) not named or identified

indignation (4) anger aroused by something unjust, unworthy, or mean

earnest (4) exhibiting a serious or intent state of mind

tchotchkes (5) Yiddish word for trinkets or nicknacks

internalize (6) incorporate within the self as conscious or subconscious guiding principles

constructs (6) things constructed by the mind, working concepts

Black Unlike Me

JANA WOLFF

1   "I hate collars," shouts my 7-year-old son into his mattress, where he has thrown himself, 20 minutes before we need to leave for school. I just woke him and we're in the middle of a fight I can't remember starting. It's no surprise that a second-grade boy would prefer to wear an oversize sleeveless jersey—Chicago Bulls red, No. 23—rather than a button-down shirt with a collar. But this is a school day, I explain to Ari, and you go to school not to play but to learn.

2   I didn't like the mini-sermon I felt coming on, but I couldn't stop myself. I chose that moment to make the connection between collared shirts and racism to my black son. I said that it was really important for him to look his best and do his best because there were idiots in the world who actually thought that people with dark skin were not as clean, or as smart, or as good as others. My son could prove them wrong on all counts.

3   Even before I finished, Ari crumbled before my eyes. From face down on his mattress, where he was trying to dig a cave under his blanket, came his muffled voice: "I hate this." And I knew just what he meant. He has heard me talk about prejudice since he learned his colors at 2½: "People with pink skin aren't always nice to people with brown skin." Truth is, the beginnings of this dawn-hour diatribe started many years ago, when my husband and I adopted our infant son. That's when I woke up from a deep, white sleep. Suddenly, racism, which had always existed outside my focus, became my focus. When children of color become your children, anonymous struggles become personal ones with names and faces that you know.

4   I wanted to walk out of Ari's bedroom and go back in as if none of this had happened. But it was too late. I had already done that thing again. That thing that white parents who have black children do: we move from racially clueless to racially conscious in the most clumsy of ways, never turning off our radar or putting down our dukes. Then we pass along our loaded agendas to our children and scare them with an edginess that is characteristic of late learners. I jumped in to fight the battle against racism with an indignation that was earnest but not earned.

5   It must be very hard for a child to have, as tour guides, parents who are tourists themselves. The risk is that the culture being visited will be reduced to its souvenirs. All I have to do is look around Ari's room—past the clutter of Lego pieces, open books and plastic swords—to see my son's life as a pathetic collection of props: the Michael Jordan poster on the wall; the knitted Senegalese cap hanging from the doorknob; the framed autograph of Tiger Woods by his bed. The process of becoming black must lie somewhere beyond ethnic tchotchkes like these. I'm just not sure where. Ari's preference for peers over parents at this age gives me more satisfaction than most mothers experience as their young children mature. In looking toward his black friends for clues, he lands on the symbols that they value most, and he makes them his own. The day he got his hair cut exactly the way he wanted—a severe buzz on the sides with just enough hair left on top for the barber to carve a Nike swoosh—Ari walked out of that shop as if he had grown a foot taller. I had his buddies to thank for that boost.

6   I want to expand the ways for my son to be black, beyond cool haircuts and athletic heroes. The images of success in Ari's bedroom invite him to aspire to narrowly defined black standards; I'd rather my son experience the white privilege of believing that there are no limitations on who he can be and what he can do. I want Ari to internalize truths that aren't yet true: that to get straight A's is a black thing; that to set a positive example is a black thing; that to be a success in any arena is a black thing. But you can't decorate your room with these constructs. It dawned on me that morning that you can't rely on collared shirts to ward off bigotry or enhance self-esteem. "It's O.K. with me, Babe, if you wear a different shirt." Ari started heading for the dresser, when I added that it couldn't be sleeveless and it had to be clean. From the top drawer he pulled out an oversize black T-shirt with Grant Hill's picture on it. Then he sped downstairs for breakfast before I could change my mind or bring up the subject of racial pride again.

7   It is with a mixture of sadness and relief that I've begun to understand this much: becoming black is an inside job—my son's job. I can help by bringing black friends and customs and even props into our

lives, but Ari's evolution into a proud black man will occur largely outside the walls of our home. And most of his growing, I'm convinced, will happen well beyond the reach of my loving white arms.

Understanding the Content

Feel free to reread all or parts of the selection to answer the following questions.

1. Why does the author object to her son wearing an oversize sleeveless jersey to school?

2. How does her son react to her "mini-sermon"?

3. What does the author say "white parents who have black children do"?

4. What does Ari have in his room that the author classifies as "ethnic tchotchkes"?

5. Why, toward the end of the essay, does the author compromise with Ari about the type of shirt he wants to wear? What has she learned by evaluating her reaction to Ari's choice of shirt?

Looking at Structure and Style

1. How does the author use the first two paragraphs to illustrate some of the deeper struggles she has with her son's ethnicity and its impact on his life?

2. How does the author develop the incident that begins in paragraph 1 throughout the essay? Why does she choose to let her son pick out his own shirt at the end of the essay?

3. How does the author use the retelling of the disagreement with her son to discuss the larger issue of racism? What examples does she give of how she thinks her son will be affected by racism in his life?

4. The author quotes her son twice. How do the two quotes illustrate the conflict between mother and son?

5. What is the significance of a shirt with a collar? What does the author think it will say about her son if he wears that type of shirt?

Evaluating the Author's Viewpoints

1. The author has taught her son about prejudice by telling him that "people with pink skin aren't always nice to people with brown skin." Do you agree with her statement? If you had to introduce your child to the subject of racism, how would you do it?

2. How does the author think white parents with black children can help the children develop their own identities?

3. What attempts has the author made to bring symbols of black culture and pride into her son's life? Do you agree with how she has gone about this? Why or why not?

4. Why does the author call herself and her husband "tour guides" and "tourists" with regard to their parenting of Ari?

5. In general, how does the author think black men are viewed in today's society? Do you agree with her assessment? Why or why not?

Pursuing Possible Essay Topics

1. Have you ever been a victim of racism? If so, describe what happened and how you reacted to the situation.

2. With what issues would you be confronted if you adopted a child of a different race? How would you help your child assimilate into your culture and society in general?

3. Write an opinion piece on one of the following:

   a. Why is it a good idea for people from one race to adopt a child of a different race?

   b. Why is it a bad idea for people from one race to adopt a child of a different race?

4. Pick one of the following topics for an essay:

   a. Do you think people should be judged by the way they dress or by their overall appearance?

   b. Do you think people are judged by the way they dress or by their overall appearance?

5. Brainstorm or freewrite on one or more of the following:

   a. racism in America

   b. multiculturalism

   c. adoption

   d. ethnicity

6. Pick your own topic on family or relationships and write an essay about it.

Preparing to Read

Take a minute or two to look over the following reading selection. Note the title and author, read the opening paragraph, and check the essay's length. Make certain you have the time now to read it carefully and to do the exercises that follow it. Then, in the spaces provided, answer the following questions.

1. What do you think the essay will say about fatherhood? _____

   _____

   _____

2. What is your reaction to the statistics presented? _____

   _____

   _____

3. What do you think is the answer to the question in the title? _____

   _____

   _____

   _____

Vocabulary

Good comprehension of what you are about to read depends upon your understanding of the words below. The number following each word refers to the paragraph where it is used.

monitored (2) observed closely

alienation (2) a sense of being withdrawn, separated, or divided

calamity (3) tragedy, misadventure

demography (7) study of the characteristics of human populations

substantial (10) abundant, visible

array (16) an impressively large number

egalitarian (18) believing in equal political, economic, social, and civil rights

superfluous (24) excessive, extra

empathy (28) feeling or concern for others

promiscuous (30) indiscriminate

insidiously (46) working harm in a stealthy manner

ominous (46) dangerous, threatening

Where's Papa?

David Popenoe

1   The decline of fatherhood is one of the most basic, unexpected, and extraordinary social trends of our time. Its dimensions can be captured in a single statistic: In just three decades, between 1960 and 1990, the percentage of U.S. children living apart from their biological fathers more than doubled, from 17 percent to 36 percent. By the turn of the century, nearly 50 percent of American children may be going to sleep each evening without being able to say good night to their dads.

2   No one predicted this trend, few researchers or government agencies have monitored it, and it is not widely discussed, even today. But the decline of fatherhood is a major force behind many of the most disturbing problems that plague American society: crime and delinquency; teenage pregnancy; deteriorating educational achievement; depression, substance abuse, and alienation among adolescents; and the growing number of women and children living in poverty. The current generation of children may be the first in our nation's history to be less well off—psychologically, socially, economically, and morally—than their parents were at the same age. The United States, observes Senator Daniel Patrick Moynihan, "may be the first society in history in which children are distinctly worse off than adults."

3   Even as this calamity unfolds, our cultural view of fatherhood itself is changing. Few people doubt the fundamental importance of mothers. But fathers? More and more, the question of whether fathers are really necessary is being raised. Fatherhood is said by many to be merely a social role that others—mothers, partners, stepfathers, uncles and aunts, grandparents—can play.

4   There was a time in the past when fatherlessness was far more common than it is today, but death was to blame, not divorce, desertion, and out-of-wedlock births. In early-17th-century Virginia, only an estimated 31 percent of white children reached age 18 with both parents still alive. That figure climbed to 50 percent by the early

18th century, to 72 percent by the start of the 20th century, and close to its current level by 1940. Today, well over 90 percent of America's youngsters turn 18 with two living parents. Almost all of today's "fatherless" children have fathers who are alive, well, and perfectly capable of shouldering the responsibilities of fatherhood. Who would have thought that so many men would relinquish them?

5   Not so long ago, social scientists and others dismissed the change in the cause of fatherlessness as irrelevant. Children, it was said, are merely losing their parents in a different way than they used to. You don't hear that very much anymore. A surprising finding of recent research is that it is decidedly worse for a child to lose a father in the modern, voluntary way than through death. The children of divorced and never-married mothers are less successful in life by almost every measure than the children of widowed mothers. The replacement of death by divorce as the prime cause of fatherlessness is a monumental setback in the history of childhood.

6   Until the 1960s, the falling death rate and the rising divorce rate neutralized each other. In 1900 the percentage of American children living in single-parent families was 8.5 percent. By 1960 it had increased to just 9.1 percent. Virtually no one during those years was writing or thinking about family breakdown, disintegration, or decline.

7   Indeed, what is most significant about the changing family demography of the first six decades of the 20th century is this: Because the death rate was dropping faster than the divorce rate was rising, more children were living with both of their natural parents by 1960 than at any other time in world history. The figure was close to 80 percent for the generation born in the late 1940s and early 1950s. But then the decline in the death rate slowed, and the divorce rate skyrocketed. "The scale of marital breakdowns in the West since 1960 has no historical precedent that I know of," says Lawrence Stone, a noted Princeton University family historian. "There has been nothing like it for the last 2,000 years, and probably longer."

8   Consider what has happened to children. Most estimates are that only about 50 percent of the children born during the 1970–84 "baby bust" period will still live with their natural parents by age 17—a staggering drop from nearly 80 percent.

9   In theory, divorce need not mean disconnection. In reality, it often does. A large survey conducted in the late 1980s found that about one in five divorced fathers had not seen his children in the past year and that fewer than half of divorced fathers saw their children more than several times a year. A 1981 survey of adolescents who were living apart from their fathers found that 52 percent hadn't seen them at all in more than a year; only 16 percent saw their fathers as often as once a week—and the fathers' contact with their children dropped off sharply over time.

10   The picture grows worse. Just as divorce has overtaken death as the leading cause of fatherlessness, out-of-wedlock births are expected to surpass divorce in the 1990s. They accounted for 30 percent of all births by 1991; by the turn of the century they may account for 40 percent (and 80 percent of minority births). And there is substantial evidence that having an unmarried father is even worse for a child than having a divorced father.

11   Across time and cultures, fathers have always been considered essential—and not just for their sperm. Indeed, no known society ever thought of fathers as potentially unnecessary. Marriage and the nuclear family—mother, father, and children—are the most universal social institutions in existence. In no society has the birth of children out of wedlock been the cultural norm. To the contrary, concern for the legitimacy of children is nearly universal.

12   In my many years as a sociologist, I have found few other bodies of evidence that lean so much in one direction as this one: On the whole, two parents—a father and a mother—are better for a child than one parent. There are, to be sure, many factors that complicate this simple proposition. We all know of a two-parent family that is truly dysfunctional—the proverbial family from hell. A child can certainly be raised to a fulfilling adulthood by one loving parent who is wholly devoted to the child's well-being. But such exceptions do not invalidate the rule any more than the fact that some three-pack-a-day smokers live to a ripe old age casts doubt on the dangers of cigarettes.

13   The collapse of children's well-being in the United States has reached breathtaking proportions. Juvenile violent crime has increased from 18,000 arrests in 1960 to 118,000 in 1992, a period in which the total number of young people in the population remained relatively stable. Reports of child neglect and abuse have quadrupled since 1976, when data were first collected. Since 1960, eating disorders and depression have soared among adolescent girls. Teen suicide has tripled. Alcohol and drug abuse among teenagers, although it has leveled off in recent years, continues at a very high rate. Scholastic Aptitude Test scores have declined more than 70 points, and most of the decline cannot be accounted for by the increased academic diversity of students taking the test. Poverty has shifted from the elderly to the young. Of all the nation's poor today, 38 percent are children.

14   One can think of many explanations for these unhappy developments: the growth of commercialism and consumerism, the influence of television and the mass media, the decline of religion, the widespread availability of guns and addictive drugs, and the decay of social order and neighborhood relationships. None of these causes should be dismissed. But the evidence is now strong that the absence of fathers from the lives of children is one of the most important causes.

15   What do fathers do? Partly, of course, it is simply being a second adult in the home. Bringing up children is demanding, stressful, and often exhausting. Two adults can support and spell each other; they can also offset each other's deficiencies and build on each other's strengths.

16   Beyond that, fathers—men—bring an array of unique and irreplaceable qualities that women do not ordinarily bring. Some of these are familiar, if sometimes overlooked or taken for granted. The father as protector, for example, has by no means outlived his usefulness. And he is important as a role model. Teenage boys without fathers are notoriously prone to trouble. The pathway to adulthood for daughters is somewhat easier, but they still must learn from their fathers, as they cannot from their mothers, how to relate to men. They learn from their fathers about heterosexual trust, intimacy, and difference. They learn to appreciate their own femininity from the one male who is most special in their lives (assuming that they love and respect their fathers). Most important, through loving and being loved by their fathers, they learn that they are worthy of love.

17   Recent research has given us much deeper—and more surprising—insights into the father's role in child rearing. It shows that in almost all of their interactions with children, fathers do things a little differently from mothers. What fathers do—their special parenting style—is not only highly complementary to what mothers do but is by all indications important in its own right.

18   For example, an often-overlooked dimension of fathering is play. From their children's birth through adolescence, fathers tend to emphasize play more than caretaking. This may be troubling to egalitarian feminists, and it would indeed be wise for most fathers to spend more time in caretaking. Yet the fathers' style of play seems to have unusual significance. It is likely to be both physically stimulating and exciting. With older children it involves more physical games and teamwork that require the competitive testing of physical and mental skills. It frequently resembles an apprenticeship or teaching relationship: Come on, let me show you how.

19   Mothers generally spend more time playing with their children, but mothers' play tends to take place more at the child's level. Mothers provide the child with the opportunity to direct the play, to be in charge, to proceed at the child's own pace. Kids, at least in the early years, seem to prefer to play with daddy. In one study of 2½-year-olds who were given a choice, more than two-thirds chose to play with their fathers.

20   The way fathers play affects everything from the management of emotions to intelligence and academic achievement. It is particularly important in promoting the essential virtue of self-control. According to one expert, "Children who roughhouse with their fathers . . .

usually quickly learn that biting, kicking, and other forms of physical violence are not acceptable." They learn when enough is enough.

21   Children, a committee assembled by the Board on Children and Families of the National Research Council concluded, "learn critical lessons about how to recognize and deal with highly charged emotions in the context of playing with their fathers. Fathers, in effect, give children practice in regulating their own emotions and recognizing others' emotional clues." A study of convicted murderers in Texas found that 90 percent of them either didn't play as children or played abnormally.

22   At play and in other realms, fathers tend to stress competition, challenge, initiative, risk taking, and independence. Mothers, as caretakers, stress emotional security and personal safety. On the playground, fathers will try to get the child to swing higher than the person on the next swing, while mothers will worry about an accident. It's sometimes said that fathers express more concern for the child's long-term development, while mothers focus on the child's immediate well-being. It is clear that children have dual needs that must be met. Becoming a mature and competent adult involves the integration of two often-contradictory human desires: for *communion*, or the feeling of being included, connected, and related, and for *agency*, which entails independence, individuality, and self-fulfillment. One without the other is a denuded and impaired humanity, an incomplete realization of human potential.

23   For many couples, to be sure, these functions are not rigidly divided along standard female-male lines, and there may even be a role reversal. But the exceptions prove the rule. Gender-differentiated parenting is so important that in child rearing by gay and lesbian couples, one partner commonly fills the male role while the other fills the female role.

24   It is ironic that in our public discussion of fathering, it's seldom acknowledged that fathers have a distinctive role to play. Indeed, it's far more often said that fathers should be more like mothers (and that men generally should be more like women—less aggressive, less competitive). While such things may be said with the best of intentions, the effects are perverse. After all, if fathering is no different from mothering, males can easily be replaced in the home by women. It might even seem better. Already viewed as a burden and obstacle to self-fulfillment, fatherhood thus comes to seem superfluous and unnecessary as well.

25   We know that fathers have a surprising impact on children. Fathers' involvement seems to be linked to improved quantitative and verbal

skills, improved problem-solving ability, and higher academic achievement. Several studies have found that the presence of the father is one of the determinants of girls' proficiency in mathematics. And one pioneering study found that the amount of time fathers spent reading was a strong predictor of their daughters' verbal ability.

26   For sons, who can more directly follow their fathers' example, the results have been even more striking. A number of studies have uncovered a strong relationship between father involvement and the quantitative and mathematical abilities of their sons. Other studies have found a relationship between paternal nurturing and boys' verbal intelligence.

27   How fathers produce these intellectual benefits is not yet clear. No doubt it is partly a matter of the time and money a man brings to his family. But it is probably also related to the unique mental and behavioral qualities of men; the male sense of play, reasoning, challenge, and problem solving; and the traditional male association with achievement and occupational advancement.

28   Men also have a vital role to play in promoting cooperation and other "soft" virtues. We don't often think of fathers as teachers of empathy, but involved fathers, it turns out, may be of special importance for the development of this character trait, essential to an ordered society of law-abiding, cooperative, and compassionate adults. Examining the results of a 26-year longitudinal study, a trio of researchers at McGill University reached a "quite astonishing" conclusion: The single most important childhood factor in empathy is paternal involvement in child care. Fathers who spent time alone with their children more than twice a week—giving meals, baths, and other basic care—reared the most compassionate adults.

29   It is not yet clear why fathers are so important in instilling this quality. Perhaps merely by being with their children they provide a model for compassion. Perhaps it has to do with their style of play or mode of reasoning. Perhaps it is somehow related to the fact that fathers typically are the family's main arbiter with the outside world. Or perhaps it is because mothers who receive help from their mates have more time and energy to cultivate the soft virtues. Whatever the reason, it is hard to think of a more important contribution that fathers can make to their children.

30   Men, too, suffer grievously from the growth of fatherlessness. The world over, young and unattached males have always been a cause for social concern. They can be a danger to themselves and to society. Young unattached men tend to be more aggressive, violent, promiscuous, and prone to substance abuse; they are also more likely to die prematurely through disease, accidents, or self-neglect.

They make up the majority of deviants, delinquents, criminals, killers, drug users, vice lords, and miscreants of every kind. Senator Moynihan put it succinctly when he warned that a society full of unattached males "asks for and gets chaos."

31   Family life—marriage and child rearing—is a civilizing force for men. It encourages them to develop prudence, cooperativeness, honesty, trust, self-sacrifice, and other habits that can lead to success as an economic provider. Marriage also focuses male sexual energy. Having children typically impresses on men the importance of setting a good example. Who hasn't heard at least one man say that he gave up a socially irresponsible way of life when he married and had children?

32   The civilizing effect of being a father is highlighted by a path-breaking program started in 1982 in one of Cleveland's inner-city neighborhoods by social worker Charles Ballard. Using an intensive social-work approach that includes home visits, parenting programs, and group therapy sessions, he has reunited more than 2,000 absent, unwed fathers with their children through his Institute for Responsible Fatherhood and Family Revitalization.

33   The standard theory is that if you want inner-city men to be responsible fathers, you first must find them a job. Ballard has stood this theory on its head. His approach is that you first must covince the young men of the importance of being a good father, and then they will be motivated to finish school and find work. An independent evaluation of his approach showed that it works. Only 12 percent of the young men had full-time work when they entered his program, but 62 percent later found such work, and 12 percent found part-time jobs. Ninety-seven percent of the men he dealt with began to provide financial support for their children, and 71 percent had no additional children out of wedlock.

34   Marriage by itself, even without children, is also a major civilizing force for men. No other institution save religion (and perhaps the military) places such moral demands on men. To be sure, there is a selection factor in marriage. The men whom women would care to marry already have some of the civilized virtues, and those who are morally beyond the pale have difficulty finding mates. Yet studies have shown that marriage has a civilizing effect independent of the selection factor. Marriage actually promotes health, competence, virtue, and personal well-being. Along with the continued growth of fatherlessness, we can expect to see a nation of men who are at worst morally out of control and at best unhappy, unhealthy, and unfulfilled.

35   Just as cultural forms can be discarded, dismantled, and declared obsolete, so can they be reinvented. In order to restore marriage and reinstate fathers in the lives of their children, we are somehow going to have to undo the cultural shift of the past few decades toward

radical individualism. We are going to have to re-embrace some cultural propositions that throughout history have been universally accepted but that today are unpopular, if not rejected outright.

36   Marriage must be re-established as a strong social institution. The father's role must also be redefined in a way that neglects neither historical models nor the unique attributes of modern societies, the new roles for women, and the special qualities that men bring to child rearing. Such changes are by no means impossible. Witness the transformations wrought by the civil rights, women's, and environmental movements, and even the campaigns to reduce smoking and drunk driving. What is necessary is for large numbers of adults, and especially our cultural and intellectual leaders, to agree on the importance of change.

37   There are many practical steps that can be taken. Employers, for example, can reduce the practice of uprooting and relocating married couples with children, provide generous parental leave, and experiment with more flexible forms of work. Religious leaders can reclaim moral ground from the culture of divorce and nonmarriage, resisting the temptation to equate "committed relationships" with marriage. Marriage counselors and family therapists can begin with a bias in favor of marriage, stressing the needs of the marriage at least as much as the needs of the individual. As for the entertainment industry, pressure already is being brought to bear to curtail the glamorization of unwed motherhood, marital infidelity, alternative lifestyles, and sexual promiscuity.

38   What about divorce? Current laws send the message that marriage is not a socially important relationship that involves a legally binding commitment. We should consider a two-tier system of divorce law: Marriages without minor children would be relatively easy to dissolve, but marriages with young children would be dissolvable only by mutual agreement or on grounds that clearly involve a wrong by one party against the other, such as desertion or physical abuse. Longer waiting periods for divorcing couples with children might also be necessary, combined with some form of mandatory marriage counseling.

39   Because the causes of the decline of marriage and fatherhood lie mainly in the moral, behavioral, and even spiritual realms, the decline is mostly resistant to public-policy and government cures. All of the Western societies, regardless of governmental system and political persuasion, have been beset by this problem. The decline of marriage is almost as great in Sweden, which has the West's most ambitious welfare state, as it is in the United States, the most laissez-faire of the industrialized nations.

40   Nevertheless, government policies do have some impact. While the statistical relationship of economic cycles to marriage and divorce is not particularly strong, for example, low wages, unemployment, and

poverty have never been friendly to marriage. Government can do something about that. It can also remedy the decline in the value of the income tax exemption for dependent children and erase the tax code's "marriage penalty." As a society, we have decided through a variety of government programs to socialize much of the cost of growing old, but less of the cost of raising children. At the very least, we should strive for generational equity. But more than anything else, parents need time to be with their children, the kind of time that would be afforded by a more generous family-leave policy.

41   We also should consider providing educational credits or vouchers to parents who leave the paid labor force to raise their young children. These parents are performing an important social service at the risk of damaging their long-term career prospects. Education subsidies, like those in the GI Bill of Rights, would reward parents by helping them resume their careers.

42   Government policies should be designed to favor married, child-rearing couples. Some critics argue that the federal government should not involve itself in sensitive moral issues or risk stigmatizing alternative lifestyles. But recognizing alternatives doesn't require treating them as equivalent to marriage. The government regularly takes moral positions on a whole range of issues, such as the rights of women, income equality, and race relations. A position on the need for children to have two committed parents, a father and a mother, during their formative years would hardly be a radical departure.

43   Our social order is fraying badly. We seem, despite notable accomplishments in some areas, to be on a path of decline. The past three decades have seen steeply rising crime rates, growing personal and corporate greed, deteriorating communities, and increasing confusion over moral issues. For most Americans, life has become more anxious, unsettled, and insecure.

44   In large part, this represents a failure of social values. People can no longer be counted on to conduct themselves according to the virtues of honesty, self-sacrifice, and personal responsibility. In our ever-growing pursuit of the self—self-expression, self-development, self-actualization, and self-fulfillment—we seem to have slipped off many of our larger social obligations.

45   At the heart of our discontent lies an erosion of personal relationships. People no longer trust others as they once did; they no longer feel the same sense of commitment and obligation to others. In part, this may be an unavoidable product of the modern condition. But it has gone much deeper than that. Some children now go to bed each night

wondering whether their father will be there the next morning. Some wonder what happened to their father. And some wonder who he is. What are these children learning at this most basic of all levels about honesty, self-sacrifice, personal responsibility, and trust?

46   What the decline of fatherhood and marriage in America really means is that slowly, insidiously, and relentlessly our society has been moving in an ominous direction. If we are to move toward a more just and humane society, we must reverse the tide that is pulling fathers apart from their families. Nothing is more important for our children or for our future as a nation.

Understanding the Content

Feel free to reread all or parts of the selection to answer the following questions.

1. Popenoe says "the decline of fatherhood is a major force behind many of the most disturbing problems that plague American society" (2). What are some of the problems he cites as examples?

2. What was the leading cause for fatherlessness in the past? What is the cause today?

3. Popenoe believes that fathers "bring an array of unique and irreplaceable qualities that women do not ordinarily bring" to a home (16). What are these qualities?

4. What, according to Popenoe, is the difference in the way mothers and fathers play with their children?

5. What did the twenty-six-year McGill University study reveal about adults raised by fathers who spent time alone with their children more than twice a week, giving meals, baths, and other basic care?

6. What effects does not being a father have on men? Why is family life—marriage and child rearing—considered a "civilizing force for men"?

7. What steps does Popenoe suggest be taken to re-establish marriage as a strong social institution?

Looking at Structure and Style

1. Popenoe opens his essay with some statistics. Is this a good technique, in light of his thesis and concerns? Does the opening paragraph get your attention? Explain.

2. What is the function of paragraph 2? Why does Popenoe quote the late Senator Moynihan?

3. Paragraphs 6–10 contain many statistics. Are they helpful or distracting? What audience would be interested in these statistics?

4. Popenoe compares and contrasts the importance of the roles of fathers and mothers in raising children. How clearly does he make these distinctions? What paragraphs reveal some of the comparisons and contrasts?

5. Describe Popenoe's tone and attitude. What words or phrases help establish his tone and attitude?

6. Does Popenoe end his essay with a summary, or does he draw a conclusion? Explain.

Evaluating the Author's Viewpoints

1. Popenoe argues against the theory that "if you want inner-city men to be responsible fathers, you first must find them a job" (33). Do you agree with the theory? Why or why not?

2. Popenoe says, "Marriage must be re-established as a strong social institution" and the father's role "redefined" (36). Explain why you agree or disagree.

3. Reread paragraph 37. Explain why you agree or disagree with each of Popenoe's suggestions. Would they help change the growing trend toward fatherlessness?

4. Reread paragraph 38. Do you agree with Popenoe's suggestion for changing divorce laws? Why or why not?

5. What role does Popenoe feel the government should have in stopping fatherlessness? Do you agree? How much do you think local, state, and federal government agencies should get involved?

6. Popenoe says, "People no longer trust others as they once did; they no longer feel the same sense of commitment and obligation to others" (45). Do you agree? Explain your views.

Pursuing Possible Essay Topics

Before beginning an essay on family or relationships, read the following essay, "The Father Fixation" by Judith Stacey.

Preparing to Read

Take a minute or two to look over the following reading selection. Note the title and author, read the first two paragraphs, and check the essay's length. Make certain you have the time now to read it carefully and to do the exercises that follow it. Then, in the spaces provided, answer the following questions.

1. What do you think the essay will say about fatherhood? _____

   _____

   _____

2. Do you think Judith Stacey will support or refute David Popenoe's thesis in

   "Where's Papa?" _____

   _____

   _____

3. What do you think the title means? _____

   _____

   _____

Vocabulary

Good comprehension of what you are about to read depends upon your understanding of the words below. The number following each word refers to the paragraph where it is used.

intoning (1) reciting, saying

mantra (1) a verbal formula repeated in prayer or meditation

rhetoric (1) use of language, discourse

consensus (2) feeling of agreement

temperate (2) milder, less severe

blatantly (3) obviously, openly

resoundingly (4) loudly, reverberatingly

poignantly (6) movingly, touchingly, in a heartfelt manner

castigates (7) denounces, condemns

coerce (9) force, pressure

The Father Fixation

JUDITH STACEY

1   As the electoral season hits full throttle, more and more voices are intoning the mantra of "family values." The Institute for American Values and its offshoot, the Council on Families in America, and other groups crusade on behalf of the supposed superiority of married-couple nuclear families, branding all other kinds of families second-rate—or worse. They are using the apparently objective language of social science to preach a sermon that we used to hear mainly in the fire-and-brimstone tones of the religious right. This quieted-down approach is having a major effect on Democratic Party and media rhetoric on family issues.

2   These groups pretend to speak for an overwhelming consensus of social scientists when they blame family "breakdown"—by which they mean primarily the rise of divorce and unwed parenting—for just about every social problem in the nation. David Blankenhorn, president of the Institute for American Values, for example, calls fatherlessness "the most harmful demographic trend of this generation." He writes that "it is the leading cause of declining child well-being in our society. It is also the engine driving our most urgent social problems, from crime to adolescent pregnancy to child sexual abuse to domestic violence against women." The somewhat more temperate David Popenoe [see pp. 288–297] concedes that there are many sources of social decay but insists that "the evidence is now strong that the absence of fathers from the lives of children is one of the most important causes."

3   However well intentioned and appealing, most of the claims made by family values crusaders are blatantly false as well as destructive. As a sociologist, I can attest that there is absolutely no consensus among social scientists on family values, on the superiority of the heterosexual nuclear family, or on the supposed evil effects of fatherlessness. In fact, the best research and the most careful, best-regarded researchers, among them Andrew Cherlin at Johns Hopkins University, confirm that the quality of our family relationships and resources is far more important than gender or structure. The claim that intact two-parent families are inherently superior rests exclusively on the misuse of statistics and on the most

elementary social science sins—portraying correlations as though they were causes, ignoring mediating factors, and treating small, overlapping differences as gross and absolute.

4   Take, for example, the hysteria that the family values campaign has whipped up about the "doomsday" effects of divorce. Certainly, no sociologist—no reasonable adult I can think of—would argue that divorce is a meaningless or minor event for a family. No one among the many scholars of the family who share my views would deny that some divorces unfairly serve the interests of one or both parents at the expense of their children. Still, the evidence resoundingly supports the idea that a high-conflict marriage injures children more than a divorce does. Instead of protecting children, the current assault on no-fault divorce endangers them by inviting more parental conflict, desertion, and fraud.

5   Moreover, research shows again and again that poverty and unemployment can more reliably predict who will marry, divorce, or commit or suffer domestic or social violence than can the best-tuned measure of values yet devised. A study conducted by University of California–Berkeley psychologist Ralph Catalano found, for example, that workers laid off from their jobs were six times more likely than employed workers to commit violent acts and that losing one's job was a better predictor of violence than gender, marital status, mental illness, or anything else. Those who really want to shore up marriages should fight for secure jobs and a living wage.

6   You don't need to be a social scientist to know that living with married biological parents offers children no magic shield against trouble. Indeed, a recent Kaiser Permanente study of youth and violence found that 68 percent of "youth highly exposed to health and safety threats" were living in two-parent households. Poignantly, even in two-parent families, fathers were among the last people troubled teens said they would turn to for help: 44 percent said they would turn to their mothers for advice; 26 percent chose their friends; and only 10 percent picked their fathers.

7   Harping on the superiority of married biological parents and the evils of fatherlessness injures children and parents in a wide array of contemporary families, including the millions of children who live with gay or lesbian parents. Blankenhorn castigates lesbian couples who choose to have children for promoting "radical fatherlessness" and advocates restricting access to sperm banks and fertility services to married heterosexual couples. Popenoe claims that biological fathers make distinctive, irreplaceable contributions to their children's welfare.

8   Yet here the social science record is truly uniform. Nearly three decades of research finds gay and lesbian parents to be at least as successful as heterosexuals. Dozens of studies conclude that children reared by lesbian or gay parents have no greater gender or

social difficulties than other children, except for the problems caused by homophobia and discrimination. Ironically, some of the worst risks these children suffer stem from our failure to legally recognize the actual two-parent families in which many live. For example, a child whose lesbian birth mother dies often loses a second parent too, as Kristen Pearlman did in 1985 when a Florida court placed her in the custody of her grandparents rather than her surviving co-mother, Janine Ratcliffe, who had helped parent her since birth. Anyone who cares about the welfare of children should campaign to extend full marriage and custody rights to their parents rather than belittle them for lacking a father or mother.

9   It is time to face the irreversible historical fact that family diversity is here to stay. Of course, two good parents of whatever gender generally are better than one. But no one lives in a "general" family. Our unique, often imperfect, real families assume many shapes, sizes, and characters. Each type of family has strengths, vulnerabilities, and challenges, and each needs support and deserves respect. We can't coerce or preach people into successful marital or parenting relationships, but we can help them to succeed in the ones they form. What we need to promote instead of divisive, self-righteous family values are inclusive, democratic, and compassionate *social* values.

Understanding the Content

Feel free to reread all or parts, of the selection to answer the following questions.

1. In what way does Judith Stacey disagree with David Popenoe and others regarding fatherlessness and the breakdown of family values? Why does she feel they are wrong?

2. What research does Stacey cite that she feels supports her viewpoint? What does she call "the misuse of statistics" and "the most elementary social science sins"?

3. In what ways do Stacey and Popenoe disagree regarding the relationship between job security and responsible fatherhood?

4. According to Stacey, what does research reveal about gay and lesbian parents? How does she use this research to counter Popenoe's claim that "biological fathers make distinctive, irreplaceable contributions to their children's welfare"?

5. What is Stacey's idea of "family diversity"? Does her idea of family differ from Popenoe's? Explain.

Looking at Structure and Style

1. How does Stacey use viewpoints opposite to her own to introduce her subject and thesis? Is this an effective method? Explain.

2. Reread paragraph 4. What paragraph pattern is used? How is it used as a transition from paragraph 3?

3. Both Popenoe and Stacey use statistics and references to research. Which of the two authors uses these more effectively? Why?

4. Describe Stacey's tone and attitude. What words or phrases develop her tone and attitude?

5. Reread Stacey's concluding paragraph. Is it effective? Explain.

Evaluating the Author's Viewpoints

1. In paragraph 3, Stacey says, "However well intentioned and appealing, most of the claims made by family values crusaders are blatantly false as well as destructive." Do you think she proves her point? Why or why not?

2. Stacey believes that "a high-conflict marriage injures children more than a divorce does" (4). Do you agree? Why or why not?

3. Reread paragraph 7. Who gives the better argument or better support for her or his viewpoint, Stacey or Popenoe? Why do you think so?

4. Stacey says in her concluding paragraph, "Each type of family has strengths, vulnerabilities, and challenges, and each needs support and deserves respect." Do you agree? Explain.

Pursuing Possible Essay Topics

1. Write an essay that shows why either Stacey or Popenoe offers better support for his or her viewpoint. Draw upon the essays to support your thesis.

2. Look up one or more of the research sources mentioned in either Stacey's or Popenoe's essay. How accurately was it used in supporting the author's viewpoint? Is the research too dated to be of relevance today?

3. Write an essay that supports your viewpoint on gay and lesbian parents.

4. Write an essay titled "The Mother Fixation" or "Where's Mama?"

5. Write an essay that discusses the family values that are important to you in raising your children. Why do you think they are worthwhile? Can the values be maintained? How would you go about instilling them in your family?

6. Brainstorm or freewrite on one or more of the following:
   a. fatherlessness
   d. domestic violence
   b. unwed parenting
   e. family values
   c. divorce
   f. sperm banks

7. If you don't like these topics, find one of your own on family relationships.

Student Essay

Read the following narrative essay written by a student. As you read, look for answers to these questions:

1. Does the essay fit the assignment to write on some aspect of family or relationships?

2. Is there a thesis? If so, is it well supported and convincing? Has the student considered her audience? Is the title appropriate?

3. What would you suggest to the student to make the essay better?

My Younger Sibling

Anne Rishi

1   When we were growing up, I never paid too much attention to my little sister Jill. She had her friends and I had mine, but it was almost as if we took each other for granted, like a piece of furniture that was always there. This was especially so when I became a teenager and spent more time away from home. But back then, I had no idea what an influence I was having on her. If I had, I hope that I would have done things differently, because it may be too late now.

2   In high school I started hanging out with some students you could say were less than academically oriented. We were bored and found little value in school. So we ditched as often as we could and would hang out at the beach, smoking and acting like we were cool. Of course, being cool meant having sex with a guy I thought I was in love with. And just like in some sad teenage tale, I found myself pregnant.

3   When my parents found out, they took it better than I thought they would. Not that they liked it one bit. No, I got my share of "how-could-you-do-it-what-were-you-thinking" comments. But my parents finally accepted the situation. When the boy involved found out, he agreed to marry me and we moved in with his parents. So my senior year was spent being pregnant and married to a boy I really didn't know all that well. We never did get to know each other very well. He took off after the baby was born. My parents didn't think it was a good idea for me to move back home with a baby, not while Jill was still in school. So they helped me with the paper work involved and soon I began collecting welfare checks and moved into a cheap apartment. Now I'm starting city college on a special program and hope I can complete my education.

4   At that time, I was so wound up in my problems that I don't remember what Jill thought about it all. I didn't care.

5   I should have.

6   Last week Jill came over to visit me and the baby. She told me she envied me living on my own and having a baby to love. I told her it wasn't as easy as it looked and that I was pretty lonely. She told me she is seeing a boy and hopes to get pregnant like I did so that she can leave home and live like me. She shocked me even more when she said that she feels our mother pays more attention to me and the baby now than she does to her. Jill admits she doesn't really want a baby, but she thinks the money she'd get from the government like I do would help her get out of the house and then Mom would pay more attention to her.

7   I tried to convince her she would ruin her life, but she looks at me and thinks I'm doing just fine. She can't see that I'm struggling with raising a baby alone, trying to pass my classes, and not having any fun. Now I see I've become an unwitting role model for my sister, a role I can only hope she doesn't follow. If only I'd realized the impact of my life on my little sister.

Reaction

In your journal or on a separate sheet of paper, write your reaction to the student essay. Use the questions posed before the essay as a guide for your comments.

On the Net

This chapter explores many aspects of family and relationships. If you want to learn more about your own family, check out *www.rootsweb.com/~rwguide*. This site will help you learn more about genealogy and will help you construct your family tree.

After you have had fun looking into your family's roots, do some research on a specific topic, such as adoption. Adoption is discussed in the article "Black Unlike Me" by Jana Wolff. Search the Web for resources on adoption and choose three sites that you think have the best, most unbiased information. Then answer the following questions:

1. How many sites did you explore?

2. What criteria did you use in choosing the three best sites?

3. Do you think the sites that you chose have the best information about adoption, or would you need to access more sites to compile the best information possible?

4. What is the best site you visited? Why?

If you do not want to do further research on the topic of adoption, choose another topic from the chapter and answer the questions above.

8

Viewpoints on Work

FOCUS ON WORK

To help you focus on the subject of this chapter, answer the following questions. You may want to write the answers in your journal or be prepared to discuss them in class.

1. Read the quotation by Samuel Butler on the opposite page. What do you think he means? Do you agree? Do you see your work as a portrait of yourself?

2. What do you feel is the ideal job, occupation, or profession? Why do you feel that way?

3. Look at the top photograph on the opposite page. What do you think is happening? Is he going up or down the ladder? What is he holding in his hand? Is he working or playing?

4. Look at the bottom photograph on the opposite page. What do you think is happening? What is your reaction? Explain.

5. In what kind of work or occupation have members of your family been involved? Are you interested in following in a family member's footsteps regarding work? Explain.

6. How do you define *work?*

7. What do you think are the characteristics of good working conditions? What types of jobs offer these conditions?

Peter Southwick/Stock Boston

Virginia Blaisdell/Stock Boston

309

For many people the real reason for working is not the work itself but the money or the status or the power the work may bring. Sociologists claim that the average person more or less puts up with a job because of personal and family needs that are considered to be important, such as food, clothing, and shelter.

The style of our lives is often based on the type of work we do. Some jobs allow for flexible schedules, which means we can take advantage of convenient times to meet personal or family needs; however, flexible schedules can be a disadvantage if we decide to take our work home with us. Other jobs are inflexible, even requiring us to punch time clocks. Such work means we cannot easily take time off to tend to personal or family needs, leaving only evenings and weekends. Yet, in those cases, work can be left behind at the job site. The time that we have for ourselves and our families, then, is determined by the type of job we have.

The work we do not only determines the quality of our lives by shaping our time, our leisure, our buying power, and our ability to travel; it even shapes our identities. When we meet someone for the first time, we generally ask, "What do you do?" The meaning behind the question is understood: "What do you do for a living?" And when the answer is waitress, police officer, doctor, writer, sales clerk, or whatever, we generally categorize that person to fit our stereotype of that particular jobholder.

As our economy changes, so do our jobs. Many of us find we must move from community to community to keep up with jobs that require our skills or to find new ones when laid off. Many of us attend college in preparation for a particular line of work only to discover that there are no positions available, or to realize that what we've prepared for is not what we really want to do. Many of us who have been in the same job for years suddenly find we must go back to school to retrain in order to meet the advancements made in our field.

Changes in traditional family roles are also changing our work habits. Some men are discovering they would rather stay home and raise their children while their wives go off to work. Many women are realizing they prefer a career to the traditional mother or housewife role. Such changes are redefining the term *homemaker*.

The reading selections in this unit supply a wide range of viewpoints toward work, from how to go for a job interview to attempts at defining what "real work" is. Use them to discover and to stimulate your own view on work.

 ## Preparing to Read

Take a minute or two to look over the following reading selection. Note the title and the author, read the opening paragraph, and check the essay's length. Make certain you have the time now to read it carefully and to do the exercises that follow it. Then, in the spaces provided, answer the following questions.

1. What does the title mean?_____

   _____

2. Based on the title and your reading of paragraph 1, what do you think the author's attitude toward the subject of the essay will be?_____

   _____

3. What is the author's tone?_____

   _____

   _____

Vocabulary

Good comprehension of what you are about to read depends upon your understanding the words below. The number following each word refers to the paragraph where it is used.

commissioned (3) assigned, appointed

coinciding (4) happening at the same time

attributes (4) characteristics, qualifications

flummoxing (6) confusing, perplexing

irascible (8) irritable, temperamental

What Does Your Pen Color Say About You?

Jessie Milligan

1   Just when you thought you'd heard of every possible survey, along comes one that says the color of pen ink used by American workers is linked to job performance.

2   Purple-pen users—male or female—say they pitch in to help, even when not asked. Users of red ink are the most likely to have been recently promoted or given a raise. Men who use erasable pens are least likely to work extra hours with no pay.

3   All that is according to the Pilot Pen Corp. of America's recently commissioned survey of the ink preferences and the work habits of 645 women and men. The survey, conducted by Opinion Research Corp. International of Princeton, N.J., is an unintentionally comic look into the American workplace. To Pilot's credit, the survey it paid for reports negative personality traits associated with some of the products the company sells.

4   Why would red-ink users be more likely to get raises? That's the weak point of the survey. It tells us the likelihood of certain pen colors coinciding with certain performance attributes. But it doesn't tell us why.

5   "We don't quite know what all this means. Frankly, we are quite flummoxed," says Ron Shaw, president and chief executive of Pilot, in one of the funniest and most refreshing quotes to come from corporate America in a long time.

6   If we accept that the reasons for choosing ink colors are downright flummoxing, then we can go ahead and just speculate on the hidden meanings associated with the pens we choose.

7   The pen-based personality indicator, according to Pilot:

8   Workers who preferred erasable pens were the most irascible. They were least likely to pitch in to help their bosses, and they were least likely to work extra hours with no pay. They were more likely than many others to say their jobs are boring. They were most likely to have poor job reviews.

9   Men who use purple ink don't fare as well in the workplace as women who use purple ink, if survey results hold true. Male and female purple-ink users say they volunteer to help their bosses, even without being asked.

10   Yet men who use purple pens are among the most likely to work extra hours with no pay, and are the most likely to report being criticized by their bosses.

11   Women who opt for purple ink report recent raises and promotions almost as frequently as people who use red ink. They are among the most likely to be looking for a new job. (We say that actively searching for a job indicates a certain amount of self-confidence, which is pretty much required in order to use purple ink.)

12   Red-ink users, male and female, are the most likely to report that their boss is "nice." These folks also were the most likely to have received a recent raise or promotion, which may well explain their attitude about their bosses.

13   Women who use red ink were the most likely to work extra hours with no pay.

14   Males who prefer green-ink pens are most likely to intentionally steal pens from co-workers.

15   Female green-ink users—and really, how many of these people do you know?—may be more bored on the job than anyone else, which,

we think, may explain why they have resorted to the entertainment value of green ink.

16   Women who use green ink, as well as those who use red ink, are the most likely to be "the office pen hog," with a dozen or more pens at their desks.

17   Black ink is still the power ink of the workplace, much more so than blue.

18   Men who use black ink or expensive pens of any color ink are the least likely to find their jobs boring, which must mean that they are actually doing something at work.

19   Women who use black pens are the least likely to report being criticized by the boss. Women who use expensive pens are most likely to report being criticized by their bosses, who, we suspect, may well come from the green-ink school that trains its users to steal co-workers' pens.

20   The Pilot survey says men who use blue ink are not likely to be helpful to their bosses.

21   The survey says that one in seven American workers don't use a pen at all because they are so busy working at computer keyboards.

Understanding the Content

Feel free to reread all or parts of the selection to answer the following questions.

1. What is one characteristic of a purple-ink user, regardless of gender?

2. What is the result of working with a red pen, according to the survey?

3. Describe how the survey characterizes people who work with erasable pens.

4. What happens to men who work with purple pens, as opposed to purple pen–using women?

5. Who are likely to be most bored by their jobs?

Looking at Structure and Style

1. How does paragraph 1 set the tone of the essay?

2. What is the purpose of paragraphs 4 and 5?

3. How effective is paragraph 21 as a concluding paragraph? Rewrite the paragraph so that it effectively summarizes the information presented in this selection.

4. What support does the author give for her statement in paragraph 4, "That's the weak point of the survey"?

5. Discuss whether the following statement is valid or invalid: "Men who use black ink or expensive pens of any color ink are the least likely to find their jobs boring, which must mean that they are actually doing something at work." Does the author provide support for this statement?

Evaluating the Author's Viewpoints

1. How does the author feel about the survey that is the basis for this selection? How can you tell? What words or phrases are used to give you an indication of the author's viewpoint?

2. What is your reaction to Pilot Pen's commissioned survey? Is it a useful survey? Why or why not?

3. Do you think the information presented in this selection is valid? Why or why not?

4. According to the author, why are red-ink users, male and female, most likely to report that their boss is "nice"? Do you agree or disagree with her theory?

Pursuing Possible Essay Topics

1. Based on your reading of the selection and the information provided, what does your pen color say about you and your work life? Write an essay describing how you should be, based on the survey.

2. Thinking about your pen color again, compare and contrast how you really are in a work setting as opposed to how you should be, based on the survey.

3. Go online to the Pilot Pen website at *www.pilotpen.com*. Summarize the information on the site. Ask yourself: Do different kinds of pens seem to be marketed to different consumers? If so, how? Does anything you learned in the essay relate to the Pilot Pen website?

4. Ignore these topics and find your own related to work.

 ## Preparing to Read

Take a minute or two to look over the following reading selection. Note the title and author, read the opening paragraph, and check the essay's length. Make certain you have the time now to read it carefully and to do the exercises that follow it. Then, in the spaces provided, answer the following questions.

1. What will the author probably say about work? _____

_____

_____

_____

2. What do you think would be the perfect job? _____

_____

_____

3. How would you define *work?* _____

_____

_____

Vocabulary

Good comprehension of what you are about to read depends upon your understanding of the words below. The number following each word refers to the paragraph where it is used.

hyperbolic (2) tending toward exaggeration

penchant (5) leaning, inclination, bias

synthesizer (6) person or thing that brings separate factors together

menial (14) common, base

geriatric (15) relating to the elderly

entrepreneurs (15) those who organize and operate new businesses

paraphernalia (15) equipment, gear

lucrative (23) profitable

On a Role

Lamar Graham

1   You want a what when you get out of college? A job?

2   "Jobs?" asks Nelson Thall, the hyperbolic research director of the McLuhan Center for Media Sciences, in Toronto. "*Jobs?* There won't be any jobs in the 21st century. Jobs are disappearing at a tremendous rate."

3   Don't panic, though. Just because there are no jobs, Thall says, "that doesn't mean there won't be a need for work. But you'll need a *role*, not a *job*."

4   Huh?

5   Like his mentor, the late media-studies guru Marshall McLuhan, Thall has a penchant for both bold pronouncements and semantics. "In the U.S. at the turn of this century," he says, "we were able to turn people into part of the machine through specialization and fragmentation of effort: the assembly line. Now that same process is in reverse under electronic conditions. Today you don't have to break a car into a bunch of tasks, a bunch of *jobs*—you need one person with a computer. People—jobs—are being replaced by computers, in effect."

6   Who's left? The person with enough adaptability to move on to something new. The person who sees himself not as a cog in the machine, not as a job description, but as a problem solver. The eclectic, creative thinker. The synthesizer. The role-player. "There's no need to fragment anymore," says Thall, "so you no longer have jobs—you have roles. We all have to have roles."

7   Jobs . . . roles—whatever you call them, like the man said, you're still going to have to have one. And, rest assured, they're still going to be around: According to Malcolm Cohen, Ph.D., a visiting professor at the Industrial Relations Center of the University of Minnesota, the U.S. economy will create an estimated 4 million new positions between now and the year 2000; between 1994 and 2005, according to the U.S. Bureau of Labor Statistics, America will end up gaining more than 17.7 million jobs. Er, roles.

8   But how do you know which one to pick? And how do you get it?

9   "There's no such thing as a lifetime career anymore," says Lynda Garow, director of career services at Clark University, in Worcester, Mass. "Employers are becoming smaller. Also, there's lots of contracting-out now, lots of temp work. And technology has changed what employers want—no matter what you go into now, you've got to know something about technology. And markets are getting global, so you've got to understand other cultures, other languages."

10   Don't pick a field to go into out of panic—or opportunism. "Don't choose a career based only on what looks like it's going to be the hot career four or five years from now," says Garow, "because things change." That said, it doesn't hurt to know where prospects are best.

11   Here's a look at five fields in which forecasters see good futures in the 21st century:

12   MEDICINE   Health care, futurists say, will continue to be a major growth industry, perhaps the biggest one in terms of overall

job growth for the next 20 to 30 years. The reason, in large part, is that more and more Americans are getting older and older and putting a greater and greater strain on existing health-care resources.

13   According to Cohen, there are currently about 600,000 physicians in the United States. Which would be plenty, he says, if more of them were family doctors; unfortunately, specialization was the trend in the '80s. Now, in the era of health-care reform—the age of "managed care"—the primary-care physician is the so-called gatekeeper of the system; you can't see that specialist without seeing your primary doctor first. Moral: If you want to be a doctor, Cohen says, think about getting back to basics.

14   But you don't have to be a doctor. Although the bulk of new health-care jobs will be fairly menial—the U.S. Bureau of Labor Statistics predicts there will be 640,000 new jobs for personal-care aides and home-health aides during the next 11 years—there will be plenty of work for college graduates. There are already shortages of occupational therapists and physical therapists—who regularly start at salaries as high as $50,000 a year straight out of college—as well as pharmacists, registered nurses and radiology technicians. By the year 2000, Cohen says, there will be a dearth of speech therapists, too.

15   Because so much of the health industry will be focused on caring for geriatric patients in their own homes, there will be wide-open opportunities for medical entrepreneurs. Says Art Shostak, Ph.D., a professor of sociology and the future at Drexel University, in Philadelphia: "Young college students who create small companies that will use mobile vans filled with all kinds of medical paraphernalia and paramedics will find an incredibly large market as Medicare cuts force an astronomical increase in the number of fragile elderly being cared for at home."

16   Finally, despite all that health care, those old folks are going to die. That's why the Bureau of Labor Statistics predicts an increase in demand for funeral directors.

17   TECHNOLOGY　Medicine aside, the other field in which virtually every forecaster sees big growth in the coming decade is computers. Not hardware but software and networking, especially anything to do with that mother of all networks, the Internet.

18   At present, Cohen says, "demand is greatest for people who have the ability to write the software; engineers and analysts are in high demand." Eventually, though, basic programming chores will move "offshore," as they have already begun to do, to places like India and Pakistan. The U.S. programming industry will turn its attention to what Shostak calls "the edge"—complex Internet-based applications and highly interactive multimedia software.

What's more, as the technology improves, becoming faster and more stable, there will finally be software that creates jobs for its users as well as its makers—and not just Web designers and architects, either, but advertising professionals and marketers. "Anyone who can come up with innovative ways for businesses to use the Web" will come out a winner, says Tom Duening, Ph.D., an assistant dean of the University of Houston's College of Business Administration.

19   MANAGEMENT   Are there people in your household who speak something other than English as their native language? Once upon a time, being a first- or second-generation American was a liability. Not so in the 21st century, according to labor forecasters. "I suspect that for some time to come, there will be major jobs of the globalist variety in management," says Shostak. "Fortune 500 companies continue to look for young people who are multicultural, who can move between the corporate headquarters and emerging markets." In particular, "young Americans with Chinese language facility should do very, very well.

20   "People who learned a second language at the knee of grandparents may find in the early part of the 21st century that they can leverage that to great advantage," Shostak says. "The person who has only Americana as his calling card may be significantly disadvantaged for the first time."

21   EDUCATION   Have you always wanted to work with children? If so, then consider working with rich, smart children. Teaching in public elementary and secondary schools won't be a high-growth, high-salary occupation in the decades to come, Shostak says, "but there will be new career possibilities in post-school tutoring for the children of what [former Secretary of Labor] Robert Reich calls the 'fortunate fifth': kids going to for-profit computer centers after school—like Japanese kids now and Southeast Asian kids in this country."

22   RECREATION   Not so many years ago, a student who got a degree in leisure-services management and then moved to Vail was called a ski bum. In the 21st century, that person will be known as an adventure-travel entrepreneur. Yes, now there's actually a market that justifies four years of skiing, mountain biking, backpacking and bungee jumping. "Anything involving adventure is hot," says Shostak. "Adventure travel, adventure vacations."

23   It's all about what futurists call the new high-tech, high-touch environment. That is, TV, movies and computers have raised our entertainment threshold so high that when we actually go outdoors and do something, it damn well better be exciting. "For college kids who have taken rock-climbing courses and have credentials," says

Shostak, there's real entrepreneurial opportunity, the potential to build a lucrative small business right out of school.

24   How do you prepare for a role in the 21st century? Five basic rules:

1. Develop a close personal relationship with computers. "It's critical in any job you go into," says Larry Salters, director of the Career Center at the University of South Carolina, in Columbia. "To keep yourself marketable, you've got to have technology in your background. And computer literacy means a lot more than word processing. You've got to know how to access information and use that information to support your employer's goals; you've got to use technology to gain edges in the market."

2. Learn the basic principles of running a small business. "Lots of universities are changing their core curriculums," says the University of Houston's Duening. "I think it's a real shame that basic business isn't a core requirement.

27   "Most people still think about getting into a large organization that's going to pay them a steady salary and two weeks of vacation and benefits for the rest of their lives—but that's not going to happen." In the 21st century, Duening says, there will be a lot more telecommuting, a lot more part-timers and temps and free-lancers, a lot more consulting and "outsourcing"; people will be getting more 1099s and a lot fewer W-2s.

28   "Let's assume everybody is going to run something called Me Inc., and they're going to have to run it for the next 40 years," Duening says. "People will need to know how to manage their finances, how to do their own tax returns and how to market their skills. Those who are able to package and sell their skills—and know how to price them—are the ones who will prosper. You have to be able to describe what you uniquely offer to the world." Duening recommends three to six credits of basic business courses—accounting, marketing, etc.: "the fundamental rules of our economic system."

3. Learn to work with others. "Increasingly, teamwork is becoming important" in American business, says Cohen. The distance between boss and worker is smaller nowadays; because of corporate downsizing there's less middle management. The future is about collaboration, teamwork.

30   Where do you learn those skills? Sports. Volunteer organizations. Management classes. The smartest idea of all: an internship. "Companies want work experience as well as a degree," says Salters. "A 3.2 and experience is better than a 4.0 and none."

4. Don't get bogged down in the details. Presumably the world is only getting more complicated. But that's OK. "Kids have to realize," says the McLuhan Center's Thall, "that the world is moving faster than they can make sense of it."

32   Thus, in the future, says Duening, you should avoid overspecialization. Don't get tunnel vision—be flexible, be ready to move. While a master's degree may indeed be useful and increase your currency on the job market, Ph.D.s are becoming passé. "The return on the investment in advanced degrees becomes less and less over time," Duening says, so finish your schooling early and then "let your profession dictate your next area of specialization." In the past, job security meant staying safely in the same place, but in the 21st century, security will be a function of your adaptability; moving around—moving laterally—may be just as important as moving up. "Don't rely on [academic] credentials to get you where you're going," says Duening. "Rely on skill building."

33   Don't forget problem solving, either. Indeed, although the 21st century will be more complex than any that has preceded it, "I don't think a liberal arts education is by any means dead," says Cohen.

34   Quite the contrary, in fact. "The demand for liberal arts students is growing," says the University of South Carolina's Salters. "Students who have a liberal arts degree are very marketable—provided they have career-related work experience and computer skills. Employers are very interested in students who can analyze information, and a liberal arts education can help with that critical-thinking skill."

35   Says Cohen: "When you're in doubt about a course to take, ask yourself, 'Will this help me with problem solving?' "

5. Do what you dig. While it's perhaps true that you'll have more options in the 21st century, it's also true that when you strip off the sugar coating, you're going to have to hustle a lot more than your parents did if you really want to be successful. Consequently, says Shostak, "it's more important than ever to find something—and it can be anything—that pleases you personally. Rather than go toward a growth field, spend time establishing what would pull you along. What would you wake up on Monday morning excited to go to?"

37   Also, says Shostak, just because a field isn't growing wildly doesn't necessarily mean that it's drying up. "There will still be teachers, for instance," he says. "There will just be more competition. But if teaching art to children is something you get all tingly about, for God's sake, go do it—don't let someone like me discourage you."

Understanding the Content

Feel free to reread all or parts of the selection to answer the following questions.

1. According to Nelson Thall, director of the McLuhan Center for Media Services in Toronto, there won't be any jobs in the twenty-first century. What does he mean? How is the job market changing?

2. What are the five major fields forecasters see as providing good occupational opportunities in the twenty-first century?

3. According to the author, what are the five basic rules to follow in preparing for a role in the twenty-first century?

4. Why is knowing a second language and something about other cultures going to be important in the twenty-first century?

Looking at Structure and Style

1. What technique or paragraph methods does Graham use to get the reader's attention? Are they effective?

2. For whom is Graham writing? How do you know? What are his tone and attitude? How do they relate to audience?

3. Is Graham's thesis stated or implied? If stated, where?

4. Graham's article contains two basic sections: one beginning with paragraph 11 and the other beginning with paragraph 24. What devices does he use to help the reader follow the basic points being made in each section?

5. Graham quotes heavily from other sources. Does this add to or detract from his thesis? Explain.

6. How well does the title fit the article?

Evaluating the Author's Viewpoints

1. Does Graham agree with Nelson Thall when he says that we "no longer have jobs . . . we all have to have roles" (6)? What is your opinion?

2. Most of the views expressed in this article seem to be the viewpoints of others. Are there any particular places where Graham lets his own opinion be known? If so, where?

3. How helpful or interesting did you find this article in regard to your own future "role" or occupational preparation?

Pursuing Possible Essay Topics

1. Write an essay that discusses whether or not you are attending college to get a better job. Is that the function of education? How can going to college help you reach your particular goal?

2. React to one or more of the points Graham makes in his article. What do you see as important to know? What do you think may be wrong with some of the predictions?

3. Write an extended definition that explains the difference between a job and a role. Or compare and contrast a job with an occupation or a profession.

4. Explain which of the five most promising areas—medicine, technology, management, education, recreation—appeals to you the most and why.

5. Freewrite or brainstorm on one or more of the following:

   a. menial jobs   d. the perfect job (role)

   b. blue-collar work   e. career

   c. white-collar work   f. entrepreneur

6. If none of the above suits you, find your own topic on some aspect of work or jobs.

Preparing to Read

Read aloud the poem shown below. Then answer the following questions.

1. What is the issue raised in this poem? _____

   _____

   _____

2. What kind of behavior is portrayed?_____

   _____

   _____

3. What was your first reaction to the poem?_____

   _____

   _____

For a Lady I Know

—Countee Cullen

She even thinks that up in heaven
    Her class lies late and snores,
While poor black cherubs rise at seven
    To celestial chores.

Going to the Internet

To truly understand the intent of this poem, you may want to go to the Internet to do more research on the author. Using one of the search engines, type in the keywords "Countee Cullen" to find out more about the author. Look at some of the websites devoted to this famous American poet and his work. You may be able to read more into the poem by exploring his life.

Understanding the Content

1. What is the poem about?

2. Who is the "she" in the poem? What type of person is characterized by the first two lines in the poem?

3. What do you think the author means by "her class"?

Looking at Structure and Style

1. The author uses four short lines to convey a serious message about class in America. What line strikes you as the most effective in conveying the point of the poem?

2. What is a cherub? If you do not know the definition of the word, consult your dictionary. Why does the author use this word to characterize the working class in the poem?

3. Who do you think the "lady" in the title is? How do you think the author knows her?

Evaluating the Author's Viewpoints

1. What is the author saying about the class system in America?

2. What is the author's attitude toward the upper classes in America and their view of black people?

3. Why do you think the author felt compelled to write this poem?

Pursuing Possible Essay Topics

1. Do some research to learn more about America in the 1920s, which have been characterized as the Roaring Twenties by some historians. With that in mind, and knowing what you do from your research, why do you think Cullen wrote this poem?

2. Brainstorm or freewrite about one or more of the following:

    a. race

    b. class

    c. work

3. Turn the poem into an essay, describing both the "lady" and the "cherubs."

 ## Preparing to Read

Take a minute or two to look over the following reading selection. Note the title and author, read the opening paragraph, and check the essay's length. Make certain you have the time now to read it carefully and to do the exercises that follow it. Then, in the spaces provided, answer the following questions.

1. Is the first paragraph an effective opening to the essay? Why or why not?

    _____

    _____

2. What do you think the essay will be about?_____

    _____

    _____

3. What is the "glass ceiling"? _____

    _____

    _____

Vocabulary

Good comprehension of what you are about to read depends upon your understanding of the words below. The number following each word refers to the paragraph where it is used.

mettle (3) courage, fortitude, spirit

flamboyant (4) showy

overwhelmingly (10) characterized by overpowering effect or strength

spate (12) a sudden outpouring

swath (13) path, strip

unconscionable (14) unscrupulous

Women Still Fighting for Job Equality

DeWayne Wickham

1　The first time boxing promoter Diane Fischer showed up at a prefight weigh-in, all 14 boxers in the room stripped down to their birthday suits before stepping onto the scale.

2　"They were trying to embarrass me," Fischer said matter-of-factly of that 1997 incident, "but I didn't let them get to me."

3　In the 2½ years since she got a license to promote prizefights, Fischer has tried mightily not to let the resistance she has encountered from men bent on testing her mettle or running her out of the fight game get to her. But it hasn't been easy.

4　"No doubt about it, I'm still bumping up against that glass ceiling," she said of her long struggle to win acceptance in a profession dominated by flamboyant men with large egos.

5　Last week, on the eve of Women's Equality Day, the anniversary of the constitutional amendment that gave women the right to vote, Fischer put on eight fights at The Big Kahuna, a Wilmington [Delaware] theme restaurant whose sprawling outdoor deck was transformed into a noisy boxing arena.

6　Seated at ringside were former heavyweight champions Joe Frazier and Michael Spinks, and Butch Lewis, one of this country's leading fight promoters. That they showed up to watch the fights was a small victory for Fischer, who has been told more than a few times that she's a fish out of water.

7　"I've been bad-mouthed a lot by men who say this is a man's job, not something a woman should be doing," Fischer said.

Cracking the Job Barriers

8　In fact, Fischer is a rare breed. More women in this country are employed as teachers, secretaries and cashiers than work in any other jobs. To break out of this box, an increasing number of the 64 million women in the labor force must find work in what the Department of Labor calls "nontraditional occupations"—areas of employment in which women now comprise 25% or less of the workforce.

9　This long list includes pilots, truck drivers, funeral directors, dentists, architects, bellhops, barbers, meter readers and construction workers. These are jobs women must get their fair share of as they assume a larger part of the burden of raising a family: Last year in this country, a woman headed nearly one of every four families that had children under the age of 18.

10   "The glass ceiling is thickest in areas where women are employed in jobs that are overwhelmingly dominated by men," said Elizabeth Toledo, a vice president of the National Organization for Women. "In general, jobs that are overwhelmingly male-dominated tend to have more issues."

11   Translation: They have more barriers for women to scale.

Good News—and Bad

12   It's easy to lose sight of this harsh reality, given the spate of good news about women on the employment front this year. There was a lot of happy talk about breaks in the glass ceiling when Carly Fiorina was named head of Hewlett-Packard, Eileen Collins became the first woman to command a space shuttle flight, and Karen Jurgensen got the editor's job here at *USA Today*, the nation's largest newspaper.

13   But despite these highly visible gains, there continues to be a wide swath of jobs with great earnings potential that are largely closed to women—and far too many work environments that are openly hostile to them.

14   NOW's two-year-old "Women-Friendly Workplace Campaign" has found no shortage of businesses to brand as "merchants of shame"— a tag the group bestows on firms it accuses of "unconscionable" abuse of female employees. The sex-discrimination lawsuits that have sprung from this campaign have ensnared some of the nation's biggest companies.

15   Still it's people such as Diane Fischer, not class action lawsuits, who put a human face on the sexism that robs millions of working women of the level playing field that Women's Equality Day symbolizes. Her efforts to win broad acceptance as a fight promoter will get a boost next month, when she and former lightweight boxing champion Roberto Duran team up to promote seven bouts in Panama.

16   But, sadly, her ultimate victory—like the jobs that millions of women seek in other occupations dominated by men—seems to be a long shot.

Understanding the Content

Feel free to reread all or parts of the selection to answer the following questions.

1. What did the boxers do to first-time boxing promoter Diane Fischer to embarrass her?

2. What event does Women's Equality Day commemorate?

3. What are the three occupations that the author says are the predominant occupations of women?

4. What are "nontraditional occupations"? Define the term and give a few examples.

5. What examples of breaks in the glass ceiling does the author give?

6. Where is the glass ceiling thickest?

7. What is the "Women-Friendly Workplace Campaign"?

Looking at Structure and Style

1. How do paragraphs 1–3 help Wickham develop his thesis? How does he use these three paragraphs to set up the rest of the essay?

2. What purpose do the quotes serve in the essay? Are they effective?

3. How does the author use statistics to support his thesis? Give some examples of the statistics included in the essay.

4. Are paragraphs 15 and 16 effective as concluding paragraphs? Why or why not?

5. Does the title tell you anything about the author's view on women's roles in the workplace? How can you tell?

Evaluating the Author's Viewpoints

1. Diane Fischer said, "I've been bad-mouthed a lot by men who say this is a man's job, not something a woman should be doing." Does the author support Fischer in her quest to become a successful boxing promoter? How can you tell?

2. Is there one paragraph in particular that tells you how the author feels about women in nontraditional occupations? If so, which one?

3. Do you agree with the author that jobs such as pilot, truck driver, funeral director, and dentist "are jobs women must get their fair share of as they assume a larger part of the burden of raising a family"? Why or why not?

4. Why is the glass ceiling thickest in areas where women are employed in jobs that are dominated by men?

5. Do you think the author makes a good argument for having women employed in nontraditional occupations? If not, what would be a better argument?

6. What do you think of NOW's "Women-Friendly Workplace Campaign"?

7. Does the author think that Diane Fischer will be successful in her quest to become a successful boxing promoter?

Pursuing Possible Essay Topics

1. Write an essay explaining why you think many women in this country are employed as teachers, secretaries, and cashiers.

2. What types of issues do you think women will face in "jobs that are over-whelmingly dominated by men"? Write an essay describing the types of issues women face when they hold jobs such as truck driver, funeral director, barber, and meter reader.

3. Write an essay that supports your viewpoint on women in nontraditional occupations.

4. Do you think Diane Fischer should pursue her dream of becoming a boxing promoter? Why or why not? Write an essay defending your viewpoint.

5. Brainstorm or freewrite on one or more of the following:

   a. women in the workplace

   b. jobs for women in the twenty-first century

   c. equality for women in the workforce

   d. the glass ceiling

   e. sex discrimination in the workplace

6. Find a topic of your own related to women and work, and write an essay.

 ## Preparing to Read

Take a minute or two to look over the following reading selection. Note the title and author, read the first ten paragraphs of dialogue, and check the essay's length. Make certain you have the time now to read it carefully and to do the exercises that follow it. Then, in the spaces provided, answer the following questions.

1. What do you think the essay is about? _____

_____

2. What do you think the Social Security worker will say when she gets back on

   the line? _____

   _____

Vocabulary

Good comprehension of what you are about to read depends upon your understanding of the words below. The number following each word refers to the paragraph where it is used.

dispensed (11) handed out, distributed

wooed (11) sought to marry, courted

reciprocated (11) gave in return

capital (13) any form of material wealth

to set hens (13) to put hens on eggs in order to hatch them

scrounge (13) obtain by salvaging or foraging

shuck (13) remove the shell or husk

threshers (13) people who remove the grain from the plant

shock (13) gather into sheaves for drying

rutted (13) full of grooves made by wheels

reclaimed (14) made suitable for cultivation or habitation

Canadian thistles (14) prickly weeds

flax (14) a plant from which textile fibers are taken

spaded (14) dug

cholera (15) an infectious disease

sustenance (21) livelihood, that which provides nourishment and supports life

My Mother Never Worked

BONNIE SMITH-YACKEL

1   "Social Security Office." (The voice answering the telephone sounds very self-assured.)

2   "I'm calling about . . . I . . . my mother just died . . . I was told to call you and see about a . . . death-benefit check, I think they call it. . . ."

3   "I see. Was your mother on Social Security? How old was she?"

4   "Yes . . . she was seventy-eight. . . ."

5   "Do you know her number?"

6   "No . . . I ah . . . don't you have a record?"

7   "Certainly. I'll look it up. Her name?"

8   "Smith, Martha Smith. Or maybe she used Martha Ruth Smith. . . . Sometimes she used her maiden name . . . Martha Jerabeck Smith."

9   "If you'd care to hold on, I'll check our records—it'll be a few minutes."

10   "Yes. . . ."

11   Her love letters—to and from Daddy—were in an old box, tied with ribbons and stiff, rigid-with-age leather thongs: 1918 through 1920; hers written on stationery from the general store she had worked in full-time and managed, single-handed, after her graduation from high school in 1913; and his, at first, on YMCA or Soldiers and Sailors Club stationery dispensed to the fighting men of World War I. He wooed her thoroughly and persistently by mail, and though she reciprocated all his feeling for her, she dreaded marriage. . . .

12   "It's so hard for me to decide when to have my wedding day—that's all I've thought about these last two days. I have told you dozens of times that I won't be afraid of married life, but when it comes down to setting the date and then picturing myself a married woman with half a dozen or more kids to look after, it just makes me sick. . . . I am weeping right now—I hope that some day I can look back and say how foolish I was to dread it all."

13   They married in February, 1921, and began farming. Their first baby, a daughter, was born in January, 1922, when my mother was 26 years old. The second baby, a son, was born in March, 1923. They were renting farms; my father, besides working his own fields, also was a hired man for two other farmers. They had no capital initially, and had to gain it slowly, working from dawn until midnight every day. My town-bred mother learned to set hens and raise chickens, feed pigs, milk cows, plant and harvest a garden, and can every fruit and vegetable she could scrounge. She carried water nearly a quarter of a mile from the well to fill her wash boilers in order to do her laundry on a scrub board. She learned to shuck grain, feed threshers, shock and husk corn, feed corn pickers. In September, 1925, the third baby came, and in June, 1927, the fourth child—both daughters. In 1930, my parents had enough money to buy their own farm, and that March they moved all their livestock and belongings themselves, 55 miles over rutted, muddy roads.

14   In the summer of 1930 my mother and her two eldest children re-claimed a 40-acre field from Canadian thistles, by chopping them all out with a hoe. In the other fields, when the oats and flax began to head out, the green and blue of the crops were hidden by the bright yellow of wild mustard. My mother walked the fields day after day, pulling each mustard plant. She raised a new flock of baby chicks—

500—and she spaded up, planted, hoed, and harvested a half-acre garden.

15   During the next spring their hogs caught cholera and died. No cash that fall.

16   And in the next year the drought hit. My mother and father trudged from the well to the chickens, the well to the calf pasture, the well to the barn, and from the well to the garden. The sun came out hot and bright, endlessly, day after day. The crops shriveled and died. They harvested half the corn, and ground the other half, stalks and all, and fed it to the cattle as fodder. With the price at four cents a bushel for the harvested crop, they couldn't afford to haul it into town. They burned it in the furnace for fuel that winter.

17   In 1934, in February, when the dust was still so thick in the Minnesota air that my parents couldn't always see from the house to the barn, their fifth child—a fourth daughter—was born. My father hunted rabbits daily, and my mother stewed them, fried them, canned them, and wished out loud that she could taste hamburger once more. In the fall the shotgun brought prairie chickens, ducks, pheasant, and grouse. My mother plucked each bird, carefully reserving the breast feathers for pillows.

18   In the winter she sewed night after night, endlessly, begging cast-off clothing from relatives, ripping apart coats, dresses, blouses, and trousers to make them to fit her four daughters and son. Every morning and every evening she milked cows, fed pigs and calves, cared for chickens, picked eggs, cooked meals, washed dishes, scrubbed floors, and tended and loved her children. In the spring she planted a garden once more, dragging pails of water to nourish and sustain the vegetables for the family. In 1936 she lost a baby in her sixth month.

19   In 1937 her fifth daughter was born. She was 42 years old. In 1939 a second son, and in 1941 her eighth child—and third son.

20   But the war had come, and prosperity of a sort. The herd of cattle had grown to 30 head; she still milked morning and evening. Her garden was more than a half acre—the rains had come, and by now the Rural Electricity Administration and indoor plumbing. Still she sewed—dresses and jackets for the children, housedresses and aprons for herself, weekly patching of jeans, overalls, and denim shirts. She still made pillows, using the feathers she had plucked, and quilts every year—intricate patterns as well as patchwork, stitched as well as tied—all necessary bedding for her family. Every scrap of cloth too small to be used in quilts was carefully saved and painstakingly sewed together in strips to make rugs. She still went out in the fields to help with the haying whenever there was a threat of rain.

21   In 1959 my mother's last child graduated from high school. A year later the cows were sold. She still raised chickens and ducks, plucked

feathers, made pillows, baked her own bread, and every year made a new quilt—now for a married child or for a grandchild. And her garden, that huge, undying symbol of sustenance, was as large and cared for as in all the years before. The canning, and now freezing, continued.

22   In 1969, on a June afternoon, mother and father started out for town so that she could buy sugar to make rhubarb jam for a daughter who lived in Texas. The car crashed into a ditch. She was paralyzed from the waist down.

23   In 1970 her husband, my father, died. My mother struggled to regain some competence and dignity and order in her life. At the rehabilitation institute, where they gave her physical therapy and trained her to live usefully in a wheelchair, the therapist told me: "She did fifteen pushups today—fifteen! She's almost seventy-five years old! I've never known a woman so strong!"

24   From her wheelchair she canned pickles, baked bread, ironed clothes, wrote dozens of letters weekly to her friends and her "half dozen or more kids," and made three patchwork housecoats and one quilt. She made balls and balls of carpet rags—enough for five rugs. And kept all her love letters.

25   "I think I've found your mother's records—Martha Ruth Smith; married to Ben F. Smith?"

26   "Yes, that's right."

27   "Well, I see that she was getting a widow's pension. . . ."

28   "Yes, that's right."

29   "Well, your mother isn't entitled to our $255 death benefit."

30   "Not entitled? But why?"

31   The voice on the telephone explains patiently:

32   "Well, you see—your mother never worked."

Understanding the Content

Feel free to reread all or parts of the selection to answer the following questions.

1. Why was the author's mother afraid to marry, according to one of her letters? Were her fears realized?

2. How old was the author's mother when she had her last child? How many children did she have? How old was she when she died?

3. Describe the kind of life the author's mother led. Would you call what she did work? How does it differ from what the government defines as *work*?

4. Apparently the author's mother was eligible for a death benefit and Social Security pension when her husband died. Why wasn't the author's family eligible for a death-benefit check when her mother died?

5. What is the thesis? Is it implied or stated?

Looking at Structure and Style

1. How does Smith-Yackel use the narrative dialogue at the beginning and end of the essay to tell her story? How effective is this in capturing our interest? Would the story have been as effective in making its point if we knew at the beginning that the family was not entitled to a death-benefit check?

2. What is the function of paragraph 12? Aside from being a bit ironic, what can we infer from the paragraph about the mother's character?

3. Smith-Yackel tells her story in a chronological fashion from paragraphs 11 through 24. What transitional devices does she use to help us follow along over so many years?

4. Why does the author spend so much time providing specific details, such as dates, number of farm animals, chores, the amount the death-benefit check would be, and so on? Do such details help the author make her point? Explain.

5. What attitude do you see revealed in the opening and closing dialogue passages with the voice from the Social Security office? Look carefully at the words used to describe the voice.

6. Search the essay for words the author uses to help us feel and imagine the difficulties her mother experienced. How do such words and phrases help us understand the author's definition of *work?*

Evaluating the Author's Viewpoints

1. The author apparently felt the need to write this essay after being told that her mother "never worked." How would you describe Smith-Yackel's attitude toward this statement? toward the voice on the telephone?

2. Do you think the author has negative or positive feelings toward the Social Security system? Explain why you do or don't agree with her.

3. Does the author imply that families should receive a death-benefit check? If so, do you agree? If she doesn't imply this, then what is her point?

4. What adjectives do you think the author might use to describe her mother to us? Why?

5. Why do you think the author says so little about her father? Would a discussion of him help make her point stronger?

Pursuing Possible Essay Topics

1. Compare and contrast working conditions you have known with those your parents or grandparents have known. What changes have occurred? Would you want to have lived their work lives?

2. It is a fact that women in general receive less pay than men in most jobs, even when they perform the same tasks. Why does this policy continue? Why did it begin?

3. Defend housework as "real work."

4. Research information on the Social Security system. Does it favor men over women? Are there inequities that need to be remedied? You might begin by asking the research librarian if the library has any current government pamphlets on the Social Security system.

5. Define and classify "a man's job" and "a woman's job."

6. Brainstorm or freewrite on one or more of the following:
   a. definition of *work*
   b. sexual harassment at work
   c. "A woman's place is in the home."
   d. "A woman's work is never done."
   e. workaholics
   f. classifications of work

7. If none of these works for you, come up with your own topic on some aspect of work.

Preparing to Read

Take a minute or two to look over the following reading selection. Note the title and author, read the first two paragraphs, and check the essay's length. Make certain you have the time now to read it carefully and to do the exercises that follow it. Then, in the spaces provided, answer the following questions.

1. What will the author probably say about work? _____

   _____

   _____

2. What is a workaholic? _____

   _____

   _____

3. What is a company man? _____

   _____

Vocabulary

Good comprehension of what you are about to read depends upon your understanding of the words below. The number following each word refers to the paragraph where it is used.

obituary (2) death notice

coronary thrombosis (2) a form of heart attack

discreetly (16) cautiously, modestly

The Company Man

Ellen Goodman

1   He worked himself to death, finally and precisely, at 3:00 A.M. Sunday morning.

2   The obituary didn't say that, of course. It said that he died of a coronary thrombosis—I think that was it—but everyone among his friends and acquaintances knew it instantly. He was a perfect Type A, a workaholic, a classic, they said to each other and shook their heads—and thought for five or ten minutes about the way they lived.

3   This man who worked himself to death finally and precisely at 3:00 A.M. Sunday morning—on his day off—was fifty-one years old and a vice-president. He was, however, one of six vice-presidents, and one of three who might conceivably—if the president died or retired soon enough—have moved to the top spot. Phil knew that.

4   He worked six days a week, five of them until eight or nine at night, during a time when his own company had begun the four-day week for everyone but the executives. He worked like the Important People. He had no outside "extracurricular interests," unless, of course, you think about a monthly golf game that way. To Phil, it was work. He always ate egg salad sandwiches at his desk. He was, of course, overweight, by 20 or 25 pounds. He thought it was okay, though, because he didn't smoke.

5   On Saturdays, Phil wore a sports jacket to the office instead of a suit, because it was the weekend.

6   He had a lot of people working for him, maybe sixty, and most of them liked him most of the time. Three of them will be seriously considered for his job. The obituary didn't mention that.

7   But it did list his "survivors" quite accurately. He is survived by his wife, Helen, forty-eight years old, a good woman of no particular marketable skills, who worked in an office before marrying and mothering. She had, according to her daughter, given up trying to compete with his work years ago, when the children were small. A company friend said, "I know how much you will miss him." And she answered, "I already have."

8   "Missing him all these years," she must have given up part of herself which had cared too much for the man. She would be "well taken care of."

9   His "dearly beloved" eldest of the "dearly beloved" children is a hard-working executive in a manufacturing firm down South. In the day and a half before the funeral, he went around the neighborhood researching his father, asking the neighbors what he was like. They were embarrassed.

10   His second child is a girl, who is twenty-four and newly married. She lives near her mother and they are close, but whenever she was alone with her father, in a car driving somewhere, they had nothing to say to each other.

11   The youngest is twenty, a boy, a high-school graduate who has spent the last couple of years, like a lot of his friends, doing enough odd jobs to stay in grass and food. He was the one who tried to grab at his father, and tried to mean enough to him to keep the man at home. He was his father's favorite. Over the last two years, Phil stayed up nights worrying about the boy.

12   The boy once said, "My father and I only board here."

13   At the funeral, the sixty-year-old company president told the forty-eight-year-old widow that the fifty-one-year-old deceased had meant much to the company and would be missed and would be hard to replace. The widow didn't look him in the eye. She was afraid

he would read her bitterness and, after all, she would need him to straighten out the finances—the stock options and all that.

14   Phil was overweight and nervous and worked too hard. If he wasn't at the office, he was worried about it. Phil was a Type A, a heart-attack natural. You could have picked him out in a minute from a lineup.

15   So when he finally worked himself to death, at precisely 3:00 A.M. Sunday morning, no one was really surprised.

16   By 5:00 P.M. the afternoon of the funeral, the company president had begun, discreetly of course, with care and taste, to make inquiries about his replacement. One of three men. He asked around: "Who's been working the hardest?"

Understanding the Content

Feel free to reread all or parts of the selection to answer the following questions.

1. Goodman's essay is an extended definition of "a company man." Define a company man in your own words in one or two sentences.

2. What is Goodman's thesis? What is she saying through the definition of the company man?

3. What does Phil's wife, Helen, mean when a company friend says, "I know how much you will miss him," and she answers, "I already have" (7)?

4. Why were Phil's neighbors "embarrassed" when his son went around the neighborhood asking what his father was like? Why did the eldest son need to ask?

5. What kind of relationship did Phil have with his daughter and younger son?

6. What kind of man is the company president looking for to replace Phil?

Looking at Structure and Style

1. Is Goodman's thesis stated or implied? If stated, where?

2. Reread paragraphs 1 and 15. Why does Goodman repeat this information?

3. Describe Goodman's tone and attitude. What words or phrases help develop her tone and attitude?

4. Look over the essay and find the places where Goodman uses dialogue. What effect does the use of dialogue have in those places?

5. Goodman frequently highlights certain words with quotation marks, as in paragraph 4. Why? What use does this serve?

Evaluating the Author's Viewpoints

1. What is Goodman's attitude toward Phil? Is she sympathetic? How do you know? Do you agree with her? Explain.

2. In paragraph 4, Goodman says, "He [Phil] worked like the Important People." To whom is her sarcasm being directed? Is it deserving? Explain.

3. Based on this essay, what values does Goodman seem to hold about work and its importance in the scheme of things? Do you agree with her? Explain.

Pursuing Possible Essay Topics

1. Write an essay that examines the importance of work in your parents' life. Did work take priority over family for them? Did they balance work and family time?

2. Write a plan for a better workweek (or workday, work year) than the traditional forty-hour week and hourly wage.

3. Argue the need for hard work and long hours.

4. What would you do with your life if you did not have to work?

5. Freewrite or brainstorm on one or more of the following:

   a. workaholism   d. free time

   b. work conditions   e. working overtime

   c. the ideal job   f. minimum wage

6. Lay off these ideas and fire away at one of your own concerning some aspect of work or jobs.

Preparing to Read

Take a minute or two to look over the following reading selection. Note the title and author, read the opening paragraph, and check the essay's length. Make certain you have the time now to read it carefully and to do the exercises that follow it. Then, in the spaces provided, answer the following questions.

1. What will the author probably say about work? _____

_____

_____

_____

2. How do you define *sex discrimination?* _____

_____

_____

_____

3. What is Title VII? _____

_____

_____

Vocabulary

Good comprehension of what you are about to read depends upon your understanding of the words below. The number following each word refers to the paragraph where it is used.

pervasive (2) spread throughout

curriculum vitae (2) resumés

detriment (3) loss, disadvantage

echelon (3) rank, position

litigant (4) person or party engaged in a lawsuit

plaintiff (4) person or party bringing a lawsuit to court

bona fide (11) genuine, true

What Does Sex/Gender Have to Do with Your Job?

JEFFREY BERNBACH

1   Although there have been laws against employment discrimination for more than a hundred years in the United States, they varied from state to state. Not until some thirty years ago did Title VII (in addition to prohibiting discrimination based on race, color, religion, and national origin) establish federal uniformity, making it unlawful to discriminate against females—or, for that matter,

males—on the basis of their sex. On-the-job gender discrimination occurs when an employee is treated differently from a person of the opposite sex under similar circumstances for reasons based solely on the employee's sex.

More Are Less Equal Than Others—Wage Bias

2   Historically, the most obvious example of sex bias has been paying women less than men for doing the same work. Although unlawful, the practice is pervasive, and even now, after years of strong feminist (and other) efforts to correct this inequity, women still earn only seventy cents for every dollar earned by men. This is *wage inequality,* not to be confused with the *glass ceiling,* which denies women the opportunity to *advance* up the corporate ladder (which also, of course, impinges on wage increases). Let's say you're a woman working as a publicity director for a large corporation, and you earn $35,000; your male counterpart, publicity director for another division of the same corporation, is earning $50,000. You and he have almost identical curriculum vitae—in fact, you went to the same college, worked together at another company, and then each of you got your "dream job."

3   Although you are worth as much as your male colleague in terms of employee value (or conversely, maybe he is worth only as much as *you*), nothing will be done to correct this unfair (read that *unlawful*) situation for two reasons, both very related:

1. Understandably, you don't want to quit your job—you love it, and protesting could lead to dismissal or, at the very least, rocking the corporate boat to your detriment,

and

2. Your company knows it can get away with such inequities.

So there you are: making seventy cents for every dollar your colleague makes. This goes on at every level of employment, from factory workers to upper-echelon managers. It's a sad, unlawful truth of life in the workplace. And, until recently, most women didn't challenge it because they wanted to keep their jobs.

4   Among the women who do take on such challenges, the litigant most feared by any employer is a minority female over forty years old. This is enough to make executives at even the grandest corporations quake in their boots because such plaintiffs fall into *three* categories protected by federal and state laws: age, sex, and race.

5   While women are victims of sex discrimination far more often than men, remember that if a male worker is treated less favorably than his female colleagues because of his sex, he has just as much a right to challenge this inequity. Here's a hypothetical example: A

man is hired as an editor at a fashion magazine where all the other editors are women. Although he has similar editorial experience and a similar position, on the organizational chart, the female editors are making more than he is simply *because he's a man.* So workplace discrimination based on gender (sex) can work both ways.

6   Those who do fight for on-the-job equality may find themselves in double trouble: victims first of sexual discrimination and later of sexual harassment.

7   Ironically, some of the most frequently cited sources of gender bias occur in professions where women not only do the same jobs but also wear the same or similar uniforms as men: the military, police and fire departments. And often, female protests have less to do with wage inequities and more to do with the way they are perceived, or treated by their peers.

8   One New Jersey policewoman, for example, reported that in over five years with a local police force, officers on the midnight tour watched pornographic movies at the station house while she patrolled the town—alone. Another policewoman reported that although she outscored two men on physical tests, and tied with another man on written tests, the men were hired promptly, while it took her five years (and a lawsuit) to gain her rightful place on the force.

9   Similar news reports show that women in the military are struggling for acceptance in what still seems to be a man's world. Two hundred officers in the air force, along with their supporters, have formed a group called WANDAS Watch (Women Active in our Nation's Defense, their Advocates and their Supporters). One target of their protests was the recently retired air force chief of staff, who had vocalized his opposition to women assuming increased roles in the air force. A few years ago he reportedly told a Senate panel he would "rather fly with a less-qualified male pilot than with a top-notch woman aviator."

10   Last year, when the first female astronaut to pilot a space shuttle successfully linked up with a Russian space flight, a group of former female pilots, thirteen women who called themselves FLATS (Fellow Lady Astronaut Trainees), recalled that when they had trained with NASA thirty years earlier, they were never called up as pilots. One FLAT, now sixty-five and a retired pilot, told the *New York Times,* "We could have done it, but the guys didn't want us." She remembered that one NASA official said at the time that he would "just as soon orbit with a bunch of monkeys than with a bunch of women."

11   In these "uniformed" cases, the problem is not one of wage or promotion, but of limited opportunities to perform the task for which these women were hired or were qualified to perform. The

time-worn excuse of denying certain jobs to females in order to "protect" them from damage to their reproductive systems or possible harm to an unborn fetus has been held by the courts to constitute sex discrimination. Similarly, restricting the weight that females can be required to lift on a job or the number of hours they may work, in order to "protect" them (which obviously limits employment opportunities), also constitutes sex discrimination. In the same way, height and weight standards adversely affect job possibilities for women and are illegal unless it can be demonstrated that they are a *bona fide occupational requirement of the job*, that is, necessary for performance.

12   [Former] Speaker of the House of Representatives Newt Gingrich committed "verbal discrimination" while infuriating millions of men and women in 1995 when he said, "If combat means living in a ditch, females have biological problems staying in a ditch for thirty days because they get infections, and they don't have upper-body strength. I mean some do, but they're relatively rare. On the other hand, men are basically little piglets—you drop them in the ditch, they roll around in it, doesn't matter, you know."

13   Aside from [former] Speaker Gingrich's skewed view, some common sense considerations should and do apply. For example, if a job at a trucking company requires lifting two-hundred-pound boxes for eight hours a day, an employer might justifiably refuse to give that job to a five-foot-two 110-pound woman (or man, for that matter). However, if the applicant could demonstrate that he or she could do the job, the employer would have no basis to deny it to him or her. As another instance, if a man is applying for a job as an attendant for the women's rest room in a restaurant or hotel, and is denied the job, that's not sexual discrimination; nor would a vice versa situation of a woman looking for a job as an attendant in a men's room be the case. In either of these examples, sex would be a bona fide occupational qualification.

14   If a woman has a license—and a desire—to drive an eighteen-wheeler, there's no *lawful reason* why she shouldn't have the job. If a man is licensed as a nursery school educator, there's no *lawful reason* why he shouldn't have the job. But stereotypical perceptions persist.

Understanding the Content

Feel free to reread all or parts of the selection to answer the following questions.

1. What can you infer Title VII is? How long has it been in effect?

2. How does Bernbach define "on-the-job gender discrimination"?

3. Historically, what has been the most obvious example of sex bias on the job?

4. What is the difference between "wage inequality" and "the glass ceiling"?

5. Why do many employees who are being treated unfairly due to gender bias not do anything about it, according to Bernbach?

6. In what professions do some of the most frequently cited sources of gender bias occur? Why is this ironic?

7. List some of the stereotypical perceptions of gender bias in the workplace.

Looking at Structure and Style

1. Is the thesis stated or implied? If stated, where?

2. What writing pattern or patterns do you see in paragraph 2? What is the point of the paragraph?

3. What is the function of paragraph 8? How is it used to support paragraph 7?

4. How many examples are provided to support the point made in paragraph 11? Does the support come before or after paragraph 11?

5. Describe Bernbach's tone. What words or phrases develop the tone?

Evaluating the Author's Viewpoints

1. Bernbach believes that many workers put up with gender bias on the job because they don't want to quit their jobs or the company knows it can get away with it. If you felt you were being discriminated against on the job, what would you do if you thought complaining might get you fired or lead to harassment?

2. Bernbach cites several examples of the resentment men feel toward women who take up what have traditionally been male roles, especially "uniformed positions" such as those in the military, the police, and fire departments. Do you think there are positions that women should not attempt to enter because they are a "man's world"? Explain.

3. Bernbach states that former Speaker of the House of Representatives Newt Gingrich committed "verbal discrimination" with a statement he made in 1995 (12). Do you agree? How would you respond to Gingrich's statement?

4. Reread paragraph 14. Do you agree? Explain.

Pursuing Possible Essay Topics

Unless you have a topic in mind for an essay on work, wait until after you have read the following essay, "If You Let Me Play" by Mary Brophy Marcus.

Preparing to Read

Take a minute or two to look over the following reading selection. Note the title and author, read the first *three* paragraphs, and check the essay's length. Make certain that you have the time to read it carefully and to do the exercises that follow it. Then, in the spaces provided, answer the following questions.

1. What do you think the author will say about the effect of sports on women in the workplace? _____

   _____

   _____

   _____

2. How might Marcus's thesis be different from Jeffrey Bernbach's in the previous essay? _____

   _____

   _____

   _____

Vocabulary

Good comprehension of what you are about to read depends upon your understanding of the words below. The number following each word refers to the paragraph where it is used.

tomboy (2) a girl considered boyish or masculine

spiked (5) rose sharply

metaphors (8) figures of speech in which a word or phrase that designates one thing is applied to another in an implicit comparison

nimble (11) quick, light, or agile in movement or action

befuddlement (13) confusion

If You Let Me Play . . .

MARY BROPHY MARCUS

1   Jackie Thomas, Nike's associate director of sports marketing, usually spends her lunch hour on the sports-shoe company's basketball
courts charging for the basket, always outnumbered by male colleagues. "I hold my own," boasts the 33-year-old executive.

2   She also does well playing the corporate game back inside the
headquarters offices. Thomas, a former University of California—
Berkeley college basketball point guard, says her success is due in
large part to the lessons she learned growing up playing competitive
team sports. "It's taught me that if you lose a game, you go back afterward and figure out what went wrong and how to overcome it the
next time," says the former tomboy from Kingston, Jamaica.

3   While most of America's corporations are still commanded by
male chief executives, women are gaining ground, winning vice
presidential and top management slots, and, in a few cases, the highest leadership roles. Many of these young female executives say playing team sports helped them get ahead. A University of Virginia
study conducted in the late 1980s showed that 80 percent of key female leaders from *Fortune* 500 companies said they participated in
sports and considered themselves tomboys.

4   **New opportunity.** A lot of the credit, female executives say, has to
go to Title IX, part of the Federal Education Amendments Act of 1972.
It mandated that federally funded schools give women's sports the
same treatment that men's games receive. That meant that in
schools and colleges across the United States, for every boy's varsity
soccer team, there must be a girl's varsity soccer team; for every male
basketball scholarship, there must be a female basketball scholarship of equal dollars. Since the early 1970s, the law has increased
money for new equipment, coaches and travel for women's teams.
More college scholarships have translated into more diplomas and
better jobs for women. Thomas earned a partial academic scholarship when she applied to Berkeley, one of the country's top universities, but without an additional basketball scholarship awarded in her
junior and senior years, she would have had a hard time paying for
the education.

5   Girls' participation in high school sports has spiked from about
300,000 in 1971 to 2.4 million in 1996. At the college level, where
competition is tougher, the number of female athletes has increased
to 123,832 from 80,040 in 1982, says the National Collegiate Athletic
Association.

6   "No other experience I know of can prepare you for the high-level
competition of business," says Anh Nguyen, 25, a former Carnegie

Mellon University varsity soccer star. She should know. Now she battles Microsoft as a product manager for Netscape Communications. "My colleagues can't believe how aggressive I am," she says.

7   Sports helped these women master the interpersonal skills, like teamwork, that many men take for granted. "I've seen firsthand hundreds and hundreds of times that one person can't win a soccer or softball game," says Maria Murnane, a 28-year-old senior account executive for a San Francisco public-relations firm. "Same goes for work. You have to learn to trust the people on your team, let them run with projects," the former Northwestern soccer center midfielder says. Her boss, William Harris, the president of Strategy Associates, agrees: "We don't want lone rangers. She's a team player—a captain and cheerleader."

8   Playing team sports helps with the little things, too. Women learn to speak in sports metaphors as many men do. Lisa Delpy, professor of sports management at George Washington University in Washington, D.C., also notes that in many companies a lot of business is conducted on the golf course, at ballgames, or at other sports events. Women who know the difference between a slide tackle and a sweeper at a World Cup soccer match can fit right in.

9   Stephanie Delaney, now 31, captained the varsity soccer team at Franklin and Marshall College in Lancaster, Pa., when it won the Mid-Atlantic conference championships her senior year. Now the sales manager for the Caribbean and Latin American division of ConAgra's Lamb-Weston, one of the world's largest frozen-french-fry producers, she was the only woman to play a game of basketball with potential clients at a big food conference last year in Jamaica. "I was the high scorer," she notes.

10   And yes, it helped sell french fries. "I didn't close the deal on the court, but afterward when we were hanging out drinking water and shooting the breeze, they agreed to test my product. Now we have Kentucky Fried Chicken's business in Jamaica," says Delaney.

11   **Confidence builder.** Female executives say that Title IX had another subtle, but important, effect. For the first time, many boys, coaches, and parents opened their eyes to the fact that their sisters and daughters could be just as strong, fast, and nimble on the field as their brothers and sons. Likewise, girls whose talents had formerly gone unnoticed under driveway basketball nets and on back lots began realizing their own power—that they could compete with boys and win. "When my girlfriends and I formed a softball team back in college, we were dreadful—like the Keystone Kops," recalls Penny Cate, 45, now a vice president at Quaker Oats. "There'd be four of us in the outfield and the ball would go through our legs. But after a few

years, we became very good. It built my confidence, made me realize I could accomplish anything in sports or out," she says.

12   That point is repeatedly brought home when Nike execs ask schoolgirls what they think of one of the company's TV ads. The ad begins with the voice of a young girl saying, "If you let me play..." The phrase is finished by other little girls saying things like, "I will have greater self-confidence" or "I will be more likely to stay in school."

13   The girls often reply, in a tone of genuine befuddlement, "If *who* lets me play?" They don't see any barriers between themselves and America's playing fields. Twenty years from now, might they say, "*What* glass ceiling?"

Understanding the Content

Feel free to reread all or parts of the selection to answer the following questions.

1. Where does Jackie Thomas spend most of her lunch hours?

2. To what does Jackie Thomas attribute much of her success?

3. What mandate do female executives think has helped women gain ground in corporate America?

4. According to the selection, what skills have women developed from their participation in sports?

Looking at Structure and Style

1. What is Marcus's thesis? Is it stated or implied?

2. How does the author use statistics to support her thesis? Give examples in your answer.

3. What does Marcus's title mean? How is it connected to her thesis?

4. What is the function of paragraphs 1 and 2? Do they provide an effective opening to the selection?

5. How effective are paragraphs 12 and 13 in concluding the essay? Do they effectively support Marcus's thesis?

Evaluating the Author's Viewpoints

1. Why do you think the author titled her article "If you let me play..."? What is implied by her choice of words?

2. What is the author's viewpoint about her topic? Do you think she supports the correlation between women playing sports and their success in the workplace?

3. How does the author use anecdotal information in the selection to support her thesis? Give examples of the people the author uses to support her main point.

4. Why do you think the author ends the selection with the sentence "Twenty years from now, might they say, '*What* glass ceiling?'" Is this conclusion supported by the selection? Why or why not?

Pursuing Possible Essay Topics

1. Write an essay comparing and contrasting how women in corporate America are described in Bernbach's article versus Marcus's article. Which selection holds out more hope for the future of women in corporate America? Why?

2. Write an essay describing your viewpoints about women and sports. Do you think that sports helps women succeed in other aspects of their lives? Why or why not?

3. Do you think Title IX has proved to be beneficial for women overall? Why or why not? Write an essay discussing your viewpoint.

4. Besides the examples listed in the selection, do you think women benefit from sports in any other ways? If so, write an essay describing some advantages that women who play sports have over women who do not.

5. Freewrite or brainstorm on one or more of the following:
   a. promotable women
   b. corporate ladder
   c. co-workers
   d. salaries
   e. women in the workforce
   f. gender bias
   g. women in corporate leadership positions

6. If none of these ideas interest you, create your own topic on some aspect of work.

Student Essay

Read the following narrative essay written by a student. As you read, look for answers to these questions:

1. Does the essay fit the assignment to write on some aspect of work?

2. Does the essay have a thesis and adequate support?

3. Does the essay hold your interest?

"Oh, I'm Just a Housewife"

Roy Wilson

1   After watching my mother deal with our family of five, I can't understand why her answer to the question "What do you do?" is always "Oh, I'm just a housewife." JUST a housewife? Anyone who spends most of her time in meal preparation and cleanup, washing and drying clothes, keeping the house clean, attending PTA meetings, leading a cub scout troop, playing taxi driver to us kids when it's time for school, music lessons or the dentist, doing volunteer work for her favorite charity, and making sure that all our family needs are met is not JUST a housewife. She's the real Wonder Woman.

2   Why is it that so many mothers like mine think of themselves as second-class citizens or something similar because they don't have a job? Where has this notion come from? Have we males made them feel this way? Has our society made "going to work" outside the home seem more important than what a housewife must face each day?

3   I would be very curious to see what would happen if a housewife went on strike. Dishes would pile up. Food in the house would run out. No meals would appear on the table. There would be no clean clothes when needed. Hobbed-nailed boots would be required just to make it through the

cluttered house. Walking and bus riding would increase. Those scout troops would have to disband. Charities would suffer.

4   I doubt if the man of the house would be able to take over. Oh, he might start out with the attitude that he can do just as good a job, but how long would that last? Not long, once he had to come home each night after work to more chores. There would be no more coming home to a prepared meal; he'd have to fix it himself. The kids would all be screaming for something to eat, clean clothes and more bus fare money. Once he quieted the kids, he'd have to clean the house (yes, housewives do windows), go shopping (either take the kids or get a baby sitter), make sure that the kids got a bath (after cleaning out all the dog hairs from the bathtub), and fix lunches for the next day. Once the kids were down for the night, he might be able to crawl into an unmade bed and try to read the morning newspaper.

5   No, I don't think many males are going to volunteer for the job. I know I don't want it. So, thanks, Mom! I'll do what I can to create a national holiday for housewives. It could be appropriately called Wonder Working Woman Day.

Reaction

In your journal or on a separate sheet of paper, write your reaction to the student essay. Use the questions posed before the essay as a guide for your comments.

On the Net

Chances are, at some point in your life, you'll need a resumé. If you would like to create one, revise the one you have, or get advice, visit one or more of the many sites on the Web that deal with resumés. About.com, which you can visit at *http://jobsearchtech.about.com/msub12-builders.htm*, has a complete site with help for creating a resumé from scratch or updating an existing resumé, and it will also give you information on how to create your own Web page, which may help in a future job search. There are also links on this site that might prove helpful if you are undecided on your career path.

If you are more interested in getting career advice so you don't end up like the "company man" described in the Goodman selection, visit one or more of the following sites to get the information you want: *www.ajb.dni.us* (America's Job Bank), *www.careercity.com* (Career City), or *www.cweb.com* (Career Web). Then answer the following questions:

1. What is the most important information you found on the site?

2. Which site would you visit again if you were actively looking for a job? Why?

3. Which sites, if any, were not helpful? Why? What kind of information would make them more helpful to people looking for jobs?

Now, do your own search on a topic of your choice related to "work" and answer the questions above.

9 Viewpoints on the Media

FOCUS ON THE MEDIA

To help you focus on the subject of this chapter, answer the following questions. You may want to write the answers in your journal or be prepared to discuss them in class.

1. Read the quotation by Susan Sontag on the opposite page. What do you think she means? Do you agree?

2. What media outlets rely heavily on "what we are shown by cameras"?

3. "A picture is worth a thousand words," according to an old saying. Is this true? How reliable are the photographs shown to us?

4. How much do you trust what you see in a newspaper or magazine photograph, or what you view on a television news broadcast? Do you always believe what you see? Why or why not?

5. Look at the photograph on the opposite page. What do you think is happening? Does it look like a news-making event? Under what circumstances do media photographers clamor to get photographs? How important are pictures to the news media?

6. From what media outlets do you receive most of your news? Do you generally accept what you read or see on television as factual and acceptable reporting? Why?

7. How do you define *media?* What media should be included?

"Reality has come to seem more and more like what we are shown by cameras."

—Susan Sontag

Ira Wyman/Corbis/Sygma

etting through a day without being touched by the media would be difficult. We have daily morning and evening newspapers. We have weekly newsmagazines to recap what we might have missed in the daily papers. We have digest magazines that gather articles and even books from a variety of sources and condense them for us so that we can keep up with what's new without straining ourselves. We have how-to books and magazines on everything from sex to bomb making. We stand in line for hours to be among the first to see the latest Star Wars movie; we wouldn't think of owning a car without a radio (AM *and* FM, of course), tape cassette, or CD player. We can't seem to get enough music: stores and elevators numb us with Muzak; the streets pulse with sounds from "boom boxes" on strollers' shoulders; parks fill up with runners wired to their headsets. More than 87 million homes in the United States alone have television sets, each one turned on for an average of more than seven hours a day. According to one study done by the Roper Organization, 64 percent of the American public turns to television for most of its news. And 53 percent rank television as the most believable news source.

Collectively, the power the media have over us is worth examining. Both directly and indirectly, the media have a profound effect on our lives. What we eat, what we buy, what we do, even what we think is influenced by the media.

Recent concern for the direction in which the media are taking us has prompted such books as Marie Winn's *The Plug-In Drug* and *Unplugging the Plug-In Drug,* which deal with the negative effects of television; David Halberstam's *The Powers That Be,* an account of the people who create, control, and use the media to shape American policy and politics; Norman Corwin's *Trivializing America: The Triumph of Mediocrity,* a look at the way the media have contributed to a lowering of our cultural standards; Ben Bagdikian's *The Media Monopoly,* in which it is revealed that only twenty-six corporations control half or more of all media, including book publishers, television and radio stations, newspapers, and movie companies; Mark Hertsgaard's *On Bended Knee: The Press and the Reagan Presidency,* which reveals how the press gets conned by the candidates and ignores election issues; Patricia Greenfield's *Mind and the Media,* which shows the media's effects on us; and James Fallow's *Breaking the News: How the Media Undermine American Society.*

Is all this attention uncalled-for? How believable, how revealing, how comprehensive, how good is what the media provide us? What effect is the Internet going to play on our lives? How much influence do advertising sponsors have on the media? What effect is the violence portrayed in movies and on television having on our society? Is rap music causing harm? Should we become more concerned with media effects than we are? Just what effects *do* the media have on our lives? These are questions that the reading selections in this unit may prompt you to ask. It is hoped that reading them will stimulate both your thinking and your writing.

Preparing to Read

Take a minute or two to look over the following reading selection. Note the title and the author, read the opening paragraph, and check the essay's length. Make certain you have the time now to read it carefully and to do the exercises that follow it. Then, in the spaces provided, answer the following questions.

1. What do you think the subject of this essay will be?_____

_____

_____

2. What is the author's tone?_____

_____

3. What is Poniewozik's attitude toward Dennis Pluchinsky? How can you tell?

_____

_____

_____

Vocabulary

Good comprehension of what you are about to read depends upon your understanding of the words below. The number following each word refers to the paragraph where it is used.

squelch (1) suppress, crush

mealymouthed (1) insincere, unwilling to be direct

infrastructure (1) understructure, foundation

in retrospect (4) in reviewing the past

innocuous (8) inoffensive, harmless

expeditiously (11) quickly and efficiently

conscientious (14) dedicated, devoted, thorough

fiefdoms (15) empires

prerogatives (15) privileges, freedoms

mea culpas (17) acts of contribution, amends

Calling the C-Word the C-Word

JAMES PONIEWOZIK

1   Three cheers for Dennis Pluchinsky. These days, too many people who would squelch reporting and expression couch their threats in mealymouthed terms—"watch what you say," and so on—so as to avoid being accused of favoring censorship. Not so Pluchinsky, a State Department analyst who has studied terrorism for the past 25 years. Writing in the *Washington Post* Sunday, Pluchinsky accuses the U.S. media of "treason" for reporting in detail on infrastructure and government weaknesses that make the country vulnerable to terrorists. These reports, he says, are easily available for terrorists to peruse and exploit. And he doesn't mince words about his solution: "This type of reporting—carrying specifics about U.S. vulnerabilities—must be stopped or censored."

2   You've got to admire a man who's willing to call the c-word the c-word, though his candor is not likely to win him many friends in the media. The knee-jerk journalistic reaction is to call Pluchinsky an alarmist, to say that reports in the press give no aid to terrorists that they don't already have. Considering the man's quarter-century of experience, that would be arrogant. But for his own part, Pluchinsky doesn't seem to have thought much about the utility of a free press at all. Puzzling over post-9/11 terrorism coverage of our terror vulnerabilities, he writes, "I do not understand the media's agenda here."

3   Let me try to explain it. A large part of that agenda, idealism aside, is to stay alive. The bulk of the journalists with the highest profile in covering the war on terrorism—and its occasional embarrassments—are not just in war zones overseas but in cities like Washington and New York. They rightfully see themselves as potentially the next victims of another large-scale terrorist attack. And Pluchinsky does nothing to counter the argument that aggressive reporting might actually do a thing or two to prevent one.

4   The basic failure to prevent the Sept. 11 attacks was not that so many of us imagined the possibility, but that so few of us did. In retrospect, the idea that terrorists might use airplanes as flying bombs—and were planning to do so—seems obvious to anyone looking at the pieces of information available before Sept. 11. It evidently didn't occur to the right people in the government, though, or for that matter in the media: a terrorist searching pre-Sept. 11 reporting for that scheme would be out of luck.

5   The kind of scenario-spinning that the press has engaged in since Sept. 11 can seem like reckless brainstorming. When a journalist suggests that a terrorist might give himself Ebola and spread the disease in public, or blow up one of America's numerous chemical trucks to

produce a crude gas attack, it may shock you or me. But that's because you and I are not soulless murdering bastards. The enemy that wants to kill us consists of people who look at any object they encounter—a truck, an airplane-dinner fork—and think, "How can I use this to kill as many people as possible?"

6   It flatters journalists to assume they can compete at that game. Look at one of the headlines Pluchinsky considers irresponsible: "Chemical Plants Are Feared As Targets." Can anyone plausibly argue that it never occurred to the folks who perpetrated Sept. 11 to hit a chemical plant?

7   Pluchinsky's stronger argument is that journalists endanger us when they report on specific vulnerabilities to terrorists or mistakes past terrorists have made. "Al Qaeda terrorists now know to pay a speeding ticket promptly," he writes. "They now know not to pay for things with large amounts of cash. They now know to buy some furniture for their apartments or rooms. . . . They know now that they should have a phone installed in their apartments or rooms." But he doesn't note that sales clerks, local cops and landlords now know to look for that too. In a war on terrorism that requires tips from an informed public, how else does Pluchinsky suggest getting that information to law-abiding citizens? He doesn't.

8   More disturbingly, Pluchinsky leaves the method of determining what needs to be censored open-ended. After all, he himself acknowledges that "dangerous" information is sometimes composed of many pieces of information that are in themselves innocuous. In other words, you can't tell from reading an individual story whether it's dangerous or not. So how small does a tidbit of information have to be—a security snafu at the local airport, a photo taken near a nuclear power plant—to escape government scrutiny? (And I'm not exaggerating "government scrutiny" for effect; he writes, "It seems reasonable to me that a process should be established where such articles are filtered through a government agency such as the proposed Department of Homeland Security.")

9   But most unsettling of all, Pluchinsky's attack could let our guardians off the hook for their failures, in ways that are not just self-serving but dangerous. Consider one example he gives: "Abu-Ubayd al-Qurashi, believed to be a close aide to Osama bin Ladin [sic], commenting on the 9/11 operatives, stated that 'the suicide hijackers studied the lives of Palestinian Yehiya Ayash [a Hamas bomb maker who was himself assassinated] and Ramzi Yousef [operational planner of the 1993 World Trade Center bombing] and the security mistakes that led to their downfall while they were preparing for the September 11 operation.' How did al Qaeda know about the security mistakes that led to the death of Ayash and the capture of Yousef? The media, at home and abroad."

10   It's a chilling passage, but not just for the reasons Pluchinsky argues. The "open sources" of vulnerability reporting he deplores are just that—open. They were available to law-enforcement officials, immigration officials and anyone else responsible for keeping those leaks plugged. It is at best a cop-out to claim that reporting weaknesses helps terrorists exploit them without acknowledging that that reporting also can spur changes in change-resistant bureaucracies.

11   Ah, but wouldn't it be better if we could make that information available only to the people on our side? Maybe, if we could assume that the folks on our side would act expeditiously and be held accountable, even though they know it won't get out to the public if they don't. (After all, if it's treasonous to report on a vulnerability, it's treasonous to report on someone's failure to correct it.)

12   This is more or less Pluchinsky's suggestion. He recommends that anyone who spots a potential vulnerability, rather than making it public, should instead report it to the government. "If the department determined that these vulnerabilities indeed existed," he says, "then it could award 'Homeland Security Protective Security' certificates to individuals or 'Homeland Security Gold Stars' to newspaper or Internet sites that put the country first during a time of war."

13   After issuing the gold star—or perhaps a decorative smiley-face sticker—presumably the government would fix the problem pronto. Problem is, that assumption flies in the face of what we've seen since Sept. 11, let alone before—be it intelligence sharing between the FBI and CIA, getting marshals onto airplanes or expediting the screening of bombs hidden in airplane luggage (an idea which, don't worry, occurred to terrorists long before I wrote it down).

14   The cynical interpretation is that the gold-star system would provide officials incentive to sweep their failures under the rug, knowing that a press not wishing to be treasonous would never call them on it, or that it would allow officials to label as "dangerous" reports that are merely embarrassing or politically dangerous. And I have no doubt some officials would use it that way, though I doubt that that is why Pluchinsky proposes it. Let's give him the benefit of the doubt and assume that he is not only sincere in his concern but good at and conscientious about his job: that, were a newspaper or other snoop to discover a flaw in our nation's security and bring it to his attention, he would set about to make it right, putting aside any questions of careerism, politics, pride or self-interest to act for the common good.

15   Pluchinsky seems to assume that every single one would. But a cursory glimpse at the intelligence failures before Sept. 11 and efforts to bolster America's security afterward makes clear that not everyone responsible for safeguarding the nation and its infrastructure is a Dennis Pluchinsky. Too many responsible people in government and industry have shown that nothing short of public exposure and

embarrassment will get them to take steps to improve security, if those steps endanger their business, bureaucratic fiefdoms or personal prerogatives.

16 "What also infuriates me," Pluchinsky writes, "is when the media publish follow-up reports noting that security measures or procedures around a specific target or system still have not been implemented. Not only do the media identify potential target vulnerabilities for the terrorists but they also provide our foes with progress reports!" It never seems to occur to him that, if a not for "open sources" of information, those measures might never be implemented, leaving us more vulnerable to terrorists—who, Pluchinsky himself notes, have other ways of finding vulnerabilities besides watching the news.

17 That is the main lesson of the Coleen Rowley FBI memo, which produced mea culpas and commitments to reform that plainly should have seemed obvious to FBI insiders long before her memo— and that, just as plainly, were not in the offing until she wrote the memo and it broke to the public.

18 Is Coleen Rowley a traitor? Are the journalists who reported her story? Maybe Pluchinsky would say so. But then what does that make the superiors who ignored her until she wrote it? No doubt many of them would rather she, and the journalists who reported on her complaint, would have quietly handed them her complaint, to be filed away in some bottom drawer, in exchange for a shiny new gold star.

Understanding the Content

Feel free to reread all or parts of the selection to answer the following questions.

1. Who is Dennis Pluchinsky? What is his attitude toward the U.S. media?

2. What does Dennis Pluchinsky propose and why?

3. What was, according to Poniewozik, the "basic failure to prevent the Sept. 11 attacks"?

4. How does the media, in general, feel about Pluchinsky and his suggestions regarding the dissemination of information?

Looking at Structure and Style

1. What is Poniewozik's thesis? Is it stated or implied? If stated, where?

2. What words or phrases does Poniewozik use throughout this selection to convey his feelings about Dennis Pluchinsky?

3. What is Poniewozik's tone throughout this essay?

4. What is the purpose of paragraphs 5–6? Do they help to support the author's thesis?

5. Rewrite paragraphs 17–18 so that they effectively conclude the essay, summarizing the information presented and restating Poniewozik's thesis statement.

Evaluating the Author's Viewpoints

1. What is Poniewozik's attitude toward Pluchinsky's suggestion that the media be censored?

2. What is Poniewozik's attitude toward the U.S. government and its intelligence gathering? How can you tell?

3. Based on your reading of the selection and what you know about the events surrounding September 11, do you agree or disagree that "too many responsible people in government and industry have shown that nothing short of public exposure and embarrassment will get them to take steps to improve security, if those steps endanger their business, bureaucratic fiefdoms or personal prerogatives"? Why?

4. What do you think of Dennis Pluchinsky's suggestion that "anyone who spots a vulnerability, rather than making it public, should instead report it to the government"?

5. Do you think that "journalists endanger us when they report on specific vulnerabilities to terrorists or mistakes past terrorists have made"? Why?

Pursuing Possible Essay Topics

1. Brainstorm or freewrite on one or more of the following topics:
   a. censorship
   b. the media
   c. freedom of speech
   d. terrorism
   e. U.S. intelligence
   f. airport security

2. Poniewozik mentions Coleen Rowley in paragraphs 17–18 of his essay. Do some research on Coleen Rowley. Who is she, and why does the author mention her? Write an essay describing Coleen Rowley and summarizing the latest events in her life.

3. Write an essay either in support of Dennis Pluchinsky's viewpoints or in opposition. Use facts to support your opinion.

4. What measures do you think the United States should take to ensure the safety of its citizens? Write an essay discussing one aspect or measure that should be taken.

5. Do you think the United States government could have done more to stop the terrorist attacks of September 11? If so, what could it have done?

6. Is there any time when censorship of the media should be enforced? If so, when would that be and why?

7. Ignore these topics and find your own topic related to the media and censorship.

Preparing to Read

Take a minute or two to look over the following reading selection. Note the title and the author, read the opening paragraph, and check the essay's length. Make certain you have the time now to read it carefully and to do the exercises that follow it. Then, in the spaces provided, answer the following questions.

1. What do you think the title means?_____

_____

_____

2. What subject does the essay discuss?_____

_____

3. What do you think is the author's viewpoint on the subject?_____

_____

_____

Vocabulary

Good comprehension of what you are about to read depends upon your understanding of the words below. The number following each word refers to the paragraph where it is used.

grisly (1) gruesome, horrible
allegedly (2) supposedly

Mrs. Grundy (3) an extremely conservative, prudish person

garroting (3) strangling

desecrating (4) abusing something sacred

prestigious (5) highly respected

denunciations (5) formal condemnations or accusations

advocates (7) recommends, supports

purveyors (7) distributors

lepers (7) outcasts

proffers (7) offers

Walter Cronkite (8) a popular TV news announcer, now retired

sanction (9) authorize, approve

trivial (10) insignificant

cerebral (10) intellectual, theoretical

propagandists (11) advocates, those who spread their doctrines and beliefs

rampant (13) widespread

endemic (14) prevalent, common in our society

forum (15) a medium for open discussion

bluenoses (15) puritanical people

The Issue Isn't Sex, It's Violence

Caryl Rivers

1   After a grisly series of murders in California, possibly inspired by the lyrics of a rock song, we are hearing a familiar chorus: Don't blame rock and roll. Kids will be kids. They love to rebel, and the more shocking the stuff, the better they like it.

2   There's some truth in this, of course. I loved to watch Elvis shake his torso when I was a teen-ager, and it was even more fun when Ed Sullivan wouldn't let the cameras show him below the waist. I snickered at the forbidden "Rock with Me, Annie" lyrics by a black Rhythm and Blues group, which were deliciously naughty. But I am sorry, rock fans, that is not the same thing as hearing lyrics about how a man is going to force a woman to perform oral sex on him at gunpoint in a little number called "Eat Me Alive." It is not in the same league with a song about the delights of slipping into a woman's room while she is sleeping and murdering her, the theme of an AC/DC ballad that allegedly inspired the California slayer.

3   Make no mistake, it is not sex we are talking about here, but violence. Violence against women. Most rock songs are not violent—they are funky, sexy, rebellious, and sometimes witty. Please do not mistake me for a Mrs. Grundy. If Prince wants to leap about wearing only a purple jock strap, fine. Let Mick Jagger unzip his fly as he gyrates, if he wants to. But when either one of them starts garroting, beating, or sodomizing a woman in their number, that is another story.

4   I always find myself annoyed when "intellectual" men dismiss violence against women with a yawn, as if it were beneath their dignity to notice. I wonder if the reaction would be the same if the violence were directed against someone other than women. How many people would yawn and say, "Oh, kids will be kids," if a rock group did a nifty little number called "Lynchin," in which stringing up and stomping on black people were set to music? Who would chuckle and say, "Oh, just a little adolescent rebellion" if a group of rockers went on MTV dressed as Nazis, desecrating synagogues and beating up Jews to the beat of twanging guitars?

5   I'll tell you what would happen. Prestigious dailies would thunder on editorial pages; senators would fall over each other to get denunciations into the Congressional Record. The president would appoint a commission to clean up the music business.

6   But violence against women is greeted by silence. It shouldn't be.

7   This does not mean censorship, or book (or record) burning. In a society that protects free expression, we understand a lot of stuff will float up out of the sewer. Usually, we recognize the ugly stuff that advocates violence against any group as the garbage it is, and we consider its purveyors as moral lepers. We hold our nose and tolerate it, but we speak out against the values it proffers.

8   But images of violence against women are not staying on the fringes of society. No longer are they found only in tattered, paper-covered books or in movie houses where winos snooze and the scent of urine fills the air. They are entering the mainstream at a rapid rate. This is happening at a time when the media, more and more, set the agenda for the public debate. It is a powerful legitimizing force—especially television. Many people regard what they see on TV as the truth; Walter Cronkite once topped a poll as the most trusted man in America.

9   Now, with the advent of rock videos and all-music channels, rock music has grabbed a big chunk of legitimacy. American teenagers have instant access, in their living rooms, to the messages of rock, on the same vehicle that brought them *Sesame Street*. Who can blame them if they believe that the images they see are accurate reflections of adult reality, approved by adults? After all, Big Bird used to give them lessons on the same little box. Adults, by their silence, sanction the images. Do we really want our kids to think that rape and violence are what sexuality is all about?

10   This is not a trivial issue. Violence against women is a major social problem, one that's more than a cerebral issue to me. I teach at Boston University, and one of my most promising young journalism students was raped and murdered. Two others told me of being raped. Recently, one female student was assaulted and beaten so badly she had $5,000 worth of medical bills and permanent damage to her back and eyes.

11   It's nearly impossible, of course, to make a cause-and-effect link between lyrics and images and acts of violence. But images have a tremendous power to create an atmosphere in which violence against certain people is sanctioned. Nazi propagandists knew that full well when they portrayed Jews as ugly, greedy, and powerful.

12   Violence against women, particularly in a sexual context, is being legitimized in two ways: by the increasing movement of these images into the mainstream of the media in TV, films, magazines, albums, videos, and by the silence about it.

13   Violence, of course, is rampant in the media. But it is usually set in some kind of moral context. It's usually only the bad guys who commit violent acts against the innocent. When the good guys get violent, it's against those who deserve it. Dirty Harry blows away the scum, he doesn't walk up to a toddler and say, "Make my day." The A Team does not shoot up suburban shopping malls.

14   But in some rock songs, it's the "heroes" who commit the acts. The people we are programmed to identify with are the ones being violent, with women on the receiving end. In a society where rape and assaults on women are endemic, this is no small problem, with millions of young boys watching on their TV screens and listening on their Walkmans.

15   I think something needs to be done. I'd like to see people in the industry respond to the problem. I'd love to see some women rock stars speak out against violence against women. I would like to see disc jockeys refuse air play to records and videos that contain such violence. At the very least, I want to see the end of the silence. I want journalists and parents and critics and performing artists to keep this issue alive in the public forum. I don't want people who are concerned about this issue labeled as bluenoses and book-burners and ignored.

16   And I wish it wasn't always just women who were speaking out. Men have as large a stake in the quality of our civilization as women do in the long run. Violence is a contagion that infects at random. Let's hear something, please, from the men.

Understanding the Content

Feel free to reread all or parts of the selection to answer the following questions.

1. What does Rivers mean by her title, "The Issue Isn't Sex, It's Violence"? Violence against whom?

2. Why is Rivers concerned that teenagers who were raised on *Sesame Street* might be misled by some rock videos and all-music channels?

3. Rivers says that violence is rampant in the media, mentioning the Dirty Harry movies and the now-canceled television show *The A Team.* Why does she consider this type of violence less harmful than some of the rock lyrics and rock videos? How do the heroes in these shows differ from the "heroes" in the rock videos?

4. What examples from her personal life does Rivers offer to support her view that violence against women "is not a trivial issue"? Are they persuasive examples?

5. What suggestions does Rivers offer to people in the music industry as a way to combat violence against women? Who else does she wish would speak out? Why?

Looking at Structure and Style

1. In paragraph 2, Rivers mentions that she "loved to watch Elvis shake his torso" and "snickered" at certain rock lyrics that were "deliciously naughty." What function does this serve?

2. What function does paragraph 3 serve?

3. How do paragraphs 4–6 work together to make Rivers's point? Why does she make paragraph 6 two short sentences?

4. How do paragraphs 7 and 8 work together? Why does she make it clear that she is not talking about censoring rock lyrics or videos?

5. What is the function of paragraphs 13 and 14? How do they work together to help support her thesis?

6. Concluding paragraphs 15 and 16 present Rivers's suggestions for curtailing the problem. Would it make much difference if she reversed the order of the two paragraphs? Explain.

7. Explain or rewrite the following passages from the essay:

    a. "I always find myself annoyed when 'intellectual' men dismiss violence against women with a yawn, as if it were beneath their dignity to notice." (4)

    b. "Usually, we recognize the ugly stuff that advocates violence against any group as the garbage it is, and we consider its purveyors as moral lepers." (7)

    c. "It [the media] is a powerful legitimizing force." (8)

    d. "I don't want people who are concerned about this issue labeled as bluenoses and book-burners and ignored." (15)

Evaluating the Author's Viewpoints

1. Rivers believes that some rock lyrics and music videos express a violence toward women, frequently a sexual violence. Do you agree? Have you listened to enough rock lyrics or seen enough MTV to speak from experience?

2. Look at the suggestions Rivers offers in paragraph 15. Do you think each suggestion is worth considering? Would implementing her suggestions be better than applying censorship laws? Explain.

3. In paragraphs 4 and 16, Rivers implies that men are not doing enough, that they are too silent about the problem. Do you agree? On what do you base your answer?

4. What is your response to paragraph 12? Is this a fairly good statement of her thesis?

Pursuing Possible Essay Topics

1. If you are not familiar with some recent rock lyrics or music videos, turn on the radio or MTV. Do you see or hear any violence toward women? Write an essay that agrees or disagrees with Rivers's thesis.

2. Analyze the lyrics of a popular rock song. What is being said? What is being implied? Do the words have any merit?

3. Write an essay that describes a rock video that appears on MTV (or some other all-music channel). What is happening? Do the images fit the lyrics? Are the images suggestive? What values are being portrayed that young viewers might accept simply because they admire the musician or singer?

4. Defend or refute the need for some type of censorship in the music industry as a way to protect young children and teenagers from exposure to sexual looseness or violence in songs and videos.

5. Brainstorm or freewrite on one or more of the following:
   a. MTV
   b. punk rock
   c. the Top 40
   d. rock-and-roll
   e. your favorite music group
   f. the influence of music

6. Come up with your own topic on some aspect of the media.

Preparing to Read

Take a minute or two to look over the following reading selection. Note the title and author, read the opening paragraph, and check the essay's length. Make certain you have the time now to read it carefully and to do the exercises that follow it. Then, in the spaces provided, answer the following questions.

1. What do you think the subject of the essay will be? _____

   _____

2. Did you watch the coverage of John F. Kennedy, Jr.'s death? If so, how much

   time did you spend watching television?_____

   _____

3. Do you think that there was too much coverage, not enough coverage, or the

   right amount? Explain._____

   _____

   _____

Vocabulary

Good comprehension of what you are about to read depends upon your understanding of the words below. The number following each word refers to the paragraph where it is used.

anecdote (1) short account of an interesting or humorous incident

demise (1) death

pundit (2) source of opinion, critic

backlash (6) antagonistic reaction to an earlier action

mawkish (6) excessively sentimental

saturation (6) the condition of being full

morbidity (7) gruesomeness

explication (8) explanation, analysis

aeronautical (10) having to do with aircraft navigation

offal (10) refuse, rubbish

opined (11) stated an opinion

invocations (12) calls, appeals

banal (13) predictable, trite

rampant (13) unchecked, unrestrained

angst (13) anxiety or apprehension often accompanied by depression

epochal (14) highly significant or important

gaseous (14) lacking substance or concreteness

Trauma TV

ANDREW FERGUSON

1   You'll forgive me, I hope, for beginning this little essay about television and the sad death of John Kennedy Jr. with a personal anecdote. It is only fitting, since there were many moments during the coverage when Kennedy's demise seemed little more than an excuse for people to talk about themselves on live TV.

2   And so it might have been with me, too, had I not managed to resist the temptation. As a sometime TV pundit, I am definitely third- or fourth-tier, dwelling deep in the cobwebby corners of a few talk-show producers' Rolodexes, and it was a testament to the enormous amount of airtime the cable networks felt compelled to fill that eventually, a day or two after Kennedy's body had been discovered, a producer got around to me. I was ready, of course. I had my own store of Kennedy memories—as it happens, I once saw John across the room at a party—but the producer told me she wanted me to talk instead about "how TV is overdoing the coverage of Kennedy's death."

3   I declined the invitation. Not more than an hour later, another producer for another cable network called. Would I come on her show to talk about how TV was overdoing this whole thing? I declined again. When I went home that evening, I switched on yet a third cable talk show. The guests were discussing whether TV was overdoing the coverage of John Kennedy's death.

4   Holy smokes, I thought. Even when they do a story about how they're overdoing the story, they overdo it. Which leads us to ask, "Can TV do anything without overdoing it?"

5   It's a question that arises whenever there is one of these tragedies that are deemed universally interesting. And the answer is: Probably not. A better question is, "Would we wish TV to behave other than it does?"

6   For all the backlash, for all the complaining about mawkish excess in coverage, the ratings show that TV was responding to the demands of its viewers. Ratings skyrocketed after Kennedy's plane was declared missing—on the cable news networks especially, but for the network news shows, too. And they continued to climb in the week that followed, as the coverage reached saturation levels.

7   Consider a comparison. In the week after the death of Princess Diana—a carnival of morbidity that no one thought could ever be matched—ABC, CBS and NBC carried 102 stories about her on the evening news. In the six days after Kennedy's plane disappeared, the network news shows went with 131 stories on the subject. This, of

course, does not include the round-the-clock coverage on the cable news channels, nor the nine hours of programming the networks' prime-time newsmagazines offered. (My figures come from the Center for Media and Public Affairs in Washington, D.C.)

8　　As they always do in times of national trauma, Americans flocked to their TVs, seeking—well, what were we seeking, exactly? Not information, surely. Judged strictly as a news story, the death of Kennedy and his companions was about as straightforward as they come: Plane takes off in unfavorable conditions, plane crashes, bodies are recovered and then buried. A detailed explication of the story, replete with interviews, maps and structural charts, would take up about 20 minutes of airtime.

9　　Yet long after the details had been hashed and rehashed, the programming droned on, and we kept watching. It became evident, as it had after Princess Diana's death, that the traditional "news cycle" is no more. Even on TV, the news used to come at us in spurts: a story might break during the morning shows; we'd get an update at noon; then a recap with fresh developments on the evening news. Now the incessant, "real-time" reporting of the cable news channels spurs the networks to more complete coverage; the networks in turn intensify the story; the 24-hour channels respond by keeping the story alive even longer. In place of the news cycle, we now have a news spiral, going only one way: up.

10　　In such an environment, embarrassments are inevitable. Certified "experts"—family friends, aeronautical engineers, cultural commentators—kept popping up like vultures circling a plate of offal. Reporters, with so little to report, filled the air with third-rate romance, beyond self-parody.

11　　Kennedy, said one CNN correspondent, was "the boy who so loved the ocean [that he] would one day become a part of it." Another on CBS opined: "It is a testament to [the Kennedys'] unquestioning love of these waters that this family can continue to find peace in a sea that has stolen so much from them."

12　　As unavoidable as the aquatic metaphors were the invocations of monarchy. At NBC, for example, 90-proof Camelot moonshine was the tipple of choice. "He is as close to royalty as this country had," said NBC's Tom Brokaw. "JFK Jr. is the closest thing this country had to a prince," agreed NBC's Matt Lauer. One can imagine Kennedy, by all accounts a sensible and modest fellow, cringing at this excess.

13　　So if we weren't seeking news (since there wasn't much) and if we weren't (heaven knows) seeking the banal poetry of TV journalists, what did we hope to get from the wall-to-wall coverage of Kennedy's death? It is at this point that TV deep thinkers invoke a cliché of their own: In an age of fractured community and rampant individualism, television has become our national hearth fire, the place where we gather to mourn or to celebrate—where we seek shared experience. The viewers not only watch the story, but become an essential component of it. Ironically enough, we saw the phenomenon first in the death of Kennedy Jr.'s father, then again in the moon landing, and on through Watergate, the fall of Saigon and the other markers of baby-boomer angst.

14   The difference, of course, is that those were epochal events. For all the attractiveness of the man himself, the death of John Jr., like the death of Princess Diana, cannot reasonably be judged an event of similar significance. Yet television seems no longer capable of making the necessary distinctions. We can blame the programmers or the gaseous anchors or the nature of the medium itself. But honesty (and the ratings) suggests a more discomfiting explanation: If TV invariably overdoes it, if it can't distinguish between the death of a celebrity and a genuine national tragedy, it's because we can't, either.

Understanding the Content

Feel free to reread all or parts of the selection to answer the following questions.

1. What do you think the title of the essay means?

2. Why was the author called by television producers during the coverage of Kennedy's death?

3. Why does the author think networks carry so much news on events such as Kennedy's death and the death of Princess Diana?

4. What is the "traditional 'news cycle' "?

5. According to the author, "what did we hope to get from the wall-to-wall coverage of Kennedy's death" on television?

Looking at Structure and Style

1. Why does the author begin the essay with a personal anecdote? Is this an effective opening? Explain.

2. What metaphors does the author include throughout the essay to make his point?

3. The author includes quotes from some of the newscasts that aired during the coverage of Kennedy's death. Are these effective?

Evaluating the Author's Viewpoints

1. How does the author feel about the media in general? How can you tell?

2. Why did the author decline the invitation to go on television to discuss Kennedy's death?

3. How does the author answer the question "'Can TV do anything without overdoing it?'"

4. When does the author think television first became the "place where we gather to mourn or to celebrate—where we seek shared experience"?

5. Do you agree with the author's conclusion that "if TV invariably overdoes it, if it can't distinguish between the death of a celebrity and a genuine national tragedy, it's because we can't, either"?

Pursuing Possible Essay Topics

1. How do you feel about the way the media cover events such as Princess Diana's death or John F. Kennedy, Jr.'s death? Do you feel that the coverage is excessive? Why or why not? Write an essay defending your position.

2. Write an essay discussing why you think the media cover such events as they do. What role do you think the American public plays in the amount of televised coverage?

3. Write an essay describing an event you thought the media did a poor job of covering. Was there too much coverage or not enough? Why do you think that was?

4. Choose your own topic related to the media and write about it.

Preparing to Read

Take a minute or two to look over the following reading selection. Note the title and author, read the first two paragraphs, and check the essay's length. Make certain you have the time now to read it carefully and to do the exercises that follow it. Then, in the spaces provided, answer the following questions.

1. What is the subject of the essay?_____

_____

_____

2. Based on just the title, what do you think the author's opinion of television is? _____

_____

_____

Vocabulary

Good comprehension of what you are about to read depends upon your understanding of the words below. The number following each word refers to the paragraph where it is used.

arrivederci (2) Italian for good-bye

sayonara (2) Japanese for good-bye

sociocultural (2) of, relating to, or involving a combination of social and cultural factors

pronouncements (2) formal declarations of opinion

elitism (3) the sense of superiority enjoyed by a favored group or class

humility (3) the quality or state of being humble

industriousness (3) persistent activity in work or study

ludic (3) of, relating to, or characterized by play

misbegotten (4) having a disreputable or improper origin

predicated (5) based or established on

exponentially (5) characterized by an extremely rapid increase

capacious (6) spacious, roomy

Pandora's Idiot Box

DAVID RAKOFF

1   I've just bought the first television of my adult life. The last time I lived with one was more than 10 years ago, a short while after college. And even that wasn't really like having a television. In Brooklyn at that time, adequate reception without cable was dicey at best. My roommate and I referred to ours as "the Channel 7." As in "Let's turn on the Channel 7 and see what's on."

2   The last time I had watched television in my own home I was iron-
ing a shirt as I listened to Ann Richards's remarkable speech from the
1988 Democratic National Convention (also virtually the last time I
ironed a shirt). When she nailed George Bush as having been "born
with a silver foot in his mouth," I jubilantly said to myself: "Ah, finally!
The '80s are officially over! Goodbye Decade of Greed! *Arrivederci*
Yuppies! *Sayonara* Era of the $1,000 Studio Apartment!" I was pitifully
wrong, of course. There is a danger in making sweeping sociocultural
pronouncements based upon one hour of television per decade.

3   People, upon hearing of my TV-lessness, would sneer at me, asking: "What? Are you above the medium?" Quite the contrary. It's not
elitism but humility—or rather, humiliation. I am so throughly and
profoundly beneath the medium that I feared having a television set
in my home would spell the end of any industriousness on my part.
I have no discernment. Abduct my family and shoot images of their
capture through a cathode ray, and I will watch it happily. I love it all:
the liquescently beautiful commercials; the ludic antics of happy
bands of sitcom pals; those smart-aleck kids turning the primal
scene into adorably precocious comic fodder; the wonderfully edify-
ing infomercials; tales of beloved household pets gone suddenly,
horribly wrong. I did not have a television because I was trying to
amount to something, a little plan that has essentially panned out.
And so, approaching the midpoint of the average human life expectancy at age 35, I decided finally to give in.

4   Here's just some of what I have not seen by not having a television:
the Menendez Brothers trial, the O.J. Simpson trial, "Seinfeld,"
"Friends," Princess Diana's tell-all interview, Princess Diana's funeral, "Absolutely Fabulous," "Melrose Place," "Beverly Hills 90210"
(indeed the entire misbegotten career of Tori Spelling), the Oscars,
the Tonys, the Grammys, "The People's Choice Awards," "The VH1
Fashion Awards," "The American Music Awards," Miss Universe,
Miss America, Miss U.S.A., Miss Teen U.S.A., Monica Lewinsky's interview with Barbara Walters, "Home Improvement," "Dawson's
Creek" and "Party of Five."

5   But just because I haven't seen these things doesn't mean I don't
know about them. (Although I still have no idea who the woman
known as Daisy Fuentes is, and I do not recognize any of the celebrities in the milk campaigns.) Barry Levinson's satire "Wag the Dog" was
predicated on the theory that people only knew about Desert Storm
through its coverage on television. Consequently, a phony war could
be staged through bogus video clips. But I remember the gulf war,
even without a television. I would even argue that, reading about it in
the newspaper and hearing reports on the radio, I was perhaps better
able to perceive the horror of what was actually happening, since I had
not been numbed by the bloodless images of smart bombs finding
their targets; just so much apparently unpopulated architecture being

blown to bits, action-movie-style. I am still surprised by how much it bears mentioning that, while exponentially the most powerful medium there is, television is thankfully not the only game in town.

6   My new roommate, a cunning little charcoal gray number with a VCR housed directly inside, sits atop my filing cabinet. Now I, like all other North Americans bathed in the TV's comforting blue glow, can sit of an evening upon my sofa. And using the sleep function, I can now wake the next morning, sprawled on same, my mouth tasting like a squirrel's final resting place. This is my birthright. I've still got something of a "Channel 7" (more of an 11 and sometimes 5, actually), reluctant as I am to pay for cable and convinced that with American Movie Classics I would be truly lost. But "The Simpsons" is on twice a day (Oh, joy capacious), and so I am happy. When asked by a friend recently if I'd seen the episode in which George Bush—he of silver foot in mouth—moves in across the street, I was able to lean across the table and respond knowledgeably, a Fellow Traveler at last. "Yeah!" I replied, my eyes shining, finally a member of that club we like to call these United States of America. "It was awesome."

Understanding the Content

Feel free to reread all or parts of the selection to answer the following questions.

1. According to the author, what are the reasons he never had a television?

2. What does the author think are the advantages of not having a television?

3. What is the author's opinion of television watching?

4. Why did the author finally decide to get a television?

5. What are some of the things the author missed by not having a television?

Looking at Structure and Style

1. What is the author's thesis? Is it stated or implied?

2. Describe the author's tone. What phrases help to establish the tone?

3. After reading the essay, do you think the author is being serious or humorous? Why?

4. What is the function of paragraph 4? Why does the author list all these events in one paragraph?

Evaluating the Author's Viewpoints

1. What is the significance of the title, "Pandora's Idiot Box"? What does it say about the author's viewpoints on television as a medium?

2. What do you think the author is saying when he writes, "There is a danger in making sweeping sociocultural pronouncements based upon one hour of television per decade"? Do you agree or disagree? Why?

3. Do you think that having a television in the author's home would have spelled "the end of any industriousness" on his part?

4. Why do you think the author mentions George Bush's name in paragraphs 2 and 6?

Pursuing Possible Essay Topics

1. Write an essay describing your television-watching habits. What do you watch and why? Do you ever watch television to avoid doing something else? Has your television watching ever interfered with your pursuit of other activities?

2. Write an essay describing your earliest memory of television. What is the first program you remember watching?

3. Write an essay describing what programs the perfect television channel would run every day. Would it have a variety of shows that consisted of entertaining programs and newsworthy, informative programs? Or would it be entirely one or the other? Why?

4. Given a choice, would you rather watch television or read? Why?

5. In your opinion, is it more valuable to watch the news on television, read the newspaper, or do both? Explain your choice.

6. Would you rather have a television in every room of the house so that everyone could watch his or her own shows, or would you rather have one television that everyone would share? Why?

7. Brainstorm or freewrite on the topic of television.

8. Don't like these topics? Find one of your own related to television or the media and write an essay about it.

Preparing to Read

Take a minute or two to look over the following reading selection. Note the title and the author, read the opening paragraph, and check the essay's length. Make certain you have the time now to read it carefully and to do the exercises that follow it. Then, in the spaces provided, answer the following questions.

1. What do you think the subject of the essay will be ? _____

   _____

2. What do you think the tone of this essay will be, from your reading of the first

   paragraph? _____

   _____

   _____

3. What examples does the author use to set up the thesis of this selection? ____

   _____

   _____

Vocabulary

Good comprehension of what you are about to read depends upon your understanding of the words below. The number following each word refers to the paragraph where it is used.

   epidemic (3) widespread

   saturation (3) overload, superabundance

   percolating (11) brewing, simmering

   manifested (11) displayed, exhibited

   roused (12) excited, inspired

   self-perpetuating (12) having the power to renew itself indefinitely

   analogous (16) corresponding, parallel

   promiscuous (16) lacking standards in selection, particularly of sexual partners

   mores (16) moral principles, ethics

   malefactors (17) criminals, offenders

   hyperbolically (19) distortedly, with overstatement

   inordinate (19) excessive, extreme

Summer Kidnapping Panic

Michelle Goldberg

1   Aug. 7, 2002   The news has been dominated by tales of vicious strangers grabbing young girls—Elizabeth Smart, Erica Pratt, Samantha Runnion, Tamara Brooks and Jacqueline Marris. Connie Chung's new CNN show has practically become all kidnapping, all the time, turning the Smart family into national celebrities. "It's been one after another, little kids taken out of their bedrooms or otherwise taken in unbelievable ways," says Marc Klaas, whose 12-year-old daughter, Polly Klaas, was abducted from her home in Petaluma, Calif., and murdered in 1993. "It's captured the public's attention." Visits to Klaas's Web site have gone from half a million a month to 2.5 million a month over the last year.

2   On Monday President Bush likened the problem to terrorism. "America's children and parents are also facing a wave of horrible violence from twisted criminals in our own communities," Bush said in a Rose Garden ceremony, held to announce that next month the White House is convening a conference on missing, exploited and runaway children.

3   All this might suggest that child kidnapping is on the rise. But it's not. Random child kidnappings are actually declining. The real epidemic is one of saturation TV coverage.

4   According to the FBI, the number of children stolen in nonransom, noncustodial cases has been shrinking for years. In fiscal year 1999 there were 134, while last year there were 93. In the first three quarters of this fiscal year, there have been 62, which basically works out to one *less* kidnapping a month.

5   Obviously, that's 62 too many. As Lou Palumbo, New York policeman turned private eye, observes, "It's very difficult to explain to a parent that's just had their child abducted, raped and murdered, 'The good news is that there are less cases like this this year than last year.'"

6   Palumbo is right. To a bereaved parent, statistics offer no solace. To the rest of us, though, they should. So if kids are actually safer from abductions now than they were a few years ago, why is the media behaving as if the country is suddenly crawling with predators? Why did our president announce a conference on the crisis as he departed for a controversial monthlong vacation?

7   Partly, it's because the high-profile recent cases had ratings-boosting elements. Seven-year-old Danielle van Dam, who was kidnapped and killed in February, had parents who were swingers. Fourteen-year-old Smart was lovely, blond and rich. Resourceful Erica Pratt, also 7, made an inspiring, daring escape. The harrowing drama of teenagers Brooks and Marris unfolded in hours.

8   Furthermore, says Harold Copus, a former FBI agent who founded the National Investigative and Recovery Center for Missing Children, a new nonprofit that helps poor families pay for investigators to recover parentally abducted or runaway kids, police have recently learned the importance of using the media. "In the first 36 hours of a matter such as this, it's critical that you get as much attention as you can to the child," he says. "You have to do everything you can so that the person who abducted the child realizes they have no place to go and needs to let this child return to her home."

9   In the past, Copus says, police didn't do a "very good job of handling press relations," but the recent nonstop kidnapping coverage suggests they're improving. The Amber Alert system, named after 9-year-old Amber Hagerman, who was kidnapped and murdered in 1996, displays information about child kidnappings on emergency broadcasts and electronic freeway signs. It's premised on the idea that getting the word out on abductions immediately can help save lives.

10   Yet there's probably more to the current national panic than just media-savvy cops and ratings-crazed cable news producers. After all, child snatching is always a compelling story, but it doesn't always top the news, even when reporters know about it. "In past years, we wouldn't have gotten national coverage for the two teen girls last week," says Tina Schwartz, public affairs director at the National Center for Missing and Exploited Children. Schwartz says high-profile cases feed on each other. "There's a lot of fear among parents, and the media is responding to that."

11   According to Paula Fass, a history professor at the University of California at Berkeley and author of the 1997 book "Kidnapped: Child Abduction in America," that fear has been percolating since the 1980s, when women started heading to work in large numbers. It manifested itself in the nationwide scare about satanic abuse in day-care centers as well as in media fascination with kidnapping. It's never gone away, she says, and an event like Sept. 11 can surely awaken it.

12   Once that fear is roused, it becomes self-perpetuating. "The televised media and the radio are just terrible," Fass says. "They have no historical memory and they make no attempt to inform themselves. Their only concern is exploiting emotion, and one emotion we can depend on is the fist in the gut of a parent [worried about her children]. I began my studies because of my terror in the '80s of my children being abducted. That immediate emotion is what the Connie Chungs of this world are after."

13   Furthermore, she says, though kidnapping isn't on the rise, there's a reason why we've seen a string of similar cases so close together. More than any other crime, she says, "kidnapping tends to encourage copycatting," especially in methods. That means that "the first time there's a crime where someone enters a house rather than snatching a child off the street, the publicity of the kidnapping will lead to clustering" of the same kind of crimes.

14   Judith Levine, author of the recent book "Harmful to Minors," about the hysteria revolving around kids and sex, adds that terror about child abductions tends to surface during times of political and economic turmoil, when there's a backlash against social liberation.

15   "There are two other main periods in American history where we've had similar panics about child abduction and child rape," she says. One was during the Depression in the early 1930s, and the other was during McCarthyism in the 1950s. Both came after moments when "women and youth enjoyed a lot of freedom"—the roaring '20s and World War II, when many women went to work—which were followed by anxiety about an out-of-control culture.

16   There's an analogous sense right now, Fass says, that we've become a "much more liberal, promiscuous society. There's been a major transformation of sexual mores, and people are terrified about their children's well-being."

17   Levine believes that long-simmering tension was exacerbated by Sept. 11. "We're in a period of heightened paranoia around both children and the idea that there are evil, unseen malefactors among us: terrorists, pedophiles, people who look and act just like you and me but are actually out to do evil," Levine says. "In general, people are feeling very nervous about a lot of things and we focus our anxieties onto the safety of children."

18   Even Marc Klaas, who believes the current intense coverage is long overdue, doesn't entirely disagree with Levin. "I know people have likened [the current coverage] to shark-bite frenzies, and I suspect there's something to that," he says.

19   "[Child kidnapping] has deserved attention and never received it," he says, somewhat hyperbolically. "Now it might be receiving an inordinate amount, but children are victimized in this country in the millions, and as soon as people understand that, maybe we'll be in a position to do something about it."

20   Then again, he says, "It could subside as soon as there's another terrorist attack or a high-profile celebrity divorce."

Understanding the Content

Feel free to reread all or parts of the selection to answer the following questions.

1. What is the Amber Alert, and how did it get its name?

2. When did the fear about child abductions really start "percolating," according to Paula Fass? What is the effect of that fear?

3. Why does Goldberg feel that, in the summer of 2002, media coverage of child kidnapping was on the rise?

4. According to Paula Fass, why have there been a "string of similar cases so close together"?

5. According to Judith Levine, when do child abductions usually surface?

Looking at Structure and Style

1. What is the purpose of paragraph 1 and the names provided by Goldberg?

2. What is the thesis of this selection? Is it stated or implied? If stated, where?

3. Do paragraphs 18–20 effectively conclude this essay? Why or why not? Rewrite the conclusion so that it effectively summarizes the material presented in the selection.

4. What is the purpose of paragraphs 4–7? How do they support the thesis regarding kidnapping and media coverage?

5. Why does the author cite Mark Klaas repeatedly in this selection? Are the quotes and citations effective in supporting her thesis?

6. Which experts does Goldberg use to support her thesis? Do they offer different points of view? Are they effective in supporting her thesis?

Evaluating the Author's Viewpoints

1. What is Goldberg's attitude toward the media and its coverage of child kidnapping? How can you tell?

2. Do you agree or disagree with President Bush that child abductions are like terrorism? Why or why not?

3. Do you agree or disagree with Mark Klaas that media attention with regard to child kidnapping "could subside as soon as there's another terrorist attack or a high-profile celebrity divorce"?

4. What can you infer about how Mark Klaas feels about the media based on the quotes used by Goldberg in this selection?

Pursuing Possible Essay Topics

1. Do you think the media go overboard in covering certain types of crime? Why? Do you think the profiles of the individuals involved in the crimes (either as victim or perpetrator) have anything to do with the coverage? Write an essay explaining your viewpoint.

2. What affect do you think the events of September 11 have had on Americans? Did the terrorist attacks, and the subsequent panic about terrorism, make the country more tense? Do you think, like Judith Levine, that the events of September 11 created "a period of heightened paranoia around . . . children"?

3. Do you think that media saturation helps or hinders investigations into child kidnappings? Why? Write an essay and discuss your opinion.

4. Brainstorm or freewrite on one or more of the following topics:

   a. the media
   b. media saturation

   c. how to keep children safe
   d. the Amber Alert

5. Find your own subject for an essay on some aspect of the media.

Preparing to Read

Take a minute or two to look over the following reading selection. Note the title and author, read the first two paragraphs, and check the essay's length. Make certain you have the time now to read it carefully and to do the exercises that follow it. Then, in the spaces provided, answer the following questions.

1. What do you think will be the subject of the essay? _____

_____

_____

2. What do you think the author will say about his subject? _____

_____

_____

3. Do you think there is too much violence shown on television? _____

_____

Vocabulary

Good comprehension of what you are about to read depends upon your understanding of the words below. The number following each word refers to the paragraph where it is used.

rampant (2) unchecked, uncontrolled

pernicious (3) harmful, damaging

proposition (6) proposal, plan, scheme

panacea (10) cure-all, remedy

repercussions (17) outcomes, results

lobotomy (18) surgical incision in the brain to cut nerves

pratfall (19) humiliating mistake, a fall on the buttocks

Chips Ahoy

Richard Zoglin

1   On NBC's *Law & Order* last week, a white racist set off a bomb that killed 20 people on a New York City subway train. Tori Spelling, in the CBS movie *Co-Ed Call Girl*, grabbed a gun and shot a sleazy pimp. Batman (the cartoon character) was almost thrown into a vat of flames by the Penguin. Lemuel Gulliver (the Ted Danson character) battled gigantic bees in the land of Brobdingnag. And Nick Nolte and Eddie Murphy slapped around bad guys in the umpteenth cable showing of *48 HRS.*

2   It was, in other words, a pretty typical week of TV in mid-'90s America. Another week, in the view of troubled parents and concerned politicians, in which TV continued to assault youngsters with violent images, encouraging aggressive behavior in a culture where handguns and street violence are rampant. But it was also a landmark week that brought new hope to many parents worried that scenes like the above are doing untold damage to their kids.

3   As President Clinton signed into law the sweeping telecommunications bill passed by Congress, he officially launched the era of the V chip. A little device that will be required equipment in most new TV sets within two years, the V chip allows parents to automatically block out programs that have been labeled (by whom remains to be seen) as high in violence, sex or other objectionable material. Last

week also saw the release of a weighty academic study that said, in effect, it's about time. Financed by the cable industry and conducted by four universities, the study concluded that violence on TV is more prevalent and more pernicious than most people had imagined. Of nearly 2,700 shows analyzed in a 20-week survey of 23 channels, more than half—57%—were said to contain at least some violence. And much of it was the kind that, according to the study, can desensitize kids and encourage imitation: violence divorced from the bad consequences it has in real life.

4   The study drew an outcry from network executives, who argued, with some justification, that they have reduced the amount of violence they air and have added warning labels for the little that remains. Indeed, a UCLA study (financed by the networks) last year found "promising signs" that levels of network violence are declining. And upon closer scrutiny, the new study's methodology does seem to overstate the case a bit. Nevertheless, it pins some hard numbers on a problem that is popping up increasingly in the public forum: What effect is TV violence having on kids? And what should we do about it?

5   Politicians of all stripes have jumped in. Democratic Senator Paul Simon has held well-publicized hearings on TV violence and first proposed that networks sponsor independent audits like last week's report. Bob Dole last year called for action against violence on TV as well as in movies and rock music. Democratic Senator Joseph Lieberman of Connecticut last week joined the conservative Media Research Center in urging the networks to clean up the so-called family hour, the first hour of prime time each evening. President Clinton and Vice President Gore have both embraced the V chip and called for a summit meeting on TV violence with top network and cable executives at the end of February. The antinetwork rhetoric from many reformers sounds strikingly like that directed against another industry charged with making a harmful product. "The TV industry has to be socially responsible," says Harvard child psychiatrist Dr. Robert Coles. "We're now going after the tobacco companies and saying, 'Don't poison people.' It seems to me, the minds of children are being poisoned all the time by the networks. I don't think it's a false analogy."

6   The analogy depends, of course, on accepting the proposition that TV has a harmful effect on young viewers. Researchers have been sparring over that question for years, but the debate seems to have swung in favor of the antiviolence forces. The study released last week did no original research on the effect TV violence has on children's behavior. But it summarized a growing body of research and concluded that the link between TV violence and aggressive behavior is no longer in doubt.

7   Even if true, the exact nature and extent of that link is unclear. Is the effect of watching TV violence brief or lasting? Is TV as important a factor in fostering societal violence as economic poverty, bad schools and broken homes? And in any event, is it really possible—or desirable—to manage kids' exposure to a cultural environment that can never be entirely beneficial or benign? From gangster movies in the '30s to horror comics and rock 'n' roll in the '50s, pop culture has always been strewn with pitfalls for youngsters. Sheltering kids from such things is largely futile; most seem to survive in spite of it.

8   The current wave of concern about TV violence seems oddly timed. The violent action shows that flourished on TV a decade or so ago—*The A-Team; Magnum, P.I.; Miami Vice*—have largely disappeared. The few crime shows left are cerebral dramas like *Law & Order* and *NYPD Blue*, which, though grittier than the older shows, have little overt violence. The sniggering sex talk on network sitcoms is a far more alarming trend. But even if there are some shows that young kids should be shielded from, the question is whether all TV should be held to the standard of safe-for-children. If TV were to be scrubbed clean for kids, it would be a pretty barren place for adults.

9   The V chip offers what appears to be an easy solution to this problem. Rather than removing or trying to tone down objectionable shows, it enables parents simply to keep them out of kids' reach. The current V-chip technology, developed by a Canadian engineer named Tim Collings, is essentially a computer chip that, when installed in TV sets (added cost: as little as $1), can receive encoded information about each show. Parents can then program the TV set to block out shows that have been coded to indicate, say, high levels of violence. If, after the kids have gone to bed, parents want to watch Tori Spelling on a shooting spree, they can reverse the blocking by pushing one or more buttons.

10   The V chip will be welcomed by many parents who despair of monitoring the multitude of TV programs available to their kids. The device has already been a godsend for politicians—a way of seeming to take action on TV violence while avoiding sticky issues of censorship or government control. Most children's activists welcome the device, yet recognize it is not a panacea. "The V chip doesn't do anything to decrease violence," says Arnold Fege of the National Parent-Teacher Association. "There are parents who are not going to use it at all. But it does give parents some control."

11   Widespread use of the V chip is probably years off. New TV sets are not required to have them for at least two years (legal challenges from the networks are expected to extend that further), and there are still all those chipless RCAs and Sonys currently in people's living rooms. Every set in the house would have to have the V

chip, or else kids could just go into the bedroom to watch forbidden shows. Some critics warn, moreover, that it's only a matter of time before kids learn how to break the code and counteract the blocking mechanism.

12   The trickiest problem of all is, Who will rate the shows, and how will they be rated? The telecommunications bill encourages the networks to devise their own rating system; if they haven't done so in a year, the FCC is empowered to set up a panel for creating one. One possible system is currently being tested in Canada. Programs are given a rating of from 0 to 5 in each of three categories: violence, sex and profanity. By setting their V-chip dial to numbers of their choice, parents can block out all shows with higher than that level of offensive material.

13   Some V-chip critics see the centralized rating concept as too rigid. They support instead one of several devices currently in development that enable parents to make their own choices of which shows to block out. FCC chairman Reed Hundt, a V-chip booster, contends that it will be only "the first of a slew of products. I predict remote-control devices with selection programs. There will be a variety of ways to receive TV."

14   Broadcasters, for their part, object that a ratings system mandated by the government threatens their free-speech rights. "A centralized rating system that is subject to review and approval by the government is totally inconsistent with the traditions of this country," says NBC general counsel Richard Cotton. "This legislation turns the FCC into Big Brother." Former CBS Broadcast Group president Howard Stringer argues, "The V chip is the thin end of a wedge. If you start putting chips in the television set to exclude things, it becomes an all-purpose hidden censor."

15   The rhetoric may invoke the First Amendment, but the networks' more pressing concern is the bottom line. The V chip will, inevitably, reduce the potential audience for shows marked with the scarlet letter. That means advertising revenue will go down. What's more, a violence label may scare off many advertisers and thus cause programmers to steer clear of provocative shows. "The thing nobody is taking into account," says *Law & Order* creator Dick Wolf, "is that there's going to be a V-chip warning on *Homicide, NYPD Blue, Law & Order, ER, Chicago Hope*—any of the adult dramas that deal with real-life substantive issues. Once that happens, you are going to have a television landscape that's far, far different from what you have today."

16   There is another possible scenario. If the networks and advertisers learn to live with a V rating, producers might find themselves liberated—able to produce even more adult fare, secure in the knowledge that children will be shielded from it. Which could, of

course, lead either to more sophisticated adult fare or sleazier entertainment. Says Wolf: "If all these shows have warnings on them, you could have a situation where producers are saying to standards people at the networks, 'I've got a warning. I can say whatever I want. I can kill as many people as I want.' "

17   They're already killing a lot, if the National Television Violence Study is to be believed. Billed as the "most thorough scientific survey of violence on television ever undertaken," the study not only found a surprisingly high percentage of violent shows; it also made some damning observations about the way violence is presented. According to the survey, 47% of the violent acts shown resulted in no observable harm to the victim; only 16% of violent shows contained a message about the long-term negative repercussions of violence; and in a whopping 73% of all violent scenes, the perpetrator went unpunished. These figures, however, were based on some overly strict guidelines: perpetrators of violence, for example, must be punished in *the same scene* as the violent act. By that measure, most of Shakespeare's tragedies would be frowned on; Macbeth, after all, doesn't get his comeuppance until the end of the play.

18   The study found significant variations in the amount of violence across the dial. On network stations, 44% of the shows contained at least some violence, vs. 59% on basic cable and 85% on premium channels like HBO and Showtime. Yet it was the broadcast networks that squawked the loudest. "Someone would have to have a lobotomy to believe that 44% of the programs on network television are violent," exclaims Don Ohlmeyer, NBC West Coast president. (Actually, the study referred to network stations, meaning that syndicated shows like *Hard Copy* were also included.) "Since I've been here, I can't think of a program we've had that's glorified violence, that hasn't shown the pain of violence and attempted to show there are other ways to resolve conflicts."

19   The researchers' definition of violence did, at least, avoid some of the absurdities of previous studies, in which every comic pratfall was counted. Violent acts were defined as those physical acts intended to cause harm to another; also included were verbal threats of physical harm as well as scenes showing the aftermath of violence. Thus, finding a body in a pool of blood on *NYPD Blue* counts as a violent act; Kramer bumping into a door on *Seinfeld* does not. A cartoon character whacking another with a mallet counts; but the accidental buffoonery of *America's Funniest Home Videos* doesn't.

20   Yet just one of these acts was enough to classify a program as violent. In addition, the survey covered a number of cable channels—among them USA, AMC, TNT, HBO and Showtime—whose schedules are filled

with network reruns (including many action shows like *Starsky and Hutch* and *Kung Fu*) or theatrical films. This served to boost the overall totals of violent shows while masking the fact that violence in the most watched time periods—network prime time—has declined.

21   "We didn't want to get into a show-by-show debate," says Ed Donnerstein, communications and psychology professor at the University of California at Santa Barbara, where most of the monitoring was done. "We didn't want to point fingers." George Gerbner, former dean of the University of Pennsylvania's Annenberg School for Communication and a longtime chronicler of TV violence, agrees with the study's big-picture approach. "Anytime you give a name of a program, it lends itself to endless quibbling," he says. "The question is not what any one program does or doesn't do. The question is, What is it that large communities absorb over long periods of time?"

22   Whatever its defects, the study could have a major impact as development of the V chip begins. "This is the foundation of any rating system that will be developed," says Representative Edward Markey of Massachusetts, the V chip's original champion in Congress. The irony is that some of the most objectionable shows, in the survey's view, are cartoons and other children's shows: they are the ones that portray violence "unrealistically," without consequences or punishment. "When you show a young kid somebody being run over and they pop back up without harm, that's a problem," says Donnerstein. Maybe so, but a kid who grows up without Batman or Bugs Bunny misses something else: a chance to engage in playful fantasy. And the V chip can't make up for that.

Understanding the Content

Feel free to reread all or parts of the selection to answer the following questions.

1. What is a V chip? What is the device intended to do?

2. What were the conclusions of a study financed and conducted by the cable industry and four universities regarding violence on television? What did a UCLA study, financed by the networks, find? What were the conclusions of the National Television Violence Study? On what do the studies agree and differ?

3. According to the author, politicians have found the V chip a "godsend." Why?

4. What are some of the warnings and concerns of V-chip critics? Why do they feel it is not a panacea for decreasing children's exposure to violence?

5. How did the researchers of the National Television Violence Study define violence for their study? Why is the definition of violence important?

Looking at Structure and Style

1. What writing pattern is used in the opening paragraph? Is it effective? Does it get the reader's attention? Explain how the development of the second paragraph depends upon the first.

2. What is the author's thesis? Is it stated or implied? If stated, where?

3. What is the purpose of paragraphs 3 and 4? Why is paragraph 4 necessary for fair coverage of the subject?

4. What are the major sources for Zoglin's content? Are they reliable sources? What, if anything, do the sources tell you about the audience for whom Zoglin is writing? Explain.

5. Explain the title. Is it appropriate? Why or why not?

Evaluating the Author's Viewpoints

1. According to the studies Zoglin cites, television violence is having a negative effect on children. Does he agree with the studies? Do you? Explain.

2. Many parents are hoping that the V chip will protect children from watching violent programs on television. As a parent or parent-to-be, do you welcome the device? Explain.

3. Several politicians are quoted as showing concern over violent programming on television. Do you think politicians should be involved in regulating television programming? Is doing so a form of government censorship or control of the public media?

4. According to the author, "The telecommunications bill encourages the networks to devise their own rating system: if they haven't done so in a year, the FCC is empowered to set up a panel for creating one" (12). As you read this, the time period has expired. What has the television industry done at this time to satisfy that bill?

5. In the last paragraph, Zoglin seems to think cartoons that show somebody being run over and then popping back up may be harmless. Do you agree? Explain.

Pursuing Possible Essay Topics

Unless you have an idea for an essay based on what you just read, wait until after you read the following essay by Terry Schwadron, "Filters Can't Block Out the World," for another view on such devices as the V chip.

Preparing to Read

Take a minute or two to look over the following reading selection. Note the title and author, read the first two paragraphs, and check the essay's length. Make certain that you have the time now to read it carefully and to do the exercises that follow it. Then, in the spaces provided, answer the following questions.

1. What do you think will be the subject of the essay? _____

   _____

   _____

2. What do you think the author will say about his subject? _____

   _____

   _____

Vocabulary

Good comprehension of what you are about to read depends upon your understanding of the words below. The number following each word refers to the paragraph where it is used.

honed (2) sharpened, shaped

glut (3) overabundance, excess

disseminated (8) distributed, scattered about

browser (9) a program that enables you to access the World Wide Web

credibly (12) convincingly, believably

fiat (18) order, command

eschewed (18) avoided

Filters Can't Block Out the World

TERRY SCHWADRON

1   Recently, I found myself debating a friend over how best to shield his children from books, movies, television and now Internet sites that, as a parent, he thinks are inappropriate.

2   Although I may be exaggerating a bit, he basically wants an electronic magic wand that makes bad stuff—or at least what he thinks represents bad stuff—disappear. I told him I have less faith in the magic and more in the discriminating taste of my kids (who are older than his). Their sensitivities at least were honed with our parental help.

3   Yet I am sympathetic. There's a glut of ugliness in the world, and I have no desire to see kids rushed to face it. That's why we see so much ado about V-chips for televisions, demands for more restrictive entertainment ratings and frustration over offensive song lyrics.

4   Now comes the Internet, a medium with a seemingly endless capacity to frighten parents and legislators alike.

5   I have this empty feeling that in our search for ways to make parenting easier, we're ready to accept some pretty blunt electronic instruments.

6   What these electronic tools do is block.

7   Eliminate pornography and life will be better for me because my kids won't run into it, is the theory. Block my children's access to discussion about violence or alternative lifestyles, and they will not be tempted.

8   And where demand incubates, the marketplace hatches:

- **Filters.** Developers are making software for individual computers that blocks access to a variety of Web sites. Some of these are controversial because they block more than the user may expect.

  Internet access companies are beginning to adopt such filters so they can advertise themselves as family-safe. That means families might never know what they don't get to see.

- **Regulation.** In recent weeks, there have been more notices that governments, Japan's and Dubai's among them, are considering software filters to block indecent sites. To me, countries have never been a great source of guidance on what material should and should not be disseminated.

- **Decency act.** Next month, the Supreme Court justices will hear arguments about whether the Communications Decency Act, passed last year amid a storm of congressional hysteria about Internet pornography, should take effect. Among other things, the act restricts publication of "indecent" material on the Net and establishes grounds for prosecution.

- **Commercial online services.** They long have advertised themselves as offering relatively safe content. But this promise does not cover the unsupervised opinion in chat rooms and bulletin board services, and that is scary to many parents.

- **Ratings.** There are efforts by a number of Internet industry forces, including Microsoft, to create rating systems for Web sites, as with movies and television. The proposals are for self-rating by Web publishers, following a scheme being used for electronic games.

9   My bet is that pornographers will gladly disclose their triple-X ratings and go happily about their publishing. And others will be forced to self-rate in order, say, to get listed by a directory service or to be accessible through a particular browser. It'll turn out to be a business.

10   On the other side of all this are the anti-censorship purists who oppose any government regulation of the Net, who want to ensure that all voices can be heard. They oppose software-filtering programs in general and specifically those that purport to make the Internet safe for family use but actually block more than they need to.

11   The Internet has been abuzz lately, for example, over the sale of a program called CyberSitter because, in addition to blocking pornography, it also blocks sites that advertise access to pirated software or display scenes of violence. CyberSitter even blacks out the site of the National Organization for Women because it lists links to gay and lesbian sites.

12   CyberSitter developer Brian Millburn credibly argues that he is filling a need he sees among parents, who not only don't share the complaints of his critics, but want even more restrictions for their $50.

13   With nearly a million sales of his program, he says, "the real question about free speech is whose free speech we need to protect—the pornographers' or the parents' right to control what comes into their home."

14   Why shouldn't I control what my kids see? argues my friend. Why should I oppose software that will do it for me? he asks.

15   These are awfully crude tools, I say, and reflective more of someone else's judgment than mine about what should be in my home. We're not even sure, as a society, whom we want to protect; all kids under 18 years old are not the same. Further, the experience of teens is far different from that of 7-year-olds.

16   What's more important to me is education in the home. That includes exposure to the unknown and unwanted. My contribution as a parent is the teaching of values through guidance.

17   Just clicking a software button to eliminate half the world doesn't make it go away.

18   I don't love some of the television my children choose to watch, but I am happier to have them decide on their own that it's not for them than I would have been to simply switch it off by fiat. My children have eschewed listening to lyrics that demean women not because I told them it was bad or because William Bennett scolded Time Warner, but because they decided it doesn't fit in their lives.

19   And then there is the problem of opening the front door and actually entering a world in which gangs, graffiti, harassment, abuse, crime and bullies are real. How long can we protect without informing? As a parent, I want my kids more prepared, not less, to face reality.

20   If you're sophisticated enough at computer code, you'll find software programs that can supposedly allow you to specify what to ban in your home.

21   That'll give you a personalized magic wand.

22   In my home, we've preferred another way: building taste by one painful discussion atop another.

Understanding the Content

Feel free to reread all or parts of the selection to answer the following questions.

1. How does Schwadron feel about V chips and other electronic tools used to shield children from inappropriate television, movies, and Internet sites? What are Schwadron's reasons?

2. The demand for ways to keep children from watching inappropriate movies, television, and Internet sites has, according to Schwadron, "hatched" what kinds of probable solutions?

3. What does a computer program called CyberSitter do? Why is it popular? What is the author's opinion of it? Why does Schwadron call such a tool a "magic wand"?

4. What is Schwadron's solution for keeping children from viewing inappropriate materials?

Looking at Structure and Style

1. What is Schwadron's thesis? Is it stated or implied? If stated, where?

2. This essay appeared in a newspaper; consequently, the paragraphs are short. As an editor, what paragraphs could you combine into one if the essay were to be submitted elsewhere?

3. Schwadron writes a first-person narrative, whereas the previous selection by Zoglin is written in the third person. Do you think they both selected the appropriate voice to discuss their subjects? Explain.

4. Who is Schwadron's audience? What makes you think so?

5. What is Schwadron's tone and attitude? What words or phrases help develop his tone and attitude?

Evaluating the Author's Viewpoints

1. As a parent, would you or do you go for the "magic wand" approach or Schwadron's approach? Why?

2. Explain your viewpoint regarding each of the following as described in the essay by the author:

   a. filters

   b. regulations

   c. ratings

   d. Communications Decency Actz

   e. online services

3. What does Schwadron think of "the anti-censorship purists who oppose any government regulation of the Net, who want to ensure that all voices can be heard" (10)? What is your viewpoint?

4. Reread paragraph 16. What is your reaction to this statement?

5. In paragraph 19, Schwadron says the "gangs, graffiti, harassment, abuse, crime and bullies are real. How long can we protect [children] without informing?" Is this a good argument for allowing a certain number of programs depicting these things to be seen by children? Explain your views.

Pursuing Possible Essay Topics

1. Look through the listings in a television guide for one week. How many of the programs deal with crime or "crime busting"? What crimes are featured most? Watch one of the programs and then write your opinion of its value. Could it be harmful to young children or teenagers? Why or why not?

2. Write an essay directed to parents suggesting what their children might do instead of watching television.

3. Write an essay arguing for one or more of the filters, regulations, decency acts, or rating efforts Schwadron mentions.

4. Do some research on the negative influences of television viewing by reading from such books as Marie Winn's *The Plug-In Drug* and *Unplugging the Plug-In Drug,* Jeffrey Schrank's *Snap, Crackle and Popular Taste in America,* Norman Corwin's *Trivializing America,* Mark Hertsgaard's *On Bended Knee,* or any current book or article on the subject. React to what you read.

5. Write an essay discussing answers to the following questions: Why shouldn't I control what my kids see? Why should I oppose tools that will do it for me?

6. Freewrite or brainstorm on one or more of the following:
   a. V chip
   b. Internet pornography
   c. television violence
   d. censorship
   e. television and movie rating systems
   f. cartoon violence

7. Tune in to your own subject for an essay on some aspect of the media.

Student Essay

Read the following narrative essay written by a student. As you read, look for answers to these questions:

1. Does the essay fit the assignment to write on some aspect of the media?

2. Does the essay have a clear thesis and good support?

3. Does the essay follow the writing guidelines suggested in Chapter 2, "Viewpoints on Writing Essays"?

TV News: Journalism or Propaganda?

Jim Stone

1   Not all television news organizations report the news fairly or completely. They all may begin covering stories with the basic idea of truthfulness in reporting, but by air-time this has fallen by the wayside. All news organizations face pressures from many different angles. Each sponsor has its wishes, special interest groups have theirs, the network and local station executives have theirs, and finally, the censors and "old man time" limit what can be shown. These pressures, as well as manipulation on the part of government, can all act on a news story and, in many cases, slant it by the time we get it.

2   Here's how it typically works. A news crew, usually
consisting of a reporter and a cameraman, is sent to the
scene of an incident or press conference. Today's story is
about a leaking toxic waste dump. A state spokesman is
holding a press conference at the site of the dump. The
conference is attended by most major newspapers, the major
wire services (AP, UPI, etc.), and the local TV networks.
The state spokesman presents the problem to the press in a
prepared statement, and then our illustrious reporter faces
the camera and paraphrases what the state spokesman just
said. The crew then gets some camera shots of leaking
chemical drums and proceeds to tour the neighborhood.

3   They are, of course, looking for "the man in the street"
for a "salt of the earth" impression of this latest item of
gloom and doom. The first person being interviewed, someone
who wants the dump removed from his neighborhood anyway,
begins to see some fairly lucrative lawsuits on the horizon.
When asked to describe any recurrent or frequent health
problems, the interviewee rattles off a lengthy list
including but not limited to gout, ulcers, arthritis,
hemorrhoids and many other common ailments that he feels
sure are caused by the leaking dump next door. The news crew
repeats this scene two or three times with other disgruntled
neighbors and gets almost identical answers from each
respondent. The news crew then returns to the studio and
proceeds to review the fruits of their labors in the video
editing room.

4   The editor then begins to "make" the story. This is where
the potential for propaganda comes in; the editor is the
person who bears the brunt of the pressures from special
interest groups. At this point he can downplay the story by
stressing the state's official assertion that they do not
know the extent of the hazard, while dropping the
spokesman's later comment that damage appears extensive. Or,
at the request of another interest group, such as an

environmental one, the editor can stress that damage is believed to be extensive and may even be irreversible. He drops the spokesman's comment that damage assessments cannot be made at this time. Or, the editor can stress the cost of the cleanup in order to help the state environmental protection agency secure a larger budget by the use of public furor that will no doubt occur from an incident of this sort. In this instance, he would probably tie in footage of all the other leaking waste dumps around the state as well as total cleanup costs. To add the human element, he can put in some of the footage of the neighborhood people with their assorted illnesses, or just the portion of the interview in which the people express their shock and outrage over the dump spill.

5   In most cases, if not all, the editor is trying to do us, the viewer, a favor. He is creating a news story that is digestible in the short time allotted for each news story. If time allows, and the story is really important, the network can do an in-depth story which might include history, background, further ramifications, and future dump site plans. Most of us would not want to sit and sift through the daily deluge of news items. This would quickly become a full-time job and is best left to the professionals.

6   But in a few instances, the editor does the viewing public a disservice by slanting the story in order to influence public opinion. This can be done either through omission or through emphasis of key points, as is often done in political campaigns. The editor favoring a candidate can downplay or ignore negative items while stressing the good ones. In contrast, if the editor dislikes a candidate, he can emphasize the negative items and downplay the positive ones.

7   In today's political world, television plays a huge role in who will get elected. Most of us don't take the time to

really deal with the issues. A 1998 *TV Guide* poll shows that most of us vote for the candidate who makes the most favorable impression on us. The politician knows this as well as news editors.

8   All of this leads to the conclusion that we still can't believe everything we see in print or on television. That old warning about buyer beware, caveat emptor, should be changed to include television news.

Reaction

In your journal or on a separate sheet of paper, write your reaction to the student essay. What would you tell the student about his essay? What do you like? What might improve the essay?

On the Net

Many of the selections included in this chapter are critical of the media. Research one of the following topics on the Web to find opposing views on each topic:

1. censorship

2. the V chip

3. coverage of celebrities on television

Decide whether you think the criticism contained in some of the selections in this chapter is justified, now that you have read opposing viewpoints on the same topics.

10 Opposing Viewpoints on the Death Penalty

FOCUS ON THE DEATH PENALTY

To help you focus on the subject of this chapter, answer the following questions. You may want to write the answers in your journal or be prepared to discuss them in class.

1. Read the quotation by William Hazlitt on the opposite page. What do you think he means? Do you agree? What are some "subjects of controversy"?

2. Why do you think capital punishment—the death penalty—is a controversial subject?

3. Do you believe in the death penalty? What do you know about it? Why do you hold the opinion you do?

4. Look at the top cartoon on the opposite page. What does the caption have to do with the drawing? Is the artist for or against the death penalty? What makes you think so? What is the cartoonist's reasoning for his position?

5. Look at the bottom cartoon on the opposite page. Is the cartoonist for or against the death penalty? What opinion does the cartoonist have of the ACLU (American Civil Liberties Union)? What is the cartoonist's reasoning for his position?

6. Which cartoon best expresses your viewpoint on the death penalty?

And may God have mercy on our souls.

399

Someone once said that there are three sides to every questionable issue: your side, my side, and the "right" side. In truth, there may be many sides, depending upon the issue itself, making it difficult for any thinking person to make quick decisions.

According to psychologists, numerous studies show that the urge to conform to group thinking is too powerful for most people to resist. Unknowingly, we become conditioned to ways of thinking. This usually happens because we are molded at an early age by our parents, relatives, teachers, and friends. We tend to honor their value systems because we love them and trust their judgments. If our families vote Republican, we usually vote Republican. If our families go to a particular church, we tend to continue in that church. If our parents and church leaders speak out against abortion, we tend to accept such views as "right." Their beliefs become our beliefs without much questioning or thought on our part.

As we mature, our beliefs are also molded both directly and indirectly by our peers. What we wear, what we eat, what music we accept, even what media we enjoy become tied in with our desire to be accepted as part of a group. Even when we think we are acting as individuals by rejecting the ideas of one group, we are often just accepting the ideas of another. We become self-deceptive. Our thinking process can become overruled by others' opinions that we think are truly our own thoughtful reactions because we have heard them for so long. We can become biased and forget to weigh our opinions by looking at facts or reasoning that goes against our belief system. And even when we do try to see "facts," we often don't have the experience needed to evaluate the information. In such cases, it is better to suspend our decision on which side to take until we do some more investigating.

This chapter contains pro and con essays on capital punishment. Only recently has the death sentence become thought of as "cruel and unusual punishment." In earlier times, the execution of a criminal was a public event. In some societies, food and drink were served to the spectators of beheadings and hangings. Watching the death of a criminal reaffirmed the people's belief that evil could be purged from their society.

Today, the subject of capital punishment causes heated debate. Many people believe that the death sentence discourages those who might commit horrible crimes. Others believe a civilized society has no right to put another person to death, especially when there are known instances of the wrong person being executed for a crime. Most industrialized nations have banned the death penalty. In 1972, the United States Supreme Court ruled in a five-to-four decision that "in the absence of clear specifications for when it might be used, the death sentence violated the Eighth Amendment to the Constitution." But since then, Congress passed legislation that legalized the death sentence, and the Supreme Court has not overruled. Consequently, capital punishment has been reinstated in many states.

At this point you may or may not have a particular viewpoint of your own on the topic. Once you have finished the chapter readings, you will at least know more about the issues involved and will be better able to form an opinion. If you already have a viewpoint, try to suspend your opinions as you read the selections. Avoid letting your own biases cloud any opinions that are opposite to yours—not always an easy task. We sometimes have a tendency to think our views are superior to another person's even though we may not have critically examined our own. Such tendencies limit our objectivity and keep us from learning from others.

As you read each selection in this unit, ask yourself these questions regarding the strengths and weaknesses of the arguments being made:

1. Is the **problem** being expressed too simplistically?

2. Does the author use mostly **facts** or mostly **opinions?**

3. Is the author trying to reach my **emotions** or my **mind?**

4. Are the judgments being made based on solid **reasoning** and **verifiable information?**

5. Is the **evidence** convincing and provable, or deceptive and distracting?

6. What **sources** are cited? Are they reliable?

7. Is the author an **authority** on the subject?

Use these questions to let go of your own feelings long enough to understand the author's position, especially if it is different from your own.

Even after reading the selections, you may discover you need more information than is provided here in order to take a stand of your own. That's a healthy sign that you are not being easily swayed. You will probably want to read more and discuss these subjects with others. That, of course, is why you are being asked to read these selections.

Most of us do not like to think about the subject of capital punishment—the death penalty. It disturbs us, makes us feel uneasy; it's something we would rather let other people deal with. Still, whether we like it or not, it is an issue we all should think about and must take responsibility for. Polls conducted in the early 1990s showed that a majority thought capital punishment was justified. However, the pendulum swings back and forth, sometimes with more people in favor and at other times, less.

The death penalty laws vary from state to state. A few prohibit it altogether; most permit it. But other questions are involved beyond the question of whether or not capital punishment should be available to the courts. Is capital punishment a leftover from more barbaric times? When should the death penalty be administered? If it is allowed, is there a "humane" way to do it? Should the guilty be gassed, electrocuted, hanged, given lethal injections? Can we be sure the person is guilty? Do we as a society have a right to take someone's life? Does the Bible say capital punishment is permissible? These and other questions make it obvious that the issue is a complicated one requiring more than emotional responses.

Hold your own opinions until you have read all the pieces. See if they help you understand the issue any better. You will then be asked to write an essay on your viewpoints regarding capital punishment.

One final word. New information on this and other controversial issues continues to emerge. What you think today may not be what you think tomorrow. That's healthy, too, as long as you are truly making sound judgments and critically weighing the evidence. A changing mind is better than a closed one.

Preparing to Read

Take a minute or two to look over the following reading selection. Note the title and the author, read the opening paragraph, and check the essay's length. Make certain you have the time now to read it carefully and to do the exercises that follow it. Then, in the spaces provided, answer the following questions.

1. Do you think the author will argue for or against the death penalty? _____

   _____

2. What does the author mean by "death penalty abolitionists"? _____

   _____

3. What arguments do you think the author may use to support his position?

   _____

Vocabulary

Good comprehension of what you are about to read depends upon your understanding of the words below. The number following each word refers to the paragraph where it is used.

abolitionists (1) people who want to do away with something

moratorium (1) suspension, cessation

fluke (6) a stroke of good luck

caveat (10) warning, admonition

irrefutably (10) undeniably, unquestionably

scrutiny (11) inspection, analysis

scrupulous (12) meticulous, painstaking

a fortiori (12) all the more so

Death Penalty Saves Lives *

JEFF JACOBY

1   Death penalty abolitionists don't usually mention it, but in promoting a moratorium on executions, they are urging us down a road we have taken before.

2   In the mid-1960s, as a number of legal challenges to capital punishment began working their way through the courts, executions in the United States came to a halt. From 56 in 1960, the number of killers put to death dropped to seven in 1965, to one in 1966, and to zero in 1967. There it stayed for the next 10 years, until the State of Utah executed Gary Gilmore in 1977. That was the only execution in 1977, and there were only two more during the next three years.

3   In sum, between 1965 and 1980, there was practically no death penalty in the United States, and for 10 of those 16 years—1967–76—there was literally no death penalty: a national moratorium.

4   What was the effect of making capital punishment unavailable for a decade and a half? Did a moratorium on executions save innocent lives—or cost them?

5   The data are brutal. Between 1965 and 1980, annual murders in the United States skyrocketed, rising from 9,960 to 23,040. The murder rate—homicides per 100,000 persons—doubled from 5.1 to 10.2.

6   Was it just a fluke that the steepest increase in murder in U.S. history coincided with the years when the death penalty was not available to punish it? Perhaps. Or perhaps murder becomes more attractive when potential killers know that prison is the worst outcome they can face.

7   By contrast, common sense suggests that there are at least some people who will not commit murder if they think it might cost them their lives. Sure enough, as executions have become more numerous, murder has declined. "From 1995 to 2000," notes Dudley Sharp of the victims rights group Justice For All, "executions averaged 71 per year, a 21,000 percent increase over the 1966–1980 period. The murder rate dropped from a high of 10.2 (per 100,000) in 1980 to 5.7 in 1999—a 44 percent reduction. The murder rate is now at its lowest level since 1966."

8   What is true nationally has been observed locally as well. There were 12,652 homicides in New York during the 25 years from 1940 to 1965, when New York regularly executed murderers. By contrast, during the 25 years from 1966 to 1991 there were no executions at all—and murders quadrupled to 51,638.

9   To be sure, murder rates fell in almost every state in the 1990s. But they fell the most in states that use capital punishment. The most striking protection of innocent life has been in Texas, which executes more murderers than any other state. In 1991, the Texas murder rate

was 15.3 per 100,000. By 1999, it had fallen to 6.1—a drop of 60 percent. Within Texas, the most aggressive death penalty prosecutions are in Harris County (the Houston area). Since the resumption of executions in 1982, the annual number of Harris County murders has plummeted from 701 to 241—a 72 percent decrease.

10   Obviously, murder and the rate at which it occurs are affected by more than just the presence or absence of the death penalty. But even after taking that caveat into account, it seems irrefutably clear that when murderers are executed, innocent lives are saved. And when executions are stopped, innocent lives are lost.

11   Death penalty abolitionists (and a few death penalty supporters) claim that a moratorium on executions is warranted because the criminal justice system is "broken" and the death penalty is unfairly applied. But if that's true when the punishment is death, how much more so is it true when the punishment isn't death! Death penalty prosecutions typically undergo years of appeals, often attracting intense scrutiny and media attention. So painstaking is the super-due process of capital murder cases that for all the recent hype about innocent prisoners on death row, there is not a single proven case in modern times of an innocent person being executed in the United States.

12   But the due process in non–death penalty cases is not nearly as scrupulous. Everyone knows that there are innocent people behind bars today. If the legal system's flaws justify a moratorium on capital punishment, a fortiori they justify a moratorium on imprisonment. Those who call for a moratorium on executions should be calling just as vehemently for a moratorium on prison terms. Why don't they?

13   Because they know how ridiculous it would sound. If there are problems with the system, the system should be fixed, but refusing to punish criminals would succeed only in making society far less safe than it is today.

14   The same would be true of a moratorium on executions. If due process in capital murder cases can be made even more watertight, by all means let us do so. But not by keeping the worst of our murderers alive until perfection is achieved. We've been down the moratorium road before. We know how that experiment turns out. The results are written in wrenching detail on gravestones across the land.

Understanding the Content

Feel free to reread all or parts of the selection to answer the following questions.

1. What is the "road we have taken before" that Jacoby feels that death penalty abolitionists are "urging us down"?

2. How many people were executed in the United States between 1965 and 1967?

3. During what years did "annual murders in the United States skyrocket"?

4. Why does Jacoby think that murder rates fell in almost every state in the 1990s?

5. Which state executes more murderers than any other state? What has been the effect on the murder rate?

6. Why do death penalty abolitionists claim that a moratorium on execution is warranted?

Looking at Structure and Style

1. What is Jacoby's thesis? Is it stated or implied?

2. What is the purpose of paragraphs 3–5? How do these paragraphs support the author's thesis?

3. How does the author use statistics to support his thesis? Is this an effective use of statistics? Could the statistics be viewed in any other way? If so, how?

4. How well does Jacoby support his thesis with facts? Are his arguments well substantiated?

5. What is Jacoby's tone throughout the selection? What words or phrases help develop his tone?

6. Do paragraphs 13 and 14 clearly and effectively conclude this selection? Why or why not? Write a one-sentence conclusion to this essay in your own words, summarizing the points made by Jacoby or restating his thesis.

Evaluating the Author's Viewpoints

1. Did Jacoby convince you that his viewpoint is correct? Why or why not? Did you already agree with him?

2. Ultimately, what does Jacoby think would be the end result of instituting the death penalty nationwide?

3. What can you infer about how Jacoby feels about death penalty abolitionists from reading this selection? What words or phrases does he use that let you know how he feels?

4. Do you agree or disagree with Jacoby's statement that "refusing to punish criminals would succeed only in making society far less safe than it is today"? Why?

5. Based on the facts presented by Jacoby, do you agree or disagree with him that "the due process in non–death penalty cases is not nearly as scrupulous" as that in death penalty cases? Why?

Pursuing Possible Essay Topics

Unless you already have an idea for an essay, wait until you have read all the selections in this chapter and have studied the list of ideas at the end before developing an essay on capital punishment.

Preparing to Read

Before reading this selection, make certain you have read the introduction to this chapter, pages 400–402.

Take a minute or two to look over the following reading selection. Note the title and author, read the first two paragraphs, and check the essay's length. Make certain you have the time now to read it carefully and to do the exercises that follow it. Then, in the spaces provided, answer the following questions.

1. What does the title tell you about the author's viewpoint? _____

   _____

2. What do you think you will learn about capital punishment from reading this

   selection? _____

   _____

3. Do you think you will agree with the author's viewpoint? Why? _____

   _____

Vocabulary

Good comprehension of what you are about to read depends upon your understanding of the words below. The number following each word refers to the paragraph where it is used.

clemency (1) mercy, leniency

constituencies (4) the voters represented by an elected official

heinous (4) dreadful, wicked

flagrant (6) obvious, conspicuous

sophistic (10) apparently sound but really false

ambivalent (12) uncertain, mixed

paramount (15) primary, foremost, top of the list

Death and Justice[*]

Edward I. Koch

1   Last December a man named Robert Lee Willie, who had been convicted of raping and murdering an 18-year-old woman, was executed in the Louisiana state prison. In a statement issued several minutes before his death, Mr. Willie said: "Killing people is wrong. . . . It makes no difference whether it's citizens, countries, or governments. Killing is wrong." Two weeks later in South Carolina, an admitted killer named Joseph Carl Shaw was put to death for murdering two teenagers. In an appeal to the governor for clemency, Mr. Shaw wrote: "Killing is wrong when I did it. Killing is wrong when you do it. I hope you have the courage and moral strength to stop the killing."

2   It is a curiosity of modern life that we find ourselves being lectured on morality by cold-blooded killers. Mr. Willie previously had been convicted of aggravated rape, aggravated kidnapping, and the murders of a Louisiana deputy and a man from Missouri. Mr. Shaw committed another murder a week before the two for which he was executed, and admitted mutilating the body of the 14-year-old girl he killed. I can't help wondering what prompted these murderers to speak out against killing as they entered the death-house door. Did their newfound reverence for life stem from the realization that they were about to lose their own?

3   Life is indeed precious, and I believe the death penalty helps to affirm this fact. Had the death penalty been a real possibility in the minds of these murderers, they might well have stayed their hand. They might have shown moral awareness before their victims died, and not after. Consider the tragic death of Rosa Velez, who happened to be home when a man named Luis Vera burglarized her apartment in Brooklyn. "Yeah, I shot her," Vera admitted. "She knew me, and I knew I wouldn't go to the chair."

4   During my 22 years in public service, I have heard the pros and cons of capital punishment expressed with special intensity. As a district leader, councilman, congressman, and mayor, I have represented constituencies generally thought of as liberal. Because I support the death penalty for heinous crimes of murder, I have sometimes been the subject of emotional and outraged attacks by voters who find my position reprehensible or worse. I have listened to their ideas. I have weighed their objections carefully. I still support the death penalty. The reasons I maintain my position can be best understood by examining the arguments most frequently heard in opposition.

5   (1) *The death penalty is "barbaric."* Sometimes opponents of capital punishment horrify with tales of lingering death on the gallows, of faulty electric chairs, or of agony in the gas chamber. Partly in

response to such protests, several states such as North Carolina and Texas switched to execution by lethal injection. The condemned person is put to death painlessly, without ropes, voltage, bullets, or gas. Did this answer the objections of death penalty opponents? Of course not. On June 22, 1984, *The New York Times* published an editorial that sarcastically attacked the new "hygienic" method of death by injection, and stated that "execution can never be made humane through science." So it's not the method that really troubles opponents. It's the death itself they consider barbaric.

6   Admittedly, capital punishment is not a pleasant topic. However, one does not have to like the death penalty in order to support it any more than one must like radical surgery, radiation, or chemotherapy in order to find necessary these attempts at curing cancer. Ultimately we may learn how to cure cancer with a simple pill. Unfortunately, that day has not yet arrived. Today we are faced with the choice of letting the cancer spread or trying to cure it with the methods available, methods that one day will almost certainly be considered barbaric. But to give up and do nothing would be far more barbaric and would certainly delay the discovery of an eventual cure. The analogy between cancer and murder is imperfect, because murder is not the "disease" we are trying to cure. The disease is injustice. We may not like the death penalty, but it must be available to punish crimes of cold-blooded murder, cases in which any other form of punishment would be inadequate and, therefore, unjust. If we create a society in which injustice is not tolerated, incidents of murder—the most flagrant form of injustice—will diminish.

7   (2) *No other major democracy uses the death penalty.* No other major democracy—in fact, few other countries of any description—is plagued by a murder rate such as that in the United States. Fewer and fewer Americans can remember the days when unlocked doors were the norm and murder was a rare and terrible offense. In America the murder rate climbed 122 percent between 1963 and 1980. During that same period, the murder rate in New York City increased by almost 400 percent, and the statistics are even worse in many other cities. A study at M.I.T. showed that based on 1970 homicide rates a person who lived in a large American city ran a greater risk of being murdered than an American soldier in World War II ran of being killed in combat. It is not surprising that the laws of each country differ according to differing conditions and traditions. If other countries had our murder problem, the cry for capital punishment would be just as loud as it is here. And I daresay that any other major democracy where 75 percent of the people supported the death penalty would soon enact it into law.

8   (3) *An innocent person might be executed by mistake.* Consider the work of Adam Bedau, one of the most implacable foes of capital punishment in this country. According to Mr. Bedau, it is "false sentimentality to argue that the death penalty should be abolished because of the abstract possibility that an innocent person might be executed." He cites a study of the 7,000 executions in this country from 1893 to 1971, and concludes that the record fails to show that such cases occur. The main point, however, is this. If government functioned only when the possibility of error didn't exist, government wouldn't function at all. Human life deserves special protection, and one of the best ways to guarantee that protection is to assure that convicted murderers do not kill again. Only the death penalty can accomplish this end. In a recent case in New Jersey, a man named Richard Biegenwald was freed from prison after serving 18 years for murder; since his release he has been convicted of committing four murders. A prisoner named Lemuel Smith, while serving four life sentences for murder (plus two life sentences for kidnapping and robbery) in New York's Green Haven Prison, lured a woman corrections officer into the chaplain's office and strangled her. He then mutilated and dismembered her body. An additional life sentence for Smith is meaningless. Because New York has no death penalty statute, Smith has effectively been given a license to kill.

9   But the problem of multiple murder is not confined to the nation's penitentiaries. In 1981, 91 police officers were killed in the line of duty in this country. Seven percent of those arrested in the cases that have been solved had a previous arrest for murder. In New York City in 1976 and 1977, 85 persons arrested for homicide had a previous arrest for murder. Six of these individuals had two previous arrests for murder, and one had four previous murder arrests. During those two years the New York police were arresting for murder persons with a previous arrest for murder on the average of one every 8.5 days. This is not surprising when we learn that in 1975, for example, the median time served in Massachusetts for homicide was less than two-and-a-half years. In 1976 a study sponsored by the Twentieth Century Fund found that the average time served in the United States for first-degree murder is ten years. The median time served may be considerably lower.

10   (4) *Capital punishment cheapens the value of human life.* On the contrary, it can be easily demonstrated that the death penalty strengthens the value of human life. If the penalty for rape were lowered, clearly it would signal a lessened regard for the victims' suffering, humiliation, and personal integrity. It would cheapen their horrible experience, and expose them to an increased danger of recurrence.

When we lower the penalty for murder, it signals a lessened regard for the value of the victim's life. Some critics of capital punishment, such as columnist Jimmy Breslin, have suggested that a life sentence is actually a harsher penalty for murder than death. This is sophistic nonsense. A few killers may decide not to appeal a death sentence, but the overwhelming majority make every effort to stay alive. It is by exacting the highest penalty for the taking of human life that we affirm the highest value of human life.

11   (5) *The death penalty is applied in a discriminatory manner.* This factor no longer seems to be the problem it once was. The appeals process for a condemned prisoner is lengthy and painstaking. Every effort is made to see that the verdict and sentence were fairly arrived at. However, assertions of discrimination are not an argument for ending the death penalty but for extending it. It is not justice to exclude everyone from the penalty of the law if a few are found to be so favored. Justice requires that the law be applied equally to all.

12   (6) *Thou Shalt Not Kill.* The Bible is our greatest source of moral inspiration. Opponents of the death penalty frequently cite the sixth of the Ten Commandments in an attempt to prove that capital punishment is divinely proscribed. In the original Hebrew, however, the Sixth Commandment reads, "Thou Shalt Not Commit Murder," and the Torah specifies capital punishment for a variety of offenses. The biblical viewpoint has been upheld by philosophers throughout history. The greatest thinkers of the 19th century—Kant, Locke, Hobbes, Rousseau, Montesquieu, and Mill—agreed that natural law properly authorizes the sovereign to take life in order to vindicate justice. Only Jeremy Bentham was ambivalent. Washington, Jefferson, and Franklin endorsed it. Abraham Lincoln authorized executions for deserters in wartime. Alexis de Tocqueville, who expressed profound respect for American institutions, believed that the death penalty was indispensable to the support of social order. The United States Constitution, widely admired as one of the seminal achievements in the history of humanity, condemns cruel and inhuman punishment, but does not condemn capital punishment.

13   (7) *The death penalty is state-sanctioned murder.* This is the defense with which Messrs. Willie and Shaw hoped to soften the resolve of those who sentenced them to death. By saying in effect, "You're no better than I am," the murderer seeks to bring his accusers down to his own level. It is also a popular argument among opponents of capital punishment, but a transparently false one. Simply put, the state has rights that the private individual does not. In a democracy, those rights are given to the state by the electorate. The execution of a lawfully condemned killer is no more an act of murder than is legal imprisonment an act of kidnapping. If an individual forces a neighbor to pay him money under threat of punishment, it's called extortion.

If the state does it, it's called taxation. Rights and responsibilities surrendered by the individual are what give the state its power to govern. This contract is the foundation of civilization itself.

14 Everyone wants his or her rights, and will defend them jealously. Not everyone, however, wants responsibilities, especially the painful responsibilities that come with law enforcement. Twenty-one years ago a woman named Kitty Genovese was assaulted and murdered on a street in New York. Dozens of neighbors heard her cries for help but did nothing to assist her. They didn't even call the police. In such a climate the criminal understandably grows bolder. In the presence of moral cowardice, he lectures us on our supposed failings and tries to equate his crimes with our quest for justice.

15 The death of anyone—even a convicted killer—diminishes us all. But we are diminished even more by a justice system that fails to function. It is an illusion to let ourselves believe that doing away with capital punishment removes the murderer's deed from our conscience. The rights of society are paramount. When we protect guilty lives, we give up innocent lives in exchange. When opponents of capital punishment say to the state: "I will not let you kill in my name," they are also saying to murderers: "You can kill in your *own* name as long as I have an excuse for not getting involved."

16 It is hard to imagine anything worse than being murdered while neighbors do nothing. But something worse exists. When those same neighbors shrink back from justly punishing the murderer, the victim dies twice.

Understanding the Content

Feel free to reread all or parts of the selection to answer the following questions.

1. What argument *for* the death penalty does Koch give for each of the following arguments against?
   a. "The death penalty is 'barbaric.'"
   b. "No other major democracy uses the death penalty."
   c. "An innocent person might be executed by mistake."
   d. "Capital punishment cheapens the value of human life."
   e. "The death penalty is applied in a discriminatory manner."
   f. "Thou Shalt Not Kill."

2. What do you learn about the author in the essay? Why does he tell you about himself?

3. Is Koch's argument based mostly on fact or on opinion? Explain.

4. What does Koch mean when he says, "the victim dies twice" (16) if the murderer isn't justly punished?

Looking at Structure and Style

1. Is the thesis stated or implied? If stated, where?

2. What is the point of quoting the two convicted murderers on death row in paragraph 1? Is this an effective technique? Explain.

3. Koch chooses to defend capital punishment by refuting what he says are the most prevalent arguments of those who oppose the death penalty. Is this a good method? Does it make him seem more knowledgeable on the subject? Explain.

4. What is the function of paragraph 4?

5. How well does the author use outside sources to reinforce his arguments? What are some of his sources?

Evaluating the Author's Viewpoints

1. Koch says, "If we create a society in which injustice is not tolerated, incidents of murder—the most flagrant form of injustice—will diminish." Do you agree? Why or why not?

2. Do you agree with Koch's distinction between murder and capital punishment? Why or why not?

3. Do you agree with the analogies he draws in paragraph 13 about imprisonment vs. kidnapping and taxation vs. extortion (blackmail)? Are these good analogies? Explain.

4. How well does Koch conclude his essay? Is he convincing? Explain.

5. Look through the essay for the following:
   a. factual statements that support the author's thesis
   b. opinions or emotional appeals that support the thesis
   c. the most convincing argument for the thesis
   d. the weakest argument for the thesis

6. Which argument for the death penalty is better presented, Jacoby's or Koch's? Explain your answer.

Pursuing Possible Essay Topics

Unless you already have an idea for an essay, wait until you have read all the selections in this chapter and have studied the list of ideas at the end before developing an essay on capital punishment.

Preparing to Read

Before reading this selection, make certain you have read the introduction to this chapter, pages 400–402.

Take a minute or two to look over the following reading selection. Note the title and author, read the first two paragraphs, and check the length. Make certain you have the time now to read it carefully and to do the exercises that follow it. Then, in the spaces provided, answer the following questions.

1. Do you think the death penalty issue is a moral issue? _____

_____

2. What arguments do you think the author may use to support his position?

_____

Vocabulary

Good comprehension of what you are about to read depends upon your understanding of the words below. The number following each word refers to the paragraph where it is used.

moratorium (1) a suspension of action

affronts (2) insults, offends

sentient (2) aware, conscious, having feeling

abhorrent (4) awful, detestable

de facto (4) actually, in fact, in reality

noncomplicity (6) noninvolvement

miscreants (7) delinquents, lawbreakers

modicum (13) little, small amount

restitution (15) compensation, reimbursement

Casting the First Stone

LLOYD STEFFEN

1   Once again, America has made its peace with capital punishment. Since the moratorium on executions was lifted in 1975, courts and state legislatures have worked hard, and successfully,

to reinstate the death penalty. Politically, the issue is no longer even interesting. As the 1988 presidential debates showed, what public debate exists around capital punishment is likely to be about its effectiveness as social policy, not with its status as a *moral* (or even legal) problem. And as social policy opinion polls tell us, America approves of the death penalty. Indeed, it seems to satisfy the American sense of justice and fair play. Given this context, it might seem futile even to ask whether capital punishment can still *be* a moral problem.

2   Yet even though opponents of capital punishment are in the minority today, they should not allow themselves to be placed on the defensive. A burden of moral proof in the debate over capital punishment still must be borne by those who support it. The death penalty must still be questioned as a moral act because it affronts the moral principle that the deliberate and premeditated taking of fully sentient human life is wrong. Therefore, it falls to those who support it to argue convincingly that killing convicted criminals is morally justifiable and not fundamentally destructive of the moral presumption against such killing.

3   Failure to debate the moral justifications for capital punishment could well lead to a situation where the practice of executing criminals is simply taken for granted. We may no longer demand a *particular* argument for capital punishment, one that is rationally compelling and able to withstand serious challenges; rather, we may come to assume that such an argument exists—somewhere. We could then justify the death penalty by the kind of moral "intuition" that concludes: "If it were really wrong we would not do it." At that point, capital punishment becomes a noncontroversial issue. . . .

The Innocence of the State

4   Once a society decides that it is useful to kill people—even people guilty of morally abhorrent acts—sanctity-of-life questions are no longer even arguable, since human life is de facto not sacred. Only those societies or states that have convinced themselves they can act as if they possessed absolute innocence can assume, in good conscience, the power to make premeditated killing a useful means to political and social ends. And, as history shows, when such states or societies acquire the power to decide which acts constitute crimes deserving death, the inevitable criterion is this: those acts that challenge the idea of absolute innocence.

5   Capital punishment is always potentially an instrument of social repression and political terrorism. As we have seen in China and Iran, when the state claims the power to impose this punishment, it is not the notorious on whom death is most likely to be inflicted, but the nameless and obscure. Even though Americans who support the death penalty can express outrage over the executions that have

occurred in these faraway places, the fact is that the 2000 condemned persons currently sitting on America's death rows are also nameless and obscure. The difference is that Americans can apparently justify killing those who disrupt our social order because our social order is "morally superior."

6   The myth of American innocence has suffered greatly in recent years. Yet it persists. Manifest destiny is still alive in the American consciousness. The myth of moral purity continues to affect how we who are not guilty separate ourselves from those who are; and those who are guilty continue to be predominantly poor, male, members of minority groups, now even those with mental disabilities. Are these people so painful a reminder of our national failure that we have deceived ourselves into thinking our innocence can be maintained if they are eliminated? Is capital punishment so popular today because it stands as a symbol of noncomplicity in antisocial acts? Does it serve the national will by perpetuating the illusion of American innocence, which is, after all, our ideological heritage?

7   My arguments, however, may seem to miss the point. Clearly the moral passion in support of the death penalty comes not from thinking about capital punishment in abstract ways, but as a just means of retribution for individual crimes perpetrated by individual miscreants on individual victims. Nonetheless, I want to interject a caution. While individual stories certainly activate the moral imagination, dangers always exist in allowing them to govern our thinking about issues that have profound social implications. Individual stories appeal to definite moral principles even if the principles themselves are not articulated, and when we appeal to them rather than to a formal moral argument, we beg questions regarding which principles should be invoked to help us decide that one story rather than another should govern behavior and guide action. Despite these problems, I can still imagine advocates of capital punishment defending their position simply by saying "What about Theodore Bundy?"

An Irrevocable Penalty

8   Bundy, who died in 1989 in Florida's electric chair, is as strong an anecdotal defense of capital punishment as we could find: A mass murderer who killed innocent women in several states, Bundy appeared to be a moral incorrigible, one who killed repeatedly and without inhibition, and who provided investigators with information about many of his unsolved crimes only because it was the last card he could play to postpone his execution. Seemingly incapable of remorse, Bundy was unquestionably guilty of the crimes for which he had been convicted and many for which he hadn't. If anyone embodies the kind of moral monster who deserves the most severe punishment society can inflict, Ted Bundy did.

9   But if Ted Bundy's story "argues" for capital punishment, James Richardson's argues even more strongly against it.

10   In 1968, Richardson, a black Florida fruit picker, was tried and convicted of killing his seven children. Richardson allegedly had taken out insurance policies the night before the murder. While this established motive sufficient to convince a jury of his guilt, neither the defense attorney nor the prosecutor pointed out that the unpaid policies were not in effect when the children died. When Richardson's three cell mates were brought in to testify that he had confessed the crime to them, no one bothered to mention that the sheriff had promised the three reduced jail time for their testimony. The one surviving witness of the three has finally admitted that Richardson never made such a confession.

11   Richardson's lie detector results disappeared and were never disclosed, and the polygraph operator who administered another test to him in prison stated that he had "no involvement in the crime whatsoever."

12   Richardson's next-door neighbor actually poisoned the children while Richardson and his wife were working in the fields. Yet she was never called to testify. The authorities did not want the jury to know that her first husband had died mysteriously after eating a dinner she had prepared or that she had actually served four years in prison for killing her second husband. The woman, incidentally, after being admitted to a nursing home, confessed to staff there that she was the guilty party, but the staff, fearing loss of their jobs, did not report her confession to superiors. And the former assistant prosecutor in the town of Arcadia, where Richardson was tried, deliberately concealed over 900 pages of evidence that would have brought all of these facts to light. It took an actual theft to get these documents into the hands of *Miami Herald* reporters. Once there, the case was reopened, and after spending 21 years in prison for a crime he did not commit, James Richardson was released.

13   Richardson may not have been executed, but his is a story about capital punishment nonetheless. For he was sentenced to death, sat for four years on death row, and was even put through a harrowing "dry run" execution, complete with a shaving and a buckledown in the chair. Richardson was not only a poor black man who received an inept defense. He was also an innocent man who was made a victim of lies, deceit, perjured testimony, false witnesses— and those who prosecuted him and knew of his innocence still demanded that he be executed. What the Richardson case points out is that the death penalty always holds the potential for interfering mightily with justice. In the Richardson case, guilt lies with the accusers, and the irrevocable nature of the death penalty would have prevented Richardson from receiving even the modicum of justice

he finally did receive. Despite being the result of a legal process, his death would have constituted an unjustified killing—an actual murder.

Justice and Social Murder

14 How is justice to be exacted when a murder is committed by all of society? Is guilt to attach only to the sheriff and prosecutor in the case? Would those two be appropriate targets for the death penalty today since they violated the moral prohibition against the taking of human life and sought deliberately and with premeditation to kill an innocent man—the crime for which we wish to impose death fairly and without caprice? That these events can occur leads to a question: Is killing a Theodore Bundy so necessary that we should accept the risk capital punishment poses to a James Richardson?

15 Supporters of capital punishment will say justice prevailed; Richardson did not die, and the case poses no challenge. I say, however, that Richardson's case is a fundamental challenge to capital punishment, since the only good thing to come out of the situation is the simple fact that he did not die. His innocence might have come to light even if he had been killed, so it is life, not just truth, that is at stake. Only the simple fact that Richardson is alive makes possible any hope for his seeking restitution from a system that at one point forsook justice and actually conspired to kill him.

No Moral Certainty

16 If Richardson had been executed and the truth found out, we might not even be asking whether it is morally permissible to continue a practice that by its very nature runs the risk of committing murder and depriving persons of any opportunity to redress injustice. Were Richardson dead, we would be facing social complicity in his death and probably looking for a way to justify his death in order to make it something other than murder. We would be defending ourselves with the very truths we refused to acknowledge to him: that our system of justice is fallible, that our knowledge and judgment can be swayed and distorted, that our moral certainty is neither pure nor absolute.

Understanding the Content

Feel free to reread all or parts of the selection to answer the following questions.

1. What is Steffen's basic argument against capital punishment?

2. When, according to Steffen, might capital punishment become a noncontroversial issue? Why does he want to put its supporters on the defensive and keep it an issue?

3. Why does Steffen take to task those supporters of the death penalty in this country who express outrage over executions that occur in other countries?

4. What caution does Steffen raise for those who feel the death penalty is just retribution for those who take another's life?

5. Who was Theodore Bundy? Who was James Richardson? What point does Steffen make with these two names? Why does Steffen feel that "Richardson's case is a fundamental challenge to capital punishment"?

Looking at Structure and Style

1. What is Steffen's thesis? Is it stated or implied? If stated, where?

2. How well does Steffen support his thesis? Are his arguments reasonable and persuasive?

3. What is the function of paragraph 5? What does it have to do with Steffen's thesis?

4. What writing pattern is used in paragraph 12? Does it work well and provoke thought?

5. This essay was written in 1990. Is the content dated? Explain.

6. How well does Steffen anticipate the arguments of those with opposing views?

Evaluating the Author's Viewpoints

1. Steffen's claims that "Americans can apparently justify killing those who disrupt our social order because our social order is 'morally superior'" to that in "faraway places" (5). Is he right? Explain.

2. According to Steffen, "Once a society decides that it is useful to kill people—even people guilty of morally abhorrent acts—sanctity-of-life questions are no longer even arguable, since human life is de facto not sacred" (4). Do you agree? Why or why not?

3. Steffen sees the issue of the death penalty as a moral one. Do you agree? Explain.

4. Steffen asks, "How is justice to be exacted when a murder is committed by all of society?" (14). As a member of society, are you indirectly committing murder when someone is executed through the death penalty?

Pursuing Possible Essay Topics

Unless you already have an idea for an essay, wait until you have read all the selections in this chapter and have studied the list of ideas at the end before developing an essay on capital punishment.

Preparing to Read

Before reading this selection, make certain you have read the introduction to this chapter, pages 400–402.

Take a minute or two to look over the following reading selection. Note the title and author, read the opening paragraph, and check the essay's length. Make certain you have the time now to read it carefully and to do the exercises that follow it. Then, in the spaces provided, answer the following questions.

1. What does the title tell you about the author's viewpoint? _____

_____

_____

2. What do you think you will learn about capital punishment from reading this selection? _____

_____

_____

3. Do you think you will agree with the author's viewpoint? Why? _____

_____

Vocabulary

Good comprehension of what you are about to read depends upon your understanding of the words below. The number following each word refers to the paragraph where it is used.

voir dire (4) a preliminary examination to decide if someone is eligible to serve on a jury

cerebral (4) having to do with intellect, using the mind

inherently (4) basically, intrinsically, essentially

hypocritical (5) saying one thing but meaning or acting the opposite

retribution (6) revenge, payment in return for a wrong

deterrent (6) something that stops an occurrence

recidivism (6) a tendency to relapse into a former pattern of behavior, especially criminal habits

Death Penalty's False Promise

ANNA QUINDLEN

1   Ted Bundy and I go back a long way, to a time when there was a series of unsolved murders in Washington State known only as the Ted
murders. Like a lot of reporters, I'm something of a crime buff. But
the Washington Ted murders—and the ones that followed in Utah,
Colorado and finally in Florida, where Ted Bundy was convicted and
sentenced to die—fascinated me because I could see myself as one
of the victims. I looked at the studio photographs of young women
with long hair, pierced ears, easy smiles, and I read the descriptions:
polite, friendly, quick to help, eager to please. I thought about being
approached by a handsome young man asking for help, and I knew
if I had been in the wrong place at the wrong time I would have been
a goner.

2   By the time Ted finished up in Florida, law enforcement authorities suspected he had murdered dozens of young women. He and the
death penalty seemed made for each other.

3   The death penalty and I, on the other hand, seem to have nothing
in common. But Ted Bundy has made me think about it all over
again, now that the outlines of my '60s liberalism have been filled in
with a decade as a reporter covering some of the worst back alleys in
New York City and three years as a mother who, like most, would lay
down her life for her kids.

4   Simply put, I am opposed to the death penalty. I would tell that to
any judge or lawyer undertaking the voir dire of jury candidates in a
state in which the death penalty can be imposed. That is why I would
be excused from such a jury. In a rational, completely cerebral way, I
think the killing of one human being as punishment for the killing of
another makes no sense and is inherently immoral.

5   But whenever my response to an important subject is rational and
completely cerebral, I know there is something wrong with it—and
so it is here. I have always been governed by my gut, and my gut says
I am hypocritical about the death penalty. That is, I do not in theory
think that Ted Bundy, or others like him, should be put to death. But
if my daughter had been the one clubbed to death as she slept in a
Tallahassee sorority house, and if the bite mark left in her buttocks
had been one of the prime pieces of evidence against the young man
charged with her murder, I would with the greatest pleasure kill him
myself.

6   The State of Florida will not permit the parents of Bundy's victims to
do that, and, in a way, that is the problem with an emotional response

to capital punishment. The only reason for a death penalty is to exact retribution. Is there anyone who really thinks that it is a deterrent, that there are considerable numbers of criminals out there who think twice about committing crimes because of the sentence involved? The ones I have met in the course of my professional duties have either sneered at the justice system, where they can exchange one charge for another with more ease than they could return a shirt to a clothing store, or they have simply believed that it is the other guy who will get caught, get convicted, get the stiffest sentence. Of course, the death penalty would act as a deterrent by eliminating recidivism, but then so would life without parole, albeit at greater taxpayer expense.

7   I don't believe deterrence is what most proponents seek from the death penalty anyhow. Our most profound emotional response is to want criminals to suffer as their victims did. When a man is accused of throwing a child from a high-rise terrace, my emotional—some might say hysterical—response is that he should be given an opportunity to see how endless the seconds are from the 31st story to the ground. In a civilized society that will never happen. And so what many people want from the death penalty, they will never get.

8   Death is death, you may say, and you would be right. But anyone who has seen someone die suddenly of a heart attack and someone else slip slowly into the clutches of cancer knows that there are gradations of dying.

9   I watched a television re-enactment one night of an execution by lethal injection. It was well done; it was horrible. The methodical approach, people standing around the gurney waiting, made it more awful. One moment there was a man in a prone position; the next moment that man was gone. On another night I watched a television movie about a little boy named Adam Walsh, who disappeared from a shopping center in Florida. There was a re-enactment of Adam's parents coming to New York, where they appeared on morning talk shows begging for their son's return, and in their hotel room, where they received a call from the police saying that Adam had been found: not all of Adam, actually, just his severed head, discovered in the waters of a Florida canal. There is nothing anyone could do that is bad enough for an adult who took a 6-year-old boy away from his parents, perhaps tortured, then murdered him and cut off his head. Nothing at all. Lethal injection? The electric chair? Bah.

10   And so I come back to the position that the death penalty is wrong, not only because it consists of stooping to the level of the killers, but also because it is not what it seems. Just before Ted Bundy's most recent execution date was postponed, pending further appeals, the father of his last known victim, a 12-year-old girl, said what almost

every father in his situation must feel. "I wish they'd bring him back to Lake City," said Tom Leach of the town where Kimberly Leach lived and died, "and let us all have at him." But the death penalty does not let us all have at him in the way Mr. Leach seems to mean. What he wants is for something as horrifying as what happened to his child to happen to Ted Bundy. And that is impossible.

Understanding the Content

Feel free to reread all or parts of the selection to answer the following questions.

1. Based on what you read, who is Ted Bundy? What have you learned about him? Why does the author refer to him?

2. What arguments against the death penalty does Quindlen provide?

3. What does she claim is "the only reason" (6) for the death penalty?

4. What does Quindlen mean when she says the death penalty "is not what it seems" (10)?

Looking at Structure and Style

1. In the opening paragraph, Quindlen sees herself as a possible victim of Ted Bundy. What is her purpose in doing so?

2. Quindlen tells us quite a lot about herself. Why? What has the personal information to do with the death penalty?

3. To what audience do you think the author is writing? Why?

4. Look again at her arguments for opposing the death penalty. Are they based on facts?

5. Reread paragraph 9. Why does Quindlen write so graphically here? Does this style help support her thesis? Explain.

6. Is the thesis stated or implied? If stated, where?

Evaluating the Author's Viewpoints

1. Quindlen says that she does not believe Ted Bundy should be put to death, yet she says that had it been her daughter he murdered, she "would with the greatest pleasure kill him myself." Is this contradictory? Does this statement help or hurt her thesis? Explain.

2. Quindlen says that she does not believe deterrence is what most proponents of the death penalty seek; instead, they want revenge. Is she right? With what evidence does she support this view?

3. Quindlen believes that nothing is a bad enough punishment for someone who commits fiendish murders, including the death penalty. Is she right? Is this a sound argument against the death penalty?

4. Look through the essay for the following:
   a. factual statements that support Quindlen's thesis
   b. opinions or emotional appeals that support her thesis
   c. the most convincing argument for her thesis
   d. the weakest argument for her thesis

Pursuing Possible Essay Topics

Unless you already have an idea for an essay, wait until you have read all the selections in this chapter and have studied the list of ideas at the end before developing an essay on capital punishment.

Preparing to Read

Before reading this selection, make certain you have read the introduction to this chapter, pages 400–402.

Take a minute or two to look over the following reading selection. Note the title and author, read the opening paragraph, and check the essay's length. Make certain you have the time now to read it carefully and to do the exercises that follow it. Then, in the spaces provided, answer the following questions.

1. The title tells you something about the subject of the essay, but what do you think the author will say about it? _____

_____

2. Based on the opening paragraph, what might make this essay different from the others on capital punishment? _____

_____

3. What do you think you will learn about capital punishment from reading this selection? _____

_____

4. What do you think the author's viewpoint on capital punishment might be?

_____

_____

Vocabulary

Good comprehension of what you are about to read depends upon your understanding of the words below. The number following each word refers to the paragraph where it is used.

sodden (1) soaking wet

warders (2) guards, watchmen

desolately (3) weakly, mutely, sounding thin and isolated

Dravidian (4) a member of a native tribe of southern India whose native tongue is Dravidian

magistrates (6) judges, justices

pariah (6) a social outcast

gambolled (8) behaved playfully

incuriously (8) with no curiosity or interest

servile (11) groveling, lowly, slavelike

Ram (12) probably a reference to Rama, a godlike hero in Hinduism

timorously (15) shyly

A Hanging

GEORGE ORWELL

1   It was in Burma, a sodden morning of the rains. A sickly light, like yellow tinfoil, was slanting over the high walls into the jail yard. We were waiting outside the condemned cells, a row of sheds fronted with double bars, like small animal cages. Each cell measured about ten feet by ten and was quite bare within except for a plank bed and a pot for drinking water. In some of them brown, silent men were squatting at the inner bars, with their blankets draped round them. These were the condemned men, due to be hanged within the next week or two.

2   One prisoner had been brought out of his cell. He was a Hindu, a puny wisp of a man, with a shaven head and vague liquid eyes. He had a thick, sprouting mustache, absurdly too big for his body, rather like the mustache of a comic man on the films. Six tall Indian warders were guarding him and getting him ready for the gallows. Two of them stood by with rifles and fixed bayonets, while the others handcuffed him, passed a chain through his handcuffs and fixed it to their belts, and lashed his arms tight to his sides. They crowded very close about him, with their hands always on him in a careful, caressing grip, as though all the while feeling him to make sure he was there. It was like men handling a fish which is still alive and may jump back into the water. But he stood quite unresisting, yielding his arms limply to the ropes, as though he hardly noticed what was happening.

3   Eight o'clock struck and a bugle call, desolately thin in the wet air, floated from the distant barracks. The superintendent of the jail, who was standing apart from the rest of us, moodily prodding the gravel with his stick, raised his head at the sound. He was an army doctor, with a grey toothbrush mustache and a gruff voice. "For God's sake, hurry up, Francis," he said irritably. "The man ought to have been dead by this time. Aren't you ready yet?"

4   Francis, the head jailer, a fat Dravidian in a white drill suit and gold spectacles, waved his black hand. "Yes sir, yes sir," he bubbled. "All iss satisfactorily prepared. The hangman iss waiting. We shall proceed."

5   "Well, quick march, then. The prisoners can't get their breakfast till this job's over."

6   We set out for the gallows. Two warders marched on either side of the prisoner, with their rifles at the slope; two others marched close against him, gripping him by arm and shoulder, as though at once pushing and supporting him. The rest of us, magistrates and the like, followed behind. Suddenly, when we had gone ten yards, the procession stopped short without any order or warning. A dreadful thing had happened—a dog, come goodness knows whence, had appeared in the yard. It came bounding among us with a loud volley of barks and leapt round us wagging its whole body, wild with glee at finding so many human beings together. It was a large woolly dog, half Airedale, half pariah. For a moment it pranced around us, and then, before anyone could stop it, it had made a dash for the prisoner, and jumping up tried to lick his face. Everybody stood aghast, too taken aback even to grab the dog.

7   "Who let that bloody brute in here?" said the superintendent angrily. "Catch it, someone!"

8   A warder detached from the escort, charged clumsily after the dog, but it danced and gambolled just out of his reach, taking everything as part of the game. A young Eurasian jailer picked up a handful of gravel and tried to stone the dog away, but it dodged the stones and came after us again. Its yaps echoed from the jail walls. The prisoner,

in the grasp of the two warders, looked on incuriously, as though this was another formality of the hanging. It was several minutes before someone managed to catch the dog. Then we put my handkerchief through its collar and moved off once more, with the dog still straining and whimpering.

9   It was about forty yards to the gallows. I watched the bare brown back of the prisoner marching in front of me. He walked clumsily with his bound arms, but quite steadily, with that bobbing gait of the Indian who never straightens his knees. At each step his muscles slid neatly into place, the lock of hair on his scalp danced up and down, his feet printed themselves on the wet gravel. And once, in spite of the men who gripped him by each shoulder, he stepped lightly aside to avoid a puddle on the path.

10   It is curious; but till that moment I had never realized what it means to destroy a healthy, conscious man. When I saw the prisoner step aside to avoid the puddle, I saw the mystery, the unspeakable wrongness, of cutting a life short when it is in full tide. This man was not dying, he was alive just as we are alive. All the organs of his body were working—bowels digesting food, skin renewing itself, nails growing, tissues forming—all toiling away in solemn foolery. His nails would still be growing when he stood on the drop, when he was falling through the air with a tenth-of-a-second to live. His eyes saw the yellow gravel and the grey walls, and his brain still remembered, foresaw, reasoned—even about puddles. He and we were a party of men walking together, seeing, hearing, feeling, understanding the same world; and in two minutes, with a sudden snap, one of us would be gone—one mind less, one world less.

11   The gallows stood in a small yard, separate from the main grounds of the prison, and overgrown with tall prickly weeds. It was a brick erection like three sides of a shed, with planking on top, and above that two beams and a crossbar with the rope dangling. The hangman, a greyhaired convict in the white uniform of the prison, was waiting beside his machine. He greeted us with a servile crouch as we entered. At a word from Francis the two warders, gripping the prisoner more closely than ever, half led, half pushed him to the gallows and helped him clumsily up the ladder. Then the hangman climbed up and fixed the rope round the prisoner's neck.

12   We stood waiting, five yards away. The warders had formed in a rough circle round the gallows. And then, when the noose was fixed, the prisoner began crying out to his god. It was a high, reiterated cry of "Ram! Ram! Ram! Ram!" not urgent and fearful like a prayer or cry for help, but steady, rhythmical, almost like the

tolling of a bell. The dog answered the sound with a whine. The hangman, still standing on the gallows, produced a small cotton bag like a flour bag and drew it down over the prisoner's face. But the sound, muffled by the cloth, still persisted, over and over again: "Ram! Ram! Ram! Ram! Ram!"

13   The hangman climbed down and stood ready, holding the lever. Minutes seemed to pass. The steady, muffled crying from the prisoner went on and on, "Ram! Ram! Ram!" never faltering for an instant. The superintendent, his head on his chest, was slowly poking the ground with his stick; perhaps he was counting the cries, allowing the prisoner a fixed number—fifty, perhaps, or a hundred. Everyone had changed colour. The Indians had gone grey like bad coffee, and one or two of the bayonets were wavering. We looked at the lashed, hooded man on the drop, and listened to his cries—each cry another second of life; the same thought was in all our minds; oh, kill him quickly, get it over, stop that abominable noise!

14   Suddenly the superintendent made up his mind. Throwing up his head he made a swift motion with his stick. "Chalo!" he shouted almost fiercely.

15   There was a clanking noise, and then dead silence. The prisoner had vanished, and the rope was twisting on itself. I let go of the dog, and it galloped immediately to the back of the gallows; but when it got there it stopped short, barked, and then retreated into a corner of the yard, where it stood among the weeds, looking timorously out at us. We went round the gallows to inspect the prisoner's body. He was dangling with his toes pointed straight downwards, very slowly revolving, as dead as a stone.

16   The superintendent reached out with his stick and poked the bare brown body; it oscillated slightly. "*He's* all right," said the superintendent. He backed out from under the gallows, and blew out a deep breath. The moody look had gone out of his face quite suddenly. He glanced at his wrist-watch. "Eight minutes past eight. Well, that's all for this morning, thank God."

17   The warders unfixed bayonets and marched away. The dog, sobered and conscious of having misbehaved itself, slipped after them. We walked out of the gallows yard, past the condemned cells with their waiting prisoners, into the big central yard of the prison. The convicts, under the command of warders armed with lathis, were already receiving their breakfast. They squatted in long rows, each man holding a tin pannikin, while two warders with buckets marched around ladling out rice; it seemed quite a homely, jolly scene, after the hanging. An enormous relief had come upon us now that the job was done. One felt an impulse to sing, to break into a run, to snigger. All at once everyone began chattering gaily.

Understanding the Content

Feel free to reread all or parts of the selection to answer the following questions.

1. Where did the hanging take place? Who was being hanged? Are we told why? Does it make any difference to the point of the essay?

2. Why is the superintendent in charge of the hanging in such a hurry?

3. When a dog came into the hanging yard, Orwell calls it a "dreadful thing." Why? Why do you think Orwell included the episode in his account of the hanging?

4. Orwell's attitude about the hanging seems to change when the prisoner, walking to the gallows, steps aside to avoid a puddle. Why the change?

5. How did the crowd watching the hanging act once the execution was over? Why do you think they reacted as they did?

6. What is Orwell's attitude toward capital punishment?

Looking at Structure and Style

1. Orwell includes a good deal of description in his essay. Find some examples of figurative language, such as metaphors and similes, that you feel are effectively used. What do they add to the feeling of the hanging?

2. Why does the author provide such detailed descriptions of the prisoners' cells? the Hindu about to be hanged? the preparations for the execution?

3. Discuss Orwell's description of the following: the superintendent, Francis, the prisoner, the dog, the crowd, the hangman, the hanging itself.

4. How does the episode with the dog, especially its joyous licking of the prisoner's face, add to or detract from the picture of the hanging?

5. How effective is the ending? Do such actions of the author and the crowd seem appropriate? Explain.

6. How would you describe Orwell's tone and attitude?

7. What is Orwell's thesis? Is it implied or stated? If stated, where?

Evaluating the Author's Viewpoints

1. Orwell says, "It is curious; but till that moment I had never realized what it means to destroy a healthy, conscious man." Is this abnormal? Could he be speaking for most of us? Explain.

2. As the prisoner was crying, "Ram," Orwell says "the same thought was in all our minds; oh, kill him quickly, get it over, stop that abominable noise!" What is your reaction to this statement?

3. After such an experience, do you think you might react as Orwell and the crowd did? Explain.

4. Does Orwell imply that the dog is morally superior to the humans?

Pursuing Possible Essay Topics

1. Pick one of the essays on capital punishment and write an argument against the author's viewpoint. Show the fallacies (examples of false or incorrect reasoning) in the argument. Or agree with one of the authors, but provide your own arguments. Use quotations from the essay you are reacting to.

2. Write an essay that outlines your opinion of when the death penalty is and is not appropriate.

3. Write an essay on your views of the death penalty using arguments that none of the essays in the chapter discuss.

4. Between 1930 and 1977, 3,859 people were legally executed in the United States. Of this number a slight majority were African Americans, a proportion that is far above blacks' share of the population. Coretta King, Martin Luther King, Jr.'s widow, and others argue that there is racial discrimination when applying the death penalty. Do some research on the number of legal executions since 1977. Do current statistics imply racial discrimination?

5. When former Massachusetts governor Michael Dukakis ran for president, he angered death penalty proponents when he said he wouldn't want to kill a man, even if that man raped and murdered Dukakis's wife. Explain Dukakis's position and that of his opponents.

6. In a 1986 Gallup poll, 70 percent of the people polled were in favor of the death penalty. Between 1977 and 1987, 37 states passed new death-penalty laws. Twenty years earlier, a slight majority opposed the death penalty. Should laws regarding the death penalty change based on popular opinion? Are most people well informed enough to make intelligent decisions on the subject? How important are emotions in making such a decision?

7. Research information on the death penalty that has been published since 1981. Use the sources to take a stand on capital punishment. In addition to your library's card catalog and the *Reader's Guide to Periodical Literature*, you might want to look in the *Criminology and Penology Abstracts*.

8. Brainstorm or freewrite on one or more of the following:

   a. death row
   b. degrees of murder
   c. death penalty as deterrent
   d. "an eye for an eye"
   e. punishment for crimes
   f. legal loopholes

9. If you don't like any of these ideas, write an essay on some other aspect of capital punishment.

Student Essay

Read the following narrative essay written by a student. As you read, look for answers to these questions:

1. Does the essay fit the assignment to write on some aspect of a controversial issue?

2. Is there a thesis? If so, is it well supported?

3. How well written is the essay? Does it hold your interest?

Stop Executing Juveniles

Trisha Toyoto

1   According to Tanya Coke in a recent editorial in the *Mobil Register,* the legal system has executed three juvenile offenders within the last ten years and placed 32 others to wait on death row for their execution. We are the only Western democracy to apply the death penalty to young people. As hard as it may be to believe, our laws, she says, are more harsh against juveniles than countries that use capital punishment frequently, such as South Africa and the Soviet Union.

2   In this country, only seven states disallow capital punishment for offenders under age 18 at the time of their crime. "The other 30 states which allow the death penalty have either a lower age limit or no limit at all,"

according to Coke. Our country is virtually the only one in the world that executes children. In fact, the Inter-American Commission on human rights ruled that the United States "violated international standards in allowing the execution of two teenagers" in 1986: James Roach in South Carolina and Jay Pinkerton in Texas.

3   A poll taken in Georgia revealed that while 75 percent of Georgians approve of capital punishment for murder, only 26 percent wanted the law to apply to juveniles. Most people in this country, if polled, would probably feel the same way.

4   Why should juveniles be exempt from the death penalty? Our entire legal system is set up with the understanding that juvenile offenders are different from adult offenders. We have a separate juvenile justice system. We are aware that juveniles are not capable of handling some situations and so have laws that limit when they can drive, when they can drink alcohol, or when they can enter into legal contracts. Juvenile offenders are sent to juvenile hall, not city or county jails when they break the law. Juvenile offenders are more prone to rehabilitation than hardened criminals and frequently leave their criminal careers behind. Why, then, do we put them to death if they commit crimes that call for the death penalty established for adults?

5   Some argue that the death penalty for juveniles is a deterrent. Victor Streib, an expert on juvenile execution and a lawyer who wants the U.S. Supreme Court to rule on this issue, says that "the deterrence theory is especially weak as applied to young people." He suggests that a better deterrent is the "prospect of a lengthy prison term—no telephone, no cars, no Saturday nights out—has more deterrent value for an adolescent than does a shadowy notion of death."

6   There are, according to Coke, some indications that states are changing. Indiana recently raised its minimum age for death sentencing from 10 to 16, and Maryland

```
abolished capital punishment for those under 18. Still,
this problem is one that concerns us all. We must stop
letting our courts send children to the executioner.
```

Reaction

In your journal or on a separate sheet of paper, write your reaction to the student essay. What would you tell the student about her essay?

On the Net

Find two websites—one supporting the death penalty and one opposing it—and answer the following questions:

1. Do you think the sites are biased in their reporting on the issue of capital punishment? Why or why not? How can you tell?

2. Which site does a better job of making an argument either for or against capital punishment? Why?

Write a short essay describing which site you think is better organized and better supported—regardless of whether you agree with the stance taken on the site—and how you think the other site could be better.

A | Essay Format and Proofreading Guide

Essay Format

If your instructor does not tell you what form your final essay draft should take, follow these standard rules.

If You Type or Use a Word Processor

1. Use standard 8 $\frac{1}{2}$-by-11 bond typing paper. Don't use erasable bond paper because it smears too easily. Make certain that your typewriter or computer printer makes a clear, dark imprint. Don't use script or unusual type, especially if you print out your paper on a dot matrix printer. Make certain all letters are distinguishable (for instance, some printers don't make clear *p*'s or *d*'s).

2. Double-space your paper to provide room for your instructor to make comments and corrections. This also leaves enough space for you to correct any typing, spelling, or punctuation errors you notice when proofreading your typed copy. (See proofreading correction symbols on page 437.) If your paper is very messy, re-type it.

3. Leave at least 1-inch margins all around your page.

4. Your name, your instructor's name, the course number, and the date should appear in the upper left- or right-hand corner on the first page. Double-space, then center your title, capitalizing the first letter of each word unless it is an article, conjunction, or preposition. Don't underline, italicize, or place quotation marks around your title. (If other writers refer to your essay by title in their writing, then they should place quotation marks around your title to identify it as such.)

5. Indent the first line of each paragraph five spaces.

6. Leave two spaces after every period, question mark, or exclamation mark; use only one space after commas, semicolons, or colons.

7. Use quotation marks around short quotations that run fewer than five lines when retyped in your manuscript. If the quote runs longer, then indent ten spaces from the left and right to set it off from your own writing; no quotation marks are needed, but the quote should be followed by the source cited in parentheses (see Appendix B, "Quoting and Documenting Sources"). When the quotation is completed, return to your regular margins.

8. Number all pages consecutively in the upper right-hand corner about $\frac{1}{2}$ inch from the top. You may want to place your last name next to the page number. No page number is needed for the first page unless your instructor wants a title page. In that case, ask the instructor for more details on format. Title pages are generally used for lengthy research papers, which require outlines and footnote and bibliography pages.

9. Staple your pages together in order at the upper left-hand corner only. Don't use paper clips; they fall off or get caught in other students' essays when stacked in a pile. Don't bend the corners together with a little tear—it doesn't work.

10. Don't use a binder or folder unless your instructor requests it.

11. Make a copy in case something happens to the original. If you use a word processor, be sure to make a backup copy on disk.

If Your Essay Is Handwritten

It's generally not a good idea to submit handwritten papers. If your instructor does permit it, you should follow the rules above for typed papers, with these differences:

1. Use white, wide-lined paper, no smaller than $8\frac{1}{2}$-by-11.

2. If you write on paper from a spiral notebook, cut off the ragged edges before you submit it.

3. Write on every other line, using only one side of a page.

4. Use only black or dark blue ink.

5. If your handwriting is poor, print. If you can't write or print neatly, pay a typist. An instructor has many papers to grade and has little patience with papers that are difficult to read.

Following these essay format rules is fairly safe, but it is always a good idea to ask any instructors who allow handwritten essays what format they want you to use.

First Page of Manuscript Without a Title Page

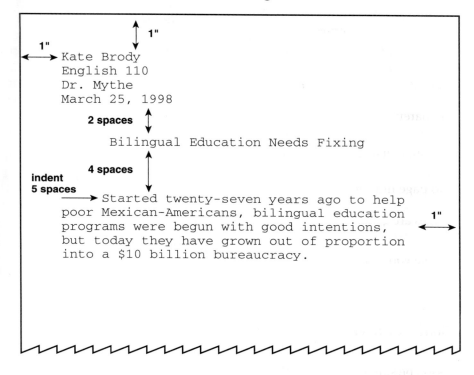

Numbering Subsequent Pages

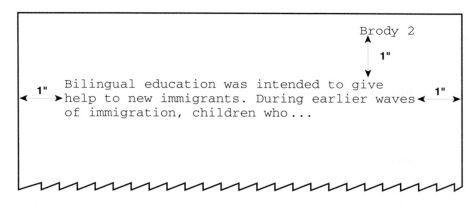

Proofreading Guide

Correction Symbols

Once you have finished typing your paper, be certain that you or someone else proofreads carefully. Read it aloud or have it read aloud to you. If you notice many mistakes, you should type it over. If there are only a few errors, you can correct them by hand using the following editing symbols. Just be neat and use dark ink.

a. to insert an apostrophe or double quotation marks

   `Is this Gingrichs book?`

b. to insert a word, letter, or comma

   `insert word, leter, or comma`

c. to insert a period

   `Insert a period`

d. to delete

   `deleéte`

e. to indicate a new paragraph

   `. . . end a sentence. The next point . . .`

f. to indicate no new paragraph

   `. . . end of a sentence.`
   `The next point . . .`

g. to insert a space

   `insert/space`

h. to close up a space

   `close up sp ace`

i. to transpose letters or words

   `revrese`

j. to indicate a capital letter

   `september`

k. to indicate a lowercase letter

   `Small Letters`

Proofreading for Mechanics

The following brief summary of some mechanical rules may be of help before you finalize your paper.

Underlining: In typing, underlining is reserved for the following:

a. to identify books, magazines, newspapers, films, or recordings (e.g., albums, tapes, CDs)

   `Gerald Graff's `<u>`Beyond the Culture Wars`</u>
   <u>`Time`</u>` magazine` (Notice that *magazine* is not underlined.)
   <u>`Los Angeles Times`</u> (Quotation marks are used around titles of chapters, articles, essays, or poems that appear in books, magazines, or newspapers.)
   `Oliver Stone's `<u>`Truman`</u>
   `The Beatles' `<u>`Sergeant Pepper's Lonely Hearts Club Band`</u> (Quotation marks are used around titles of songs in an album.)

b. to identify foreign words not found in a standard English dictionary or not in everyday use

`The Welsh call themselves ` cymry `.`

c. to call attention to a particular word

`The word ` run ` has more than twenty definitions.`

`The student used ` affect ` when she meant ` effect `.`

d. to denote sounds

`With a ` plunk `, the penny slowly dropped to the bottom of the well.`

Note: If your word processor has italic fonts, you can use italics in place of underlining.

Numbers: In general, these rules apply to writing numbers and figures:

a. Spell out numbers that can be written in one or two words.

`twenty`

`twenty-two`   (Hyphenated numbers are considered one word.)

`twenty-two thousand`

b. Use numerals for numbers that require more than two words.

`275`   (two hundred seventy-five)

`22,645`   (twenty-two thousand six hundred forty-five)

c. Numerals are almost always used for money: *$35.* Occasionally dollars and cents are written out: *one dollar.* There are times when the use of figures is more impressive looking. For instance, *one trillion* doesn't have the visual snap that the figure *$1,000,000,000,000* has.

d. When starting a sentence, it's better to spell out numbers.

`Forty-three people attended the lecture.`

e. When referring to page numbers, prices, or scores, use figures.

`From page 16 of ` Newsweek `, he learned that the tickets were $15.`

`The Giants beat the Cardinals 10-4.`

Capital letters: Use capital letters:

a. to refer to persons, places, and brand names

`Albert Einstein`

`Yellowstone National Park`

```
Porsche
Harvard University
```

b. to refer to title or rank

```
Mayor Lodge
Bishop Tutu
Queen Elizabeth
```

c. to refer to names of religions and members of them

```
Buddhism, Unitarians, Jewish
```

d. to refer to titles of written works

```
Bloom's The Lexington Reader  (book)
Smith's "What Will Become of the Latchkey Kids?"  (essay)
Frost's "Stopping by Woods on a Snowy Evening"  (poem)
```

Notice that the words "of the," "by," and "on a" in the titles are not capitalized. Unless they begin the title, articles (*a, an, the*), prepositions (*of, on, by, in, to,* etc.), and conjunctions (*and, or*) are not capitalized.

e. for the names of the days and months

```
This year, March has four Sundays.
```

Manuscript style manuals vary, but unless your instructor requires a particular style manual, these rules should be acceptable.

B

Quoting and Documenting Sources

Quoting Sources

Quotations from other sources are basically used for one of three reasons: (1) they contain authoritative information or ideas that support or help explain your thesis, (2) they contain ideas you want to argue against or prove wrong, or (3) they are so well written that they make your point better than your own explanation could. However, before you use any quotations, ask yourself what purpose they serve. Too many quotations can be confusing and distracting to a reader. Quotations should not be used as substitutes for your own writing.

There are several ways of quoting your source material. One way is to quote an entire sentence, such as:

> In her article "The State of American Values," Susanna McBee claims, "The recent U.S. News & World Report survey findings show that the questions of morality are troubling ordinary people."

Notice that the title and author of the quotation are provided before the quotation is given. Never use a quotation without providing a lead into it. Usually, verbs such as "says," "explains," "states," and "writes," are used to lead into a quotation. In this case, it is "claims." Notice, too, the placement of punctuation marks, especially the comma after "claims" and the closing quotation marks after the period.

Another way to quote sources is to incorporate part of a quotation into your own writing:

> In her article "The State of American Values," Susanna McBee claims that a recent survey conducted by U.S. News & World Report shows that "the questions of morality are troubling ordinary people."

Quotation marks are only placed around McBee's exact words. Because her words are used as part of the writer's sentence, the first word from McBee's quotation is not capitalized. Notice the way the quotation marks are placed at the beginning and end of the quotation being used.

At times, you may want to make an indirect quotation. Indirect quotations do not require the use of quotation marks because you are paraphrasing, that is, rewriting the information using your own words. Notice how the McBee quotation is paraphrased here:

> In her article "The State of American Values," Susanna McBee states that according to a recent survey conducted by <u>U.S. News & World Report</u>, the average person is bothered by what is and isn't moral.

When the exact wording of a quotation is not vital, it is better to paraphrase the quotation. However, be sure not to change the meaning of the quotation or to imply something not stated there. When paraphrasing, you must still provide the reader with the source of the information you paraphrase.

When quotations run more than five lines, don't use quotation marks. Instead, indent the quoted material ten spaces from the left and right margins and skip a line. This is called a **block quote,** and it shows that the quotation is not part of your own writing:

> In her article "The State of American Values," Susanna McBee concludes by stating:
>
>> Where individuals should be cautious, warn social scientists and theologians, is in forcing their standards upon others. In the words of Rev. McKinley Young of Big Bethal AME Church of Atlanta: "When you find somebody waving all those flags and banners, watch closely. Morality, if you're not careful, carries a sense of self-righteousness. Whenever you pat yourself on the back, it creates all kinds of cramps."

Here, quotation marks are not needed for the McBee quotation. But because McBee's quoted statement contains a quotation by someone else, those quotation marks must be included in the block quote. This is a quotation within a quotation.

Try to avoid quotations within quotations that are shorter than five lines. They are awkward to follow. But if you do need to use them, here is the way:

> McBee concludes by saying, "In the words of Rev. McKinley Young of Big Bethal AME Church of Atlanta: 'Morality . . . carries a sense of self-righteousness. Whenever you pat yourself on the back, it creates all kinds of cramps.'"

Notice the position of the first set of quotation marks (")—just before the beginning of the McBee quotation. Then, when McBee begins quoting Young's words, a single quotation mark (') is used. Because the entire quotation ends with a quote within a quote, a single quotation mark must be used to show the end of Young's words, followed by a double quotation mark to show the end of McBee's words. You can see why it's best to avoid this structure if possible.

Look in the example above at the use of what looks like three periods (. . .) between the words "Morality" and "carries." This is called an **ellipsis.** An ellipsis is used to indicate that part of the quotation is left out. When part of a quote is not important to your point, you may use an ellipsis to shorten the quoted material. Be sure, however, that you haven't changed the meaning of the original quotation. Furthermore, always make certain that the remaining quoted material is a complete thought or sentence, as in the example.

Documenting Sources

Most English instructors require that you document your sources by following the guidelines of the Modern Language Association (MLA). The following examples show how to document most of the sources you would probably use. However, it is not complete, so you may want to consult the *MLA Handbook for Writers of Research Papers* for further information.

When you use quotations, you must identify your sources. Documenting your sources lets your readers know that the information and ideas of others are not your own. It also lets readers know where more information on your subject can be found in case they choose to read your sources for themselves. You cite your sources in two places: in your paper after the quotation and at the end of your paper under the heading "Works Cited."

Citing Within the Paper

Here's how you would show where the examples above came from.

> In her article "The State of American Values," Susanna McBee claims, "The recent U.S. News & World Report survey findings show that the questions of morality are troubling ordinary people" (54).

The number in parentheses (54) refers to the page number in the McBee article where the quotation can be found. Since the author and article title are provided in the lead-in to the quote, only the page number is needed at the end. Readers can consult the "Works Cited" page at the end of your paper to learn where and when the article appeared. Notice that when the source ends with a quotation, the parentheses and page number go *after* the quotation marks and *before* the period.

When paraphrasing a quotation, use the following citation form:

> In her article "The State of American Values," Susanna McBee states that according to a recent survey conducted by U.S. News & World Report, the average person is bothered by what is and isn't moral (54).

Here the parentheses and page number go after the last word and before the period.

If the quote is not identified by author, the author's name and page number should be included in the parentheses.

```
A recent survey shows that the average person is bothered by what
should be considered moral (McBee 54).
```

By including the author's name and page number, you let the reader know where to look on the "Works Cited" page for the complete documentation information.

Works Cited

All the sources used for writing the paper should be listed alphabetically by the author's last name on the "Works Cited" page. If no author's name appears on the work, then alphabetize it using the first letter of the first word of the title, unless it begins with an article (*a, an, the*). Here are the proper forms for the more basic sources. Note especially the punctuation and spacing.

Books by one author:

```
Bloom, Alan. The Closing of the American Mind. New York: Simon, 1987.
```

As usual, two spaces are used after periods; single spacing is used elsewhere. A colon is used after the name of the city where the publisher is located, followed by the publisher's name. Book publishers' names can be shortened to conserve space. For instance, the full name of the publisher in the example above is Simon and Schuster. A comma is used before the date and a period after it.

If two or more books by the same author are listed, you do not need to provide the name again. Use three hyphens instead. For example:

```
---. Shakespeare's Politics. Chicago: U of Chicago Press, 1972.
```

Books by two or three authors:

```
Postman, Neil, and Steve Powers. How to Watch TV News. New York:
Penguin, 1992.
```

The same punctuation and spacing are used, but only the name of the first author listed on the book's title page is inverted. The authors' names are separated by a comma.

Books by more than three authors:

```
Gundersen, Joan R., et al. America Changing Times. 2nd ed. New York:
Wiley, 1993.
```

The Latin phrase *et al.*, which means "and others," is used in place of all but the name of the first author listed on the book's title page. Notice its placement and the use of punctuation before and after.

Books that are edited:

```
Dupuis, Maw M., ed. Reading in the Content Areas. Newark: International
Reading Assoc., 1994.
```

The citation is the same as for authored books except for the insertion of *ed.* to signify that it is edited rather than authored by the person named. If there is more than one editor, follow the same form as for authors, inserting *eds.* after the last editor's name.

Magazine articles:

```
McBee, Susanna. "The State of American Values." U.S. News & World
Report 9 Dec. 1995: 54–58.
```

When citing magazine articles, use abbreviations for the month. The order of the listing is (1) author, (2) article title, (3) magazine title, (4) date, and (5) page number(s) of the article. Note carefully how and where the punctuation is used.

Newspaper articles:

```
D'Souza, Dinesh. "The Need for Black Investment." Los Angeles Times
24 September 1995: M2.
```

The citing is basically the same as that for a magazine article. The difference here is that you include the letter of the newspaper section with the page number ("M2" in the sample).

Scholarly journal articles:

```
Clair, Linda H. "Teaching Students to Think." Journal of College
Reading and Learning  26 (1997): 65–74.
```

Citation for a scholarly journal article is similar to that for a magazine article except that the journal volume number (26 in the example) and the date (only the year in parentheses) are cited differently. Volume numbers for journals can usually be found on the cover or on the table of contents page.

Encyclopedia articles:

```
"Television." Encyclopedia Americana. 1995 ed.
```

Since encyclopedias are written by many staff authors, no author can be cited. Begin with the title of the section you read, then the name of the encyclopedia and the date of the edition you used. No page numbers are needed. Notice the position of the punctuation marks.

Interviews that you conducted yourself:

```
Stone, James. Personal interview. 9 Jan. 1997.
```

Lectures:

Dunn, Harold. "Poverty of the Arts in an Affluent Society." Santa
Barbara City College. 3 May 1997.

If a lecture has no title, substitute the word *Lecture.*

Movies and videos:

Jules and Jim. Dir. François Truffaut. With Jeanne Moreau, Oscar
Werner, and Henri Serre. Carrose Films, 1962.

The listing order is title, director, actors, distributor, and year the film was made.

Television shows:

ABC Nightly News. With Peter Jennings. KABC, Los Angeles. 2 May 1997.

CD-ROMs (original printed source):

West, Cornel. "The Dilemma of the Black Intellectual." Critical
Quarterly 29 (1987): 39-52. MLA International Biography. CD-ROM.
SilverPlatter. Feb. 1995.

The listing order for material that has a printed version is the same as it is for
the printed source with the addition of the database title (underlined), the
publication medium, the name of the vendor (if available), and the publication
date of the database.

CD-ROMs (no printed source):

Reemy, Paul. "Company Disclosures," 13 October 1995. Compact
Disclosure. CD-ROM. Disclosure Inc. 6 June 1996.

The listing order for material that has no printed source is the author's name (if
provided), title of the material (placed in quotation marks), the date of the material, then the database information as in the example for database material
with a printed version (shown above).

CD-ROMs (nonperiodical publication):

Mozart: String Quartet in C Major. CD-ROM. Santa Monica: Voyager. 1991.

Online databases (printed source):

Mooney, Christopher. "Who Is Responsible?" Christian Science Monitor
6 July 1995: 9. Online. Dialog. 12 Jan 1996.

The listing order includes what you would provide for a printed source, plus the
medium (such as Online), the name of the computer service (such as Dialog,
CompuServe, or America Online) or network (such as Internet), and the date of
access.

Acknowledgments

Magdoline Asfahani. "Time to Look and Listen," by Magdoline Asfahani, from *Newsweek*, December 2, 1996. All rights reserved. Reprinted by permission.

James Baldwin. "If Black English Isn't a Language, Then Tell Me, What Is?" by James Baldwin, *New York Times*, July 29, 1979. Copyright © 1979 by The New York Times Co. Reprinted by permission.

Toni Cade Bambara. "The Lesson," copyright © 1972 by Toni Cade Bambara, from *Gorilla, My Love*, by Toni Cade Bambara. Used by permission of Random House, Inc.

Jeffrey M. Bernbach. "What Does Sex/Gender Have to Do with Your Job?" by Jeffrey M. Bernbach, from *Job Discrimination: How to Fight, How to Win*, 1996, Crown Trade Paperbacks, pp. 43–48 (top). Copyright © 1996 by Jeffrey Bernbach. Reprinted by permission of the author.

David Biro. "Silent Bond," by David Biro, *New York Times*. Copyright © 1998 by David Biro. Reprinted with permission.

Gwendolyn Brooks. "We Real Cool," by Gwendolyn Brooks © 1991, from the author's book *Blacks* published in 1991 by Third World Press, Chicago.

Countee Cullen. "For a Lady I Know," by Countee Cullen. Reprinted by permission of GRM Associates, Inc., Agents for the Estate of Ida M. Cullen, from the book *Color* by Countee Cullen. Copyright © 1925 by Harper and Brothers; copyright renewed 1953 by Ida M. Cullen.

Amy Dickinson. "Spoiling Our Kids," by Amy Dickinson. © 2000 Time Inc. Reprinted by permission.

Phil Donahue. "My God, My Constitution," by Phil Donahue. Copyright © 2002 by Phil Donahue. Reprinted with permission.

Barbara Dority. "Ratings and the V-Chip," by Barbara Dority, from *The Humanist*, May/June 1996, pp.16–19. Reprinted with the permission of the author.

Alan Ehrenhalt. "I'm Not a Dork," by Alan Ehrenhalt, from *USA Today*, 8/17/99. Reprinted with the permission of the author.

Barbara Ehrenreich. "Cultural Baggage," from *The Snarling Citizen: Essays* by Barbara Ehrenreich. Copyright © 1995 by Barbara Ehrenreich. Reprinted by permission of Farrar, Straus & Giroux, LLC.

Larry Eichel. "School Vouchers Don't Seem the Answer," by Larry Eichel, *Philadelphia Inquirer*, June 28, 2002, p. A27. Copyright © 2002 Philadelphia Newspapers. Reprinted with permission.

Andrew Ferguson. "Trauma TV," by Andrew Ferguson, 9/18/99. Reprinted with permission from *TV Guide*, 1999 © TV Guide Magazine Group, Inc.

Francis Flaherty. Article "The Ghetto Made Me Do It," by Francis Flaherty from *In These Times*, April 5, 1993. Reprinted by permission of *In These Times*, a bi-weekly news magazine published in Chicago.

David Gergen. "Keeping Faith in Kids," by David Gergen, from US News, 5/31/99. Copyright 1999, U.S. News & World Report, L.P. Reprinted with permission.

Nikki Giovanni. "On Holidays and How to Make Them Work," by Nikki Giovanni, from *Sacred Cows and Other Edibles*, by Nikki Giovanni. Copyright © 1988 by Nikki Giovanni. By permission of HarperCollins Publishers, Inc.

Michelle Goldberg. "Summer Kidnapping Panic," by Michelle Goldberg. Reprinted with permission of Salon.com. All rights reserved.

Paul Goldman. "Vouchers Answer New Segregation in Our Schools," *Los Angeles Times*. Copyright © 2002 by Paul Goldman. Mr. Goldman was the campaign manager for Governor Wilder in 1989. Reprinted with permission.

John Gonzales. "College Brings Alienation," by John Gonzales, from Family Friends, from *Los Angeles Times*, January 20, 1996, p. B7. Copyright 1996 *Los Angeles Times*. Reprinted by permission.

Ellen Goodman. "The Company Man," by Ellen Goodman, from *At Large*, 1981 Washington Post Co. © 1981, The Washington Post Writers Group. Reprinted with permission.

Lamar Graham. "On a Role," by Lamar Graham, from *Rolling Stone*, March 21, 1996, pp. 71-ff, by Straight Arrow Publishing Company, L.P. 1996. All rights reserved. Reprinted by permission.

Kevin Gray. "House of Cards," by Kevin Gray, *New York Times Magazine*, 8/1/99, pp 68–69. Copyright © 1999 by Kevin Gray. Kevin Gray is the senior features writer at *Details* magazine. His work has appeared in the *New York Times Magazine, The Washington Post*, and *Newsweek*. He is a former producer at CNN. Reprinted with permission.

Christy Haubegger. "The Legacy of Generation Ñ," by Christy Haubegger, from *Newsweek*, July 12, 1999. © 1999 Newsweek, Inc. All rights reserved. Reprinted by permission.

Alice Hoffman. "The Perfect Family," by Alice Hoffmann, *New York Times*, November, 1 1992. Copyright © 1992 by The New York Times Co. Reprinted by permission.

Jeff Jacoby. "Death Penalty Saves Lives," *Boston Globe (Staff Produced Copy Only)*, June 6, 2002, by Jeff Jacoby. Copyright 2002 by Globe Newspaper Co. (MA). Reproduced with permission of Globe Newspaper Co. (MA) in the format Textbook via Copyright Clearance Center.

Rachel L. Jones. "What's Wrong with Black English," by Rachel L. Jones, from *Newsweek*, December 27, 1982, from "My Turn" column. Reprinted by permission of the author, a reporter for the *St. Petersburg Times*.

Bel Kaufman. "Sunday in the Park," by Bel Kaufman, author of the best-seller, *Up the Down Staircase*. Reprinted with the permission of the author.

John F. Kennedy, Jr. "Big Ideas for a Better America," by John F. Kennedy, Jr., *USA Weekend,* June 11–13, 1999. Reprinted with the permission of the Estate of John F. Kennedy, Jr.

Mari Kinney. "Teen Sex: 'Too Scary Out There for Me,'" by Mari Kinney, from *Los Angeles Times,* December 7, 1996. Copyright 1996 Los Angeles Times. Reprinted by permission.

Edward I. Koch. "Death and Justice," by Edward I. Koch, from *The New Republic,* April 15, 1985. Reprinted by permission of *The New Republic.* © 1985 The New Republic, Inc.

Jim Lichtman. "Ethical Tightrope," by Jim Lichtman, *Santa Barbara News-Press.* Copyright © 2002. Reprinted with permission of the author.

Mary Brophy Marcus. "If You Let Me Play . . ." by Mary Brophy Marcus, from *U.S. News and World Report,* October 27, 1997. Copyright 1997, U.S. News & World Report, L.P. Reprinted with permission.

H. Bruce Miller. "Severing the Human Connection," by H. Bruce Miller, from the *San Jose Mercury News,* August 4, 1981. Reprinted with permission from the *San Jose Mercury News.*

Jessie Milligan. "What Does Your Pen Color Say About You?," *Fort Worth Star Telegram,* by Jessie Milligan. Copyright 2002 by *Fort Worth Star Telegram.* Reproduced with permission of *Fort Worth Star Telegram* in the format Textbook via Copyright Clearance Center.

George Orwell. "A Hanging," from *Shooting an Elephant and Other Essays,* by George Orwell, 1950, copyright 1950 by Sonia Brownell Orwell and renewed 1978 by Sonia Pitt-Rivers, reprinted by permission of Harcourt Inc.

Jeanne Park. "Eggs, Twinkies and Ethnic Stereotypes," by Jeanne Park, *New York Times,* April 20, 1990. Copyright © 1990 by The New York Times Co. Reprinted by permission.

Linda Pastan. "My Grandmother," from *The Five Stages of Grief* by Linda Pastan. Copyright © 1978 by Linda Pastan. Used by permission of W. W. Norton & Company, Inc.

Leonard Pitts. "Your Kid's Going to Pay for Cheating—Eventually," by Leonard Pitts, *Miami Herald Online.* Copyright 2002 by *Miami Herald.* Reproduced with permission of *Miami Herald* in the format Textbook via Copyright Clearance Center.

James Poniewozik. "Calling the C-Word the C-Word," by James Poniewozik. © 2002 Time Inc. Reprinted by permission.

David Popenoe. "Where's Papa?" by David Popenoe. Reprinted with the permission of The Free Press, a division of Simon & Schuster Adult Publishing Group, from *Life Without Father: Compelling New Evidence That Fatherhood and Marriage are Indispensable for the Good of Children and Society,* by David Popenoe. Copyright © 1996 by David Popenoe.

Anna Quindlen. "Our Tired, Our Poor, Our Kids," by Anna Quindlen. Reprinted by permission of International Creative Management, Inc. Copyright © 2001 by Anna Quindlen. First appeared in *Newsweek*.

Anna Quindlen. "Death Penalty's False Promise," by Anna Quindlen, *New York Times*, Dec. 23, 1979. Copyright © 1979 by The New York Times Co. Reprinted by permission.

Michael Quintanilla. "The Great Divide," by Michael Quintanilla, from *Los Angeles Times*, November 17, 1995, page E7. Copyright 1995, Los Angeles Times. Reprinted by permission.

David Rakoff. "Pandora's Idiot Box," by David Rakoff, *New York Times Magazine*, July 18, 1999. Reprinted with the permission of the author.

James Reiss. "Suenos," by James Reiss, originally published in *The New Yorker*, October 1975. © 1983 University of Pittsburgh Press. Reprinted by permission.

Rochelle Riley. "Pledge Words Do No Harm to Nonbelievers," by Rochelle Riley, *Detroit Free Press*. Reprinted by permission of the Detroit Free Press.

Caryl Rivers. "The Issue Isn't Sex, It's Violence," by Caryl Rivers, from *The Boston Globe*. Reprinted by permission of the author.

Arthur Schlesinger, Jr. "The Cult of Ethnicity, Good and Bad," by Arthur Schlesinger, from *Time*, July 8, 1991, p. 21. © 1991 The Time Inc. Reprinted by permission.

Terry Schwadron. "Filters Can't Block Out the World," by Terry Schwadron, from *Los Angeles Times*, February 24, 1997, Section D, p. 1. Copyright 1997 Los Angeles Times. Reprinted by permission.

Mary Seymour. "Call Me Crazy, But I Have to Be Myself," by Mary Seymour, from *Newsweek*, July 29, 2002. All rights reserved. Reprinted by permission.

Mary Sherry. "In Praise of the F Word," by Mary Sherry, from *Newsweek*, May 6, 1991. All rights reserved. Reprinted by permission.

E. R. Shipp. "Why Must Everything Be Black or White?" by E. R. Shipp, *SB News Press*, 5/14/2002. Copyright © 2002 New York Daily News, L.P. Reprinted by permission.

Debra Sikes and Barbara Murray. "The Practicality of the Liberal Arts Major," by Debra Sikes and Barbara Murray. Reprinted by permission: *Innovation Abstracts* Vol. IX, No. 8; Austin, Texas: The University of Texas and the National Institute for Staff and Organizational Development (NISOD).

Bonnie Smith-Yackel. "My Mother Never Worked," by Bonnie Smith-Yackel. Reprinted by permission of Bonnie Smith-Yackel, a Minneapolis writer who is currently working on a book of essays and stories of life on a family farm.

Judith Stacey. "The Father Fixation," by Judith Stacey, which was found in the *Utne Reader*, September–October 1996 and is adapted from her book, *In the Name of the Family: Rethinking Family Values in a Postmodern Age*. Reprinted by permission of the author.

Brent Staples. "Night Walker," by Brent Staples from *Los Angeles Times Magazine*, December 7, 1986. Reprinted by permission of Brent Staples, Assistant Metropolitan Editor of the *New York Times*.

Lloyd Steffen. "Casting the First Stone," by Lloyd Steffen, from *Christianity and Crisis*, February 5, 1990. Reprinted by permission of Lloyd Steffen, University Chaplain and Associate Professor of Religion Studies at Lehigh University, Bethlehem, PA.

Anastasia Toufexis. "Seeking the Roots of Violence," by Anastasia Toufexis, from *Time* Magazine, April 19, 1993. © 1993 Time Inc. Reprinted by permission.

Robert W. Tracinski. "The Bible Belt's Assault on Education," by Robert W. Tracinski, *Santa Barbara News Press*. Reprinted with the permission of the author.

Roger von Oech. From *A Whack on the Side of the Head*, by Roger von Oech. Copyright © 1983, 1990, 1998 by Roger von Oech. By permission of Warner Books, Inc.

DeWayne Wickham, "Women Still Fighting for Job Equality," by DeWayne Wickham, *USA Today*, 8/31/99. Copyright 1999 by DeWayne Wickham. Reprinted with permission.

Jana Wolff. "Black Unlike Me," by Jana Wolff, *NY Times Magazine*, 2/14/99. Jana Wolff, the author of *Secret Thoughts of an Adoptive Mother*, lives in Honolulu. Reprinted with permission.

Richard Zoglin. "Chips Ahoy," by Richard Zoglin, from *Time*, Feb. 19, 1996. © 1996 Time Inc. Reprinted by permission.

Index

451